GCSE
SOCIOLOGY

Swindon College

Stephen Moore
Senior Lecturer in Sociology
Anglia Polytechnic University

EDUCATIONAL

Every effort has been made to trace copyright holders and to obtain their permission for the use of copyright material. The author and publishers will gladly receive information enabling them to rectify any error or omission in subsequent editions.

First published 1985
Revised 1989, 1992
Reprinted 1992, 1994, 1995

Text: © Stephen Moore 1985
Design and illustrations: © BPP (Letts Educational) Ltd 1985

Letts Educational
Aldine House
Aldine Place
London W12 8AW
0181 743 7514

British Library Cataloguing in Publication Data
A CIP record for this book is available from the British Library

ISBN 1 85758 311 6

Acknowledgements

My heartfelt thanks to Hatti and Tuan, owners of Solidisk Technology Ltd of Southend-on-Sea, for their word processing facilities. Thanks also to Richard Wadge and his staff at Southend College library, and to Brian Dutton and Peter Hallam who contributed most helpfully to this book.

Acknowledgement is made to the following examination groups for their permission to reproduce examination material:
London East Anglian Group
Midland Examining Group
Northern Examining Association
Southern Examining Group

Printed in Great Britain by Martin's the Printers Ltd, Berwick upon Tweed

Letts Educational is the trading name of BPP (Letts Educational) Ltd

CONTENTS

INTRODUCTION AND GUIDE TO USING THIS BOOK

The GCSE examination requires you to know the subject matter of sociology; to be able to analyse issues based on this information; and to be able to carry out an enquiry in the field of sociology which shows you have mastered the research techniques of the subject.

This book contains all the information and coverage of issues necessary to gain grade A in GCSE. There is all the information you need to plan and carry out an excellent piece of coursework, plus advice on what types of examination questions occur and practice in how best to answer them. There are also self-test questions which you can ask yourself at the end of each chapter to see if you have really understood what you have read.

Use the book carefully throughout your examination course and you will enter the examination well-prepared and with confidence, and also with the knowledge that you have completed a good piece of coursework.

Using this Book

1 First, check which examination board you are following. Ask your teacher or, if you are a private student, write to the board for the copy of the syllabus. Incidentally, if you are a private student, you have to be registered and accepted by a recognized educational institution. Check with the Board on this. The addresses of the Boards are on page **228**.
2 Turn to pages xi–xiv and find out from the tables the areas which you need to study for your syllabus. (If you are studying for the Midland Board, please read the note concerning the core and options).

As sociology is a wide ranging subject, the topics have been divided into very broad areas and you may find that your syllabus or teacher lays greater stress on certain topics than others. Remember the syllabus analysis is only a very general guide and you should always consult your teacher.

3 Work your way through all the relevant units. Try to do this at the same time as you are studying that particular subject at school, rather than in a panic at the end of your course!
4 When you finish each unit, turn to the appropriate **self-test questions**. Compare your answers with those provided. Do not worry if your answers are not always the same, though they should be similar.
5 After you have got some way through the book, turn to the section **Types of Examination Questions** (page 181). Find out the types of examination questions asked by your Board and study the techniques which are suggested for answering them.
6 When you have finished all the units in the book, go through the examination questions section (page 191) and select relevant questions. Compare your answers with those given— again they need not be exactly the same, although they should be similar in both content and standard.
7 Your teacher will tell you when he/she wants to begin the project work. At this time, please turn to page vii, and in the section **Coursework** you are provided with help and advice. In selecting topics for a possible project, flick through the book and tackle an issue that interests you.

Studying and Revising

When you are studying and revising sociology, here are some simple guidelines that will help you to get the most out of the book.
1 Once you know what the relevant topics are, work through them steadily.
2 Do not try to study in a room with the television on but go somewhere where you can be alone, or at least fairly quiet, and really try to concentrate. A half hour of hard work is worth a whole evening of sitting with one eye on the television and one on your *Revise GCSE Sociology*.
3 It is very useful to write on books and add in extra notes or underline/use marker pen on areas of special importance or difficulty. But only if you own the book. If it is a library book, think of others.
4 Everything in this book is written in the clearest way possible, but if anything confuses you or is difficult to understand ask your teacher.
5 It is pointless trying to learn all the information in this book off by heart, and it is not what the examiners are looking for. You should aim to understand the material, and use this as a

springboard for developing your ability to analyse problems through a sociological perspective.

6 Use the self-test questions and the examination practice questions to the full. It is only by being forced to use your knowledge that you can see how much your know.

7 Do not rush your revision at the last moment if you can help it. If your examination is in June, start your revision in April.

COURSEWORK

You will have to write at least one piece of coursework during your course. Below are details of the coursework for your examination board. Remember that a high mark in your coursework will provide you with an excellent base for you examination. You can enter the exam confident that if all goes well you are likely to emerge with a high grade.

A most important point to remember in doing your coursework is that different examination boards have their own system for awarding marks. You can only be awarded marks according to the mark scheme laid down by the Examination Boards. In the following analysis, I have used the mark scheme the Boards give the teachers, but I have simplified the language slightly. Study the system of your examination board carefully and write your coursework according to the headings provided below.

London East Anglian Group

Number of pieces of coursework: One.

Length: 2500 words approximately.

Content notes: You can work with others on the 'design of the enquiry and in data collection' but the Board states that 'the writing up of the material is to be the work of the individual candidate alone...The final presentation of the enquiry must include a clear statement of the contribution of the individual candidate'.

The bulk of the work will generally be in written form, but 'diagrams and other graphic material, photographs and transcriptions of tapes should be included where appropriate'.

A list of sources should be provided.

Percentage of marks in the examination: 25%.

Marks to be awarded for the following:

1 To identify, with guidance from the teacher, a general area for investigation and then to focus within that on a specific issue. **15 marks**

Here you should show the reasons for your choice of general area and specific issue. You should be able to show that you can organize a clear and feasible study. There should be a clear hypothesis.

2 Identify and evaluate the most appropriate sources of information for your enquiry.

15 marks

Here you should show you are aware of the varieties of both primary and secondary sources and you should indicate why you finally discarded some methods as inappropriate and chose others for your research.

3 Identify and use appropriate methods of collecting and recording data from such sources.

25 marks

(a) You need to show the examiner that you know how best to collect material – which implies that you know sociological methods in some detail. You also need to demonstrate real competence in actually doing the research. Remember – do not rely solely on questionnaires and interviews, or copying from textbooks. You should combine reading books and magazines with a variety of other methods. Remember also that you must always state the sources of your information and back up any statements you make with evidence.

(b) You must prove to the examiner that you know best how to present your material. Written work may include sources, pie charts, bar charts, graphs, tables, photographs and possibly tape-recordings. Do not forget to present your material in a clear manner, with appropriate headings and clear explanations of your actions.

(c) Finally, to obtain maximum marks in this section, you should explain the importance of the findings and draw any appropriate conclusions. Do not forget to be self-critical.

4 Present the results of the enquiry accurately and briefly, showing that you are aware of other relevant studies made by sociologists. **15 marks**

This is the summary and you are expected to draw together everything that you have written so far in your enquiry. Points you should cover should include a selection of the statistical information you have already given, but summarized in a new format.

5 Draw reasoned conclusions from the evidence obtained in the enquiry and relate these to your original hypothesis. **30 marks**

The point here is to try to pull together all your information in a way that relates it to your original hypothesis or area of research. Ideally, you are showing how relevant the information you have found is to the hypothesis. You must very carefully and clearly assess the results of your enquiry. How do they bear out your original ideas, or not, as the case may be? What alternative lines of enquiry could you have followed? Do your results only partially bear out your hypothesis? Why is that? Do not forget to be detailed and precise.

Midland Examining Group

Number of pieces of coursework: One enquiry and two assignments set by the teacher.
Length: The enquiry should be 2000–3000 words. The assignments should be 500 words each.
Content notes: You must present your work on A4 paper. In terms of presentation, most of the report should be in written form, but 'diagrams, illustrations, statistical tables, photographs and work in other media such as video and audio-tapes should be encouraged so that the most appropriate form of presentation should be adopted'.

Group and collaborative work may be carried out, especially in the design of the enquiry and the collecting of the information, but all candidates must produce their own written report which identifies their own contribution to the group report.

The subject of the enquiry should be 'directly related' to the syllabus content, and students should be given encouragement to base their enquiry on their own experience or personal interest.

Percentage of marks in the examination: 50%

The assignments: (20% of marks)
These can take a variety of forms, depending upon the decisions of the teacher. They are both designed and marked by your classroom teacher.
Assignment one: Examples of possible assignments could be an essay, a stimulus exercise with questions that become increasingly more difficult, or even a class discussion.

Whatever form the assignment takes, the teacher is looking to see how much you know and understand about sociological topics, concepts and issues.

In practice this means that you will understand the meaning of sociological terms, such as *social class*: you will also understand how these can be *applied to the real world*, for example in looking at social class differences between families

Assignment two: This may take the form of a series of questions on a number of stimulus items, which are linked by a common theme, or you may be asked to undertake a very limited research activity. Students will then be asked to analyse and interpret the information, drawing conclusions, and evaluating the strengths and weaknesses of the material studied.

Whichever form is chosen for the assignment, the student is required to produce evidence of his/her ability to analyse, interpret and evaluate sociological evidence.

In practice this means that you are able to take a piece of sociological information and to be able to interpret this and draw conclusions but at the same time to be aware of the biases and the weaknesses, as well as the strengths of the information.

The enquiry: (30% of the marks)
The teacher will mark you on the basis of five assessment objectives:
1 You need to show that you understand the topic or issue you have chosen for your enquiry. This involves being aware of the appropriate sources of information for your study. You also need to show that you understand sociological concepts (such as gender, social class, etc). **4 marks**
2 You must demonstrate your ability to use the information you have collected in order to produce some results. You also need to be able to interpret these results. Most importantly, you should be aware of the strengths and weaknesses of your research methodology.
9 marks
3 You must be able to identify a clear area of interest. You must then evaluate the different research methods you could use, and justify which one(s) you have chosen. Ideally, you should undertake a *pilot study*. **6 marks**
4 This refers to the actual collection of the data, that is the conduct of the research process itself. Marks are therefore awarded on finding/collecting the information in the most appropriate way, and recognising the difficulties/weaknesses and, of course, being able to overcome these problems. **9 marks**
5 Marks are awarded for the ability to produce a clear and well-organised study, which addresses all the issues in points 1–4 in a detailed and informed manner. **3 marks**

Northern Examination Association

Numbers of pieces of coursework: One.

Length: 1000–3000 words.

Content notes: 'It is anticipated that many reports will include illustrative material such as diagrams, tables, quotations, etc and that some may include audio and video recordings and photographs.'

Group investigations may be carried out, but 'appropriate arrangements will have to be made to ensure that a valued assessment can be made of the individual's contribution to the work of the group'.

Percentage of marks in the examination: 30%

Marks to be awarded for the following:

1 A detailed formulation of the investigation being undertaken and a comprehensive outline of the methods to be used to undertake the investigation. **15 marks**

The examiners are looking or a clearly stated description of the investigation you are going to make. You should identify the methods you propose to use and explain why you chose these in particular. Explain how these methods help you to answer to question or hypothesis you have set yourself. Prove to the examiner that you have a well-planned enquiry.

2 A comprehensive and detailed presentation of the investigation. **15 marks**

These marks are awarded for a report of the investigation in which the information is presented in a very clear and logical way. There should be a wide range of data which has been obtained through a variety of different research methods. The way the original plan of the study was altered in the light of the actual process of research should be included.

3 Analysis and interpretation of data gathered. **20 marks**

You should concentrate on showing the range of data you have collected and explaining what the information actually means. Then you need to show how the information is related to the research you are carrying out. You should also show how the work you are doing relates to the course in general. Finally, you need to point out problems and defects in your research and data.

4 Presentation of conclusions. **10 marks**

In this section you should draw conclusions solely from the information you have collected, showing clearly what you have learned from the investigation. Ideally you should relate you findings to the wider study of sociology which you have covered in the GCSE course.

Southern Examining Group

Numbers of pieces of coursework: One.

Length: 1500–3500 words.

Content notes: Students can collaborate in the *early stages* of planning and collecting data, but the *analysis and writing up* of the topic must be the work of each individual candidate.

The work must be presented in written form, which has to include a table of contents; clear separation of chapters; good layout and clear use of language; where relevant diagrams, graphs, photographs and recorded tapes and cassettes should be included (clearly labelled). There should be a detailed bibliography.

Percentage of marks in the examination: 30%

Marks to be awarded for:

1 Aim: you need a clear hypothesis or to have asked a relevant, useful question. **4 marks**

2 Methodology: you must use one or more sociological methods in some depth, and show clearly why you chose your methods and why alternative methods were inappropriate.

5 marks

3 Sources: you need to recognise, and use, the relevant primary (first hand) and secondary (other research, books, official statistics, etc) sources for your enquiry. You must clearly relate them to the aims of the enquiry to show that it is relevant material that you are using.

4 Content: you must clearly cover the aims of the project in your content, making a clear analysis of the material you have collected. **4 marks**

5 Presentation: your enquiry must contain the following: table of contents, separation of chapters, planned layout, a bibliography (list of books and articles you have used) and be clearly written using good English. **4 marks**

Welsh Joint Education Committee

Number of pieces of coursework: One.

Length: 3000 words.

Content notes: A number of candidates may choose the same topic, but the teacher must 'supply the necessary evidence to ensure that a valid assessment can be made of the individual's contribution to the work of the group'.

If the investigation uses audio and video recordings, photographs, diagrams and tables, etc, then 'they must be accompanied by the appropriate supporting written material, e.g. video script'.

Candidates **must** demonstrate the use of **two** of the following methods in their enquiry: (i) observation, (ii) interviews, (iii) questionnaires, (iv) secondary documents and statistics.

Percentage of marks in the examination: 40%

Marks to be awarded for:

1 Aims: a clear introduction which describes in detail the aims and hypothesis to be tested. There should be a clear explanation of why the study is being undertaken (a 'rationale').
5 marks

2 Methodology: you need to show in a clear manner how the two methods you have chosen are used throughout your investigation, and to explain the role of the research in your enquiry. **15 marks**

3 Results: you must provide information which relates the study to the wider context of society. You must analyse the data and draw any conclusions. The study should include comparisons with available information and any critical comments about the enquiry and the information gained. **10 marks**

4 Conclusion: you need to discuss the methodology in some detail. You should examine the strengths and weaknesses of the methodology, and the alternative methods that you could have used. You should ideally refer to any other published studies and their methods and results. **10 marks**

Table of analysis of examination syllabuses

	London	Midland	Northern	Southern	Wales
Examination papers (time in hours for each paper)	1hr10mins+1½	2 + 1½	1½ + 1	1½ + 1 hr 10 mins	2
Marks allocated for exam papers	75%	50%	70%	70%	60%
Marks allocated for teacher-assessed coursework	–	} 20%	–	–	} 40%
Marks allocated for enquiries	25%	30%	30%	30%	
1 Socialization					
The meaning of socialization	●	●	●	●	●
Instinct or socialization?	●	●	●	●	
People without socialization	●	●	●	●	●
The process of socialization	●	●	●		●
Socialization in specific settings	●	●	●		
Variations in socialization in modern society	●	●	●		
Culture	●	●	●		●
The components of culture	●	●	●	●	●
Culture in other societies	●	●	●	●	●
2 Research Methods					
The steps in scientific research	†	*	●	●	●
Sampling	†	*	●	●	●
Types of sample survey	†	*	●	●	●
Collecting sociological information	†	*	●	●	●
Questionnaires	†	*	●	●	●
Interviews	†	*	●	●	●
Asking questions	†	*	●	●	●
Secondary sources	†	*	●	●	●
Subjective sociology – observation	†	*	●	●	●
The reasons influencing the choice of research methods	†	*	●	●	●
Values in research	†	*	●	●	●
3 Family					
The various forms of the family – marriage	●	○	●	●	●
Industrialization and the changing form of the family	●	○	●	●	●
Functions of the family	●	●	●	●	●
The negative side of family life	●	●	●	●	●
Changing relationships in the family	●	●	●	●	●
Varieties of family in Britain	●	●	●	●	●
Alternatives to the conventional family	●	○	●	●	●
Family life in another society			●		
Marriage	●	○	●	●	●
Divorce	●	○	●	●	●
4 Education					
Socialization and education	●	●	●	●	●
Educational change	●	○	●	●	
Public schools	●	○		●	
The functions of education for society	●	○	●	●	
Social class and educational achievement	●	○	●	●	●
Intelligence	●	○	●	●	●
The role of the home in educational attainment	●	○	●	●	●
The role of the neighbourhood	●	○	●	●	●
Cultural deprivation	●	○	●	●	●
The role of the school in educational attainment	●	○	●	●	●
Gender and education	●	○	●	●	●
Race and education	●	○	●	●	●
5 Social Stratification					
The meaning of stratification	●	●	●	●	●
Comparative forms of stratification	●	●	●	●	●
Life chances and social class	●	●	●	●	●
Explanations of social class	●	●	●	●	●
Measuring social class	●	●	●	●	●
Changes in the class structure	●	●	●	●	●
The working class	●	●	●	●	●
The middle class	●	●	●	●	●
Ownership of wealth and income	●	●	●	●	●
Social mobility	●	●	●	●	●

	London	Midland	Northern	Southern	Wales
Examination papers (time in hours for each paper)	1hr10mins+1½	2 + 1½	1½ + 1	1½ + 1 hr 10 mins	2
Marks allocated for exam papers	75%	50%	70%	70%	60%
Marks allocated for teacher-assessed coursework	–	} 20%	–	–	} 40%
Marks allocated for enquiries	25%	30%	30%	30%	
6 Gender					
Gender roles	●	●	●	●	●
The significance of gender	●	●	●	●	●
The changing status of women	●	○	●	●	●
Women and employment	●	●	●	●	●
Housework	●	○	●	●	●
7 Age					
Childhood	●	●	●	●	●
Childhood in another society		●	●		
Youth culture	●	●	●	●	
The origins of youth culture	●	●	●	●	
The nature of youth culture	●	●	●	●	
The importance of the peer group	●	●	●	●	
Youth culture and unemployment	●	●	●	●	
Old age	●	●	●	●	●
The elderly in another society: Japan		●	●		
8 Race and Ethnicity					
Race and ethnic group	●	●	●	●	
Immigration control		○	●		
Patterns of immigration	●	○	●	●	
The demography of ethnic minorities	●	○	●	●	
Reasons for immigration		○	●		
The problems faced by ethnic minorities	●	●	●	●	
Preventing discrimination		●	●		
9 Work					
The meaning of work		○	●	●	●
Why do people work?		○	●	●	●
The occupational structure	●	●	●	●	●
Changing technology	●	●	●	●	●
The division of labour	●	●	●	●	●
Mechanization to automation	●	●	●	●	●
Work satisfaction	●	○	●	●	●
Attempts to make work more fulfilling	●	○	●	●	●
Industrial relations	●	○	●	●	●
Representative organizations	●		●	●	●
Work in other societies: a comparative approach			●		
The growth of industrialization in Japan			●		
The influence of work on our lives		○	●	●	
10 Unemployment					
The extent of unemployment	●	●	●	●	●
The duration of unemployment	●	●	●	●	●
Differences in unemployment between groups	●	●	●	●	●
Unemployment by region	●	●	●	●	●
The causes of unemployment	●	●	●	●	●
The implications of unemployment for society			●	●	●
The experience of unemployment	●	●	●	●	●
11 Leisure					
Defining leisure	●	○	●	●	
The growth of leisure	●	○	●	●	
Factors affecting leisure activities	●	○	●	●	
The future of leisure	●	○	●	●	
Social implications of retirement				●	
12 Population					
Collecting information		○		●	●
The importance of demography		○		●	●

	London	Midland	Northern	Southern	Wales
Examination papers (time in hours for each paper)	1hr10mins+1½	2 + 1½	1½ + 1	1½ + 1 hr 10 mins	2
Marks allocated for exam papers	75%	50%	70%	70%	60%
Marks allocated for teacher-assessed coursework	–	} 20%	–	–	} 40%
Marks allocated for enquiries	25%	30%	30%	30%	
12 Population continued					
Population size	●	○	●	●	
Changes in the number of births	●	○	●	●	
Changes in the number of deaths	●	○	●	●	
Changes in migration	●	○	●	●	
The gender balance	●	○	●	●	
Changes in population	●	○	●	●	
Consequences of an ageing population	●	○	●	●	
Consequences of population changes	●	○	●	●	
Changes in the distribution of the population in Britain	●	○	●	●	●
Changes in the world population		○			
13 Urbanization and Community					
Urbanization and industrialization	●		●	●	●
Community and association	●		●	●	●
Housing zones	●				
Patterns of life	●			●	●
The inner city	●			●	●
The suburbs	●			●	●
14 Poverty					
Defining poverty		●	●	●	●
The extent of poverty		●	●	●	●
Who are the poor?		●	●	●	●
Causes of poverty		●	●	●	●
Policy implications of the different explanations of poverty				●	
Living in poverty: the poverty trap			●	●	●
The Welfare State and poverty – the role of Government				●	
15 The Welfare State					
Development of the Welfare State				●	●
The debate on the Welfare State	●			●	●
National benefits	●			●	●
Local benefits	●			●	●
Voluntary organizations				●	
16 Politics and Power					
Power and authority		●	●		
Different political systems	●	●	●	●	
British political parties	●	●	●	●	●
Voting behaviour	●	●	●	●	●
Political socialization	●		●	●	●
Types of voter			●	●	●
Voting and opinion polls	●		●	●	●
Politics and the mass media	●	●	●	●	●
Pressure groups (interest groups)	●	●	●	●	●
The role of the state	●	●	●	●	●
The civil service	●		●		
17 Social Control					
Meaning of social control	●	●	●	●	●
Informal control	●	●	●	●	●
Formal control	●	●	●	●	●
The nature of social control	●	●	●	●	●
Social control in other societies			●		
18 Crime and Deviance					
The distinction between legal and deviant	●	○	●	●	●
Variations in the definition of deviance	●	○	●	●	●
Why definitions of deviance vary	●	○	●	●	●
Reasons why some deviant acts are criminal	●	○	●	●	●

	London	Midland	Northern	Southern	Wales
Examination papers (time in hours for each paper)	1hr10mins+1½	2 + 1½	1½ + 1	1½ + 1 hr 10 mins	2
Marks allocated for exam papers	75%	50%	70%	70%	60%
Marks allocated for teacher-assessed coursework	–	} 20%	–	–	} 40%
Marks allocated for enquiries	25%	30%	30%	30%	
18 Crime and Deviance continued					
Patterns of crime	●	○	●	●	●
Types of offenders	●	○	●	●	●
Sociological explanations of crime and delinquency	●	○	●		
Alternative explanations for crime and deviancy		○	●		
Labelling	●	○	●	●	●
Labelling and deviancy amplification	●	○	●	●	
Understanding criminal statistics	●	○	●	●	●
19 Religion					
Religion and social control	●	●	●	●	●
Secularization: the declining importance of religion			●		●
The significance of non-Christian religions in Britain			●		
The significance of religion in a simple society			●		
20 Media					
Types and characteristics of the media	●	●	●		
Socialization, social control and the media	●	●	●	●	●
Women and the media	●	●	●		
Race and the media	●	●	●		
Criminals and the media	●	●	●		
The media, labelling and moral panics		○	●		
Explanation of media influence on behaviour		●	●		
Mass media and political opinion		○	●	●	
Contents of the media	●	●	●		
Reasons for style of the media's contents	●	●	●		
Patterns of ownership and control		○	●		

The addresses of the examining boards can be found on page 228.

Notes on syllabus analysis

The Midland Examination Group syllabus is composed of two elements, a *core* and a number of *options*. Teachers will cover the whole of the *core* and then select from the options. However, the core overlaps with some of the options, with the option going into greater depth. The syllabus analysis given above shows all the core areas (indicated by ●) and separately the option areas (indicated by ○).

* There is no research method element in the Midland Examining Group syllabus. Nevertheless you must do an enquiry that shows (amongst other things) you have 'awareness of some of the main methods of sociological enquiry and the uses to which they can be put.' In short, you must know research methods.

† The London East Anglian Group say that 'there is no separate section on the methods used in sociological enquiry. It is intended rather that awareness of and the capacity to use such skills and techniques be developed in the course of undertaking substantive studies.' So although you may not specifically be *taught* research methods you are expected to know them.

Note

External syllabuses are mainly the same as those given above – the difference is that coursework enquiries are not required.

1 SOCIALIZATION

1.1 The Meaning of Socialization

At birth children have few of the qualities, apart from the physical ones, that we expect of human beings—they cannot walk or talk, they do not know how to eat and they have no opinions on religion, politics or sport.

Sociologists believe that human beings are not just created in a physical manner, but also in a social manner. If people were left on their own after birth, merely being fed and physically cared for, they would not develop into recognizable human beings. They would not be able to talk, perhaps even to walk, to laugh, or to understand others. In effect they would merely be animals.

As soon as a child is born the members of society begin to influence and mould the child's beliefs, personality and behaviour.

What changes human beings from animals into the *social actors* (a term to describe people living in society) whom we recognize as members of society, is the process of *socialization*.

The learning process begins in childhood, but continues throughout life. The growing child, through contact with others of the society, gradually learns the language, beliefs and behaviour of the group in which he or she is brought up. The values and behaviour of groups vary, so that the socialization process is different from one society to another.

1.2 Instinct or Socialization?

It is a basic belief of sociology that the major part of all human behaviour is learned and is not the result of some *biological drive*. For example, it is often claimed that women have a natural *mothering instinct*: sociologists firmly deny this, arguing that women are taught in our society that as they bear the children they ought to take the main responsibility for looking after them. The proof as far as sociologists understand it can be found by comparing patterns of behaviour across societies. The argument is that if certain forms of behaviour are *natural*, then all 'normal' people in all societies ought to show that particular form of behaviour. For example, it is natural to feel pain, to be able to walk, to eat (although even here people need to be shown how). However, if the patterns of action vary considerably, being absent in one society and present in another, it cannot be argued that that behaviour is 'natural' to human beings.

An example: the female role

Until recently it was widely assumed that women were 'naturally' less violent and tough than men, that they had a natural mothering instinct and that women were naturally the ones to stay at home to look after the children. However, in recent years in Britain this view of the nature of women has been undermined; in other societies it was never held at all. In *Sex, Gender, Society*, Ann Oakley describes the expectations of women in three simple societies in the past:

1 The Kgatla tribe of South Africa Here women and girls did all the heavy manual labour, such as building and repairing walls, and this involved carrying large baskets full of earth. On the other hand the men had little work, except occasionally thatching the roofs.

2 The Tchambuli of New Guinea (South Pacific) In this society, the women had the 'looks' and behaviour men traditionally have in Western societies. They wore short, cropped hair, with no make-up or jewellery. The men were extremely concerned about their looks and would spend hours arranging their long hair, even adding false pieces to make it look better. They wore jewellery and make-up. They were highly strung and spent much of their time dancing and gossiping.

3 The Manus tribe of New Guinea (South Pacific) As soon as the child had stopped breast feeding (at about one year), the father took over the complete raising of the child, undertaking all the tasks that are thought of as normally done by the woman in British society. The woman in the Manus tribe is then expected to 'return to work'.

The point of these three examples is to show how behaviour that is regarded as natural to men and women is in fact the result of socialization. (There is a detailed discussion of female socialization in the unit on 'Gender'.)

1.3 People without Socialization

To make the point quite clear concerning the power and importance of socialization, it is worth looking at the behaviour of some people who have not been through the process of socialization into human society.

There are a number of famous examples, two of which are given below. They all show how humans who are not socialized into the normal behaviour of society are almost unrecognizable as humans in their behaviour. This shows that our behaviour is not natural but learned.

The case of Anna

In 1978 a girl of about five years of age was discovered on a farm in the United States. Since birth she had been completely isolated, locked up in a room by herself. This was done because she was illegitimate and the grandparents were ashamed. When disovered she could not walk, talk or feed herself and had no control over her bladder or bowels. She had great difficulty in understanding anything that was explained to her or done for her. After being taken from the farm and looked after, she made some progress, learning to feed herself, to speak a few sentences and to dress herself. Unfortunately, she died about three years after being discovered. (Source: Kingsley Davis *Human Society.)*

The case of Shamdev

In 1978 a boy of about five was discovered playing with wolf cubs in the Musafirkhana forest in India. He hid from people and would only play with dogs. At night he grew restless and it was necessary to tie him up to stop him going out to follow the jackals that prowled around the village at night. If people cut themselves, he would smell the blood and rush across to it. His favourite food was chicken. He caught them, killed them and ate them raw. (Source: *Observer*, 30 August 1978.)

1.4 The Process of Socialization

Sociologists distinguish between two aspects of socialization: *primary socialization* and *secondary socialization*.

PRIMARY SOCIALIZATION

This refers to the process of socialization that takes place between an individual and a group of people with whom he/she has intimate contact, such as the family and the peer group (which is a group of people close to an individual, against whom he/she measures his or her own behaviour).

The family

This forms the most important agency of socialization for most people. Children identify with their parents and copy them. Their behaviour is conditioned by the responses of their parents. Because most children want to please their parents, they repeat behaviour that gains approval. Gradually, they learn to *internalize* the correct patterns of behaviour, so that instead of winning the approval of their parents, they *know themselves* when their behaviour is correct or not.

Within the family, the children are generally socialized along gender lines, with girls being encouraged to copy their mothers and boys their fathers.

The peer group

The second important influence a child encounters is the peer group. A child's play patterns with other children influence the way he/she thinks and acts later. Children play together at adult roles, such as cops and robbers, shopkeepers, and mothers and fathers. By playing together in this way they learn the appropriate roles of behaviour for later life.

Piaget, a famous Swiss psychologist, suggested that children pass through various stages in their play as they grow older. In the game of marbles, which he studied, children of two and three at first play with the marbles having no idea of a game. At the age of four or five they begin to understand the idea of rules. The rules are rigidly interpreted. At the age of seven or eight the rules are regarded as flexible and changes can be made. Finally, in adolescence, the rules may be adjusted to give handicaps to even out players' chances.

Conformity among the peer group is strongly maintained and those who in some way fail to meet expectations are picked on, and may be rejected. (The importance of the peer group in adolescence and the formation of a youth culture is discussed on pp 63–6.)

SECONDARY SOCIALIZATION

Secondary socialization usually occurs in more formal situations, which are not so personal – the two most powerful are the school and the mass media.

Schools

In complex modern societies, the wide variety of different home backgrounds and values can lead to children being socialized in different ways. One of the roles of the school is to provide a common pattern of socialization. Thus teachers teach the skills, knowledge and behaviour considered vital for survival in society (the *curriculum*). As well as this, sociologists suggest, children learn the *hidden curriculum* of values and skills that permeate the school. These may include such things as finding out the expectations of males and females in society, through the unintentional comments of teachers, plus the activities of other children in the class (there is a further discussion on this on pp 28–9).

The mass media

Apart from the direct experiences we have, which for the majority of us are rather limited, our knowledge about the wider world comes from what we read, hear on the radio or see on film or television. Attitudes towards other countries, ethnic groups and political events are all influenced by what information we receive about them and how this information is presented to us.

1.5 Socialization in Specific Settings

Socialization, however, is not limited to just the family, peer group, education and mass media. Throughout life, people are undergoing new experiences and new processes of socialization. Two examples illustrate this: socialization in work and socialization in total institutions.

Socialization in work

When people enter the world of work, they must learn the appropriate forms of acceptable behaviour. On the shopfloor in many manual jobs, the newcomer must learn the right pace of work. Someone working too fast or too slow will disrupt the workrate adjudged 'right' by those already there.

For example, employees paid by the amount they produce (piece rate) will limit the quantity turned out to an informally agreed level. The advantage is that the bonus level at which a higher rate of pay is given can be reached without too great a difficulty. A newcomer working fast to earn as much money as possible will mean that the employer will realize the true possible output, and will raise the number of units to be completed to achieve the bonus.

Newcomers who break the rules are made the butt of practical jokes; if they continue then they are 'sent to Coventry'.

It is not just output that is involved. Other workers demand conformity in attitudes towards management, in solidarity with workmates, and in most instances doing the job well.

People in the professions have very strong socialization processes. Doctors, for example, are taught the rules of professional conduct and can be thrown out of the profession for not obeying them. Informally, too, doctors have their own rules – it is extremely rare, for instance, for one doctor to criticize another; this is 'just not done'. Patients, too, help to socialize doctors. They expect them to have a middle class accent and to dress smartly (and until comparatively recently they expected them to be male).

Total institutions

There exist in society certain institutions in which people have all their choice taken away. Exampes of these are monasteries, convents, the armed services, mental hospitals and prisons. In these institutions the individual is often 'stripped' of his or her identity outside the institution and given a new one. Thus the monk is renamed and instead of being Mr Moore becomes Father Stephen; or the prisoner becomes 11657. The person is then encouraged or even forced to accept the rules and values of the new institution. The prisoner must eat and exercise at fixed hours; he/she must learn the appropriate ways of addressing those in authority (to their faces and behind their backs). Total institutions are unusual in that they take people who are already socialized and then completely resocialize them; but they still illustrate the extent of the power of socialization over individuals.

1.6 Variations in Socialization in Modern Society

In modern complex societies socialization patterns are different between different groups. The complexity of life is matched by a complexity of patterns of socialization. People are socialized differently by social class; by ethnic group; by workplace and type of job; by the region of the country; and by age group. However, although there are differences in Britain (unlike some other countries), these differences are not so great as to prevent the society holding together.

Social class

The values of the working class are different from those of the middle class, although the extent of those differences is a matter of debate. Goldthorpe and Lockwood suggested that the values of the working class included believing in stressing the need for the working class to stick together (particularly at work); (b) that those who are unemployed are simply unlucky; (c) that society is composed of two classes and that most working class people are stuck where they are.

By contrast the middle class believes (a) in individuality; (b) that the unemployed are generally lazy; (c) that where you get in life depends upon hard work. We could add, too, that the working class tends to have clearer-cut ideas concerning the roles of men and women and a greater stress on traditional ideas of 'masculinity'.

Research

Work by the Newsons (*Seven Years Old in an Urban Community*) has suggested that working class children are brought up in a more rigid way by their parents: they are not supposed to question their parents' authority and are not given reasons why they ought to do a particular thing – they must just obey.

The Newsons suggest there is less stress upon academic success and the working class children do not receive as much help with reading and writing as the middle class children. All this has consequences for their future success at school and their future employment.

Ethnic group

Britain is a multicultural society. About 7 per cent of the population are immigrants or the children of recent immigrants, from a wide variety of nations. These bring up their children to have specific values that differ from the 'mainstream values' of British society. For example, the children of Indian immigrants to Britain will most likely follow the Hindu or Muslim religions. They have very different views about the role of the family and the correct behaviour for females. The family is very important and obedience to parents is generally absolute. Females are expected to be extremely modest. Marriages may be arranged by parents.

Age

In particular different youth cultures emerge for each generation and divisions occur within each generation. Thus a variety of competing groups exists at any one time. These reflect in turn class, ethnic and regional differences and the present problems that groups face.

1.7 Culture

Culture is the whole of the knowledge, ideas and habits of a society that are transmitted from one generation to the next. Culture is not static, however, and is always changing. The beliefs and values that we hold are not the same as those held in medieval or even Victorian Britain. Sociologists often use the terms **society** and **culture** interchangeably, for a society is generally a group of people **sharing** a culture.

Humans are guided far less by instinct than any other animal. It may be natural to eat and to make love, but *how* these things are done is a reflection of the expectations and values of a particular society.

An example of the importance of culture is the activities of the Japanese *kamikaze* pilots in the Second World War. Near the end of the war, as Japan seemed doomed to lose, volunteers were called for who would fly aircraft packed with explosives into American and allied ships. In the resulting explosion, the pilot was guaranteed to lose his life. Yet there were too many volunteers for the planes available. The pilots considered it a great honour to die for their country and their Emperor. Here the *culture* had completely swamped the *instinct* of self-preservation.

However, clear variations exist in the values that people hold and the patterns of behaviour they engage in. When there is an overall shared culture, but within it there are clearly distinguishable sets of values and behaviour, sociologists use the term **subculture**.

Subcultures are linked to ethnic, social class, and age divisions in our society.

A typical example would be the youth subculture: in each generation there is a variety of styles of dress, types of music, special language and attitudes that distinguish youth from older people and from children. These values make youth distinct from society, but rarely do they represent complete rejections of the overall culture.

1.8 The Components of Culture

1 Beliefs These are general, vague opinions held about the world and about the nature of society. They vary by society and sometimes by subcultures, e.g. Westerners are encouraged to think that Russians are intent on taking away our freedom and are therefore enemies. Russians are encouraged to think the same thing about Westerners.

2 Values These are vague beliefs about what is right and correct in the world. They imply that there are certain appropriate forms of action which ought to be taken, e.g. life is precious therefore it is wrong to kill anybody.

3 Norms These are socially expected patterns of behaviour. (Actions that are regarded as *normal*). A norm of our society is to say 'Hello!' on meeting someone, or to stand in a queue without trying to push in front. Norms that are vital to a society and have a certain moral content are sometimes referred to as **mores**.

4 Roles Social roles are patterns of behaviour expected of certain people according to the occupation or position they hold in society. The role of a clergyman is to be sympathetic, well-mannered, well-spoken, religious and charitable. A swearing, heavy-drinking, party-going clergyman would be regarded with astonishment by most people.

5 Role conflict There are innumerable social roles – father, mother, child, shopkeeper, footballer, old age pensioner, etc. All of us occupy a number of roles, which are generally complementary, but sometimes they may conflict, for instance, the role of being a policeman and of being a friend. If a policeman apprehends a friend who is speeding, does he treat him as a friend or as an offender? This is known as **role conflict**.

6 Status This refers to the position of a person or social role in society according to the amount of prestige received from others. In different societies/cultures, status varies. In Britain those with the highest status are the best educated and the rich, although this will obviously vary within subcultures. In traditional Japan, it was the *samurai* warriors who received the greatest prestige, after the Emperor.

1.9 Culture in Other Societies

It is important to remember that there are and have been a wide variety of different cultures. It is wrong to see British culture as the *normal* culture and to measure all others alongside ours. This is known as **ethnocentrism** and is a common error of those who have no knowledge of sociology.

The Cheyenne Indians

1 The Cheyenne existed for thousands of years in the west of what is now the United States;

2 Unlike our society, wealth was regarded as a bad thing and there was no status attached to owning goods;

3 On the other hand, to give things away was regarded as an action worthy of admiration;

4 Therefore in special ceremonies those more successful members of the tribe gave away most of their possessions to others;

5 The greatest prestige was attached to bravery in battle. This did not necessarily mean killing enemies, but simply showing bravery in whatever respect; for example, an individual brave might ride towards the enemy alone and attack them;

6 Power in the Cheyenne nation was held mainly by men and they achieved positions of authority through acts of bravery which impressed other members of the 'tribe'. Powerful positions could not be inherited;

7 Children were brought up to be very tough, receiving regular beatings from their parents. This was not done from cruelty but in order to strengthen the children for the extremely tough life they would face.

1.10 Summary

1 Socialization consists of the process of becoming a full member of a society, accepting all of its ideas, values and patterns of behaviour.

2 Socialization is more important than the biological drives or instincts that we have.

3 Animal behaviour in general is determined by instinct, very rarely by learning. On the other hand, human behaviour is largely determined by learning.

4 This can be seen in the variety of different forms of human behaviour in different cultures.

5 People who are not socialized lack most of the attributes we normally associate with being human.

6 There are two aspects of socialization: primary and secondary.

7 Primary socialization is learning that takes place within intimate groups, such as the family and the peer group.

8 Secondary socialization is the more formal learning patterns that take place in the school and through the peer group.

9 In modern, complex societies it is possible to have differences between the values learned in secondary and primary socialization.

10 Socialization takes place throughout life and in specific settings – for example, the workplace. People learn to act according to the way that is normal for those within the work organization.

11 There are differences in socialization according to class, gender and ethnic group.

12 Culture is the set of values and ways of acting that mark a particular society.

13 Variations within the culture are known as subcultures.

14 Culture is more powerful than instinct.

15 Culture is learned through the socialization process.

16 Beliefs are general opinions and understandings about the world.

17 Values underpin how we act by providing the moral framework within which we make decisions.

18 Norms are the accepted patterns of behaviour in a society.

19 Roles are expected patterns of behaviour linked to particular statuses.

20 Role conflict is when two or more roles go against one another.

21 Status is the position of a particular person or social role in society.

1.11 Keywords (*as they appear in the unit*)

biological drive, instinct, primary socialization, secondary socialization, internalize, peer group, hidden curriculum, multicultural, culture, subculture, beliefs, values, norms, roles, role conflict, status.

2 RESEARCH METHODS

In order to discover information about society, sociologists have developed a wide range of research techniques. Unlike journalists or politicians, these allow them to make unbiased, accurate statements about social life, and allow them to make tentative predictions, based on their research, of how people will act in particular situations.

Within sociology there is some debate between those who believe sociology should aim to follow the lead of the traditional sciences (e.g. chemistry, biology, etc.) and those who feel that as sociologists study people's **attitudes** as well as their actions, this makes it different. They advocate placing less stress on much of the scientific method that follows. Usually they argue for participant observation (pp 11 – 12). Those who adhere to the scientific methods are known as **positivists**, while those who stress understanding attitudes are known as **subjective sociologists**.

However, increasingly this division is being bridged with sociologists using a mixture of both types of method.

2.1 The Steps in Scientific Research

When engaging in scientific research, it is customary to follow a number of stages. This is as true for physics as it is for sociology. The stages are: (1) observation (2) hypothesis (3) research planning (4) collecting the information (5) analysing data and drawing conclusions.

Moore and Hendry, in *Sociology*, have analysed a well-known piece of research by Howard Newby (*The Deferential Worker*) under these headings. The research concerned the lives of Suffolk farmworkers.

Observation Whilst studying local community life in Norfolk, Newby noticed the poor pay and conditions of farmworkers; he also noticed little evidence of resentment even though most farmers who employed the labourers were affluent.

Hypothesis Newby tried to find an explanation for this, and finally put forward **the possible explanation** (a hypothesis) that farmworkers hold an attitude called **deference** which resulted, among other things, from working closely with the farmer – this stops them feeling resentful.

Research planning Newby had to find a typical agricultural area without too many commuters who alter the rural community. He therefore moved his research to Suffolk. He next found a **sampling frame**–the *Yellow Pages*.

Collecting the information Newby originally wrote to 312 farmowners, but was only successful in obtaining interviews at 71 farms with 233 farmworkers. He filled out his information using **secondary sources** such as official statistics. He also lodged with a farmworker's family for six months to gain better knowledge of the community.

Drawing conclusions Newby took three years working on his information before he could see if his original hypothesis was correct. He concluded that although much of his hypothesis was comfirmed, there were many new areas he had not originally perceived, and so his results were rather different from what he could have foreseen.

2.2 Sampling

1 Sample

Sociologists frequently make **general** statements about the population, such as 29 per cent of the population think companies make too much profit, while 80 per cent of the population think trade unions have too much power.

Clearly sociologists cannot interview the whole of the British population–the cost and time required make that impossible. Instead sociologists use a **sample** of the population. A sample is a small, representative group selected from the population. The survey that gave the information mentioned above was based on a sample of 1828 people which reflects the general population of Britain.

It is very important that the sample is representative; any error here will be magnified greatly if we use it to make statements about the whole population. Sociologists have therefore developed a considerable number of techniques for ensuring that their information is correct and drawn from a representative sample of the population.

2 Sample frame

This refers to the source from which the informants have been drawn. To find out people's voting intentions, a useful source (and hence the sample frame) would be the electoral lists. To study workers' opinions about their employers, a useful sampling frame would be the factory personnel records. It is used with random sampling (see below). Oakley (*Housewife*) studied women's attitude to housework, and used the patients' lists of two London doctors to find names and addresses of married women aged 20–30 years old with at least one child under five years of age.

3 Pilot sample

Before undertaking the full sample survey, sociologists usually take a very small 'sample of their sample'. They then test the correctness of their sampling, the usefulness of their questions and, finally, any possible problems. This is a **pilot sample**.

4 Snowball sample

Sometimes it is not possible to find a sample frame or simply to stop people in the street to ask them questions–particularly if the sociologist is studying a 'deviant' group. In this case the sociologist may find one 'deviant' and then ask him/her to introduce him to a friend. Thus the sample grows rather like a snowball rolled in the snow. (Martin Platt did just this in his study of drug taking.)

5 Types of sampling methods

There are two types of sampling methods: random sampling and quota sampling.

Random sampling Individuals are chosen entirely at random from a sampling frame, rather like the idea underlying a lottery–everybody has an equal chance of being selected. Usually sociologists choose at random from a relevant sample frame, by selecting every 10th or 20th name that appears–depending upon the size of the sample required–or they choose from the sample frame by random number. There are three subtypes of random sampling:

(a) Strata sample: this involves dividing the population according to relevant factors such as age, gender or social class, and once this division (into strata) is complete, taking a random sample within each stratum. This ensures that the sample will be safely representative of the population. It is particularly useful where the sample is very small.

(b) Multistage (sometimes known as **cluster sampling**): if the survey is of a widely dispersed population, it is easier to subdivide (by random sampling) the sample into **clusters**. For example political constituencies (MP's districts), upon which electoral lists are based, are subdivided into **wards** which are in turn subdivided into **polling districts**. By choosing certain wards at random, then certain polling districts within those wards, and finally certain people within those few polling districts – the result is a geographically close, random selection of people over 18. The information can then be collected easily.

(c) Multiphase: when the survey is completed the sociologists randomly select a sample of the full sample, to ask further questions. This is useful when further depth is required.

Quota sampling This is not based on the principle of randomness to ensure a representative sample. If we know a lot of information about the population to be studied (*population* in sociological language means any group which we wish to study), then it can be subdivided proportionately according to important social factors (gender, age, class) and interviewers told to question a specified number (a quota) from each group. This is the type of sampling used by most market research companies.

6 *Random versus quota sampling*

Advantages of random sampling:
(i) statistically very reliable
(ii) there are ways of checking that the sample is representative
Disadvantages of random sampling:
(i) expensive   (ii) time consuming   (iii) complex
Advantages of quota sampling:
(i) simple   (ii) relatively cheap   (iii) relatively quick
Disadvantages of quota sampling:
(i) relies too much on the interviewer's selection of people. If the interviewee chosen does not truly fit the category given to the interviewer, then the sample is ruined
(ii) no possibility of checking accuracy of sample.

2.3 Types of Sample Survey

1 *Cross-sectional studies* A study of a representative cross-section of the population at any particular time. This is generally known as 'a survey', e.g. opinion polls. A famous example is Schofield's 1960's study of young people's sexual behaviour – in which 2000 13–18 year-olds were questioned on their attitudes and behaviour. The main disadvantage of these studies is that they represent only a *snapshot* picture of what is happening at one time. There is no attempt to look at changes.

2 *Case studies* These limit themselves to in-depth study of one particular place or event, e.g. Beynon's study of Ford car workers (*Working for Ford*), in which Beynon talked to Ford production line workers about their attitudes to their work and the management. The main disadvantage of these studies is that as they are restricted to one occurrence it is difficult to generalize from them.

3 *Longitudinal studies* These are studies conducted over an extended period of time. The researchers study a selected group of people over time noting the changes and differences between them, e.g. The National Children's Bureau Study of 17 000 children born in the week ending 9 March 1958. This study has followed their lives, to understand the factors influencing educational attainment.

The main problem is the large loss of the sample over time so that it becomes increasingly difficult to make generalizations when so many are missing and there is no information for them.

2.4 Collecting Sociological Information

Sociologists use a wide variety of techniques in order to gather information about society. There is a division among sociologists about the best method to capture the truth about society.

1 One group of sociologists stresses the importance of following scientific method.
2 The other group argues that sociology is slightly different from other sciences, and the task of sociology is to find out how people live and what they think, not by asking questions, but by observing them in their daily life (subjective sociology).

Sociologists who prefer *scientific sociology* (or *positivism*) tend to use (a) questionnaires (b) interviews (c) experiments (all of which are types of *primary sources*, so called because they are found out at first hand by sociologists) and (d) secondary sources (sources that have been created by others and which sociologists use).

2.5 Questionnaires

These are sets of written questions which are either mailed to individuals (postal questionnaires) or simply handed out. The respondent completes it alone and then returns it to the researcher. Answers are either **closed** (tick the appropriate box) or **open** (write answer in own words). The advantages are:

(a) they can be mailed to a widespread sample;

(b) they are quick to do. All the researcher has to do is to write the questionnaire, hand the copies out (or mail them) and then collect them afterwards for analysis. Interviews on the other hand can take a long time to complete and so the amount of time must be expanded or the number of interviews cut down;

(c) people are more likely to answer embarrassing questions (as there is no interview or personal contact).

There are also disadvantages to this method:

(a) they cannot be used for complex issues;

(b) the researcher can never be certain who actually completes the questionnaire. Is it the person he or she wants?;

(c) most people cannot be bothered to return questionnaires (high non-response) – which means that the researcher is never certain what the opinion is of those who do not respond.

2.6 Interviews

These are where an interviewer asks a respondent a number of questions and writes down the answers. The interview can fall between the two extremes of the structured interview, which is rather like an oral questionnaire, or the unstructured, where the interviewer converses with the respondent. Within these extremes is a whole range of techniques. As in questionnaires, questions can be **closed** or **open-ended**. The advantages are that the interviewer:

(a) can examine complex issues;

(b) can compare the answers with personal observations;

(c) obtains a lower non-response rate.

The disadvantages are that:

(a) the interviewer may influence the replies of the respondent by his presence, or inadequate interviewing skill. This is known as **interviewer bias**;

(b) the technique tends to be relatively expensive.

2.7 Experiments

These are not commonly used in sociology, as sociologists generally argue that individuals in isolation from their normal daily lives do not act in a **natural** manner. Experiments place individuals in closely controlled situations where they can be observed; they then create a particular event to observe the subjects' response. For example, Asch conducted a series of famous experiments which illustrated the power of group pressure. A group of students were asked to estimate the lengths of a series of lines on individual cards. All the students except one were told to give a pre-arranged incorrect answer. The student who did not know would often change his estimate of length to agree with his fellow students. This occurred in 37 out of 100 cases.

2.8 Asking Questions

As we have just seen, questions used in interviews and questionnaires tend to be of two types, open-ended or closed. Let us consider them in more detail.

Open-ended These are the type of questions which are 'open' in the sense that there is no choice or guidance to the answer – this is left entirely up to the respondent. These sorts of questions are usually asked when an opinion is sought, e.g. 'What do you think about . . . ?'

They are very useful in getting people to talk in their own words and they allow people to express quite complicated ideas and feelings. However, they are very difficult to code, and so are complicated to use.

Closed questions These are much simpler and involve giving the respondent a limited choice of answers, e.g. how many hours each week do you spend studying sociology? One hour or less, more than one hour but less than three, more than three? These are simple to code, but they often simplify issues too much (for instance you might spend 20 hours one week doing sociology and then nothing for a fortnight).

They do not allow people to reply in detail.

They do not allow people to reply in their own words.

They guide the respondent in answering in a certain way, thus possibly biasing the response.

Structured and unstructured interviews

The degree of structure in an interview can have a considerable bearing on its outcome.

The structured interview is good for simple issues and provides clear answers which are easy to code.

The unstructured interview can probe an issue in depth and the skilled interviewer can follow up interesting points finding out the true meaning behind the reply of the respondent.

Coding

When a number of questionnaires or interviews have been completed, they need to be put together and analysed. It is much easier if the replies can be grouped in some way. Coding is simply the simplifying and grouping of answers. For example, if questions are being asked about the degree to which people like their jobs, then the type of response can be grouped into three possible boxes, 'like', 'neutral' and 'dislike'. The replies of the respondents are then analysed and placed into the group that is nearest to their reply. Great attention must be paid to ensure that the coding (grouping) by the sociologist reflects the real opinions of the respondent.

2.9 Secondary Sources

These are any sources of information that the sociologist has not obtained for him/herself. Secondary sources include:

OFFICIAL GOVERNMENT REPORTS AND STUDIES

The **Census** is an example – a national survey of the population conducted every ten years by the government. This, along with regular studies such as the *National Household Survey* keep the government (and sociologists) up to date with changing trends in British society and allow social policy to be planned.

Problems **1** The government statistics are collected for official purposes – they are not intended for use by sociologists. The definitions and classifications used by these statistics may not be ideal for the sociologist (see, for example, the discussion on measuring social class on pp 44 – 6).

2 The figures may be the subject of some controversy, as it may be felt that the government is defining the figures in such a way as to benefit its political image. Criticism was levelled against the Conservative government in 1985 after it changed certain definitions of who was to be counted as unemployed, thereby 'reducing' the numbers of the unemployed (for a discussion of this see p 87). Poverty statistics, too, are the subject of heated debate (see pp 110 – 13).

3 The source of the official statistics may be dubious, as is the case with the official statistics on wealth and income. Many people lie to government officials to avoid tax, or figures are presented in such a way for tax purposes that they make the ownership of wealth seem less concentrated than it is.

4 Some statistics tell us more about the activities of officials than they do about the actual occurrences they are supposed to represent. Thus crime statistics tell us about the activities of the police more than anything else (see pp 142 – 3).

HISTORICAL DOCUMENTS

(a) Official: such as parish records of births and deaths historically kept by clergy in Britain. These were used by Laslett in *The World We Have Lost* to study family changes in Britain between the sixteenth and nineteenth centuries.

(b) Unofficial: such as diaries and novels; these give a picture of how people felt and lived at a particular time. Here, however, the researcher has to be very careful as the contents will reflect the bias of the writer.

NEWSPAPER REPORTS

These are useful to fill in information for a researcher and to give the background to an event; they may also be useful as a piece of research in themselves. This form of studying events through newspapers is sometimes called *content analysis*. Often it is the only way to find out information about the activities in the past of certain groups without an official history, such as gangs of delinquents or criminals.

Problems The problems of bias are particularly strong in content analysis.
(a) Newpapers need to sensationalize events in order to sell copies and so facts are often distorted.
(b) Newspapers are generally politically biased, in the majority of cases towards the Conservative Party. Political reporting may not therefore be 'balanced'. (See p 154 for a discussion on the bias of newspapers.)

2.10 Subjective Sociology – Observation

This is sometimes called observational sociology.

Earlier we saw that some sociologists believe it necessary to observe, or even join in, social activities in order fully to understand them. This does not mean they are opposed to the stricter scientific methods, it is just that they place less emphasis on statistics and more on their own observation. Sociological knowledge has traditionally come from blending the two approaches.

Observational methods are particularly useful:
(a) in digging below people's answers to questions, in order to see how they actually behave;
(b) for certain **deviant** groups, delinquents etc., who may not reply to questionnaires or interviews;
(c) where it may be inappropriate to use interviews or questionnaires, at a football match for instance when the sociologist may be trying to understand football crowd violence.

There are two types of observational method: **1** nonparticipant and **2** participant. In practice the two method are often intermixed.

1 Nonparticipant: The observer watches the behaviour of a group, perhaps following them around and asking questions. He does not join in group activities. It often happens, however, that the observer gets drawn into the group through his close contact. In certain circumstances the observer may use mechanical methods of recording information such as a tape recorder or a video camera.

Advantages:
(a) the researcher is able to observe a group who could not be studied in any other manner;
(b) the researcher exerts minimal influence on the group's actions;
(c) the researcher is able to study the group as they behave normally.

Disadvantages:
(a) observations are only superficial if the observer does not join in the group activities;
(b) lack of statistical evidence – all based on observation.

The most famous example of observational research is the Hawthorne Studies of 1924 conducted by Elton Mayo. He examined the effects of changing the working environment on the productivity levels of a group of workers. He found that virtually any change in working conditions improved productivity. Apparently the influence of Mayo's presence actually encouraged the workers to greater efforts. This illustrates the influence of the researcher.

Today researchers overcome this by using various forms of recording. Stanworth tape-recorded lessons in a number of Cambridge schools to illustrate the point that boys receive more attention in class than girls. The tape recorder was far less obtrusive than her presence would have been. (*Gender and Schooling*).

2 Participant observation: Here the observer joins the group as a full member and is accepted by them. The researcher also participates in all group activities.

Advantages:
(a) deep contact with the group who confide in the observer as group member;
(b) full understanding of the reasons behind group's actions, as the observer is participating.

Disadvantages:
(a) the observer may lose his/her objectivity and become biased through too much contact with the group under study. This makes any observations very suspect;
(b) lack of statistical information to confirm the observer's conclusions;
(c) the group may be influenced by his/her presence, for instance an older middle class sociologist joining and observing a group of working class delinquents may end up advising them, so altering the **natural** pattern of events.

For example, James Patrick (*A Glasgow Gang Observed*) joined a violent Glasgow gang without telling them his true identity as a sociological researcher. He stayed with the gang over a period of months, joining in their criminal activities and behaving similarly to them.

The result is an in-depth description of gang life and beliefs. It is clear that Patrick disliked the gang, and this dislike may perhaps have biased his conclusions and observations.

3 Participant versus nonparticipant observation: when choosing the particular form of observation, the sociologist must be aware that participant observation:

(a) gives a greater depth of information;
(b) is more likely to be coloured by his/her identification with the group;
(c) is more likely to influence the group under study.

Nonparticipant observation:

(a) gives more superficial observable information only;
(b) there is less chance of influencing the group or
(c) being influenced by it.

2.11 The Reasons Influencing the Choice of Research Methods

In the review of research methods which I have given, the methods seem clear cut. One sociologist uses nonparticipant observation and another questionnaires. Yet in reality it is not like this. Sociologists have to adjust their research methods to the particular situation they find themselves in.

They may prefer to give out questionnaires or conduct formal interviews with a group of 'troublemakers' in a school, but the lads themselves may not want this – so the researcher is forced into a kind of observational study. Therefore it is important to realize that various factors will determine the choice and practice of actual research. These could include:

(a) specific settings (in a school or on a street corner);
(b) the amount of time;
(c) the willingness of the people under study – housewives were pleased to talk to Ann Oakley in her study of their lives. They were glad of a sympathetic person to talk to and wanted people to become aware of the problems of mothers;
(d) the amount of financial resources – there are various grant-giving bodies such as the Nuffield Foundation which support research. Some researchers receive this and so can expand their work, some do not and have to struggle through alone;
(e) personality of the researcher – when Howard Parker wished to study a group of youths who stole car radios, he was allowed to join the group, because he looked young, he was outward-going, could play football and liked drinking in pubs – all important characteristics needed to win acceptance.

2.12 Values in Research

In a subject like sociology dealing with the ideas and opinions of people on social issues, there is always the problem of sociologists' own values intruding. Sociologists are highly aware of this issue.

1 Sociologists always try to keep their own values and biases out of the actual research process;

2 However, they are aware that this is not always possible, therefore they often mention their own biases at the beginning of the piece of research so that this is clear to the reader. The readers can then judge whether they think some subconscious bias has crept in. Lea and Young in *What Is To Be Done About Law And Order* make their political beliefs very clear;

3 The best way to avoid bias is to publish not only one's own political views but also full details of the research so that other sociologists may criticize and form their own opinions;

4 Sociologists accept that the values of the researcher will determine in the first place which areas of social life are to be studied.

2.13 Summary

1 There is a wide range of techniques used by sociologists to understand society. Sociologists select whatever methods seem most appropriate.

2 There is a division between those sociologists who stress more the method of using social surveys and those who stress more the use of observational methods.

3 There are specific steps to be followed in conducting a survey. These are observation, hypothesis, research planning, collecting of information, the drawing of conclusions.

4 When studying society, sociologists use sample surveys, which are representative selections of the population.

5 A sampling frame is the list from which the sample is drawn.

6 Pilot samples are small samples taken before the main sample to check for problems that may be encountered.

7 There are two main types of sampling technique – random and quota.

8 There are various ways within these two methods of varying the data collection – snowball sampling, cluster sampling, multiphase, etc.

9 There are different types of studies which vary in depth and width. Types of study include cross-sectional, case, longitudinal.

10 Sociologists collect sociological information using questionnaires (written questions), interviews (oral questions) and experiments, and secondary sources (material collected by other people).

11 Questionnaires and interviews are dependent on the quality of the questions asked. The sociologist must beware of making them confusing, or biased.

12 Experiments are not commonly used in sociology because they do not reflect the situation of real life.

13 Secondary sources provide many problems for the sociologist – in particular the sociologist has to be aware of the reasons why the information was originally collected and the biases built into that information.

14 Some sociologists prefer to use the observational approach because they argue that it gives them greater understanding of what people actually do, rather than what they say they do.

15 There are problems with observational studies in that the sociologist often becomes too involved in the group and therefore becomes biased.

16 Sociologists choose the best research method available for them under the circumstances – there is no one correct or best method.

17 Sociologists must always try to keep their own biases and values out of the studies they do, otherwise the study will be of little value.

2.14 Keywords *(as they appear in the unit)*

positivism, subjective sociology, hypotheses, sample, sample frame, pilot sample, snowball sample, random sampling, multistage sampling, cluster sampling, quota sampling, cross-sectional studies, case studies, in-depth studies, longitudinal studies, questionnaires, interviews, closed questions, open-ended questions, coding, interviews, secondary sources, nonparticipant observation, participant observation.

3 THE FAMILY

3.1 The Various Forms of the Family – Marriage

FAMILY

When sociologists speak of '**the family**', they generally mean a group of people living together, who are generally related by blood or marriage ties, and who support each other economically and emotionally.

Kin means a wider collection of people who are related by blood, and who extend beyond the immediate family.

There are two main types of family form:

The extended family

This consists of a large number of people; typically three generations (grandparents, parents, children) who live together or close by each other. It is sometimes found in pre-industrial societies such as the Bedouin of the Negev desert.

The nuclear family

This consists of few people, typically two generations (parents and children) who live together.

It tends to be a much weaker, more flexible family type than the extended. It is usually found in modern industrial societies such as Britain today.

Authority: (a) If the father is regarded as the head of the family, it is known as a **patriarchal** type. The Bedouin of the Negev mentioned earlier are patriarchal; (b) If the mother is regarded as the head of the family, it is known as a **matriarchal** type. The traditional society of the Trobriand Islands (South-West Pacific) has always had the mother as the head of the household and her wishes are followed by husband and children.

MARRIAGE

All forms of the family as we describe it here are based on a sexual relationship between at least one member of either sex, producing children.

The relationship is based on some form of religious or cultural ceremony which marks them as married – this can take two different forms:

1 Monogamy

Marriage of one man and one woman only (e.g. Britain).

2 Polygamy

This is the general term for the situation where one of the partners has more than one partner from the opposite sex. In particular:

Polygyny

This is the marriage of one man with a number of wives. The Koran (the sacred book of Islam) permits Muslims to have up to four wives at the same time. Polygyny is common in the Muslim Arab states of the Middle East, such as Saudi Arabia, and in Africa, such as Senegal.

Reasons for polygyny

1 In many societies the balance of males and females may not be more or less equal. Usually there is a shortage of males because male infants are weaker than females and more likely to die. As adults, it is generally men who engage in warlike or dangerous behaviour. As a response to this polygyny absorbs the surplus of females.

2 In pre-industrial societies, the mortality rates are very high. In order for the society to continue, the maximum possible number of children must be born. Women who are able to bear children, but who are 'surplus', must therefore have a sexual partner.

3 Religion and culture are extremely important influences. Many societies, for example ones based on the Muslim religion, allow more than one wife.

4 Polygyny is useful for a family in an agricultural society where it produces more children to help in planting and harvesting crops.

5 Although polygyny is stressed as ideal in certain societies, in fact it is often only the better-off males who can afford to have more than one wife.

Polyandry

This is marriage of one woman with a number of husbands at the same time. Polyandry is much more unusual than polygyny.

It occurs in Tibet, where there is little land suitable for agriculture. In order to keep the population down to realistic survival levels, one woman will marry a number of brothers. This means that all the brothers are restricted to the number of children that one woman is able (or willing) to bear, rather than each one having a wife to bear children.

3.2 Industrialization and the Changing Form of the Family

THE FAMILY BEFORE INDUSTRIALIZATION

There are two extreme (or 'ideal') types of family, as we saw earlier – the extended and the nuclear. Both types have existed throughout history and coexist today.

Studies of the family in Britain before industrialization suggest that the extended family was *not* typical here. Instead only a small proportion – about 10 per cent – of families was of the extended type. The extended family seemed to be typical of the better-off families and the nobility, whereas among the peasants the nuclear family was typical.

Research

Peter Laslett in *The World We Have Lost* studied the parish records of English country villages from 1564 to 1821. He concluded:

1 Late age of marriage combined with the shortness of most people's lives meant that the three-generation extended family was rare in Britain in this period. Only about one household in twenty was composed of more than two generations, so grandparents were much rarer than today.

2 There were large households as opposed to large families over the period studied. What Laslett means by this is that the slightly better-off families would take the children of poorer families into their homes or farms where they would work as a type of domestic servant (although they were also regarded as partly 'kin'). Almost 40 per cent of all children were domestic 'servants' of this type in their childhood and youth.

THE FAMILY IN THE EARLY INDUSTRIAL SOCIETY

The coming of industrialization had a major impact on the family, in particular for the working class.

The working class

The siting of the factories in towns meant that workers left the country to live in towns near their work. There developed a local working class community which was based upon the kinship or extended family network.

Research

Michael Anderson studied the town of Preston, Lancashire, using census data for the year 1851. He concluded that there was an increase in the numbers of elderly parents living with their children, and that the extended family as we know it now probably expanded considerably among the working class at this time.

As the wages were low in the cotton industry of Lancashire, the working class had to have as many family members as possible working. The greater the number of incomes coming into the house, the higher the standard of living for everybody and the more help that could be given to those who fell ill or became unemployed.

Elderly parents were useful for baby minding when the mother worked, and for a wide range of household duties.

The middle and upper class families

These continued to be of the extended type, as the increased wealth allowed the three-generation family to exist with the grandfather as the family head, controlling the family finances. On his death the eldest son took over and controlled family finances.

THE FAMILY STRUCTURE IN THE TWENTIETH CENTURY

The working class

In this century the mutual need of the working class family members for help slowly declined.

1 The state took over some of the family functions, by providing pensions, decent health care and social security in times of unemployment.

2 Family size declined, as children became less of an economic asset and more of a burden, and the cultural stress on care and love of children changed attitudes to family life.

3 Geographical mobility increased and so the inner city working class extended family network declined.

The result was that the nuclear family became much more evident.

The middle class

The middle class were the first to move away from the extended family. The reasons were much the same as for the working class, but they happened to the middle class 20–30 years before they influenced the working class.

The rich

The available evidence from studies by many sociologists is that the extended family is still normal among the rich.

The nuclear family is the dominant family type today among the middle and working classes. However, cars and telephones allow contact between family members dispersed throughout the country.

3.3 Functions of the Family

The family, in whatever form, performs a number of important **functions** for its members. The extent of these functions depends primarily on the economic nature of society. On the whole, it appears that more functions are performed by extended families in simple tribal societies than by nuclear families in modern industrial societies like our own.

THE FUNCTIONS OF THE MODERN FAMILY

Families perform the following functions in society:

1 Regulate sexual behaviour
2 Reproduction
3 Socialization
4 Economic
5 Emotional support.

1 Regulate sexual behaviour

Firstly, uncontrolled sexual activity is a possible source of conflict in any society as disputes can easily break out between rivals for the same lover. Therefore, by restricting sexual activity to one's married partner the degree of conflict is lowered. Secondly, if blood relatives are clearly marked by family membership, so that everybody knows his/her relationship to others, there is less risk of incest.

2 Reproduction

Every society needs to reproduce itself in order to continue. The family is the culturally approved unit in which we have children. If the family is stable then the infants are guaranteed a safe and secure early life. The family, therefore, ensures that enough healthy children survive to continue the society.

3 Socialization

Fundamental to any society is the need to teach each new generation the socially correct ways of behaving and acting. Without these common standards of values and behaviour societies could not continue. Shared forms of behaviour ensure that we are able to live together with a minimum of conflict.

The family is the first and perhaps the most significant agency of socialization that most people encounter. Parents teach their children:

(i) who they are, e.g. their social class, their gender, their colour of skin;
(ii) the behaviour expected of them by society according to who they are;
(iii) the values of the society in general, which they must know and copy.

4 Economic

The family is an economic unit of **consumption**, by which we mean that family members dispose of much of their earnings on buying items for the family, as opposed to individuals. From house purchase through to daily groceries, the family members may well pool most of their earnings together. This is different from agricultural societies where the whole family worked together as a unit of **production**.

5 Emotional support

Modern Western societies are highly competitive – and, many think, unfriendly. Our contact with others is generally superficial. In this sort of world, the family ideally provides the warmth and emotional support that is missing in the wider society. Often, the closest social bonds are between family members.

3.4 The Negative Side of Family Life

The functionalists in the previous section make a crucial assumption that the **family is beneficial** (good) **for its members.** Many sociologists criticize this assumption. Although there is certainly good in the family, they balance this out with comments on the harm the family can do its members:

1 Emotionally intense The narrowness of the nuclear family and the intense bonds between the few family members can lead to great strain and conflict. The rise in divorce rates is seen as evidence of this.

2 The repression of women Feminists state that the family as we know it operates to the benefit of men. Women are expected to do most of the housework and cooking and to disrupt their working lives in order to raise the children.

3 Violence in the family This is linked to the two previous points. Wives and children are physically abused in the family and in the last 15 years there has been a growth in the women's refuges where they can go to escape from violent husbands; however, there are no refuges for children regularly beaten by parents. In 1985 the National Society for the Prevention of Cruelty to Children estimated that the numbers of cases of serious violence against children by parents had more than doubled.

4 Psychological disorders The psychiatrists Laing and Cooper, among others, have suggested that certain psychological disorders such as schizophrenia are closely linked to family life. When intense pressure is put upon children to conform to the parents' wishes, it can lead to psychological disturbance.

The Marxist view of the family

A completely opposite approach to family life to that of the functionalists mentioned earlier is taken by the Marxists, who see the family as performing a very useful role for the rich in controlling the population.

1 Social control The family passes on the very conservative values of society, teaching children to obey and not to question the world outside. This attitude remains in people as adults and they accept the economic system without criticism.

As adults most people are too concerned about their own family, caring for it and making sure that its members do well rather that causing 'trouble' by joining in radical political movements.

2 Economic effect The family is useful as the new generation is created and trained by the adults, ready for employment, without any cost to the owners. The male wage is generally seen as the one necessary to bring up the whole family.

3.5 Changing Relationships in the Family

HUSBANDS AND WIVES

At the beginning of the century the relationship between husband and wife could be described as **male dominated.** The father was the undoubted head of the household, his needs, his values, his viewpoint were always considered first.

Women were regarded as inferior and spent their lives as mothers, looking after the children; as wives, looking after the husband; and as housewives, looking after the home. The wife's **role**, that is the typical pattern of behaviour expected of a wife, reflected the attitudes held about women at that time. These attitudes were basically that women were naturally inferior to men and should accept their authority.

There were, however, considerable differences between the **social classes** which persisted over time.

Traditional working class relationships in the 1950s

Marriage was regarded as an exchange of economic provision (the wage, house, security) from the male for sexual and domestic services from the female. There were no joint leisure activities as these were prevented firstly by the long working hours of the men (10–12 hours per day) and secondly by working class culture, which stressed that separate leisure activities were normal and correct.

Middle class relationships in the 1950s

In their 1950's study of a middle class London suburb (Woodford) Willmott and Young argued that middle class family relationships were closer than working class ones because:

(a) middle class families generally had to move from one place to another for the man to gain promotion. This isolated them from the wider family and community, and, as a result, they were forced closer together;

(b) home ownership meant that the middle class family had an incentive to improve their home. As a result of working on the home to improve it, and the fact that it became a pleasanter place to live in, middle class men spent much more time at home and were therefore in contact with their wives and children for longer periods.

The symmetrical family

Much has happened since the 1950s. The values and relationships that were traditionally regarded as middle class:

1 equality between husband and wife
2 a sharing of domestic tasks
3 leisure time spent together as a family
4 a greater pride in the home

are being increasingly accepted by working class families.

The following factors have shifted the working class towards the middle class pattern of life:
1 The increasing importance of the home to working class couples (and this is especially true with the rapid growth in home ownership among the working class) has meant that the working class man lavishes more time and money on his home.
2 The increased geographical mobility of the working class
(a) as they move to seek work or better quality of work;
(b) as rehousing schemes break up the traditional inner city working class communities;
(c) as the decline in traditional industries such as coal and steel has eroded those solid working class communities.

All these factors have isolated the nuclear family pushing its members closer together.
3 The general rise in the status of women is reflected in legal and social changes. This acceptance of the equality of women with men has affected family relationships.
4 The increase in the number of women working has led to a degree of financial independence, so that they no longer have to rely solely on a husband's earnings.
5 Decrease in family size has led to reduced stress, higher standards of living and greater freedom for the woman.

All this has led Young and Willmott to describe the modern family as **symmetrical** which means simply that the modern family gives equality in all areas to husband and wife.

Friendship networks and family relationships

Although we can describe most familes now as in the stage of **the symmetrical family**, there are still many couples in both the middle and working class who do not share household tasks and who lead relatively separate lives.

Elizabeth Bott in *Family and Social Network* explains why some couples share domestic tasks and act jointly on most matters (what she calls a '**joint role relationship**') while others act independently ('**segregated role relationship**').

In an in-depth study of 20 London families, Bott found that if a couple shared the same group of friends before marriage – what she calls a '**close-knit social network**', then they were more likely to have a segregated role relationship irrespective of their social class.

She explains this by suggesting that if the husband and wife marry from within the same circle of friends and keep these after marriage, then the marriage does not have to provide them with close emotional support and mutual dependence. The friends are always there to help and to support. The life that the couple had before marriage continues.

However, if a couple come from separate groups then they are rather more isolated, and the marriage provides an abrupt change for both partners. In this situation the couple are more likely to rely on each other and develop a closer, shared pattern of life.

THE FEMINIST APPROACH

The idea that the relationship between husband and wife can best be described as **symmetrical** has been severely criticized by feminists, who point out that women benefit far less from marriage than men.

Women are expected to shoulder the larger proportion of the housework, to take the responsibility for the children, and to cook. They point out that violence against women is still common in family life and that this is generally ignored by the police unless it is extremely violent.

Research
1 Ann Oakley in *The Sociology of Housework*. Oakley studied 40 London housewives in the mid-1970s. Her findings included:

(a) 70 per cent of housewives were dissatisfied with their role;

(b) most felt isolated and lonely, as young children tended to cut them off from others, trapping them in the home;

(c) most felt that they had a very low status as a 'housewife';

(d) on average the women in her sample worked 77 hours each week;

(e) husbands regarded housework as the wives' job and they saw themselves as 'helpers'. Very few husbands actually took the main responsibility for any household chore.

2 In 1981, the Equal Opportunities Commission found in a survey of 175 working class women that in virtually every household task women were expected to take the main responsibility. This is illustrated in Table 3.1.

Table 3.1 Husband's participation in household tasks and child care

1 Household Tasks (percentages)

	Cleaning	Shopping	Cooking	Washing-up	Washing	Gardening	Household repairs	Decorating
Never	25	43	27	17	61	27	15	18
Occasionally	38	22	38	35	18	26	35	15
Regularly	21	17	20	30	6	17	19	21
Always	3	4	2	5	2	16	15	32
No husband	14	14	14	14	14	14	14	14
	101	100	101	101	101	100	98	100

2 Childcare (percentages)

	Looks after children on his own	Puts children to bed on his own
Never	15	24
Occasionally	48	42
Regularly	37	35
N=146 relevant cases	100	101

Source: Equal Opportunities Research funded by Equal Opportunities Commission and SSRC, 1981; Quoted in: P. Mayes *Gender*, 1986

Note: The column totals do not always equal 100 (as could be expected) since individual items may be rounded up or down.

3 A 1986 study by the Metropolitan Police uncovered 28,000 cases of violence against wives in London that year – the researchers suggested this may have been as little as ⅓ of all actual cases.

4 Women's careers are interrupted by child-bearing and rearing. This means that they may miss out on promotion at a crucial period in their working lives (25–32).

5 It has been suggested by Marxists that the housewife who stays at home to look after her children and husband, helps employers by providing free services on their behalf. By washing clothes, cooking, etc., a fresh, looked-after employee is fit and ready for work each day.

CHILDREN AND PARENTS

Changes in the relationships between parents and children in this century

At the beginning of this century children were very much under the authority of their parents, particularly the father. Factors which caused the acceptance of parental authority were:

(a) cultural stress on the inferiority of children. Children were 'to be seen and not heard';

(b) the fact that economic power was in the hands of the father (especially in the middle class) meant that he controlled the spending pattern of the family.

There were differences, however, between the middle and working class girls and boys.

In upper middle class homes children were often brought up by a nanny and were later sent to public schools. Here the boys learned the knowledge necessary to obtain entry into professional occupations. Girls were taught the skills considered more necessary to be good wives and accomplished hostesses. As a result of the long separation from parents, relationships between parents and children tended to be cool and distant.

In working class homes children were often sent out to work at the earliest age they could leave school (in 1901 it was 12 years of age), consequently childhood was much shorter for them. They soon began to contribute to the family income and this gave them some small measure of independence. Relationships between mother and children were usually close and affectionate. The father was less involved in family life and tended to be a figure of authority.

The roles expected of boys and girls were clearly distinct. Boys were expected to prepare themselves for a life of normal employment; girls to become efficient housewives and mothers.

Today, there has been a convergence between the middle and working classes in the way that parents and children act towards each other:

(a) there are closer emotional bonds between parents and children;
(b) children are treated more as responsible individuals;
(c) children have greater freedom of action;
(d) the distinction between boys' and girls' future roles in life is no longer as strong as it once was;
(e) the father is regarded far less as a figure of authority.

Factors that have caused these changes in relationships include:

(a) the changing child-rearing patterns of parents who give a higher level of care, and show greater interest in their children. This creates strong emotional bonds later in life;
(b) the growth of youth culture which stresses the freedom and independence of youth (see 'Youth Culture' pp 64–6);
(c) smaller families led to greater interest in and care of children.

Research

1 John and Elizabeth Newson in *Four Years Old in an Urban Community* studied the socialization patterns of a group of parents in Nottingham. They found clear social class differences in the way that parents treated their children:

(a) middle class parents were more likely to use verbal control rather than physical control to discipline their children;
(b) middle class parents explained why children should behave in certain ways and this led to the children feeling less frustrated at home and causing fewer problems to their parents.

SOCIALIZATION OF CHILDREN INTO GENDER ROLES

Traditionally parents in Britain have socialized their male and female children in very different ways. In particular girls have been raised:

1 To learn household tasks, traditionally associated with women; practising this by helping their mothers;

2 To see themselves in terms of their physical attractiveness; adjectives such as pretty, attractive, beautiful, etc. are more often used in describing girls than boys. This also involves developing in girls a greater interest in clothes;

3 To see tough or dirty games or work as not being appropriate for them – they learn that they are weaker and gentler than boys;

4 To see educational success and high job aspirations as being unimportant for them. Instead they see their futures as getting married and having children.

These elements of socialization have been reinforced in **books** that children read which have traditionally stressed the different roles expected from girls, and by the different **toys** that are given to girls (dolls) and boys (guns).

(For more details on female socialization see pp 54–6.)

THE OLDER GENERATION AND THE FAMILY

In pre-industrial societies it was rare for individuals to reach the age of 60. Today it is normal to live into one's seventies, so that over 16 per cent of the population are now over 65.

The implication for the family is that there are many more aged grandparents alive. Whether they are an asset to the family or a weight on its resources depends upon their health, which is often, in turn, dependent upon their age. As a general rule grandparents under 65 are useful to the family as:

1 They can care for children in the absence of parents, especially useful in periods of illness of the mother or if she wishes to go out to work;

2 If they live near by then they can provide day-to-day assistance;

3 According to Colin Bell in *Middle Class Families*, middle class grandparents who live some distance away still provide assistance to the younger generations by financial gifts such as presents for their grandchildren or articles for the house.

In a study by Hunt in 1976, over a third of elderly people visited their relatives at least once a week and one fifth said that they were 'able to do things to help' when they visited.

When grandparents become feeble and infirm, their usefulness to the family declines; they lose their authority. However, it does not mean that they are rejected or isolated from the wider family.

1 Old people are very often taken back into their family. Only about a third of over sixty-fives are living alone. The majority are either still living with their spouse or with the younger generation. Only 2 per cent live in residential homes.

2 Even those who do not live with the younger generation are not necessarily isolated. Hunt's survey showed that of the elderly with relatives alive, over 50 per cent received a visit at least once a week, and almost a third 'several times a week'.

3 Only 5 per cent of the elderly on average 'never received a visit'.

4 Where the younger generation is separated from their aged relatives, the telephone and post keep them in contact.

3.6 Varieties of Family in Britain

Most people hold an image of the typical British family as consisting of a wife and husband plus two or three young children. The wife stays at home looking after the children and the husband goes out to work—yet only about 30 per cent of households in Britain are composed of a married couple and their young children.

Table 3.2 Household types in Britain

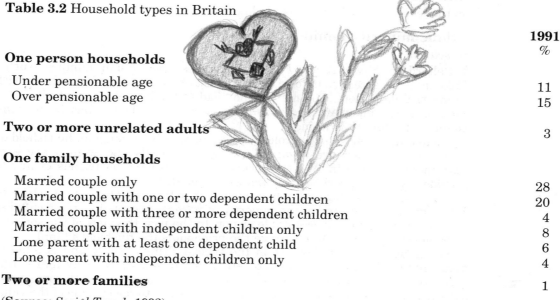

	1991 %
One person households	
Under pensionable age	11
Over pensionable age	15
Two or more unrelated adults	3
One family households	
Married couple only	28
Married couple with one or two dependent children	20
Married couple with three or more dependent children	4
Married couple with independent children only	8
Lone parent with at least one dependent child	6
Lone parent with independent children only	4
Two or more families	1

(**Source:** *Social Trends* 1992)

As Table 3.2 shows, 28 per cent of households are composed of married couples with no children, 29 per cent of households do not live in a family at all, 8 per cent are married couples with their grown-up children, and the remaining 10 per cent are one-parent families.

EXPLANATIONS FOR THE VARIETY OF FAMILY LIFE IN BRITAIN

1 Increasingly, the availability of contraceptives and the possibilities of careers for women have meant that women reject the traditional role of mother. They prefer not to have children and to pursue their careers.

2 The number of lone parent families has been increasing over the last ten years, as divorces increase and women do not necessarily choose to marry when they become pregnant outside marriage.

3 It is most important to remember that a family is a **dynamic institution**, which is changing all the time. Each family will typically go through a **family life cycle**, passing from one stage to the other. These stages may typically include:

(a) young marrieds, both working, no children;

(b) young marrieds with children;

(c) middle aged with older children leaving home;

(d) old with all children living independently;

(e) one remaining original partner (usually the wife), with other original partner dead.

An analysis of family life would have to take into account all these stages. So although there are only 24 per cent of households with young children, many of the 28 per cent of married couples without children may be in stages (a) and (d) of the family life cycle. Furthermore, many of the 15 per cent of one-person households over pensionable age may be the widow/widower in stage (e).

Single-parent families

The increase in single-parent families has been a result of:

1 increasing divorce rates;

2 the increasingly common decision of women who become pregnant not to marry – reflecting a change in the attitudes of women to marriage and their role in society.

The rise in single-parent families has been seen by some as a threat to marriage and the conventional family. They argue that the children need two parents ideally and that one parent is unable to look after the children adequately if he/she works (for he/she will be out all day). This has led to a growth in child minding. On the other hand, if the single parent does not work and lives on state benefits he/she will be unable to provide an adequate standard of living.

Against this it is argued that:

(a) only a very small proportion of families are headed by one parent;

(b) unhappily married partners give their children an unstable home background, which is often linked to later social problems with the children;

(c) the level of state benefits is too low.

Ethnic minority families

Research

1 Ballard in *South Asian Families* has described Asian families (such as Indians and Pakistanis) as extended in form. They consist of man, sons and grandsons with their wives and unmarried daughters. The man is the head of the household, controlling family finance and making most important decisions. The style of family life has been transferred from the country of origin to Britain.

Women have very distinct roles from men, mainly working on household duties and having to accept that men are regarded as superior. Girls and women are expected to behave extremely modestly in Western terms and not to have boyfriends or any form of social life outside the kin network. This is known as **purdah**.

Marriages are **arranged**, which means that the parents find a partner for their children, although in practice today the majority of parents accept that their children will have some say in which partner is acceptable or not. In the past the view of the son or daughter has not been very important. On marriage the bride joins the husband's family.

The family is much closer than the typical British family and is often not just a unit of consumption, for they may work together in a business, in a way that is rare in Britain.

There is the beginning of conflict between the generations, with some younger Asian people influenced by the Western values. They have begun to reject some of the values of obedience to parents, of extreme modesty and arranged marriages that are expected of them by the older generation. However, the majority of those studied simply adapted their behaviour, behaving as expected at school and then switching to the values of their ethnic community in their private lives.

2 Oakley studied Cypriot families in London (*Cypriot Families*). She concluded that here the male dominates and the women are trapped in the house with a purely domestic role to play. The husband has all the dealings with the wider world and effectively makes all decisions. The honour of the family is very important and neither male nor female should do anything that could be regarded as staining this honour – such as sexual promiscuity on the part of the females. The family is of the extended type.

3 Driver studied families of West Indian origin (*West Indian Families*). He suggested that there are two types of Black family structure in Britain. The first is the nuclear family in which both partners share all domestic tasks. However, there is another form – the **mother-centred family**. This is the result of lack of stable employment for the men, and a cultural norm borrowed from the West Indies. The mother is left on her own to bring up the children and provide an income. The husband is a person who appears only occasionally and provides little regular support for the family. The mother is the dominant figure in the household and it is around her that the family forms. This form of family accounts for about one third of families in the West Indies.

3.7 Alternatives to the Conventional Family

The family is not the only form of group life possible. There have been, and still are, alternatives to it.

Historical alternatives

The Oneida community

In 1848 John Humphrey Noyes created the Oneida community, based on communal living. Noyes believed that individualism and the narrow nuclear family was bad and that there had to be greater stress on wider social bonds.

All males and females had sexual access to one another, although this was conducted in a very formal way. Any advance had to be through an older, respected member of the community.

Sexual pleasure was distinguished from the creation of children. A selected group of men and women only were allowed to bear children and these offspring were the children of the whole family community. Strong feelings between parents and their children were discouraged.

Disputes and disreputable behaviour were controlled by a committee of people who confronted the wrongdoer and criticized him/her.

Twentieth-century alternatives

The Kibbutz

Kibbutzim (the plural of *kibbutz*) were set up in Israel soon after its foundation in 1948. These were communes which, like the Oneida community, stressed the community and not the individual or the family. Children were brought up together in a nursery under the charge of nurses and the community not the parents had the final say in the lives of the children. Parents spent part of each day with their children and might eat with them, but they did not sleep or live separately with them.

Marriage was simple – a couple moved into a room together. Divorce was simple, too – one person moved out.

However, in the last 15 years it seems that the family has made a limited comeback in the *kibbutzim* and there are now special arrangements in most of them for married couples with children so that they spend some of their time together and may even have separate living quarters.

3.8 Family Life in Another Society

THE JAPANESE FAMILY

Pre-industrial Japan

The family was the most important institution of Japanese society before the coming of industrialization. Even relationships between employer and employees were viewed in family-type terms, similar to that between father and son.

The traditional Japanese family controlled every aspect of life of its members, and the laws of the state supported this. The father was the undisputed head of the household and property was passed from him to the eldest son. Other sons, on getting married, were expected to start a separate household, and they received help to do this from the eldest son. For example, the eldest son would give his younger brothers a piece of property, or a small part of the family business.

The family of the father/eldest son would be known as the **stem family** and those of the younger brothers/sons were called the **branch families**. The decisions of the head of the stem family were binding on all family members. Obedience to the head of the stem family was far more important than the ties of marriage.

Clearly, in this male-dominated society, women had a subordinate role.

Households were often expanded by the addition of the children of poor people, who 'sold' their children to the rich. These children became full, if lowly, members of the household (they were called *fudai*) and were treated as family members. (This bears some resemblance to the situation in England described by Laslett, see p 15.)

The marriages of all family members, including the *fudai*, were arranged by the head of the family.

Industrialization This occurred in Japan in the late nineteenth century, and was connected with the rapid rise of cities, trade and manufacturing. The result was to weaken the stem/branch family relationship. People left to move to the cities, and there was the possibility for a branch family of creating an independent economic unit for itself.

As in Britain, in the initial stages of industrialization (see p 15), kin often helped each other to cope with the uncertainty of work and life in the cities. However, as prosperity increased, the extended family weakened and the nuclear family form developed.

The importance of the stem/branch family remained embedded in the law until the new constitution was introduced after the Second World War, when the traditional legal powers of the head of the family were abolished.

Many of the values of the traditional family remain, however. In particular the attitude to the role of women in the family has changed little. They are expected to give way to the authority of the male and to stay at home to look after the children and do the housework. The proportion of married Japanese women working is much smaller than in Britain, although it is gradually increasing. The modern Japanese family still stresses the importance of the obedience of children to their parents – far more so than in Britain.

3.9 Marriage

This century the number of marriages steadily increased until the early 1970s and overall has been on the decline since then. This is illustrated in Table 3.3.

Table 3.3 Total number of marriages in Britain (thousands)

1901	1921	1951	1961	1971	1972	1973	1974	1975	1976	1977	1978	1980	1981	1982	1983
360	360	400	387	447	470	450	425	420	396	360	407	415	398	387	389

Source: *Social Trends* (adapted)

This is not the full story, however, as the **total** number of marriages includes remarriage by divorcees and widows/widowers. If we subtract these from the total number of marriages, as illustrated in Table 3.4, then a clear pattern emerges. There has been a marked overall decline in first marriages and an *increase* in remarriages. Indeed one area of noticeable growth is in third or even fourth marriages. This tendency to marry, divorce, remarry (and perhaps repeat the cycle of divorce/remarriage) is known as **serial monogamy**.

Table 3.4 Total number of first and second marriages in Britain

Year	1961	1966	1971	1976	1979	1980	1984
First marriage for both partners (thousands)	331	358	357	273	270	270	259
Second marriage for one or both partners (thousands)	56	68	90	123	137	139	137
Remarriages as a percentage of marriages	15	16	20	31	34	34	35

Reasons for the decline in first marriages

1 Changing values – it is not now regarded as wrong for a couple to live together (cohabit). However, marriage still remains the socially more approved relationship.
2 Demography – there are fewer people in the marriageable age groups (20–30), so the numbers marrying for the first time would decrease.
3 Later marriage – people are marrying later in life. This means that for a number of years the total numbers of people marrying declines – there is a time lag before the numbers pick up again. This may be happening now.

Age at marriage

The median age of marriage dropped in the 1960s but has steadily increased during the 1970s and '80s. However, this includes the remarriages we discussed earlier. If we take the median age of first marriages, the figure declines, e.g. the median age of marriage for a single man marrying a single woman was 25.5 in 1970 and 23.7 in 1979.

Number of children

Throughout this century there has been a clear decline in the number of children in the family. In 1900 the average number of children was 3.3, by the 1980s it had fallen to 1.9. The **average** figure, however, masks differences between the social classes, as middle class family sizes have always been smaller than working class family sizes. (Family size is discussed on pp 15–16.)

3.10 Divorce

There has been a clear rise in the divorce rate this century, as illustrated in Figure 3.1.
It ought to be noted that divorce is **not** the only form of marital breakdown. There also exist the following:

1 **separation** where spouses live entirely apart but remain legally married. Many Catholics are in this situation as the Catholic Church does not allow divorce. A rise of 60 per cent occurred in the decade 1960–70, according to a study by R. Chester;

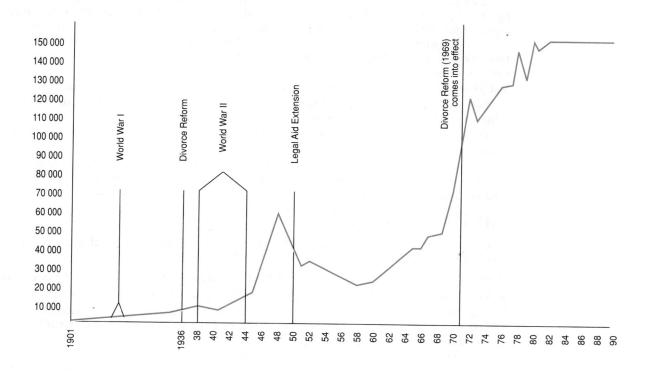

Fig. 3.1 Changes in the number of divorces in England & Wales, 1904 – 90

Oynastit / oli '23:1/

2 desertion where one partner simply walks out on the family. Often the deserted spouse never actually bothers to divorce the missing partner;

3 unhappy marriage—two partners may continue to live together, even if they intensely dislike each other. This may be 'for the sake of the children', or for financial reasons.

There are no reliable figures for these last two categories of marital breakdown.

SOCIAL FACTORS CAUSING THE RISE IN THE DIVORCE RATE

1 Legal changes   2 Attitude change
3 Expectations of marriage   4 Specific historical factors
5 Urbanization   6 Increasing independence of women

1 *Legal changes* The divorce rate is an almost exact reflection of the gradual liberalization of divorce this century. There appears to be a **dam effect** with a build-up of people wanting divorce leading to a change in the law, and as a result a sudden rise in divorce.

1857 Divorce available for the first time in the courts, although the law for men was different from that for women, allowing men to obtain divorces more easily.

1937 Divorce made easier, with one partner having to **prove** that the other partner had committed some offence against the marriage vows such as adultery or cruelty.

1950 Extension of legal aid to divorce. This meant that many people, particularly women, who previously could not afford to start divorce proceedings were able to proceed.

1969 The law was changed so that the **irretrievable breakdown of marriage** became the only reason for divorce. This meant separation for two years if both partners wanted the divorce, or separation for five years if only one partner wanted the divorce. It has to be remembered that changes in the law reflect changes in public opinion, so we cannot say that the changes in divorce laws **caused** a rise in divorce, rather they **allowed** a rise in divorce.

2 *Attitude change* At the turn of the century divorce was considered disgraceful and there was a stigma attached to being a divorcee. These attitudes towards divorce were strengthened by the values of the established churches. However, there has been a definitive shift of opinion.

3 *Expectations of marriage* William Goode, an American sociologist, argues that the partners expect too much from each other in modern marriages. He points to the fact that traditionally, in Europe, and still today among many Asian families, arranged marriages are common. As the partners have relatively low expectations of their partners, they are prepared to be far more flexible in their relationships.

4 *Specific historical factors* The first of these may be seen as the fivefold increase in the number of divorces after the Second World War. This was mainly due to the disruption caused by the war. The second occurred in the late 1950s and early '60s, when the freedom, early sexual maturity and affluence led to a sudden rise in teenage marriages, with over one third of all brides being under 21 in this period. The highest rates of divorce are among young marrieds, so in the 1960s and '70s, part of the sharp rise in divorce can be attributed to this fashion of early marriage.

5 *Urbanization* The move into large-scale, impersonal city life has meant that:

(a) there is a greater chance of meeting a partner with a different class or ethnic background which may lead to eventual problems with a clash of cultures;

(b) there is less pressure from the community to stay together as the scale of city life makes the individuals feel anonymous.

6 *Independence of women* Nowadays 70 per cent of divorces are filed by women. This reflects the rise in the independence of women this century and their refusal to accept the traditional role of housewife and mother.

THE END OF MARRIAGE ?

In recent years it has been argued that we are witnessing the end of marriage as we know it. Evidence to support this includes:

1 Since the mid 1970s the number of people marrying has declined by 15 per cent;

2 The number of divorces has increased in the last ten years by 30 per cent;

3 One child in eight is now born outside marriage, compared to one in seventeen in 1961. This has occurred despite introduction of abortion and the widespread use of contraception, with the consequent control of unwanted pregnancies;

4 A third of abortions are performed on married women, indicating a possible rejection of the traditional child-bearing role. This rejection of the traditional role is reinforced by the fact that 70 per cent of divorces are started by wives;

5 The number of lone parent families is growing steadily. By this is meant those families with only one parent. Today, one family in eight is headed by one parent only;

6 Dominian's survey of divorce revealed that couples are less likely than in the past to see their wedding vows binding them to their partners for life. If they are unhappy they see it as their right to separate.

EVIDENCE FOR THE CONTINUING STABILITY OF MARRIAGE

1 Divorce rates do not reflect unhappy or broken marriages. Some people may separate but never divorce, for a variety of social or financial reasons. In the past when it was difficult to obtain divorce, unhappily married couples merely separated or lived together in a dreadful atmosphere. Today the more liberal divorce laws may reflect more accurately the number of unsuccessful marriages, but there is no evidence to suggest that the number of those marriages has actually increased.

2 Although large numbers of young people cohabit, this does not mean that they reject marriage. Of women marrying in the late 1970s, over 20 per cent had previously lived with their husbands. This indicates that cohabitation is seen as a first step towards marriage, rather than as an alternative.

3 For the majority of divorcees, remarriage is almost a certainty. Today three quarters of divorcees remarry. The average length of time before remarriage for a woman of 25–29 years of age is two years. This indicates that marriage has not declined in popularity, but that people increasingly wish to change partners. The **institution** of marriage is therefore still stable.

(However, those remarrying are twice as likely to divorce again as first-time marrieds.)

4 In *Values and the Changing Family* (1982) the **Study Commission on the Family** points out that the majority of people questioned firmly believed in the family and regarded family life as the ideal to be aimed at.

3.11 Summary

1 There are two extreme family types, extended and nuclear; most societies have a mixture of both.

2 There are a number of different forms of marriage, including polygamy, polyandry and monogamy.

3 The type of marriage varies with the culture and economic situation of the society.

4 The typical family in Britain before industrialization was the nuclear type. However, better-off households were larger because orphans, related kin and child servants all lived in.

5 Early industrialization brought an increase in the number of extended families living in

industrial towns and giving mutual assistance. These lasted right up to the 1950s in some cases.

6 The family performs some functions for society and its members, including the regulation of sexual activity, socialization, production of children, economic activity and emotional support.

7 However, it is also agreed that the family can be harmful to its members, because of the intense emotional ties within it.

8 There is a debate among **functionalist** sociologists about the extent to which the family has lost its functions. It is probably true to say that it is less important to people today than in pre-industrial societies.

9 Relationships have changed considerably among family members. In particular –

10 children are treated with greater consideration and there is an acceptance of their right to have a viewpoint and a say in the affairs of the family.

11 However, girls and boys are brought up very differently to have clear **gender roles**.

12 Women have gained a greater measure of equality in the home (and in society generally). Some sociologists have gone so far as to argue that there is now equality in the household and that men do as many household chores as women. This form of relationship has been called the **symmetrical family**.

13 Feminist sociologists have argued that this is an exaggeration and that women have to do the bulk of housework and child rearing.

14 The idea that the elderly are isolated from the wider family seems to be untrue. Most of the elderly who have family are in regular contact with them.

15 There is a wide variety of family forms in Britain today, including lone parent families, families formed through divorce and remarriage, couples without children, etc and the families of ethnic minorities.

16 Families as we know them are not the only form of group life – there have been communes and there are *kibbutzim*, for example.

17 Industrialization has also affected family life in other societies – for example in Japan, where the authority of the male head of household has been undermined, and the extended or 'stem/branch' family has given way to the nuclear family.

18 Marriage: people are marrying later and are more likely to live together before marriage.

19 They are having fewer children.

20 Divorce has increased rapidly since the 1960s.

21 The increase in divorce reflects changing attitudes and expectations from marriage and the fact that divorce is now easier to obtain.

22 Marriage still remains very popular, with 90 per cent of the population marrying.

3.12 Keywords (*as they appear in the unit*)

kin, extended family, nuclear family, patriarchal family, matriarchal family, monogamy, polygamy, polygyny, polyandry, conjugal roles, symmetrical family, privatized (family), joint role relationship, segregated role relationship, family life cycle, commune.

4 EDUCATION

4.1 Socialization and Education

Learning about society does not start or finish at school, but happens throughout our lives. Schools contribute to this learning process in two ways, through **formal learning** and through **informal learning**.

FORMAL LEARNING

1 This is the academic or practical knowledge taught to us at school and college.

2 It consists of clearly defined skills or bodies of knowledge taught in an organized manner (the lesson), which can be graded and tested (examinations) after a set period (the length of the course). Each subject we are taught at school, such as mathematics or history, is an example of formal learning.

3 Formal learning is the official reason for the existence of schools.

INFORMAL LEARNING

1 This form of learning is part of the socialization process, in which we learn social skills and values that are necessary in order to function as a normal person in society.

2 Informal learning is not organized or examined (except that if we are badly socialized we may be regarded as deviant by others).

3 It is learned in our daily lives through interaction with other people and through the mass media. The most important people who influence our informal learning are family, the peer group (people of our own age), and especially our friends and teachers.

All complex industrial societies have education systems for formal education in order to train people how to carry out the tasks necessary to maintain the economic system of a rapidly changing society. The education system trains scientists, clerks and tradespeople.

In simpler societies without industrialization and rapid social change, there was no need for a formal education system. All learning took place informally through the family, religion and the peer group. Knowledge of farming or hunting useful to one generation was also of use to the next.

Informal learning in the school: the hidden curriculum

The distinction between the two forms of learning is not totally clear, however. Formal learning may occur in the home, e.g. where a mother teaches her child to bake a cake or repair a car; while in school informal learning takes place alongside formal learning. An English lesson may be about a comprehension exercise, but the teacher may choose an extract on old age. Through the lesson the pupil may be socialized informally to expect certain patterns of behaviour from the elderly.

In fact informal learning as a part of the process of socialization occurs as much in the school as does formal learning. All the things that the pupils learn at school which are not officially part of the lessons are known as the **hidden curriculum**. The term is used because all the lessons that form the typical school timetable are collectively known as the curriculum.

EXAMPLES OF THE HIDDEN CURRICULUM

1 Gender roles Through the actions of teachers in responding to girls and boys differently and expecting different forms of behaviour from them (see pp 54 – 6) children learn the behaviour expected of the sexes.

2 Racial differences Just like gender roles, children also become aware of the differences in ethnic groups. This is partly through the attitudes and expectations of teachers, and partly through the content of books and lessons they study. For example, very few books, if any, studied at school have a black heroine or hero (see pp 38 – 9).

3 Class differences Research by Sharpe and Green indicates that teachers are more sympathetic towards middle class children and find it easier to relate to them, possibly because the teachers come from middle class backgrounds themselves.

4 Streaming and examinations These prepare children for the inequality of later life when some groups take the better jobs with higher prestige and better rates of pay. Children come to regard it as natural that people are graded.

5 Language Working class children and those from the ethnic minorities discover that the

FORMAL ·LEARNING * INFORMAL LEARNING

forms of English they use are inferior to the middle class language of the school books they study.

6 Social control Children learn that they must do what they are told, even if this is not what they want to do. They are therefore prepared for work later when they must obey their bosses even if the work seems pointless and boring.

7 The peer group Pupils of the same age are known as the **peer group** and they are extremely important in influencing the attitudes and behaviour of their colleagues. In lower streams, for instance, it is not regarded as 'the done thing' to be helpful and polite to teachers. This can lead to anti-school groups who will help develop values that will lead to school failure.

The research of Paul Willis (*Learning to Labour*) is important here. He shows how lower stream pupils learn to see school as completely unimportant. They develop values that enable them to cope with the boredom and irrelevance of school—for instance, they muck around, playing tricks on teacher, and the result is they fail. However, these very values that led to their certain failure also allow them to cope with the boring work they might later obtain.

4.2 Educational Change

THE TRIPARTITE SYSTEM

The 1944 **Butler Act** emerged as the Second World War neared its end and as a new concept became accepted in educational circles, i.e. **meritocracy** (defined as a society in which every child is given the maximum help to develop his/her own talents. Education is not seen as something to be bought, but as every child's right). Among its reforms it introduced:

1 An intelligence examination at the age of 11 (11+) to grade children by ability. This was based on IQ (intelligence quotient);

2 Three types of schools which were to cater for three types of child that the Act claimed existed in Britain:

(a) **Grammar schools** for the academic child, taking the top 30 per cent;

(b) **Secondary Technical schools** for the technically minded;

(c) **Secondary Modern schools** for the less academic.

Because there were three different schools it was called the **tripartite system**. Each type of school was meant to be equal in prestige.

Reasons for the Act

The aim of the Act was to give each child the best education appropriate to him/her, irrespective of financial circumstances. In this way it was hoped to break down the rigid class structure of British society. An equal opportunity to succeed was to be given to each child. The belief was that Britain would benefit, too, as a result of the mushrooming of untapped working class talent.

At the same time the Government was aware that the industrial development of Britain lay in training a highly educated, technically and scientifically skilled workforce. The Butler Act responded by radically overhauling the education system.

Criticisms of the tripartite system

By the late 1950s educationalists had serious doubts about the value of the tripartite system.

1 Most middle class children attended grammar schools; most working class attended secondary moderns. Class barriers were not being broken down.

2 The 11+ examination was shown to be inaccurate, up to a figure of 10 per cent according to Vernon in a study of IQ tests. This meant that large numbers of children were being sent to the wrong type of school.

3 The division of children into different schools at 11 was too early, limiting their later development. In particular late developers were often trapped in secondary moderns.

THE COMPREHENSIVE SCHOOL DEBATE

In 1965 the Labour government wrote to Local Education Authorities (in 'Circular 10/65'), requesting a move towards a comprehensive system of schooling. A comprehensive school is a secondary school that takes all children within a particular neighbourhood, regardless of ability.

The road to comprehensive schooling has not been simple and has been blocked on occasion by Conservative governments, then advanced rapidly by Labour administrations.

In support of the comprehensive system

1 Comprehensive schools allow pupils to develop at their own pace, rather than restricting them to one particular type of school at the early age of 11;

2 If all children attend comprehensive schools there will be a mixture from every social background. This will destroy class divisions;

3 The larger size of the comprehensives makes it financially possible to provide better facilities such as swimming pools, craft workshops, computing laboratories, etc.;

4 No child will be labelled a failure at 11 and will be spared the humiliation and frustration that occurred among many secondary modern pupils.

Criticisms of the comprehensive system

1 More intelligent children are held back by the less academic environment. The country is therefore wasting its best young talents;

2 The schools are far too large and impersonal;

3 Comprehensives do **not** break down class barriers. They draw their intake from the immediate neighbourhood. If the local neighbourhood is middle class, for instance, the school becomes a middle class preserve with no mixing with working class children.

Research findings

1 The National Children's Bureau studied 16 000 children born in March 1958. They were all tested at the age of 11, on entry to secondary school, in reading ability and maths. They were tested again at the age of 16. The results indicated no difference whatsoever in the results at 16 of the brigher children, whether they attended grammar or comprehensive schools. However, lower ability children performed better at 16 if they attended a comprehensive rather than a secondary modern.

These results give strong support to those in favour of the comprehensive school, because in many areas at that time, grammar schools and comprehensives existed in the same district and many of the brighter children were sent to the grammars, thus depriving the comprehensives of some of this potential. (This is known as **creaming**.)

2 Auriol Stephens (*Clever Children in Comprehensive Schools*) concluded that the most able children may have suffered slightly, but the majority of pupils have benefited from comprehensives. She found, too, that comprehensives have given far more children confidence to enter public examinations. This may indicate that the feeling of being failures among the lower ability children is being overcome.

3 Julienne Ford (*Social Class and the Comprehensive School*) argued that all schools can do is to **mirror society**. Inequalities of class, gender and race cannot be solved by changing the type of school, as these inequalities are so deep rooted in the wider society.

RECENT CHANGES IN THE EDUCATION SYSTEM

The Assisted Places Scheme This was introduced by the Conservative government to encourage children of high ability to apply for free places in public schools. The effects have been (a) to deprive the state schools of a number of their cleverest children; (b) to give support to the public schools by making it seem that their examination results are far superior to the State schools, when in fact they are simply taking some of the better State-educated pupils, who would have got good examination results anyway.

Vocational preparation There has been a major shift away from the traditional courses, such as GCSE, towards more **vocationally orientated** courses (courses which are basically to train people in skills necessary for jobs), such as BTEC.

Funding Increasingly the money for education is coming direct from the government, through TECs which are only willing to pay for education that trains people in skills for work. The idea of education as a means of widening people's horizons is losing favour.

City technical colleges: in order to train pupils in technical and vocational skills, these secondary specialist technical schools have been introduced where the stress is on engineering and science.

4.3 Public Schools

There are 218 public schools in Britain. They are all private, fee-charging institutions, which belong to an exclusive organization called the Headmasters' Conference.

There is disagreement over the desirability of private schools in general and public schools in particular.

Supporters of the public schools claim that:

1 It is the right of all parents to choose to pay for their child's education. Furthermore, most of the population could afford to pay if they made small sacrifices;

2 Public schools provide better facilities, particularly in the form of smaller classes;

3 Staff are generally more highly qualified than in state schools;

4 Examination results are better than in state schools, e.g. 25 per cent of university places go to public school pupils, yet they make up only 5 per cent of secondary school places.

Critics argue that:

1 Only the affluent can afford to send their children to public schools and that this maintains the clear social divisions between the rich and the rest of the population;

2 The public schools, which are mainly for the well-off, are classified as charities and so receive considerable tax benefits. In effect they are supported by the taxpayer in general;

3 The Assisted Places Scheme, which allows clever children from state schools to enter public schools by having their fees paid by the Local Education Authorities, effectively creams (takes away the brightest pupils) from the state schools.

4 A greater number of university places are awarded to public school boys because the schools have close connections with the universities. In particular, this is true of the Universities of Oxford and Cambridge, where almost 50 per cent of the undergraduates come from public schools;

5 There exists an **old boys' network** which ensures that top jobs are provided for ex-public school boys by others already in important positions. Thus the rich perpetuate their wealth and influence.

4.4 The Functions of Education for Society

The functionalist school of sociology analyses each social institution (e.g. the family, the political system, religion, education) in terms of **the functions** it performs for the existence of society, in much the same way that to understand the purpose of a heart, we look at the function it performs for the existence of the body.

Functionalists conclude that there are four functions of the education system:

1 the transmission of culture   2 social control
3 economic training   4 social selection

1 The transmission of culture (or socialization)

To exist every society needs a basic set of shared beliefs and values. In order for society to continue, it is necessary to pass on these values from one generation to the next. It is a particularly important function in our complex form of society, where many different cultural groups must exist together. The school transmits a core set of values around which society adheres.

This cultural transmission function may be reinforced by other agencies such as the family or the mass media. However, in certain cases, such as among the children of immigrants, the school alone teaches them the values of our society (see Socialization and Education pp 28–9).

2 Social control

Closely allied to the transmission of culture is the need for each society to regulate the activities of its members. We cannot be allowed to do just what we want. Schools teach us the specific behaviour expected of us. We learn about acceptable and unacceptable, perhaps even illegal, behaviour. Part of this social control function is to pass on an acceptance of the political system of our society.

3 Economic training

Each society needs to produce its economic necessities in order to survive. Our economic system, based upon industry, needs a wide variety of skills varying across the range from scientist to plumber to chef. The education system produces an adequate supply of trained manpower for every skill required.

4 Social selection

Society needs the more able children to perform the more complex jobs. Ideally, the education system should grade children according to their ability, so that they may learn the level of skill best suited to their ability. In such a way society best uses its available talents.

The Functions Of Education: A Criticism

The functionalist viewpoint we have just read implies that the education system benefits everybody in society equally. Many sociologists – particularly those influenced by the Marxist approach – disagree with this viewpoint. They argue instead that powerful groups in our society use education to *impose* beliefs and values that benefit them on the rest of society. So children are taught at school to do what they are told, to accept society as it is without questioning why it is organized so that a few are extremely rich and the rest work for a wage in order to keep the few rich.

In reality education does not reflect the needs of society, but the needs of the owners of industry and commerce for a docile workforce with enough skills to do the jobs needed.

Bowles and Gintis (*Schooling in Capitalist Society*) studied 237 final year US secondary school pupils. They found that pupils who received the highest grades were more likely to be the hardworking, quiet, reliable ones who did what they were told without question. On the other hand, low grades were associated with students who were creative, aggressive and independent. There was no evidence to suggest that the aggressive, low-grade students were less intelligent than the high-grade obedient ones. Schools are not then rewarding intelligence, but conformity.

4.5 Social Class and Educational Achievement

THE FACTS OF DISADVANTAGE

Research has shown that the higher a child's parents are in the class structure, the greater that child's chances of educational success.

1 At the age of seven, 48 per cent of children with parents in unskilled manual jobs were found to be poor readers for their age. This compares to only 8 per cent of children with parents employed in the professions.

2 By the age of sixteen, 34 per cent of those with parents in non-manual occupations had obtained five or more O Levels compared to only 11 per cent of those with parents in manual jobs.

3 Over 60 per cent of children from non-manual backgrounds stay in education after the age of sixteen, compared to only 27 per cent of those from manual backgrounds.

4 Since the 1944 Education Act, 27 per cent of children from professional backgrounds obtained degrees compared to less than 3 per cent from unskilled manual backgrounds.

THE EXPLANATIONS FOR EDUCATIONAL DIFFERENCES

In explaining why there are differences in educational achievement, sociologists have stressed:

1 The influence of the home;
2 The influence of the neighbourhood;
3 The influence of the school.

However, before we look at sociological explanations we need to look at the issue of intelligence, which is often used as an explanation of educational disadvantage.

1 Intelligence

Psychologists such as H Eysenck argue that differences in educational attainment reflect the fact that individuals inherit their intelligence from their parents in much the same way that a person inherits his facial features. (The term used to describe this view of intelligence is **innate intelligence**.) Furthermore, intelligence can be measured by IQ tests such as those used in the 11+. A person's IQ can be measured by dividing his mental age by his chronological age, and multiplying by one hundred. So a person with a mental age of twelve but a real age of ten has an IQ of 120 (12/10×100). Most sociologists argue that although we inherit a degree of mental capacity from our parents, most of our intelligence is determined by our culture and our upbringing. In particular they make the following points:

1 What is considered to be intelligence varies from society to society. An intelligent person in a tribal society may be considered stupid in ours;
2 IQ scores vary over time and a person can improve them with practice;
3 IQ tests measure only the ability of the person tested to conform to the tester's idea of intelligence. This varies with class and background culture.

2 The role of the home in educational attainment

In explaining why certain children, usually from the working class, achieve poor academic results, many sociologists point to *three* areas of disadvantage linked with the home background of working-class children.

(a) *The values and behaviour of a child's family* Parents may have little interest in their children's education and may incline a child to a lack of enthusiasm for learning that may ensure his later failure.

The National Children's Bureau conducted a nationwide survey of children born in a week of March 1946. The study followed the children throughout their schooldays. Among its many conclusions it found that middle class parents are more likely to be interested because:

(i) they are more aware of the importance of education;
(ii) they are usually in a better position to encourage and advise as they are well educated themselves.

(b) *The form of language used in the home* In order to benefit from an academic education, a wide vocabulary and an ability to communicate clearly and cogently are crucial. Basil Bernstein has suggested that parents pass on vocabulary and ability with language to their children. The more clearly parents reply to children's questions and explain things to them, the better the children will be in their use of language.

Bernstein distinguishes between two codes of speech:

(i) **elaborated**, where a wide vocabulary is used with the child and he is encouraged fully to explore his language potential. This code is most often found in middle class homes;

(ii) **restricted**, where the child is spoken to with a narrow range of vocabulary. This is more often found in working class homes.

The result is that middle class children are more likely to be adept at language when they attend school and this gives them a great advantage when speaking or writing.

(c) *The physical conditions of the home* Many children from poorer homes suffer physical deprivation, which affects their school progress; for example, undernourishment leads to a feeling of tiredness and an inability to concentrate. Damp and overcrowded homes cause regular illnesses and consequent absences from school.

Wedge and Prosser (*Born to Fail?*) in a national study of children born in one week in 1958 found that three important factors influenced school success:

(i) large families
(ii) low income
(iii) poor housing

In total more than 1 in 16 children suffer from all three of these disadvantages.

FACTORS·INFLUENCING·EDUCATIONAL ·ATTAINMENT·

3 The role of the neighbourhood

The local environment in which we live is a powerful influence on our lives. If there is general support for the values of the school, then it can only help school progress.

As the values of schools are generally seen as being *middle class*, then the values of working class neighbourhoods may well clash with those of the school. For example, schools stress sacrificing short term gain now (such as wages and employment) for longer term aims (A Levels, then a degree and at the end of studying a good job). Yet the values of the working class neighbourhood stress immediate pleasure (go out and find a job, get a car, have a bit of money to spend, why wait five more years?).

Pupils in predominantly working class neighbourhoods are faced with a difficult choice, especially if they see their friends and neighbours (their **peer group**) out enjoying themselves while they stay in to study. Also, it is unlikely that in an inner city working class area there could be many people who had been highly educated to give help and encouragement.

CULTURAL DEPRIVATION

Most of the disadvantages we have mentioned so far accumulate, creating cultural barriers that prevent certain groups of children, particularly the poor and some of the ethnic minorities, from benefiting fully from attendance at school. The culture of the home and neighbourhood simply does not provide the sort of support that is necessary if a child is to succeed in the education system. There may be no books in the home, or no encouragement to read. In the case of children of immigrants, the language of the home may not be English. The parents may be illiterate, or uninterested in education. Sociologists refer to this sort of situation as one of **cultural deprivation**.

The term first became used in Britain as a result of the **Plowden Report**, a government enquiry which reported in 1967. The conclusion of the Report was that cultural deprivation was the main reason for education failure of poor and immigrant children. The report argued that unless the child was helped at a very early age to overcome the culturally barren home or community life, then he/she was doomed to fail.

As a result of this, a programme of **compensatory education** (or **positive discrimination**) was instituted. The idea here was that if enough extra education resources were pumped into poor, inner city areas, then the extra education provided would help the children to overcome the deficiences of their home background. The extra facilities provided included:

(a) more nursery schools;

(b) extra teachers with slightly higher pay;

(c) more school equipment.

The areas that received the extra help were known as **educational priority areas**. The whole approach was closely connected with the **culture of poverty** (discussed on p 110) and the **cycle of poverty**.

A similar programme had already been running in the United States, when the Plowden Report was being prepared. There was a much greater input of resources into the deprived inner city areas of America under the title of Operation Headstart than in Britain.

Criticisms

The whole area of compensatory education has been attacked:

1 By Bernstein, who argues that it makes no sense to improve the schools when the homes and neighbourhoods the deprived children come from are so lacking in amenities. It is the poverty of the home and neighbourhood that should be tackled first.

2 By the American sociologist Valentine, who argues that calling the children of the poor and of immigrant backgrounds 'culturally deprived' is an insult. What they have are *different* cultures, and it ought to be recognized that Britain (and the United States) are multicultural societies and the subjects and style of teaching in the school ought to take account of this. For example, there ought to be more classes on Asian history and African studies.

4 The role of the school in educational attainment

Sociologists are aware of the importance of factors within schools in encouraging or discouraging pupils in their studies.

(a) *Good teaching* Organized, interested teachers provide an excellent learning situation for children. Rutter (*Fifteen Thousand Hours*) studied 12 inner London secondary schools over six years. He found that differences in examination results between the schools could be traced back to good teachers who motivated their pupils, working within a school environment that had a consistent set of aims and values.

(b) *Labelling* How a teacher acts towards a pupil can strongly influence his behaviour in school and his attitudes towards his studies. If a teacher labels a pupil as a troublemaker or chatterbox then the teacher may act in a different manner towards him than towards a pupil he has labelled as intelligent. The pupils then respond to the teachers' labels, either being discouraged or encouraged in their studies. The importance of teachers' labelling of pupils has been stressed by a school of sociology called **interactionism**.

Numerous studies have illustrated the way that pupils are influenced by teachers' labels. Rosenthal and Jacobson (*Pygmalion in the Classroom*) gave a test to a number of children in a Californian school. They then told the teachers they had identified a number of children who would suddenly surge forward academically. The teachers did not know that really the children had been chosen at random and were not different from any other child. After a few months these children were found to have improved dramatically compared to their peers. This was because the teachers acted differently towards them, without being aware of it. When pupils act the way teachers expect them to act (as a result of teachers' expectations) we call this a **self-fulfilling prophecy**.

(c) *Streaming* Streaming is the division of children into teaching groups according to their general ability.

According to those who support streaming its advantages are that children receive the correct level of teaching for their ability and that the whole class can be taught at the same pace.

But most of the interactionists suggest that labelling by teachers and the pupils themselves leads to the following problems:

Once in a class children adjust themselves to the general academic and behaviour standards of that class;

Children in lower streams feel failures compared to higher stream pupils. This leads to frustration and behavioural problems;

Teachers subconsciously look down upon lower stream pupils and may make less effort with them.

Lacey (*Hightown Grammar*) studied a grammar school in Manchester. He found that lower stream pupils developed strong anti-school values as a result of their frustration and humiliation. In a later follow-up study, when the school had abolished streaming, he found most of this anti-school feeling had disappeared.

According to the national study by the National Children's Bureau, no evidence exists to show that examination results vary for a pupil attending a streamed or unstreamed school.

(d) *The peer group* If the actions of teachers are important in creating attitudes towards education, the actions of other pupils are probably even more powerful. The **peer group** is composed of pupils of the same age. Generally, the pupils split into two kinds of groups. One type rejects the school and sees it as just a waste of time. The pupils in these peer groups may simply 'muck about' in class, trying to pass the day enjoying themselves. Teachers generally view these pupils as bad and in need of strict control. A second type of peer group may see the school as a fairly pleasant place, although they may moan about it. They will do all the work set and are generally keen to support school clubs and teams. Teachers like and reward these pupils.

Corrigan (*Schooling the Bash Street Kids*) found that most pupils simply accepted school without really giving it support or strongly rejecting it. This can be described as acquiescence.

Willis (*Learning to Labour*) studied a small group of secondary school boys in the Midlands. He found that the peer group played a very important part in success and failure. The 'lads' in his study felt that they were wasting their time at school. They knew that all that lay ahead for them was low-skilled, labouring work (today, it is more likely to be unemployment). As a result they simply played around at school, making fun of teachers and pupils ('ear'oles') who wanted to work and pass their exams.

Willis points out that although the 'lads' were indeed very likely to fail at school and to go on to dead-end jobs, their peer group attitudes *guaranteed* this. Sharpe (*Just like a Girl*) found that the peer group was just as influential in the case of girls. Lower stream girls also saw school as irrelevant. More important were getting boys, looking attractive and knowing musical trends.

4.6 Gender and Education

THE FACTS OF GENDER DIFFERENCES IN EDUCATION

The 1975 Sex Discrimination Act prohibits preference for one sex at the expense of the other, yet evidence shows that the final educational achievement of women falls behind that of men. Although girls show greater learning abilities in their early years, they leave school less well qualified.

1 At GCSE, girls are slightly more successful than boys overall: 54 per cent of girls obtained one or more GCSEs compared to 49 per cent of boys. However, there were clear differences in entry and success rates between the sexes. Girls were more successful in certain subjects such as English, modern languages and biology, while boys were more successful in maths, physics and chemistry.

2 At A Level, males are slightly more successful than females: 10 per cent of males get 3+ A Levels, compared to 8 per cent of females. Again differences in subject entry appear as at GCSE.

3 There are also marked differences in higher education; of those qualified to enter higher

education, approximately 1 in 9 men and 1 in 4 women do not go on. Women are less likely therefore to go onto further study; in fact in universities women only form 40 per cent of undergraduates.

4 In other forms of training, there are clear differences, particularly in the vocational courses followed by males and females. For example, over 5 per cent of female school leavers take secretarial courses whereas the figure is 0.01 per cent for males, and twice as many females as males take catering courses.

EXPLANATIONS FOR EDUCATIONAL DIFFERENCES

1 Parental socialization Parents have different expectations of their children. Boys are expected to be tougher and more boisterous, girls to be quieter and neater. They are given different types of toys and encouraged to play different games. This creates the basis for differences in interests and attitudes.

2 Curriculum differences Curriculum means the combination of subjects followed by school pupils. There are two levels, the ordinary (or overt) curriculum and the hidden curriculum:

(a) *Overt curriculum* Although schools have to offer girls and boys equal access to all courses, clear differences in choice emerge. Girls are less likely to choose to follow CDT (craft, design and technology) or science or computer courses, and are more likely to take home economics, modern languages, social studies and secretarial studies. Therefore the official curriculum varies by gender.

(b) *The hidden curriculum* This refers to the way that certain ideas and values of the teachers and the wider society permeate through the school. These values influence the way teachers act towards girls and encourage them in certain forms of behaviour. Blackstone and Weinreich-Haste, two feminists, argue that as a result of the attitude of parents and teachers, girls learn to 'under-achieve'. By this they mean that sex stereotyping occurs in which teachers (and parents) know what sorts of jobs girls do, and have been traditionally successful in, and they counsel girls to follow courses which would lead to careers in these areas.

3 The wider culture As we have seen, females tend to have inferior status to males in society in general, to receive lower wages on average, and to have less chances of promotion. Futhermore there are clear gender roles expected of girls, e.g. to be **feminine**, to want to marry and to have children and to follow only a relatively narrow range of occupations in social work, nursing and office work, etc. These views are strengthened by the media, which portray women as sex symbols, nurses or housewives. From an early age girls are being socialized into appropriate behaviour. In a study of reading schemes, Lobban found that girls were rarely portrayed as the central character and rarely showed initiative. Boys were far more often shown as the central character and tended to engage in more exciting activities.

The result of all this is to trap girls into a self-selected choice of careers and educational courses that maintain their low status and less exciting activities.

Sue Sharpe's research (*Just Like a Girl*) studied a group of secondary girls in Ealing. She found that they were primarily concerned about boyfriends and their future prospects of marriage. School, and education in general, were seen as largely irrelevant in their eyes, as they would only be working for a few years at the most before **settling down** into marriage and child bearing.

Michelle Stanworth (*Gender and Schooling*) tape-recorded a number of classes. She found that boys dominated classroom discussion, while girls were allowed to sit quietly. This occurred with both male and female teachers. When she interviewed the teachers, she found that they had lower expectations of the girls and were less likely to know what careers they wanted. Overall, the teachers were found to underestimate the potential of girls. When she interviewed girls, she found that they were more likely to exaggerate the ability of boys and underestimate that of the girls. The result is, she claims, a lack of confidence in themselves by the female pupils and this affects their career aspirations and their studies.

4.7 Race and Education

THE FACTS OF UNDER ACHIEVEMENT

In 1985 *The Swann Report*, a Government study of educational achievement by the ethnic minorities, reported the following facts:

1 That in all GCE and CSE exams, only 6 per cent of pupils of West Indian origin obtained five or more higher grades (A to C at O Level), compared to 17 per cent of Asians and 19 per cent of all other school leavers.

2 That at A Level, only 5 per cent of West Indian origin pupils got at least one pass, compared to 13 per cent of Asians and 13 per cent of all other leavers.

3 That only 1 per cent of West Indians went on to full-time degree courses in higher education compared to 5 per cent of Asians and 5 per cent of all other school leavers.

4 That overall Asian children do about as well as white children, except in English language. However, children of Bangladeshi origin perform worst of all the ethnic minorities, including those of West Indian origin. This shows that:

(a) West Indian origin children obtain very poor examination success rates, compared to Asian and white children;

(b) There are considerable variations within the various ethnic minorities, with some children of Asian origin performing exceptionally well in the education system – especially the children of African Asians – and other children performing particularly badly: for example, the children of Bangladeshi origins.

(c) Research by Driver has suggested that West Indian girls do particularly well in the education system.

(d) It is therefore wrong to say that all children from the ethnic minorities do badly at school.

REASONS FOR THE POOR PERFORMANCE OF CHILDREN OF THE ETHNIC MINORITIES

1 *Low IQ* Some psychologists, such as Eysenck, have suggested that West Indian children have a lower IQ than white children. However, the Swann Report could not find evidence for this at all;

2 *Family background and material circumstances* We have already seen that working class children do less well in the education system than middle class children, because of differences in the home background. Children from the ethnic minorities are generally working class and so suffer from exactly the same problems as white working class children. Ethnic minority children from middle class backgrounds have no differences in their educational attainment from white middle class children;

3 *The hidden curriculum* (a) The contents of the school textbooks are often racist, denying, for example, the fact that Africa has any history at all and concentrating on Western European history only. This can make students feel inferior. Books also contain stereotypes of Blacks and Asians which constantly lower their self image. (b) The form of English spoken at home is often rejected by the school as incorrect, so the student has difficulties in expressing him/herself. For the West Indian children it is a matter of their dialect of English, but Bangladeshi children, for example, may speak a completely different language (Bengali) at home;

4 *Teacher expectations* Teachers have been shown by Tomlinson to hold stereotypes of children from the ethnic minorities. For example, they have lower expectations of West Indian children – they see them as more excitable and less academic than most children. We know that low expectations can lead to low attainment;

5 *Racism* Not only is there direct racism in school, both by other pupils and certain members of staff, but there is also racism in the wider society which the West Indian child frequently meets. This can lower the West Indian child's self-esteem and make him/her feel rejected by society. This can lead to a rejection of school and the dominant culture. (Racism is when people are disliked only because of their membership of an ethnic minority.)

Reasons for the relatively better performance of Asian compared to West Indian children

1 *Family background* There is generally a very great stress in the Asian family on obtaining good qualifications. The Asian family is very closely knit and provides an exceptionally stable background for study;

2 *Rejection of racism* Although Asians face racism just as much as West Indians, they seem better able to reject it. It has been suggested that this is because they have a greater sense of cultural identity than West Indians. They have managed to retain a sense of community and independence of culture which makes them sure of their own worth;

3 *Children of African Asian backgrounds* These generally have middle class educated parents who had professional jobs in Africa before coming to Britain. They therefore receive all the same advantages as middle class white children.

Combating racism in schools

Ways in which racism and discrimination in education can be defeated include:

(a) Training of teachers (and through them the teaching of white pupils) to understand the cultural background of the ethnic minorities and to learn to respect their cultures;

(b) More and better language lessons for the children of the ethnic minorities;

(c) A thorough checking of teaching materials to eliminate racism;

(d) More teachers from the ethnic minorities need to be recruited;

(e) **Positive discrimination** could be practised, with more resources going into those schools with high proportions of pupils from the ethnic minorities.

4.8 Summary

1 Socialization is the process whereby a person learns the expectations and rules of society. Primary socialization takes place in the home and family. Secondary socialization takes place in the school.

2 The curriculum consists of all the subjects taught at school that prepare the pupil for adulthood.

3 The hidden curriculum consists of all the values and expectations that are taught to the pupil in the informal relationships between teachers and pupils and among pupils themselves. These may actually conflict with the official curriculum. Pupils learn expectations regarding social class, gender and race in particular.

4 The education system in Britain has developed mainly as a result of the need for more and better skilled manpower. Recent developments today such as CPVE, TVEI and YTS all show that education is closely related to skill training.

5 However, it is not just the demands for skilled workers that caused the changes in the education system. Political demands by the working class for better schools for their children were also important.

6 There is some dispute about the wisdom of abolishing grammar schools and replacing them with comprehensives. However, comprehensive schools appear to have had some (limited) success in helping the children of the working class to do better in the educational system.

7 There is a division between **functionalists** and **Marxists** over the functions of the education system. Functionalists argue that the education system has four functions: the transmission of culture, social control, economic training, and social selection. These all benefit society. Marxists disagree; they argue that the education system operates to the benefit of the rich and simply trains an obedient, skilled workforce.

8 Working class children are less successful in the education system. Sociologists have explained this by the facts that (a) the home background is often not as helpful for educational success as that of the middle class; (b) the neighbourhood may also weaken the chances of the working class child; and (c) what happens inside the school, particularly the actions of the teachers and the peer group, can help the middle class child and harm the working class child.

9 Girls perform differently in the educational system from boys. It has been suggested that this is mainly due to the way society creates **gender roles** which stress how males and females ought to behave. The result is that girls are directed towards caring and secretarial types of courses.

10 The ethnic minorities differ in their educational performances from whites. Although some Asians in particular perform exceptionally well, others, such as West Indians and Bangladeshis, perform poorly. Explanations vary, but it is generally agreed that as the

majority of people in the ethnic minorities belong to the working class, the same explanations are useful for their failure. On top of this, intentional and unintentional racism are important.

11 Britain cannot be said to be a **meritocracy** as so many of the children of the working class, the ethnic minorities and many girls fail to achieve their full potential from the education system.

4.9 Keywords (*as they appear in the unit*)

formal learning, informal learning, the hidden curriculum, tripartite system, comprehensive schools, assisted places schemes, vocational preparation, Manpower Services Commission, public schools, functions of education, intelligence, elaborated and restricted codes, cultural deprivation, compensatory education, positive discrimination, educational priority areas, labelling, streaming, peer group, equality of opportunity.

5 SOCIAL STRATIFICATION

5.1 The Meaning of Stratification

Social stratification means the division of people into various social groups who have different levels of prestige, economic rewards and power according to their membership of these groups. Most societies have some ways of dividing people into social groups. The main ones are:

> Caste
> Estates (Feudalism)
> Slavery
> Social class

However, running alongside these forms of social divisions are those of:

> Age
> Gender
> Ethnic group

In this unit we will concentrate mainly on **social class,** as it is generally accepted to be the most significant influence on our lives. In the following units we will concentrate on **gender, age** and then **ethnic divisions**.

5.2 Comparative Forms of Stratification

1 CASTE

Caste stratification is based on the principle that people are born into a group and nothing they can do in their lifetime alters their group membership – different groups receive greater or lesser rewards and prestige as their birthright. This idea that you are born into a particular group is called **ascription**.

The caste system exists in India, although it is being increasingly weakened by industrialization. It is based on the **Hindu** religion which preaches that people are reborn (**reincarnation**), i.e. have more than one life. The form of life and the caste you are born into depends upon your conduct in your previous life; the worse your conduct the lower your caste.

The various castes are rigidly separated; contact with a lower caste member **pollutes** a higher caste person. Thus social intercourse and marriage are strictly forbidden.

Each caste is traditionally associated with a form of work. The castes are in descending order of status:

(a) Brahmin	Priests
(b) Kshatryas	Soldiers
(c) Vaishyas	Merchants
(d) Shudras	Servants and manual workers
(e) Untouchables	Regarded with disgust by the rest of the population

The Indian system of caste is the classic example, but it has also been applied in other countries where strict unbreakable divisions are enforced.

In South Africa, for example, people are born into groups and divided by skin colour, and life for whites is far better than for blacks. No possibility exists to change the colour of one's skin, and therefore one's caste.

2 FEUDALISM

This system of stratification is traditionally associated with medieval Europe – but it also existed in Japan, Russia and Eritrea until this century.

The basic principles are very simple. Ownership of the land was in the hands of a small group of **nobles**. Each noble divided his land and allowed a lesser noble to have that land as long as he swore personal loyalty to the senior noble, swearing to provide him with fighting men in the event of war. The lesser noble then subdivided his land in return for personal oaths of allegiance. The resulting system was rather like a pyramid with the king at the top and working through all the nobility right down to the serf who swore personal allegiance to his local lord in order to have the right to work on the land. In an agricultural society to have land meant to have wealth.

Each layer of the society was known as an **estate**, and like the caste system each estate was based on ascription (or the assigning of land/wealth/loyalty to other groups in society).

3 SLAVERY

One of the earliest and most widespread forms of stratification was slavery. In societies such as Ancient Greece or Rome it was customary for the society to be divided into freemen (among whom great differences in wealth existed) and slaves – who were owned by freemen. This ownership of one man by another existed until the nineteenth century.

4 SOCIAL CLASS

In modern industrialized societies the dominant form of social stratification is social class. People are grouped according to a **hierarchy** (a series of steps) based on economic and status differences.

The main differences between social class and other forms of stratification are that:

(a) Social class is **open** in the sense that one can move up or down the hierarchy, as opposed to the **closed** stratification systems of slavery and caste etc. This is known as **social mobility**;

(b) The basis of class is primarily economic;

(c) The separate strata are not clearly marked off from each other;

(d) Social class, unlike caste, is not formally legalized;

(e) Intermarriage between social classes is possible in a social class system.

5.3 Life Chances and Social Class

Social class is probably the most significant influence on our lives. It affects us in two ways: *objectively*, that is in such things as health, possessions and general life style; and *subjectively*, that is in our ideas and values.

OBJECTIVE

(a) *Birth and infant mortality* Children of unskilled working class parents are three times more likely to die in the first year of life than children born to professionally employed parents;

(b) *Health* Working class people are three times more likely to have long-term serious illness compared to middle class people. They are twice as likely to have a disease of the respiratory system, and six times as likely to get arthritis and rheumatism;

(c) *Death* Over 75 per cent of social class I survive to 65, less than 65 per cent of social class V (unskilled working class) do. A professional man can expect to live, on average, seven years longer than an unskilled working class man;

(d) *Family life* Working class people are more likely to marry younger and traditionally have larger families. In 1976, of families that had completed their child rearing, professional couples had on average 2.0 children, and unskilled manual couples had on average 2.3 children;

(e) *Housing* Whereas 85 per cent of social class I are house owners, only 24 per cent of social class V are;

(f) *Education* Class differences are fully discussed on pp 33 – 5, but suffice to note here that 60 per cent of social class I are graduates, whereas at the other end of the scale 47 per cent of unskilled manual workers have no educational qualifications at all;

(g) *Income* Income varies by occupation, for example in 1984 the average gross weekly wage for male manual workers (usually factory workers or labourers) was £180, while the wage for non-manual male workers was £210;

(h) *Possessions* The higher income groups have considerably greater income to spend. This shows itself in higher levels of ownership of consumer goods, such as cars and videos, and a more expensive social life, such as dining out, and travel abroad;

(i) *Job security* Working class people are three times more likely to be unemployed than middle class people.

The nine factors mentioned are simple examples of the tremendous importance of social class in our lives. We ought to be aware that it influences our opinions and views of the world on the one hand (subjective influence), and it limits or promotes our chances of a good life style through educational opportunities, income and occupational differences (objective influence).

SUBJECTIVE

(a) *Politics* (discussed on p 121). Voting behaviour is related to social class. Conservative support is more likely the higher the social class – on average 68 per cent of professionals vote Conservative;

(b) *Leisure* The middle class tend to have different leisure interests from the working class. This is partly a reflection of greater income, longer holidays and higher levels of education. The middle class are more likely to read novels, to go to the cinema, theatre and restaurants, and less likely to watch television. They are more likely to play sports of any kind, but particularly golf and squash. However, there is considerable overlap by the social classes in their leisure pursuits;

(c) *Views on social issues* The middle class are less likely to be sympathetic to trade unions, and to those who are unemployed, than the working class. According to Goldthorpe and Lockwood, the middle class look upon social class as a ladder of opportunity. Those who work hard are able to climb up and are eventually successful. The working class see a person's social class as largely fixed at birth and those who are successful are regarded as lucky and the exception to the rule.

These are only a few of the wide range of subjective and objective differences between the social classes.

Sociologists use the term **life chances** for these differences in a person's chances of success or failure in life. They conclude that in Britain our life chances are strongly influenced, if not determined, by the social class that we are born into.

▮ 5.4 Explanations of Social Class ▮

Although it is clear that social class exists and that it influences our lives, sociologists have disagreed about how it developed and exactly what the basis of class is. There are three different explanations:

1 The ideas of Karl Marx (often known as **conflict theorists** or **Marxists**);

2 The ideas of Max Weber;

3 The **Functionalist** approach.

KARL MARX

The basis of Marx's explanation of social class is economic. Marx, who lived and wrote in the nineteenth century, argued that although the class structure appeared very complex, in reality a clear distinction could be made between two groups who formed the only two classes in society:

(a) Those who own wealth and property – the **Bourgeoisie**;

(b) Those who sell their labour to the wealthy – the **Proletariat**.

The bourgeoisie Marx argued that anybody who owns wealth and property (he used the term **the means of production**) is in a fundamentally different position from those who have to work for a wage. They have power and influence to shape the political and social nature of society. He sees society as a reflection of their interests. They pass on their wealth and power to their children.

The proletariat Everybody who works for a wage or salary falls into this social class. Marx argued that the distinctions between groups as far apart as doctors and unskilled labourers are really unimportant. Both groups have to work for their living, and have little power compared to the wealthy bourgeoisie.

The origin of classes according to Marx Marx's division between bourgeoisie and proletariat is only part of his explanation of the political and social history of man. According to Marx in every society two classes exist – one that owns the wealth and the other that is exploited by the wealthy.

(a) In Ancient Greece and Rome – there were freemen and slaves;

(b) In feudal societies – nobility and serfs;

(c) In industrial societies – bourgeoisie and proletariat.

The struggle between the wealthy and the workers has caused most social change.

False consciousness Many people criticize the Marxists' view of the class structure by arguing that if the people really were so exploited they would rise up in revolution. However, Marxists believe that the bourgeoisie control the television and newspapers, as well as the educational system. These all promote ideas which benefit the bourgeoisie, creating the belief that what is good for the rich, is good for everybody. Because they are constantly told this, people believe it. There is therefore no revolution. Marxists call this acceptance of the views of the bourgeoisie **false consciousness**. If people are aware of their exploitation this is **class consciousness**.

Criticisms of Marx

Among the many criticisms (and replies to the criticisms) of Marx's work are the following:

1 Marx argued that there are only ever two social classes, but in practice the class structure is much more complicated, with a wide variety of groups existing in society. It seems a mistake to group doctors with production line workers.

2 He claimed that a revolution must occur in industrial societies when the tension between proletariat and bourgeoisie becomes too intense. Yet no signs of such potential revolutionary activity exist, instead the Labour Party and the trade unions have developed to look after the interests of the working class.

Marxism today

Modern Marxists accept the criticism that Marx's stress on only two social classes in society needs to be modified. They suggest that although the basic division between owners (bourgeoisie) and non-owners (proletariat) is correct, there are a number of splits within them, which they call **social class fractions**. For example, they see white-collar employees, such as junior managers working in offices, as having different views and life styles from many factory workers, even though they both work for the same employer. Marxists suggest that these are still members of the proletariat (because they do not own), but are different fractions of it.

MAX WEBER

Weber lived shortly after Marx and his work on class was influenced by him. Although he agreed that a small group of people had excessive power and wealth, he disagreed that the most important division was into two groups based on ownership of wealth.

Weber suggested three elements that divide people in our society:

(a) *Economic factors* How much wealth or income a person has or inherits from his parents;

(b) *Status* The amount of prestige we give to a person based on such characteristics as occupation, accent, education, etc.;

(c) *Power* The amount of power and influence a person has.

When all three are added together they indicate a person's **life chances**, that is a person's chances of success in life. Weber argued that the divisions between people in society are very complex and the class structure resembles a ladder with a long series of small steps.

Weber points out that although the three elements (economic factors, status and power) usually go together (for example, a rich person is often powerful and has high status in society) this is not always the case. There are many rich people who do not have high status, and some people who are powerful without being very well off, for instance Labour politicians. So people are ranked on each element separately. The important point here is that Marx only stressed one (economic factors) of the three elements that form class according to Weber, and saw the other two as deriving from it, which Weber saw as wrong.

THE FUNCTIONALIST APPROACH

In the 1940s Davis and Moore put forward what has now become the classic **functionalist** explanation of social class. Functionalists see society as similar to a human body. Each part of society performs a function to keep the society 'alive', just as each part of the body has its role to play.

Clearly there are some parts of the body that are more important than others. For example, the heart is much more important than the little finger. In society there are certain jobs that are more important for society than others. Functionalists would claim that doctors are more important, for example, than car salesmen. In order to persuade the very best people to take these difficult but very important jobs, such as the doctors, they need to be paid more and receive higher social status. The result is the differences in status, power and prestige to be found in our society. According to this explanation of stratification, the differences in income reflect differences in the importance of those jobs to society.

Functionalists see little conflict among classes.

Criticisms of functionalism

This explanation of the origins and basis of social class has been criticized because it seems a justification by the better paid for their higher incomes. Although some jobs are clearly more important than others, it is extremely difficult to grade most jobs.

The levels of income reflect less the social importance of the jobs than the success of trade unions, professions, or simply individuals by their wits, to negotiate high wages. A simple comparison of some obvious jobs shows the weakness in the argument.

Doctors, for example, earn much less than advertising executives on average, but most people would see the doctor as more important to society.

5.5 Measuring Social Class

The importance of occupation

In investigating society, sociologists need to use a simple measurement of social class – as a result most surveys have been based upon occupational differences. We know that occupation is related to:

1 Differences in income;

2 Differences in prestige – for example, people rank doctors as more prestigious than factory workers;

3 Differences in education – usually the higher educated a person is the higher his occupation;

4 Life style – different incomes earned in different levels of occupation are generally reflected in different spending patterns, and therefore different life styles. Differences in education are important here, too;

5 Differences in speech and dress – differences in occupation reflect educational differences, and this shows itself in different types of speech patterns. It also influences taste in and ability to pay for different types of clothes.

Problems with using occupation as the only measure of social class

In using occupation to measure class as the following classifications do, there are some problems; these include:

1 Classifications based on occupation omit the very rich who own the factories, and commercial institutions;

2 They ignore the fact that some people in similar occupations may have very different backgrounds and resources. For example, a teacher from a rich family, who is given regular financial help by his/her family, is in a very different situation from a teacher from a working class background;

3 These classifications ignore the unemployed;

4 Classifications based on occupation ignore or gloss over the fact that the same job title can mean very different things in different circumstances. For instance, a doctor can mean a very successful general practitioner with a 'practice' in a pleasant part of a city, with some private patients; or it can mean a junior hospital doctor in an inner city hospital earning low wages.

CLASSIFICATIONS USED

Based on the assumption that occupation is the most useful indicator of class, the following classifications are used.

The Registrar-General's classification

Class	Type of occupations
1	Professional and higher administrative e.g. lawyers, architects, doctors, managers, university teachers
2	Intermediate professionals and administrative e.g. shopkeepers, farmers, actors, musicians, teachers
3	Skilled (a) Non-manual e.g. draughtsmen, shop assistants, clerks (b) Manual e.g. electricians, coalminers
4	Semi-skilled e.g. milk roundsmen, bus conductors, telephone operators, fishermen, farm workers
5	Unskilled e.g. nightwatchmen, porters, refuse collectors, cleaners, labourers

The Registrar-General's classification divides the workforce into five groups, with a further division in class three between manual and non-manual workers. This division reflects the fact that sociologists are aware that manual workers (those who work with their hands) and non-manual workers (those who work in clerical or professional occupations) have a very wide gap between them in values held and life styles, even though their incomes may not differ greatly.

The Registrar-General's classification is the one used in official government studies.

The Hope-Goldthorpe classification

Hope and Goldthorpe have developed a refined version of the Registrar-General's classification of occupations. It divides the eight groups into three classes, service, intermediate and working, reflecting the changing occupational structure of Britain. In particular, it divides the white-collar workers with some degree of power and control over their working situation, such as accountants or managers (the service class), from those white-collar jobs that are routine and have relatively lower wages (the intermediate class). Included in this class are manual workers who have authority, such as foremen. Finally, there is the working class composed of the rest of the manual workers.

Eight occupations	%	Classes
1 Higher-grade professionals, administrators, managers and proprietors	7.7	
2 Lower-grade professionals, administrators and managers		Service
Supervisors and higher-grade technicians	6.0	
3 Clerical, sales and rank-and-file service workers	7.4	
4 Small proprietors and self-employed artisans	12.6	Intermediate
5 Lower-grade technicians and foremen	11.3	
6 Skilled manual workers in industry	27.2	
7 Semi- and unskilled workers in industry	22.6	Working
8 Agricultural workers and smallholders	5.2	
All	100	

3 Manual/non-manual division

In practice the classifications of the Registrar-General and Halsey may be too complicated, so often the simple division between manual and non-manual workers is used. Goldthorpe and Lockwood have suggested that this distinction is true; on the whole, the two groups differ on grounds of (a) income, (b) beliefs, (c) life styles.

(a) *Income* Non-manual workers earn, on average, £30 a week more than manual workers. They are also more likely to have longer holidays, shorter working hours, better pensions, the possibility of promotion and generally a pleasanter working environment;

(b) *Beliefs* Manual workers and non-manual workers tend to hold different beliefs about society. Non-manual workers tend to be optimistic about their future career, to believe that hard work will be rewarded, to look out for themselves and to value education. Manual workers tend to stress that they can only improve their pay and conditions through union action, to see unemployed people as 'unlucky' rather than as 'lazy' and to undervalue education;

(c) *Life styles* Each group tends to keep to itself in terms of friendship and club membership. Furthermore speech, dress and spending patterns are noticeably different.

Criticisms

This simple division between manual and non-manual workers is rapidly becoming out of date as the number of people involved in manual work declines. The changing nature of industry and commerce means that the number of jobs requiring physical strength alone is declining. Increasingly the jobs available are routine white collar, such as clerks in offices. Very often these routine white collar workers are from manual backgrounds and in the past would have done manual work – but it is no longer available.

Increasingly the real divisions are those between the higher paid managers and professional workers and the rest.

5.6 Changes in the Class Structure

THE CHANGING NATURE OF BRITISH SOCIETY

In order to understand the changes in the nature of social class in Britain, first it is necessary to see the changes that have taken place in British society over the last 30 years.

1 *Affluence* In the 1950s many of the consumer goods we now take for granted either did not exist, or were owned by a tiny proportion of the population. Today, 61 per cent of the population own at least one car, 66 per cent have central heating, 83 per cent colour televisions, and 61 per cent have a deep freeze. For those in employment these are the most affluent years in history.

2 *Unemployment* There are at least 3½ million unemployed in Britain. Alongside the affluence of those in employment there is the growth of people who are living on supplementary benefit. There is a real division occurring between those in secure employment and the rest of the workforce.

3 *Housing* Today two thirds of the population own or are buying their own homes. Thirty years ago the figure was only one third.

Where people live has also been changing. The move from the inner cities has been very marked in the last 30 years, with the decline of the traditional inner city working class neighbourhoods (such as the area inhabited by the *EastEnders*) and the growth of outer city suburbs and new towns (such as *Brookside*).

4 *The educational system* This has become more open, with more opportunities for the children of the skilled working class to obtain high qualifications, which allow them to compete for the professional jobs available.

5 *The occupational structure* This is certainly the most important change that has taken place in the wider society to influence social class.

First, there has been a major movement away from manual work to white collar work. Thirty years ago, two thirds of the workforce were in manual jobs. Today, it is less than half.

Second, within manual work, there has been a much greater decline in unskilled work than in skilled work. Technological changes and the introduction of automation have taken away much of unskilled work.

Third, the biggest growth in occupational groups has been in the professional and junior management area. This, plus the widening of educational opportunities for the skilled working class, has meant that there has been a significant growth in the numbers of people of working class origins in professional employment.

Fourth, the number of women in employment has been increasing consistently and today women form over 40 per cent of the workforce. It is estimated that by 1995 women will form half of the workforce. Women are mainly stuck in the lower grades of work both in the manual and non-manual groups.

Conclusion

The discussion of class that follows must be seen against the background of the changing nature of Britain. Class still exists and is a very powerful influence on our life chances, but it is changing in appearance like the society it reflects.

5.7 The Working Class

EMBOURGEOISEMENT

The term embourgeoisement comes from the French *bourgeois* meaning middle class—embourgeoisement means to **become middle class**.

In the 1950s the spread of affluence to the working class, and the consequent purchase of houses (instead of renting), the emergence of **consumer durables** such as washing machines, fridges, cars, etc., followed later by foreign travel and eating out at restaurants, seemed to indicate that the better-off sections of the working class were joining the middle class; not only in terms of possessions, but also in terms of their values, patterns of behaviour and expectations for their children.

Research

Goldthorpe and Lockwood (*The Affluent Worker in the Class Structure*) decided to test the embourgeoisement theory. In the early 1960s they studied a group of Vauxhall car workers in Luton. These men were earning high wages, owned their own houses and most of the consumer goods available at the time. However, Goldthorpe and Lockwood concluded that there was little evidence to support the view that these affluent workers were breaking away to any significant extent from the traditional working class.

The major differences between the middle and working classes still remained and according to Goldthorpe and Lockwood these were:

(a) *Income* The manual workers earned a lower basic wage than non-manual workers, had less security and little possibility of promotion;

(b) *Beliefs* The view of society of the manual workers ('**us**'–the working class, against '**them**'–the bosses) was very different from the non-manual workers who saw society as a 'ladder' (anyone can climb up society if he works hard). The manual workers sought and found little satisfaction from their work–unlike the non-manual workers;

(c) *Life styles* Few common bonds of leisure activities or friendships could be found between manual and non-manual workers.

THE DECOMPOSITION OF LABOUR AND THE GROWTH OF THE NEW WORKING CLASS

Although the idea that the better-off working class were becoming middle class was rejected after Goldthorpe and Lockwood's study, in recent years a new argument has been put forward. The claim is that the working class has divided, and there are now two clearly distinguishable groups within the working class. (This has been called the **decomposition of labour**). The first of these is the **traditional** working class, and the second is the **new working class**.

The traditional working class They maintain a completely different life style to that of the middle class. These people (a) live in council houses and rent their homes; (b) live in the traditional working class communities, in inner cities or in industrial towns; (c) work in manual occupations; (d) solidly support the Labour Party; (e) are more likely to become unemployed.

The new working class They are (a) likely to own their own homes; (b) likely to live on new housing estates in the suburbs; (c) likely to be affluent, owning many consumer durables such as cars, videos, etc.; (d) less likely to give their total support to the Labour Party; (e) more likely to be in secure jobs.

Research

R. Pahl in *Divisions of Labour* studied working class households in Kent. He concluded that there was a growing gap between those families with and those without regular employment. They were achieving a higher standard of living than ever before. The other group in his study, those who were in more precarious work and became unemployed, found it increasingly difficult to survive.

The working class: conclusions

The working class is less solid than it once was. It has *fragmented* or *decomposed*. In particular we can distinguish:

1 The growing numbers of the unemployed and the poor, who are being left behind. These are most often drawn from

2 The 'traditional' working class, who are working in the declining manufacturing industries and who still hold traditional working class values;

3 The 'new' working class who are more likely to live in the South, to be buying their own homes and to be working in the more secure jobs of light industry.

5.8 The Middle Class

THE TRADITIONAL MIDDLE CLASS

Traditionally, the middle class was composed of white-collar workers, such as clerks at the lower end and managers/traditional professionals, such as solicitors and doctors, at the other end. They tended to live in different areas of the towns and cities from the working class, had greater job security and higher wages (although the wages of highly skilled manual workers and clerks overlapped) and better working conditions. The values of the middle class stressed individual hard work and the desire for a career. Although the income levels varied within the middle class, those engaged in office jobs saw themselves as having higher status in society and felt that they did form a clear class.

Changes in the middle class

The middle class, like the working class, has been fragmenting and is nowhere near as cohesive as in the past.

Two major changes have been discussed by sociologists:

1 The **proletarianization** of clerical workers;

2 The growth of the **professions.**

Proletarianization

The wage position of the clerk in respect of skilled manual workers has declined consistently since 1914. By 1971 some unskilled manual workers had also overtaken clerical workers in their weekly wage levels. This has led to the claim that clerical workers have undergone a process of **proletarianization** (have sunk into the working class).

However, clerical workers still enjoy some clear advantages over manual workers:

(a) Their working conditions are more pleasant – warm offices etc.;

(b) They more often receive fringe benefits such as special pension schemes, better sick pay provision, flexible working hours, etc.;

(c) They have some, though decreasing, chances of promotion;

(d) They tend to see themselves as middle class.

Weir (*Class Consciousness Amongst Clerical Workers*) studied 1400 clerical workers in Hull over a five-year period. He found that the clerks tended to see themselves stuck in their present jobs, and a third saw a decline into the working class. However, they were aware of themselves as a distinctive group in relation to both management (the middle class) and manual workers (the working class).

Roberts *et al* (*The Fragmentary Class Structure*) conducted a survey of 243 Liverpool white-collar workers in a variety of jobs. The group most likely to define themselves as working class were routine clerical workers with little chance of promotion.

Proletarianization conclusion There has clearly been a decline in the earnings and status of clerical workers. It seems that where chances of promotion exist they are likely to see themselves as middle class or at least not working class, if there are no possibilities of promotion then they see themselves as working class. Whereas traditionally clerical workers were part of the middle class, they now form a **marginal group**, straddling the borderline between the working and middle classes. It should be remembered that as manual work declines an increasing proportion of the whole labour force is in low level white collar employment. Also, an increasing proportion of the workers are female.

The growth of the professions

Between 1971 and 1981 the numbers of people working in manufacturing industries (actually making things) fell by a quarter. At the same time the numbers of people engaged in the service industries (providing services, such as insurance, banking, etc.) rose by a quarter.

The occupational group that benefit most from this growth in services are the professions, who increased their numbers by over a quarter in this period. Since the turn of the century the proportion of the workforce in the professions has increased from only 4 per cent to over 12 per cent.

The rise of the professions is related not just to the expansion of service industries owned by private companies, but also to the growth of the state. The biggest expansions have taken place in the areas of education, health and welfare. Within the professions, however, there is a clear division between the 'traditional' professions of solicitor and doctor, who are generally well paid and enjoy great status, and the 'newer' professions of teacher and social worker, who are less well paid and have lower status in society.

The middle class: conclusions

Just as the working class has begun to show divisions within it, so, too, has the middle class.

1 Clerical workers are now in a *marginal* position, and are not clear members of the working class;

2 There has been a significant growth of the professions.

CHANGES IN THE CLASS STRUCTURE: CONCLUSION

The various studies on embourgeoisement and proletarianization have led many writers, but most noticeably Roberts *et al* (*The Fragmentary Class Structure*) and Halsey (*Change in British Society*), to argue that the class structure of Britain is becoming increasingly **fragmented**, that is, less clearly divided into (a) the working class composed of manual workers, and (b) the middle class composed of white-collar and professional people. We can distinguish:

1 The unemployed and poor;

2 The traditional working class, based in areas of traditional employment such as mining, docks and heavy industry, all of which are in decline. The belief is in working class solidarity and Labour voting. Most of these workers are semi-skilled;

3 The affluent working class employed in the new industries of advanced technology and light industry. Well paid, although overtime is needed to earn the high wages. Tend to own their own houses and be less committed to seeing themselves as working class. Less likely to vote Labour;

4 Clerical workers – split in their views of themselves between (a) those with little chance of promotion, who see themselves as working class and who come from working class homes, and (b) those who see the possibility of promotion and who cling to a middle class view of themselves;

5 Management and professional employees. Regard themselves as solid middle class and have high incomes and job security. Solidly Conservative. Mainly from middle class backgrounds;

6 The rich – those who own stocks and shares.

5.9 Ownership of Wealth and Income

Britain is a **capitalist** society in which companies, banks, insurance companies as well as the small business are owned and controlled by a relatively small proportion of the population. This small group is extremely wealthy in proportion to the rest of the population. The top 1 per cent own 23 per cent of marketable wealth.

1 WEALTH

Wealth means assets that are worth money if sold. The main forms of wealth are: **1** property; **2** stocks and shares (part ownership) of companies.

Distribution of personal wealth

	England and Wales			United Kingdom			
% of wealth owned by:	1923	1938	1950	1976	1981	1986	1989
	%	%	%	%	%	%	%
Most wealthy 1%	60.9	55.0	47.2	21	18	18	18
Most wealthy 5%	82.0	76.9	74.3	38	36	36	38
Most wealthy 10%	89.1	85. 0	–	50	50	50	53
Most wealthy 25%	–	–	–	71	73	73	75
Most wealthy 50%	–	–	–	92	92	90	94
Least wealthy 50%	–	–	–	8	8	10	6

(**Source:** *Social Trends* 1992)

The table above shows the changes in wealth distribution over this century. Three points need consideration.

1 The proportion of wealth held by the top 10 per cent has declined this century.

2 The proportion of wealth held by the top 10 per cent is extremely high, 53 per cent of all wealth. Indeed this figure is put into a much more vivid perspective when one realizes that 50 per cent of the British population only owns 6 per cent of all wealth between them.

3 There is considerable evidence to show that these figures are not totally accurate as they are based upon the official Inland Revenue Tax figures. We know that extremely rich people are able to avoid paying taxation by a number of methods. According to A. B. Atkinson the rich have redistributed their wealth among themselves giving the appearance that more people own wealth but in reality it goes to more members of the same rich families.

Who are the wealthy?

1 *The landowners* The British aristocracy owns 40 per cent of British land. The richest man in Britain, the sixth Duke of Westminster, owns 138 000 acres of land including 300 acres of Belgravia, Mayfair and Westminster and some of the world's most exclusive land. This group of the rich has obtained its wealth exclusively through inheritance.

2 *The entrepreneurial rich* Many British companies are owned and controlled by relatively few families – these include the Guinness family (brewing), the Cowdray family (banking and publishing), the Sieff family (Marks and Spencer), the Vestey family (meat). Most of these families have inherited their wealth, like the landowners – few entrepreneurs become rich from humble origins. Those who do are held up by the media as examples to us, as to how open British society is. However, the self-made man's wealth is more precarious than inherited wealth, as the 'Laker' saga illustrates.

3 *Research* Harbury compared the wills of men leaving large amounts in various years between 1950 and 1970 with their fathers' wills; 60 per cent of those leaving £100 000 or more had rich fathers. Wealth, he concludes, is generally inherited.

2 INCOME

Income is the money or benefits which a person receives. It may come from **1** employment (earned income); **2** investments (unearned income); or **3** the state in benefits (social income).

According to The Diamond Commission (1974–9), a Government study of income and wealth distribution, the top 10 per cent of income earners received 26 per cent of pre-tax income compared to 2.5 per cent earned by the bottom 10 per cent. Indeed the bottom 50 per cent of income earners receive only 24 per cent of all income.

These figures have not changed substantially in the last 30 years. In 1949 the top 10 per cent earned 33 per cent of all income and the bottom half 24 per cent – exactly the same as today.

The influence of taxation

Taxation seems to have very little redistributive effect (i.e. taking money from the rich and giving it to the lower income groups). Figure 5.1 indicates the tiny effect of taxation.

Population divided into fifths

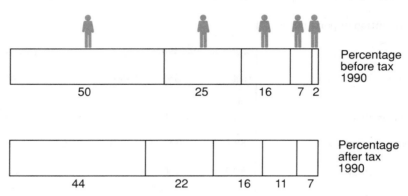

Figure 5.1

As the figure clearly shows the top 20 per cent of income earners lose only 6 per cent of their income after tax in proportion to the rest of the population, while the lowest group only receive an extra 5 per cent of income.

Overall, very marked differences in income still exist, with those in managerial and professional occupations (social class 1) still receiving 3½ times the earnings of unskilled workers (social class 5).

According to Westergaard and Resler (*Class in Capitalist Society*) progressive taxation (the more you earn the more you pay) and the Welfare State have done little or nothing to redistribute income. What the highest earners lose in direct taxation, they regain in various tax concessions for mortgages, insurance policies and pensions. Furthermore, **fringe benefits** such as cheap holidays, subsidized education, and so on are not subject to tax and so these actually increase the differences between the highest and lowest income groups as shown in the table.

Attempts to redistribute wealth and income

Inheritance Tax This is a tax paid when wealth is passed from one person to another. It has many loopholes so is not effective in preventing inherited wealth.

Income Tax The more you earn the more you pay.

Welfare State The higher taxes on the better paid, plus the National Insurance contributions, should pay for the welfare benefits of the poor.

5.10 Social Mobility

THE MEANING AND MEASUREMENT OF SOCIAL MOBILITY

The main distinction between caste and class societies is that in a class-based society, such as

Britain, there is social mobility. Social mobility means the movement of people up and down the social scale.

1 There are two types of social mobility (sometimes called *vertical mobility*);

(a) *Intragenerational* movement within the occupational structure by one person over a period of time. In other words a person's career;

(b) *Intergenerational mobility* – occupation of a person compared to his/her father.

2 The **measurement** of social mobility is usually based upon either the Registrar-General's scale, or the Hope-Goldthorpe classification (see p 45), and so it is based upon **occupation**.

3 The **extent** of social mobility is usually described in terms of:

(a) *Long-range mobility,* which is movement of two or more occupational groups up or down the social scale;

(b) *Short-range mobility,* which is movement up or down by only one occupational group;

(c) *Self-recruitment,* the situation when children are in the same occupational group as their parents.

Example: (i) a man is working as a doctor, and his father was a labourer on a building site. This type is *intergenerational mobility* (parent/child being compared), and the extent is long range (he moved more than two occupational groups up, compared to his father); (ii) if the man was a labourer, this would be an example of *self-recruitment.*

Problems in measuring social class

In measuring social mobility in research, certain problems arise:

1 Most studies use occupation, and so encounter the same problems as are discussed on pp 44 – 9 in creating categories of class, as they ignore the differences within occupations, and they assume that all non-manual work is 'higher' than manual work (whereas many manual workers earn more than routine white-collar workers);

2 Over time the status and significance of certain jobs change. For example, a clerical worker in 1900 had a job considered to be of far higher status than today. Any comparison over time needs to take this into account;

3 At what point in a person's career do you measure his/her social mobility? For example, if the son/daughter of a rich London stockbroker has his/her first employment as a manual worker on a building site for a year, while he/she waits for a suitable opening in the City of London as a stockbroker, do we measure the mobility from the first job or from the second job in the city?

SOCIAL MOBILITY IN BRITAIN

In 1972 a group of sociologists at Nuffield College, Oxford, studied the extent of inter-generational mobility in Britain. The *Oxford Mobility Study,* as it is known, was based upon interviews with 10 000 men, from all social classes. They compared the social mobility patterns of men born between 1908 and 1917 with those born between 1938 and 1947, in order to obtain a view of the changes in social mobility this century.

In order to simplify the results of the survey, the seven occupational groups were put into three classes (which are given in detail on p 45):

The service class, composed of those in professional and managerial positions – that is the most successful;

The intermediate class, which includes those in routine white-collar jobs, the self-employed, technicians and supervisors;

The working class, which includes most manual workers. The results are illustrated in the diagram below.

Likelihood of ending up in service class

Men born 1908–17   If father was

14% WORKING	
25% INTERMEDIATE	
55% SERVICE	

Men born 1938–47   If father is

18% WORKING	
30% INTERMEDIATE	
62% SERVICE	

Fig. 5.2

Figure 5.2 shows that for all groups the chance of going into the service class has increased.

1 18 per cent of the 1938–47 generation who were born into the working class achieved the service class, compared to 14 per cent of the 1908–17 generation.

2 30 per cent of the 1938–47 generation who were born into the intermediate class achieved the service class, compared to 25 per cent of the 1908–17 generation.

3 62 per cent of the 1938–47 generation who were born into the service class succeeded in staying in this class, compared to 55 per cent of the 1908–17 generation.

This means that upward mobility has certainly increased.

At first sight it would seem that by 1972, the class structure was more **open** (there was greater movement, so that talented people from working class backgrounds could be successful) than previously. Indeed, 25 per cent of all higher professionals (the highest occupational group in the survey) came from working class backgrounds.

However, the **relative** chances of children of each group entering the service class did not alter over time. The sons of the service class have four times the chance of following their fathers into the service class themselves compared to the sons of the working class, and twice the chances of the sons of the intermediate class. This has been dubbed 'the 1:2:4 rule'.

The explanation for the movement of so many people, according to Halsey and Goldthorpe, who led the survey, is that the changing *occupational structure* means that there are many more jobs available in the service class than ever before. So, there is a lot more room at the top. There are also fewer working class jobs. This is illustrated in Figure 5.3.

Men born 1908–17			Men born 1938–47
13%	SERVICE	25%	
33%	INTERMEDIATE	30%	
54%	WORKING	45%	

Figure 5.3

The diagram shows that of all jobs:

(a) the proportion of service class occupations has increased from 13 per cent to 25 per cent;
(b) the proportion of intermediate class occupations has decreased from 33 per cent to 30 per cent;
(c) the proportion of working class jobs has decreased from 54 per cent to 45 per cent.

WOMEN AND SOCIAL MOBILITY

There have been few studies of the patterns of social mobility of women. This is mainly because of the fact that sociologists have traditionally taken the social class of wives from the class of the husbands – even though it is known that women often marry 'outside' their class.
Research Heath in *Social Mobility* found that single women tend to be more upwardly socially mobile than single men, although in a more restricted range of professions. This reflects the concentration of women working in a few areas of the professions. He suggests that in order to be successful in their jobs women have to make a choice between marriage and children (and the consequent disruption of their careers during child raising) and concentrating all their attention on work. For men, on the other hand, it is accepted that they ought to concentrate on their jobs. So for men, careers and marriage fit together. For women, they are opposed.

WHAT ARE THE CAUSES OF SOCIAL MOBILITY?

(a) *Occupational change* As the occupational structure alters in response to economic and technological change, different types of employment arise. These may be of higher or lower status. Since the end of the Second World War, there has been a considerable expansion in middle and high status jobs and a decline in labouring work. (For a full discussion of occupational change in Britain, see p 76.) This has meant that there is more 'room at the top' and less at the bottom. Individuals who may have entered manual work 20 years ago will not enter clerical positions. This appears to be intergenerational mobility, although some sociologists have suggested that there has been a decline in the status of clerical work, so that no 'real mobility' is taking place. It is just low paid, low status work adapted to changed technological circumstances (see 'Proletarianization' p 48);

(b) *Differential fertility* If the top groups fail to produce enough children to fill all the top positions, then there is space for the children of lower groups. (This argument is based on the fact that there is a high rate of self-recruitment in the class structure.) Since the turn of the century the expansion of the non-manual job sector has been greater than the birth rate of the middle class;

(c) *Educational change* Since the 1944 Education Act there has been greater opportunity for intelligent working class children to succeed. The introduction of comprehensives, the expansion of university and polytechnic provision have been further attempts to expand the chances of working class children. Today 25 per cent of the professions are from working class backgrounds. However, the education system in Britain has never fully succeeded in eliminating the differences in the success rate between the middle and working classes. (For a full discussion of this, see pp 33–6.) It should be noted that in the last 10 years there has actually been a drop in the proportion of working class children attending university;

(d) *Individual motivation and aspiration* Although sociologists stress that social mobility is mainly outside a person's control, it is true that certain people may be more motivated to succeed. The different ways in which middle class children are socialized from working class children is an example of this. Middle class children may have been brought up with higher aspirations and have received greater encouragement to be successful;

(e) *Gender* As a woman's social class position is usually measured by her husband's occupation, it is therefore possible, and common, for women to switch social class through marriage. Many women have their careers interrupted, however, in order to have children.

THE SIGNIFICANCE OF SOCIAL MOBILITY

There are two very different views on social mobility: the **functionalist** and the **Marxist**.

The functionalist view This is that the greater the amount of social mobility in society, the greater the degree of reward exists for ability. Those who are able and hard working can move upwards and the less able sink down. This is known as a **meritocracy** or an **open society**, as opposed to a **closed society** where the higher classes ensure that their children will follow them into those occupations.

The Marxist view is that social mobility is really a smokescreen that obscures the fact that only a tiny proportion of the population own significant wealth in Britain. People compete against each other in order to reach managerial or professional jobs, yet hardly anyone progresses beyond this to join the ranks of the owners. Social mobility operates within a fairly small range of incomes.

The result of social mobility is that people see their success/failure in *individual terms*, competing against one another for a small proportion of 'the cake', failing to see that benefiting from all of their efforts are the owners. The owners get the very best people into the managerial jobs to look after their interests for them.

5.11 Summary

1 Social stratification means the division of people into various social groups having different status and prestige.

2 The main types of divisions are: **caste** (as in India); **estates** (as in feudal times); **slavery** and **social class**. Other divisions are based on age, gender or ethnic group.

3 Social class is the main form of social stratification in modern industrialized society. It is based on economic and status differences.

4 Social mobility occurs between different classes, i.e. movement between classes in a social class system; but not in a caste system.

5 Objectively, **life chances** are affected by social class. Unskilled working class people will have poorer health and larger families. People in social class I will have better education and more material possessions.

6 Subjectively, **views and ideas** on politics, leisure and social issues will be very different, although there is overlap in attitudes between classes.

7 There are three different explanations of social class:

(a) **The Marxist theory** based on economics where society is divided between those who own wealth (the bourgeoisie) and those who sell their labour to the wealthy (the proletariat); such theories have been developed from the work of Karl Marx.

(b) Followers of **Max Weber** say that three elements divide people: economic factors, status and power; and these together influence a person's life chances.

(c) **The Functionalist explanation** compares society to the human body with some parts more important than others.

There are criticisms of all three explanations.

8 In measuring social class **occupation** is very often used as the most important factor. This leads to the **Registrar-General's classification** and the **Hope–Goldthorpe classification**.

9 It has been suggested that a simple division between manual and non-manual workers is adequate, though this division between manual and non-manual is criticized as being out of date.

10 Certain factors have caused changes in the class structure in British society. Such factors include the growth of affluence; unemployment; far more people owning their homes; changes in the educational system giving increased social mobility.

11 Embourgeoisement means 'to become middle-class'. This was rejected in a study by Goldthorpe and Lockwood.

12 Others maintain that there is a 'new' working class as well as the 'traditional' working class which still exists. **Fragmentation** of the working class has taken place.

13 The middle class has also been fragmented or decomposed, e.g. clerical workers have undergone a process of **proletarianization** (have sunk into the working class). Their importance has decreased.

14 The growth of the professions—but here again there is a distinction between the traditional professions, such as doctors or solicitors, with their income and status higher than that of the newer professions, such as social workers or teachers.

15 Britain is a **capitalist** society. The top 1 per cent in Britain own 23 per cent of wealth. Wealth means assets that are worth money if sold, made up of property or stocks and shares.

16 Attempts to redistribute wealth have been largely ineffective.

17 Social mobility is movement up or down the class structure. There are a number of political difficulties in trying to measure social mobility.

18 In Britain social mobility has involved more people entering the 'service class', i.e. the professional and managerial occupations.

19 Heath in *Social Mobility* suggests that for women to become upwardly mobile they have to make a choice between marriage/children and concentrating on their careers.

20 Other factors affecting social mobility are individuals' motivations and aspirations—the 'will to succeed'.

21 The **functionalist** view of social mobility is based on a **meritocracy**, where those who are able can succeed and move upwards.

22 The Marxist view says that really only a tiny proportion of the population own significant wealth and nothing changes this. Nobody joins the owners, but the owners simply benefit from this limited social mobility by getting the best managers to run things for them.

5.12 Keywords (*as they appear in the unit*)

social stratification, caste, estate, slavery, social class, age, gender, ethnic group, ascription, hierarchy, open and closed systems of stratification, life chances—objective and subjective, functionalist, Marxist, false consciousness, class consciousness, Weber, status, power, classifications of social class (Registrar-General, Hope—Goldthorpe), occupation, embourgeoisement, the traditional working class, the 'new' working class, fragmented, working class, proletarianization, professions, wealth, income, social mobility, intragenerational, intergenerational, long range, short range, self-recruitment, élite recruitment.

6 GENDER

6.1 Gender Roles

Definitions
Sociologists use the term **sex** to refer to the biological differences between males and females. The term **gender** is used to refer to the social expectations (or roles) which are related to the physical differences.

In British society, there are certain forms of behaviour that are regarded as appropriate for one gender and inappropriate for the other. For example, it is seen as normal for women to be gentle and emotional by nature; to wear dresses, skirts and make-up; to be better at cooking and dressmaking. On the other hand, men are supposed to be less emotional than women; to be tough and physical; to have a strong sex drive; to regard clothes and their appearance as less important than they are for women; to have mechanical and decorating abilities, etc. These differences of behaviour which we expect from men and women are known as **gender roles**. It is also commonly felt by men that women are inferior in some ways to men as a result of these differences.

Gender roles are learned Gender roles are so obvious and common that often we fail even to think about them, simply accepting them as somehow 'natural' ('Boys will be boys'). The reasons normally given for these differences are that they reflect biological differences between men and women and that it is quite impossible for them to be changed. For example, men are supposed to be naturally stronger than women, and women are said to have a natural 'mothering' instinct for their infants.

Sociologists disagree. They argue instead that the differences in the way men and women behave is the result of socialization into a culture that artificially stresses whatever differences there are between men and women. They point out, for instance, that there is no reason why men should do all manual work in society – in Britain in the past, and in the USSR and much of Africa today, women perform just the same sort of hard, physical labour as men. As for the 'mothering instinct', if it were natural, then all women in all societies would show a natural 'mothering instinct' to their young. Yet no clear pattern emerges; in some societies mothers are gentle and caring with their children as in Britain today, in others they are hard and apparently uncaring as was the case with the Ik tribe of Northern Uganda (studied by Colin Turnbull in the mid-1960s).

GENDER SOCIALIZATION

This is performed by (a) the family, (b) the school, (c) the media and (d) is reinforced by the general culture of society.

The family The most important institution to teach us the values and expectations of society is the family. Gender roles are taught here, too. In the hospital as the birth is about to begin the midwives will ask conversationally whether the couple would prefer to have a girl or a boy? The birth of a girl is often greeted with disappointment by the father, who wants a son to 'carry on the line'. The congratulations cards sent often contain pictures of little girls or boys on the front. If it is a boy the picture invariably shows a boy with a football and a toy plane, and dressed in scruffy jeans. The picture of the girl on the other hand will show a beautifully dressed young child clutching a doll. These models of behaviour are then reinforced throughout a child's life (a) in the sorts of toys given – ball for a boy, doll for a girl; (b) in the language used – 'Stop crying, you're behaving just like a little girl! (c) in the activities they are encouraged to engage in – boys to help their fathers and girls to help their mothers; (d) in the clothes they wear – boys in active clothes such as jeans and tracksuits, girls more carefully dressed in dresses with hair long and combed; (e) as they grow older the boy will be allowed greater freedom; (f) in some families the education of the boy will be regarded as more important than that of the girl, as it is argued that the girl will most likely marry and have children rather than a career.

The school At school the differences between boys and girls are strengthened. In some places they even send children to boy or girl only schools. Inside the school girls are often encouraged to follow subjects seen as appropriate to them. So far more girls than boys study languages, human biology, typing and commercial arts (and sociology!). Boys are more likely to take science and maths subjects. This reflects both the attitudes of the pupils themselves, and also the advice given by teachers.

Apart from the official choices of subjects given by the school (the **curriculum**), there is also a **hidden curriculum**, which refers to the way certain ideas and values of the teachers about the way the girls and boys ought to act are imposed upon pupils in the school. These values influence the way teachers talk and behave towards girls and boys, encouraging them in certain forms of behaviour and discouraging them in others. Girls learn to see their future in terms of low-level jobs while they wait for a husband. They see that teachers pay more attention to males and expect higher grades from them – this often discourages them from trying. They may also learn that good looks and flirting can actually achieve far more popularity than being a 'swot'.

Although the performance of males and females in school examinations is now roughly equal, the subsequent choices for girls is less often one of staying on for academic qualifications such as 'A' Levels, it is more likely that they will go straight into work, or take a fairly low level course such as secretarial studies.

The media The images presented of women in newspapers, radio and television (the media) are either of their (a) 'sexiness' or (b) 'motherliness'.

(a) Newspapers such as the *Sun* print a daily 'page 3' pin-up picture. Women are described as 'attractive blonde' or 'beautiful brunette', even in quite serious papers, yet it is rare to have a man described in such a way. There are women's magazines that are devoted to explaining how women can (and should) make themselves more attractive to men. In such ways as these women come to see themselves as desirable or not, depending upon their attractiveness to men.

(b) The other major role of a woman is to be a good mother and wife. Certain women's magazines are filled with knitting patterns, recipes, child care and domestic hints. Often, too, romance stories are published which strengthen the ideal of true love and the importance of finding a good husband.

Both these images are strengthened by the millions of pounds spent on advertising. The advertisers stress how alluring certain perfumes, clothes and make-up can make a woman. On the other hand, the advertisers present women in the home feeling proud and fulfilled because their children's clothes are really white.

The wider culture Gender roles are strengthened in the wider culture of British society. For example, the Christian religion stresses the role of the woman as mother and wife. In daily life girls are complimented on their good looks and encouraged to seek this approval from men. Certain attitudes towards sex are expected from females, which are not expected from men.

THE SIGNIFICANCE OF GENDER

In childhood girls are expected to help their mothers in housework and parents keep much stricter control over them.

In books and magazines girls are rarely shown as the central characters. Usually they are seen in the role of helper to the male. Magazines written for girls are usually based on romance stories about 'getting their man'.

Education Girls are generally more successful than boys at school, but they study different subjects from boys – less often maths and science, more often languages and commercial subjects such as typing. After school they are less likely to go into further training or higher education.

Employment Females are concentrated in a few areas of work, such as 'caring' jobs (e.g. nursing) and clerical work. They earn less than men – on average about two thirds the male wage – and are less likely to be promoted into positions of responsibility.

Family Care of the children and the running of the household are seen as more the responsibility of the wife than the husband. Women are much more likely to give up jobs and careers to stay to look after the home and bring up the children.

6.2 The Changing Status of Women

Today, men and women have equal legal rights and most men regard women as their equals. This has not always been the case, and 120 years ago women's political rights were almost non-existent. They were effectively prevented by legislation from many types of work and were regarded as inferior by most men.

THE DECLINE IN STATUS

When we examine the move towards equality over the last 100 years, we need to bear in mind that women's status reached its lowest point about 120 years ago and that today we are simply restoring the situation of 220 years ago.

Ann Oakley has pointed out that in pre-industrial Britain, women and men had similar legal rights and regarded each other as equals. Most people at that time worked in agriculture, and the work was shared between men and women, with women doing much of the back-breaking physical work. As the type of work shifted from agricultural and domestic (work produced in the home for sale) to factory employment, women were gradually edged out of employment and forced to stay at home caring for children for at least part of their lives. Oakley actually argues that the restrictions imposed upon women were the result of competition for the available jobs between men and women – and the men won.

There then occurred a gradual decline in the status of women, with women being seen as basically inferior creatures who were to be treated in much the same way as children. Among better-off families it became fashionable for the husband to use his wife as a way of showing how successful he had become. The wife's clothes, her jewellery and the number of servants indicated just how well the husband had done. In poorer households, women looked after children, worked in factories and as servants for the rich.

One other reason for the decline in the status of women, suggested by Hannah Gavron, was the *excess* of women over men in Britain in the nineteenth century. This was a result of war and emigration. There were always unmarried women chasing too few men and so they were in a weak position.

THE IMPROVEMENT IN STATUS

In 1837 a woman had no vote and belonged with all her possessions to her husband. Any children of the marriage belonged to the father. Divorce was only possible if started by the husband. Wives, in fact, had the same legal standing as lunatics.

1 *Property* Although Acts in 1880–2 (Married Women's Property Acts) gave a woman rights to property belonging to her before marriage, and to earnings from her work, it was not until 1925 that a husband and wife were treated as separate individuals in property transactions (Law and Property Act). Only in 1970 (Matrimonial Proceedings Act) did wives have an automatic right to half of the marital assets.

2 *Parental rights* Only in 1886 was a mother allowed to be the sole guardian of her children on the death of her husband (Guardianship of Infants Act). Before that time the family of the husband also had a legal claim to the children. In 1925 the principle of the prime importance of the welfare of the child was established. In practice this meant that the wife almost always obtained custody of the children in cases of divorce or separation.

3 *Divorce* It was not until 1875 that women could divorce men (Matrimonial Causes Act). But whereas men could divorce women for adultery, wives could only divorce husbands when they had committed **both** adultery and cruelty. Only in 1937 were equal rights of divorce granted. In a judgment in 1977, common-law wives obtained the same property rights as married women.

4 *Politics* Women had no voting rights in national elections until 1918, when they were granted to women over the age of 30 (it was 21 for men). In 1928 voting rights were also granted to women between 21 and 30. However, the representation of women in Parliament is extremely low. In 1986 there were only 25 female Members of Parliament.

5 *Education* Obstacles existed until 1944 to prevent girls attending secondary schools. As there were a limited number of free grammar school places, they were generally given to boys who, it was argued, would be able to use their education instead of staying at home to run the household and look after the children.

6 *Work and pay* Until very recently there was no protection for women against discrimination in terms of employment, promotion and pay. Then came a series of Acts to cover these three areas.

(a) 1970 The Equal Pay Act meant women were to receive equal pay for equal work.

(b) 1975 The Employment Protection Act gave women the right to have paid maternity leave.

(c) 1975 The Sex Discrimination Act. This states that nobody can be discriminated against on the grounds of sex in areas such as employment, education, provision of goods, services and housing, public appointments and certain related matters such as discriminatory advertisements. There were specific penalties set out for those who did discriminate.

(d) 1975 The Equal Opportunities Commission. This body was set up to enforce the laws relating to discrimination. It has the power to initiate action against those who do discriminate, it can also support individual complainants in the Courts and Industrial Tribunals. It promotes equality through education and research.

(e) In 1984 there was an amendment to the 1970 Equal Pay Act, which stated that women doing work of equal value to men, even if the work was different, must be paid the same rate as men. By 1986, this amendment had taken effect and forced employers into raising the wages of many women workers.

THE HISTORICAL OPPRESSION OF WOMEN

NO VOTE until 1918 (women over 30) | NO CUSTODIAL RIGHTS until 1886 (on death of husband) | NO RIGHT TO DIVORCE (till 1875- then only adultery & cruelty) | THE SAME LEGAL STANDING AS LUNATICS (1837) | NO PROPERTY RIGHTS AFTER MARRIAGE (until 1882) | FEWER EDUCATIONAL OPPORTUNITIES | DISCRIMINATION IN EMPLOYMENT

Reasons for the improvement in women's status:

(a) There has been a consistent *decline in the average number of children born to each family*. It has declined from 6+ children in the 1860s to about 2 children per family in the 1980s. This has been caused largely by the increased use of birth control. The result has been to free women to a certain extent from a life of childbearing when they were forced to remain at home to care for their children;

(b) *Increasing educational opportunities* which occurred with the general expansion of education;

(c) The *expansion of social services* provided assistance and support for women at specific stages in their lives, particularly in and shortly after childbirth. This helped to free women from dependence on men;

(d) *Legal changes*, although a reflection of women's increasing status, further strengthened their position, giving them in particular property rights and equal rights in divorce;

(e) Women are commonly *in charge of the household finances*. They are therefore of great importance in a consumer society. This has implications for the content of newspapers and magazines which need to attract women. Many feminists dispute this and argue that magazines and newspapers actually lower the status of women by concentrating on trivia, e.g. women's magazines, or by degrading them, e.g. the *Sun's* page 3 photographs;

(f) The single biggest cause of the rise in women's status has been their *economic importance at any particular time*. It is clear that some of the most significant gains by the women's movement were the legal and political rights obtained after the First World War (1914–18). Before that war there were 15 million women in Britain, but only 5½ million were in paid employment, and of these 1½ million were domestic servants. The war led to a massive recruitment of women from all classes into all fields of employment. At the end of the war it was no longer possible to claim that women were incapable of doing these jobs or that they were in any way inferior to men. This led (as the result of female pressure groups) to women obtaining property rights and the vote. However, women were strongly encouraged to return to their household duties after the war, giving their jobs back to men.

The Second World War led to a similar recruitment of women, but after this war there was an increasing demand for female labour as there was a labour shortage. It could be argued that the importance of women in the economy allied to feminist pressure groups has led to the changes that have taken place in the last 20 years;

(g) Although economic factors are of the greatest importance, *women's political activity* and their struggle for their own rights have combined with their economic position to change the climate of opinion regarding women.

Although there had been political protest by women from about 1850, it was not until 1903, with the formation of the Women's Social and Political Union under the leadership of Emmeline Pankhurst, that they engaged in militant action. They were commonly known as **suffragettes.** They were involved in marches, protests, hunger strikes, a systematic campaign to destroy shop windows in London, and one woman killed herself in public to protest. However, it was only their pressure **combined with** their importance in the war economy that led to their obtaining the vote.

The *contemporary women's movement* has no clear structure as its predecessors had, rather it belongs to a broad movement which manifests itself in magazines such as *Spare Rib*, or in local women's groups who organize women's studies.

The position today is that although women have achieved legal equality with men this does not mean that they have full equality. Women still have particularly restricted roles in society which are based upon a notion of **femininity**. Women have to be attractive to men, to be sexually desirable, to be good mothers, to be good housewives, to be good cooks. Men's roles are different and, some would argue, are treated as having higher status than those of women. Any women's magazine immediately shows the major concerns and social role of women.

6.3 Women and Employment

The best way to illustrate the inequality of women's position in society today is to examine in detail their situation in the world of work.

THE NUMBERS OF WOMEN WORKING

1 This century there has been a strong increase in the numbers of women going into paid employment.

In 1901 women formed only 29 per cent of the workforce; after the Second World War, however, the numbers in employment began to increase and by 1961 women formed 32 per cent of the workforce; today it is over 44 per cent and increasing.

2 There are now 10.4 million women working, compared to less than 8 million 20 years ago.

3 The increase in the numbers of women working has largely been taken up by *married* women. In the last 20 years, the total labour force has increased by 2½ million, and this was entirely due to a 70 per cent increase in the number of married women working. While this has been happening the number of male workers has been declining.

4 Indeed, the most noticeable trend since the end of the Second World War has been the increase in married women working. Today, of all married women approximately 50 per cent are in some form of employment compared to under 30 per cent 20 years

Table 6.1 The percentage of each age group within each gender working

Age	16–19		25–44		45–54	
	Male	Female	Male	Female	Male	Female
	74%	70%	95%	62%	90%	68%

ago. And if we restrict the proportion to married women of working age only, then the figure reaches 60 per cent.

5 Women are far more likely to have part-time employment than men; in fact 90 per cent of part-time employees are women. It has been estimated that 3½ million women work part-time.

WOMEN, WORK AND THE FAMILY CIRCLE

There is a close relationship between family life and female employment. As women are expected to stay at home to look after their children, they generally leave full-time work for a few years while bearing and raising them and then undertake part-time employment. Today, on average, women return to work 3½ years after the birth of their last child.

Table 6.2 The numbers of men and women workers and the numbers of married and non-married females in the workforce (millions)

	Married females	Non-married females	All females	Males	Total (millions)
1961	3.9	3.9	7.7	16.1	23.8
1971	5.8	3.4	9.2	15.9	25.1
1976	6.7	3.3	10.1	15.9	26.0
1979	6.8	3.5	10.3	15.8	26.1
1981	6.7	3.7	10.4	15.9	26.3
1983	6.9	3.8	10.7	15.5	26.2
1988	–	–	10.9	14.4	25.3
1990	–	–	11.5	14.8	26.3

(**Source:** *Social Trends* 1992)

REASONS FOR THE INCREASE IN THE NUMBERS OF WOMEN WORKING

1 The changing economic structure since the 1950s has seen a shift in Britain from heavy industry (e.g. steel, engineering) towards light industry (e.g. electronics) and service industries (e.g. shops, catering). Employers were more likely to accept women in the growing industries.

2 There was an acute labour shortage until the early 1970s, and married women were encouraged to enter the workforce.

3 Women were/are a cheap source of labour; on average, women earn only 70 per cent of the wage of men. This has made them economically attractive to employers.

4 Women are a far more **flexible** form of labour than men, and can be employed part-time. 90 per cent of all part-time workers are women.

5 An increase in educational opportunities for women has meant that they are better able to compete for work and less content to remain at home as housewives.

6 A general rise in the status of women has meant that they are more likely to want, and to be given, work.

7 Smaller families in a shorter period means greater freedom for women who are less tied to the home.

THE SITUATION OF WOMEN IN WORK

The types of work women do

Two thirds of all working women are concentrated in just three types of work:

1 clerical work, which is generally routine office work;

2 service work which covers a range of occupations such as shop assistants, receptionists, etc.;

3 professional and technical services – this sounds impressive, but for women it usually means the lower-paid professional and technical work such as nursing (92 per cent of nurses are female), technicians and typists (98 per cent are female). It is interesting to note that women form less than a quarter of self-employed workers (that is people who work for themselves and who have no boss).

In general women are employed in a narrow range of occupations and in work that is considered to need less skill (and can therefore often be more boring).

This situation of low skilled jobs in a restricted range of occupations reflects the wider role of women in society. Women are encouraged to see themselves as primarily mothers and housewives rather than as career women. This is different from the situation of men who see their work as most important.

Research In her investigation of secondary schoolgirls in Ealing, West London (*Just Like a Girl*), Sue Sharpe found that their main ambition was to get married and have children; careers were seen to be of little importance. Sharpe argues that this is because the girls are constantly encouraged to think this way by the education system, the media and the wider culture, which stress the differences between traditional male and female roles.

Promotion and level of work

In 1985 only about 10 per cent of working women were in the higher grades of professional, managerial or white-collar work, compared to 23 per cent of men, and 53 per cent of working women could be found in low-level, routine white-collar work, compared to only 18 per cent of men.

When it came to manual work (for instance, physical work in a factory) only 13 per cent of workers classified as 'skilled manual' (the higher grade of manual worker), were women.

Table 6.3 shows the proportions of men and women in 10 professions.

Table 6.3 Men and women in ten selected professions, 1977

Profession	% women	% men
dentists	15	85
family doctors	14	86
veterinary surgeons	10	90
barristers	6	94
architects	5	95
university professors	2	98
chartered surveyors	1	99
civil engineers	1	99
bank managers	under 1	over 99
mechanical engineers	0	100

(**Source**: A. Oakley, *Subject Women* Fontana, 1981)

It shows for instance that only 15 per cent of dentists and 14 per cent of family doctors were women.

In a study by Greenhalgh (*Male/Female Wage Differentials in Great Britain*), 60 per cent of married men with qualifications above A Level standard had a professional or managerial occupation, compared to only 16 per cent of married women with similar qualifications.

Women's chances of promotion are less because they still have to combine the twin roles of mother and employee. Usually they have to leave work for a period to have children and this lowers their chances of promotion. It is also true to say that male employers (the majority) are often wary of giving women promotion because they believe that they will leave their jobs at some point to have children and this will cause disruption.

Hours of work

(a) Of part-time workers 90 per cent are female and 42 per cent of women in employment have part-time as opposed to full-time work.

The main reason for women working only part-time appears to be family obligations. Evidence supporting this comes from a survey by Klein which showed that many mothers restrict their working hours to the school hours of their children. In another survey it was found that 90 per cent of married women who would have liked to work, but did not, gave responsibility for their children as the main reason. This reflects the fact that wives, as opposed to husbands, are seen as the people mainly responsible for the welfare of children. This emphasis on child welfare also influences women's attendance at work. Women have considerably higher rates of absence from work than men. This reflects the fact that if children are ill, it is generally believed to be the mother's duty to stay at home to look after the child. The husband will still go in to work.

(b) The amount of overtime worked by women is (i) affected by this role of mother and housewife; (ii) affected by the fact that women tend not to work in industries offering high levels of overtime. On average, whereas women work less than one hour per week in overtime, men work about 3½ hours.

Wages

Sixty per cent of women are found in the 10 lowest-paid occupations. In 1984, men earned £4.21 per hour compared to women's £3.09. In 1983, the average male wage per week was £163, whereas it was only £109 for women. Women therefore earned about 66 per cent of male wages – little changed from previous years. It is important to remember that it is illegal to pay women less than men as a result of the 1970 Equal Pay Act (which came into force in 1975).

The differences in earnings occur because women are concentrated in lowly paid, low-status work and have little opportunity (or possibility) of doing overtime. One particular example of low-paid work is the situation of some *homeworkers*, that is people who are given work to do at home rather than in a factory, who are engaged in tasks such as sewing clothes, constructing toys or filling envelopes. It has been estimated by the Low Pay Unit that many of these are earning less than 50p an hour.

Women workers and unemployment

The overall figures for unemployment are lower than those for men. This can partially be explained by the fact that as women are generally more lowly paid than men, employers are more likely to dispose of the more expensive male workers first. However, it should be remembered that (a) women are more likely to accept part-time work than men; (b) married women are less likely to sign on the official unemployment register as they do not receive any social security benefits, so they do not appear in the unemployment figures.

HOUSEWORK

It is commonly believed that when we talk about 'women working' it means paid employment in offices, factories and shops. But the job of being a **housewife** involves just as much work as any form of labour outside the home. In *The Sociology of Housework* Ann Oakley has suggested a number of characteristics of housework:

(a) it is unpaid—women rarely receive any form of regular salary they can call their own in exchange for all the cooking, cleaning, and ironing, etc. they do;

(b) it is low-status work—most men do not even regard housework as work, as they have an untrue image of its consisting of playing with the children, cooking a meal and watching television. In reality the tasks of cleaning, shopping, cooking and caring for children can be exhausting labour;

(c) it is monotonous. Oakley's study of housewives in North London found that they found their work to be more boring and repetitive than assembly line workers in factories;

(d) housewives are isolated, tending to be cut off from people other than their young children. They are often trapped in the home most of the day apart from visits to the shops;

(e) long hours of work. Oakley estimated that housewives worked an average week of 77 hours—more than any group of workers employed in factories or offices. She points out that the activities of clearing up, of cooking and ironing continue well into the evening, long after the hours of outside employment have finished;

(f) housework is female work. The role of housewife, as the word suggests is almost exclusively female. It is women who give up their jobs to stay at home to care for children and this is expected of them. The occasional husband who does this is regarded as highly unusual. (This exclusivity to women is closely linked to the whole idea of male and female roles as discussed on pp 54–5.)

Women and education: please turn to the 'Education' unit, pp 36–8.
Women and the family: please turn to the 'Family' unit, pp 13–27.
Women and social class: please turn to the 'Stratification' unit, pp 40–54.
Women and crime: please turn to the 'Crime and Deviance' unit, p 137.

6.4 Summary

1 Gender roles are how sociologists describe the idea that there are certain different activities, attitudes and ways of dressing which society regards as appropriate for males and females.

2 Sociologists argue that these differences are not natural, but are learned in childhood and constantly strengthened in everyday life.

3 The most important influences in forming gender roles are the family, the school and the media.

4 The attitudes held towards women have changed considerably over the last 400 years. When Britain was a nation based on working on the land, men and women were regarded as equal. Later, as Britain became a society based on factories, women were regarded as inferior to men and lost many of their rights. In the last 100 years women have been fighting to regain equality with men.

5 Today women are legally equal to men, but they still suffer some disadvantages, particularly in the world of work.

6 Women work in low-paid, lower-grade occupations than men.

7 Women, unlike men, have to combine the responsibility of running a household, looking after their children and working – this means that they are more likely to do part-time work and more likely to give up all paid employment for a few years while they have their children and bring them up.

8 The job of housewife is performed almost exclusively by women and, although it is hard work, it is often not seen as work at all.

6.5 Keywords *(as they appear in the unit)*

sex, gender, gender roles, status, housework.

7 AGE

7.1 Childhood

Aries has argued that the idea of childhood is a relatively new phenomenon. He points out that for the bulk of the population, the notion of treating a child as someone in need of care and protection derives from the eighteenth century. Before this time children above the age of 5 were treated as little adults.

The Middle Ages

The peasants expected their children to help work the land. As soon as they were old enough to help they started to work. The children were an absolutely essential part of the economy; without them the family would have been unable to cope. Children wore the same clothes as adults and both age groups played games together (games were not just for children then). There was no organized education and learning was a matter of copying skills from the parents.

For the wealthy a lengthy training for their duties, such as running the family estates, began early on. Some sons were sent to monasteries to learn to become clergymen. Girls were expected to learn how to run households.

The early eighteenth century

The newly rich traders began to treat their children rather differently, in particular giving them a longer education so that they could run the family business efficiently when it came to their turn.

At this time the idea that children were born pure and innocent emerged among the wealthy and people began to supervise the bringing up of children of the rich to ensure that they were not harmed or corrupted by bad influences. Clothes specifically for children were introduced for rich families at this time.

The nineteenth century

Under the influence of new religious ideas, there was a change in the attitude to children, in particular it was now believed that they were born corrupt and wicked and had to be firmly controlled and taught the best way to behave. If they were 'naughty' they were beaten.

In Victorian England the lives of *middle class children* were tightly controlled. They were brought up by governesses and taught to regard the authority of adults as total. Boys were sent away to public schools to become gentlemen and girls were taught to become good wives and mothers.

The lives of *the peasantry and later the working class* continued much as before. Children were regarded as a necessary part of the economy of the family and were put to work as soon as possible. With the coming of industrialization, they worked up to 14 hours a day in mines and factories.

The awareness of childhood as a truly distinctive period for all social classes finally emerged without any doubt with the passing of various employment acts, controlling the hours of work of children (which indicated that in people's minds children were clearly a separate group in need of protection) in the 1820s onward, and the eventual introduction of a national system of schooling in 1870. However, the ideas of child rearing in which children were often beaten and regarded as having no views worth listening to carried on well into this century.

The twentieth century

It was not until the 1950s that the present idea that children are deserving of love and attention was common to all social classes. However, important differences appear in the way children are socialized in childhood today.

Gender Girls are more closely supervised and their primary role as mother/wife is still stressed (see pp 37–8 and pp 55–6).

Class Research by the Newsons (*Seven Years Old in the Home Environment*) suggests that:

(a) Working class parents are more liable to give commands to their children, while middle class mothers are likely to explain their wishes. According to Bernstein, this has important consequences for the development of learning and writing skills later in life;

(b) They are less likely to ask for the views of children;

(c) They are more erratic in their punishment of children than the middle class (see p 20).

Ethnic group West Indian and Asian parents are stricter with their children and place a higher value on obedience.

Childhood in contemporary Britain is viewed as a period of great innocence. The 'realities' of life, such as sex and violence, are generally hidden from children. The general view is that they are human beings who are to be 'moulded' into the values of society through socialization. It is not considered correct for them to undertake certain activities that are regarded as only for adults, which vary from voting through to taking alcohol. All this is based on the notion that children are not able to make sensible choices for themselves, but as they grow they become more 'mature' and better able to exercise choice.

7.2 Childhood in Another Society

In the 1960s, Colin Turnbull studied the lives of a tribe living in the mountains between Uganda and Sudan (in *The Mountain People*). The Ik, as the tribe was called, had been transferred to the mountain area because the authorities had decided to make their traditional homeland into a game reserve. Although hunters, the Ik were forced into a life of agriculture, even though conditions in the mountains were extremely harsh and hostile to the growing crops. The Ik were always short of food and so had developed a new culture to cope with their conditions. One element of the culture was a completely changed attitude to children.

Children were regarded as a curse, as they meant more mouths to feed. If they survived birth, they were treated extremely harshly, in the hope that they might die. On at least one occasion children were stolen by leopards and eaten. This pleased the Ik enormously as it meant that the leopard would be very full and would probably sleep while digesting the child. The leopard was then tracked down, killed and eaten.

Children were thrown out of the 'home' at the age of three, when they were expected to look after themselves. The three-year-olds would band together in a group to survive. At eight they would progress to the next age group and so on until full adulthood. Young girls often survived by acting as 'prostitutes' in exchange for food.

Childhood here contained none of the ideas of purity and innocence, and the need for protection, which we have in our society.

7.3 Youth Culture

YOUTH AS A DISTINCT PHASE IN LIFE

Traditionally, individuals moved directly from childhood to adulthood—there was no intermediate stage of **youth** as there is now.

This transition from childhood to adulthood, with its assumption of rights and responsibilities, was clearly marked in a ceremony known as a **rite of passage**.

A well-known example of a rite of passage is the traditional initiation ceremony for males in the Murring aboriginal tribe in Australia. The adolescents were initiated by having a tooth wrenched out, during a ceremony which involved special dancers and the wearing of masks. The missing tooth was a symbol of manhood and an indication of the ability to withstand pain.

For women, the initiation ceremony was usually one related to onset of puberty and the first period. Among the Wanomani Indians of South America, for example, girls were expected to retire to a specially constructed hut for their first period and to be attended by older women.

In contemporary Western society there are no rites of passage linked to the movement from childhood to adulthood – instead there is the period of youth. In this period, the individual is not expected to behave like a child, but is denied the status and rights of an adult. There is also no clear age at which childhood and youth end or adulthood begins. The only accepted age of adulthood is 18, which marks the right to legal powers, voting, borrowing money, and purchasing alcohol.

Although the boundaries of youth are unclear, it is accepted that it now forms a distinctive phase in people's lives, and those boundaries are expanding in both directions, so that youth begins earlier and ends later.

SUBCULTURE

Since the early 1950s, young people have adopted certain values and patterns of behaviour that are noticeably distinct from those of the older generation, particularly in dress and music. This had led some sociologists to argue that a separate **youth culture** exists.

When sociologists use the term **culture** they mean the whole way of life and set of beliefs of a particular society. The anthropologist Ralph Linton describes culture as 'the way of life of its (a society's) members: the collection of ideas and habits which they learn, share and transmit from generation to generation.' Youth culture therefore refers to the distinctive values and activities of young people. It should more correctly be referred to as either of the following:

1 *Subculture* This means a distinctive way of life *within* a wider social culture. After all, youth may have a **distinctive** way of life but it takes place *within* the wider culture of our society;

2 *Contra-culture* This is where a set of values arises in *opposition* to the wider culture. The **punks** and **hippies** in different ways opposed the dominant society.

7.4 The Origins of Youth Culture

Although adolescence as a stage of life was often regarded as a period of difficulty as a result of the individual's need to establish personal independence and sense of identity, the idea of a youth culture with its own particular values and beliefs first emerged during the 1950s. The following reasons have been suggested.

Pace of change

The increasing pace of social change since the Second World War has meant that social patterns regarded as normal for the older generation are not relevant to new social, technological and economic conditions. As parents cannot provide a **role model** for their children, the younger generation has to create its own culture to cope with the new conditions.

Length of education

The extension of compulsory education to 15 after the war and to 16 in 1972 and the massive growth in sixth forms, further education and higher education has kept people in education up to the age of 18–21. This isolation from the discipline of work and the large number of young people concentrated together in educational institutions has, according to *The Adolescent Society*, by Coleman, an American sociologist, led to the creation of a specific lifestyle and set of values among young people.

Affluence

In a study of adolescents' incomes in the 1950s, Abrams (*The Teenage Consumer*) concluded that their incomes had more than doubled in this period. As they did not have to spend their incomes on household items, they represented an enormous market for the new leisure industries of fashion and pop music. Although youth today is far less affluent the industries still remain, exerting considerable influence on spending patterns.

Growth of the media

The affluence of youth in the 1950s coincided with the growth of the new media of television, the music industry, radio and specialist teenage/pop music magazines. The result of this explosion of the media was the development of a self-image of youth as a distinct group with its own **generational consciousness**.

This consciousness has been reinforced throughout society, according to Stanley Cohen (*Folk Devils and Moral Panics*), because the media in general find youth a useful source of news providing interesting stories and images. Thus the category of mod, rocker, skinhead, punk, etc. may be as much a creation of the media as of young people themselves.

7.5 The Nature of Youth Culture

As the focus of sociological research has come to bear on youth culture two viewpoints have emerged:

1 that youth culture is one culture shared by all youth of every social class and has led to a clear-cut **generation gap** between the younger and older generations;
2 that youth culture is really an **umbrella** term that covers a wide range of divisions *within* youth. The divisions are based on social class, gender and race.

1 THE SINGLE YOUTH CULTURE VIEW

Early sociologists studying youth culture, such as Talcott Parsons, argued that the period of adolescence is one in which young people are passing through a transitional stage between childhood and adulthood. This transitional stage gives the chance to rebel against parental and adult authority; it also allows society in general to change its values slightly to cope with changing social conditions. The variations within youth are not regarded as being very significant: they are viewed merely as different reflections of the same youthful rebelliousness and the search for pleasure.

Youth culture and the activities of the peer group serve a very important psychological function for young people. As they are unsure of themselves and their developing identity, they look to others in the same situation with the same fashions and values for guidance, reassurance and support.

2 YOUTH CULTURE AS AN UMBRELLA TERM

The idea that there is *one* all embracing youth culture has come in for considerable criticism in recent years. In particular it is argued that there are a number of *different* youth cultures which reflect the particular problems (and advantages) of youth of the different social classes. Middle class, working class, and black youth have their own distinctive subcultures.

(a) Middle class youth culture

Middle class youth are more likely (i) to stay on in education and (ii) to have good chances of future success in life. The result is that their versions of youth culture focus on student life and political protest. Very often they develop clear-cut alternatives to the present system, e.g. the hippies of the 1960s.

(b) Working class youth culture

Working class youth have a wider variety of subcultures than the middle class. Sociologists such as Mike Brake argue that their versions of youth culture (from Teds to Punks etc.) 'attempt to infuse into this (working class) bleak world excitement and colour, during the respite between school and settling down into marriage and adulthood'. For working class youth, school is largely irrelevant as most will leave at the minimum age with low academic qualifications to undertake manual work or be unemployed. Their cultures are far more of a **response** to their **experiences** of life, which are very different from the middle class student. For example Jeff Clarke, writing about skinheads, argues that the clothes they wear, the shaved hairstyle, braces, boots, etc., all reflect a conscious copy of the traditional working class male dress. They are, in a particular way, maintaining the working class community and tradition which have been destroyed through rehousing and changes in the nature of employment. Football violence reflects the need for working class youth to belong to a definite neighbourhood of their own (the football club) which they **defend** against intruders (other teams' fans). Other versions of working class youth culture (Teds, Mods, Punks, etc.) stress the need to escape from the bleak working class life, so fashion, style and excitement are stressed.

(c) Black youth culture

The explanations sociologists have put forward for working class youth culture also apply to West Indian youth. They return to their parents' culture for their image of themselves. In the way that skinheads take traditional working class dress, the Rastafarians have gone back to West Indian culture for an alternative model and have adopted the dreadlocks, the marijuana smoking and the reggae music.

Black youth music Stuart Hall, himself a black sociologist, points out the close links between the origins of reggae, which is based on the poverty and exploitation of blacks by whites, and the current situation of West Indian youth in Britain. Reggae music gives black youth their

own way of expressing themselves independently of *white* pop music. Like punk music, however, reggae has been *refined* and popularized by the music industry.

(d) Asian youth culture

Young Asians have kept a remarkably low profile in Britain. It appears that the strength of family life, tradition and racism keeps them separate from mainstream white youth culture. It appears that music and films, etc. are imported from India, to cater for the youth audience. Female Asians are closely controlled by parents and strictly forbidden from social mixing with boys or outside the controls of the community.

(e) Female youth culture

Clearly there are major class and ethnic divisions between girls, as between males. However, all female youth seem to share a similar situation in that there are very different expectations of them than males – reflecting the expectations attached to different gender roles in British society in general.

Studies by McRobbie and Garber, and by Sue Sharpe, indicate that the main centre of female youth is romantic – basically, getting a boyfriend (though it does not indicate a desire to marry). An analysis of the different contents of magazines aimed at the male and female market illustrates this. The female magazines stress such things as romantic stories, make-up, fashion, etc. Male magazines are more likely to stress particular interests such as music or motorbikes.

In addition, females have greater restraints placed on them by parents – they are allowed out less and expected to return relatively early at night. Those females who do experiment sexually (in much the same way boys are encouraged to do) are labelled as sexually permissive and not seen as respectable girlfriends to have.

7.6 The Importance of the Peer Group

A **peer group** is a group of people of similar characteristics who identify with each other. The term is generally used to refer to youth – although, as can be seen from the definition, this is not necessarily the case.

A peer group usually plays an important part in the **socialization process**:

(a) It teaches people how to behave in groups outside the family;

(b) It is often in youth peer groups also that individuals learn how to treat others of the opposite sex;

(c) Peer groups develop their own norms and values and those in the group who break the informal rules may well be punished;

(d) Status differences appear within peer groups. These can be based on a wide variety of factors, but in adolescence it is typically such things as attractiveness, wit, toughness and ability at sport;

(e) At its most powerful, in adolescence, the peer group may actually develop its own subculture (as discussed earlier) and so in a wider sense some people use the term *peer group* to refer to *youth subcultures*.

Research

Paul Willis in *Learning to Labour* studied the influence of the peer group in education. His study was of a group of secondary school, lower stream boys. These rejected the school system and instead committed themselves to an anti-school culture of avoiding work, being tough, having a laugh, and making fun of the teachers and those pupils who worked hard. Each member of the peer group measured his behaviour against his fellow anti-school group and no one else was of real importance to him. The 'lads', as they were called, egged each other on to be the most awkward or the toughest at school.

7.7 Youth Culture and Unemployment

About 20 per cent of those under 25 are registered as unemployed – a figure that grossly underestimates the number of young people who would like to work, but cannot. Many go into further education, trying to get better qualifications; others opt for the Youth Training Programme. It has been estimated the true rate of youth unemployment in Britain is in the region of 40–50 per cent.

This has had an impact on youth culture which was created in a period of affluence and is based very much on **style** and **consumption**. There are two views on this spread of unemployment.

The optimistic view

This perspective argues that:

1 As youth have never had jobs, there is no loss of identity as there is with a middle-aged person who has come to see him/herself in terms of his/her employment;

2 The income level of youth often increases on leaving school and being unemployed. Unemployed school leavers are entitled to benefits which they did not receive at school or college, where they had only received an allowance from parents (plus, of course, part-time employment income);

3 As the group of young people leaving school are unemployed together, there is little or no disruption of the social life, or loss of friends.

The pessimistic view

This is associated with Paul Willis and his study of youth unemployment in the Midlands. He argues that:

1 Employment is the key that unlocks the door to adulthood among the working class;

2 It means that the person can afford independence from parents and the ability to buy all the 'props' considered important in our society (a car, fashionable clothes, etc.);

3 In working class culture, traditional views of 'masculinity' in particular are associated with employment;

4 The result according to Willis is to throw youth into crisis. They cannot look forward to marrying, to having their own home. Indeed, the dependence of youth on parents, beyond the age at which the working class traditionally have financial independence, has caused conflict in the home.

7.8 Old Age

The rite of passage of retirement marks the end of a person's economically useful life to the community. Old age has become the phenomenon of modern society, as before this century, the numbers surviving to old age were very small. Today there are over 10 million people of retirement age in this country. In contemporary Britain, the elderly have low status and are regarded as having little to contribute to society.

As a person's employment often gives him/her an identity, the movement out of paid employment often creates problems of self-identity. Modern Britain has not yet developed an adequate status for the elderly (see p 101 in the unit on 'Population' for further discussion on the elderly in Britain).

In a comparative study of 14 different societies, ranging from the simple tribal (the Aborigines of Australia), through the underdeveloped (Mexico) to the modern industrialized (Britain), Cowgill and Holmes found that:

1 Being elderly is seen in most societies not just as having lived for so many years, but as achieving the status of a tribal elder or of becoming a grandfather. Actual age, which is important to us, is not generally seen as so important.

2 There are many more elderly people in modern industrialized societies than in tribal or underdeveloped ones. This can be explained by better standards of living and to a lesser extent improved medical services.

3 The status of the aged is at its lowest in modern societies.

4 In simpler societies older people hold most positions of power. This is generally not true in modern societies.

5 The faster the rate of social change, the lower the status of the aged in society. This is because the skills and knowledge they have are not relevant to the younger generation – so they are not regarded as having worthwhile knowledge. In agricultural societies where the knowledge of one generation is generally useful to the next, the old therefore have high status.

6 Retirement is a modern invention. Traditionally, the elderly gradually withdrew from active manual tasks as their ability declined – but there was no abrupt stopping of work. This is important, as in modern societies an individual's status and self-perception is related to his/her job. On retirement, the person has lost his/her identity.

7 In modern societies, there is a process called **disengagement**, which is the gradual withdrawal of old people from other people's company. This does not occur in other societies.

7.9 The Elderly in Another Society: Japan

In Japanese society, before industrialization (which took place at the beginning of this century), the extended family structure was the backbone of the social structure. The eldest male was the head of the family and absolute obedience was expected from all family members.

Although the power of the eldest male of the family derived from his position as head of the family, it is also true to say that anybody of great age was treated with respect. Thus status increased with age, and did not decline as it does now.

As the extended family formed the basis of economic and political power in the Japanese society of this period, it meant that all major decisions were taken by the elderly.

One point should be made—Japanese society was **patriarchal** in that it was male dominated and although elderly women received respect, the effective power was in the hands of the men.

The reasons why the elderly received so much respect was basically that they were in effective control of the economy. In each household or extended family, the male owned everything and allotted tasks to family members. Whatever they received for their work was dependent on him, as there was no such thing as a wage.

Finally, as Japanese society remained relatively unchanged until the industrial revolution there, the knowledge of the elderly was useful for the young—unlike our society where the skills of one generation are rapidly outdated.

Japanese society today still demands that great respect must be given to the elderly.

7.10 Summary

1 The idea of appropriate behaviour being attached to certain ages is a social creation and is not the result of biology.

2 Childhood as we know it now developed over a long period—starting in the eighteenth century.

3 Before that time children were seen as 'little adults'.

4 There have always been class differences in the way that children have been treated. Possibly the greatest gap was in the early part of the nineteenth century, when the children of the working class were forced to work longer hours and in much worse conditions than even adults today.

5 The proof of the social creation of childhood comes from comparing childhood in different cultures and over time. In one culture (of the Ik) children are expected to look after themselves at the age of three.

6 Rites of passage are the ceremonies that most societies have to mark the transition from one age grade to another—for example, from childhood to adulthood.

7 British society has lost most of its rites of passage relating to age—although the 18th birthday is still commonly marked by a party.

8 The idea of youth is a new invention that occurred in the 1950s.

9 The main factors influencing the growth of youth culture were: (a) pace of change (b) length of education (c) affluence (d) growth of the media.

10 Subculture means to have a distinctive set of values within the wider culture, but not, however, opposed to it.

11 One group of sociologists has argued that youth culture is a way for young people to cope with the change from childhood to adulthood, by giving them confidence.

12 A different approach is taken by most other sociologists who argue that there is no one youth culture at all, and that youth culture is really closely related to differences in class, gender and ethnic group.

13 The peer group is a group of people of the same age or situation against whose behaviour we measure our own. The peer group is particularly important to youth.

14 The idea that there is a clear generation gap is not proved by research. It seems that most youth are conventional in their attitudes.

15 The number of the elderly is increasing in society, so there are now more of them than ever before.

16 The status of the elderly has never been so low in advanced industrial societies.

17 This low status is related to the fact that the skills and knowledge of older people is of restricted value in a rapidly changing world.

18 However, the degree of status of the elderly is not equal in all advanced societies; in Japan the elderly have considerably higher status than in Britain.

7.11 Keywords (*as they appear in the unit*)

socialization, rite of passage, subculture, youth culture, contra-culture, generational consciousness, generation gap.

8 RACE AND ETHNICITY

8.1 Race and Ethnic Group

Race is the term that has been used to indicate a group who are assumed to share some common biological and social traits. It is an extremely difficult concept to define, as it has been used in a number of ways. Perhaps the most infamous attempt to define race was by the Nazis in the 1930s in Germany, who claimed that one could distinguish pure races. However, they were unable to substantiate this claim in practice.

A commonly accepted division of people into races is into Negroid, Mongoloid and Caucasoid. Interestingly for those who argue that Indians are of a different race from the British, they are both, in fact, Caucasoid. Over the millions of years of man's existence and various migrations over the earth these three groups have become intermixed.

Ethnic groups (ethnic minorities) are groups of people who share a common culture which is different from that of the majority of society. Sometimes this is the result of migration from one country to another. The new society to which they move is known as the **host society**. Ethnic minorities usually only remain noticeable if their culture, form of dress or skin colour make them stand out, and if they form a distinctive community slightly separate from the main host society.

8.2 Immigration Control

Since 1962 there has been a series of Acts which have progressively tightened controls on the entry of immigrants to Britain. These are closely related to the declining numbers of job vacancies and rising unemployment.

8.3 Patterns of Immigration

Historically, Britain has been characterized by fairly frequent waves of immigration coupled with a steady outflow through emigration. For example, the period between 1825 and 1905 was characterized by high levels of immigration of the Irish, and later of Central European Jews. In this period, approximately 700 000 Irish came to live in England. After the passing of the 1905 Aliens Act immigration was much reduced until 1948 and the liberalizing effect of that year's British Nationality Act. After 1950 the pattern of British immigration overall is as follows:

1 Between 1951 and 1961 there was a sharp increase in immigration of people from West Indian and Asian backgrounds, as well as a smaller number of Chinese origin. In 1951 of a total population of 49 million there were approximately 75 000 non-whites or 0.2 per cent of the population. By 1962 it had increased to 200 000 or 0.5 per cent of the population.

2 Between 1962 and 1971 there was an overall decrease in the numbers entering Britain. This was the result of the 1962 Act. However, numbers remained fairly high because the wives and children of immigrants were coming to join them.

3 In 1972–84 there was a continuing decrease in immigration from the New Commonwealth and Pakistan except for sudden **emergency** influxes – for instance in 1976 Uganda forced Asians to leave. Today, about 50 per cent of all immigrants come from the New Commonwealth and Pakistan, and these are almost all dependents of people already living here. There are now 2½ million Blacks and Asians living in Britain forming about 5 per cent of the total population.

West Indians and Asians

From 1951 onwards immigrants began to arrive from the West Indies, India and Pakistan. The urban pattern is illustrated in the Figure 8.1.

It illustrates that:
1 Immigration was significant until the early 1950s.
2 People from the West Indies were the first to start coming here in large numbers; their numbers rose until 1957 when about 16 000 immigrants arrived; there followed a sharp drop and then in 1960–2 there was a sharp increase to about 37 000. The reason for this sudden increase reflected the panic to enter Britain before the introduction of the 1962 Act. After 1962 the numbers entering dropped again, just as sharply as they had risen, and since 1970 the number of West Indians entering Britain has been negligible. In 1981, 250 male West Indians, 360 women and 280 children migrated here.

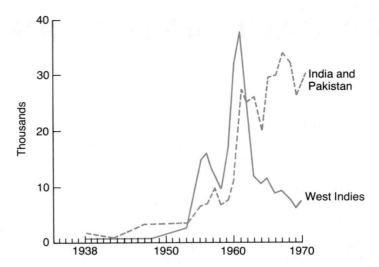

Fig. 8.1 Source: *The Economist* 'Britain's Urban Breakdown'

3 Workers from India and Pakistan began to arrive in Britain later than, and carried on arriving longer than, West Indians. This reflects the facts that they were either better qualified or that employers in certain industries (such as textiles and metal-working) continued asking for them. The result was that they were more likly to get vouchers. A second factor was that the Asian tradition of arranged marriages and larger families meant that marriage partners and dependent relatives have continued to enter Britain in relatively large numbers (compared to West Indians).

8.4 The Demography of Immigration

It is estimated that there will be 3.3 million non-white people (6.7 per cent of the population) in the year 2001.

1 West Indians Between 1970 and 1979, live births to West Indian-born mothers declined by 48 per cent to bring them roughly equal to the UK-born mothers. It seems that West Indians in Britain have adopted British cultural norms over the number of children regarded as appropriate. There is unlikely to be any change in this as today the overwhelming majority of young Blacks were born, and have lived all their lives, in Britain.

2 Asians The situation is different for those of Asian origin. Births to mothers of Asian origin (Indian and Pakistani) increased slightly between 1970 and 1979. This reflects the fact that as women join their husbands here, often after long separation, they tend to become pregnant very quickly. Furthermore, with the inflow of dependents continuing longer for those of Asian origin than for West Indians, they have not yet had time to adapt to British cultural norms regarding family size. For a number of years they retain Third World fertility patterns where large families are seen as necessary.

3 Age structure Overall the non-white population tends to be younger than the white one. This means that the non-white population is likely to increase in size proportionately more rapidly than the white population, simply because it has a greater proportion of fertile women.

4 Settlement patterns Immigrants went to the areas where there were jobs in the 1950s and 1960s. There are practically none in Northern Ireland and few in the areas of declining heavy industry in the North-East, Wales and Scotland.

Most moved to:

1 West Yorkshire and East Lancashire to work in the low-paid jobs in the textile industries;
2 The West Midlands for manual work in the foundry trades or in Birmingham for the labour-intensive service trades;
3 The South-East, and especially London, to take over all the jobs that British workers did not want to do.

Within these broad areas, they settled in the inner city areas, not necessarily through choice, but because of:

(a) discrimination;
(b) the high cost of housing relative to their incomes;
(c) the need to be near their work.

The result is that in most cities there are clearly definable areas with a high immigrant population.

8.5 Reasons for Immigration

We can divide the reasons that people migrate to another country under the headings **push** and **pull**.

Push reasons

1 Poverty and unemployment at home If there is widespread poverty and unemployment in the home country, with little prospect of the situation improving, then people search elsewhere for a better life. In the ex-colonies of India, Pakistan and the West Indies, Britain had left little industry and poorly developed agriculture. These, combined with high birth rates, led to widespread poverty.

2 Persecution If certain groups are undergoing persecution then they will attempt to flee. It was for this reason that Jews came to Britain near the end of the last century, and in smaller numbers in the 1930s. Most of the Asians who came here in 1972 and 1976 were escaping from policies of Africanization followed by the Ugandan government, which wanted to replace Asian British passport holders with locals to limit unemployment.

Pull reasons

1 Recruitment Britain was undergoing an acute labour shortage in the early 1950s. This was the result of the take-off of the economy after the end of the Second World War. The limits of the British workforce had been reached and so Britain turned to the West Indies (and later India and Pakistan). Immigrants were encouraged to come; and some institutions such as London Transport and the National Health Service actually set up recruitment offices in the West Indies. The immigrants who came generally took the jobs that nobody else wanted. In recent years, only the long hours of work and low pay of Pakistani workers has kept the British textile industry in existence. As nobody else wanted to do this work, the employers continued to recruit from Pakistan right through the 1970s.

2 To join relatives If part of the family is living in one country and part in another, then there is an understandable desire to reunite; 70 per cent of immigrants from the New Commonwealth and Pakistan are wives and children of immigrants already settled here.

The amount of immigration has been dependent on:

(a) the economic situation and needs of Britain compared to the immigrants' country of origin;
(b) the legislation limiting immigration, which is heavily influenced by the economic situation;
(c) the number of dependents of those immigrants settled here.

8.6 The Problems Faced by Ethnic Minorities

The root of most problems experienced by non-white immigrants is **racial prejudice**, which means that a person is disliked immediately on the simple grounds of his or her skin colour. The personal qualities of the black person are ignored. The British Social Attitudes survey in 1984 found that 35 per cent of a sample of people were prejudiced. In an opinion poll (1975) it was found that younger people and women were least prejudiced. Racial prejudice then leads to **discrimination**, which means to treat a person in a worse manner on the grounds of his colour. So a person may be denied a house or a job just because he or she is not white.

Causes of prejudice

1 The authoritarian personality Certain people are brought up in such a way as to be rigid in their beliefs and intolerant of weakness. Adorno claims that these people have **authoritarian personalities**. A further aspect of the authoritarian personality is to be prejudiced against minority groups, so they are anti-semitic (anti-Jewish) and anti-black.

2 Stereotyping Many people regard all Blacks as having certain negative characteristics. These characteristcs confirm to the person that he or she is superior. Stereotyping is very useful because it allows people to treat the stereotyped group in a worse way without feeling guilty. Before independence was granted to Zimbabwe the ruling white regime would say that it could not possibly give political control to the Blacks as they were 'just like children' and could not be expected to behave sensibly. This allowed white people to continue owning the bulk of the land, exploiting African workers and controlling the political system.

Many of the stereotyped views held of non-Whites are a result of our colonial past, when the repression of other independent nations and their exploitation was justified by their natural inferiority. This has been perpetuated in Britain in the media images of non-Whites as stupid and subservient to Whites.

3 Scapegoating In periods of economic decline or social tension certain groups are picked on to be blamed for the problems. This provides a simple, understandable explanation for far more complex issues which may be too difficult to be fully understood. In Germany in the 1920s and 1930s, Jews were blamed for the economic chaos which really occurred as a result of the repercussions of the First World War. The result was Nazism.

In Britain black people are often used as scapegoats for unemployment, inner city deprivation and high levels of crime. This idea of *scapegoating* has been taken further by Marxist sociologists. They have suggested that when there is competition among poorer groups for scarce resources, such as housing and jobs, in order to avoid seeing the real reason for deprivation, that is exploitation by the rich, poor Whites are encouraged through the media to blame non-Whites. As a result there is hostility between the races that prevents them from joining together to seek a common solution to their problems.

Discrimination

There are a number of areas in which Blacks and Asians are discriminated against, but possibly the two most important are (i) employment and (ii) housing.

1 Employment

(a) Occupations: overall, blacks and Asians are far more commonly found in lower level jobs than white workers. For example, whereas 19 per cent of white males are in professional and managerial jobs, the figure is as low as 5 per cent for those of West Indian background.

However, it is a mistake to bracket all Blacks and Asians together, for there are huge differences in education and culture between various groups from immigrant backgrounds. People from African Asian backgrounds (Asians who were brought up in the ex-British colonies in Africa) have high levels of educational success, and are successful in obtaining decent jobs. For example, 22 per cent of these are in professional and managerial work – a figure higher than that for Whites. When it comes to employment levels for females from the ethnic minorities, there is more of a similarity with white women. Both groups tend to be concentrated in low-level white-collar work and semi-skilled manual work. This reflects the low levels of women's jobs throughout the population.

A detailed breakdown of the employment patterns of male workers is given in Table 8.1.

Table 8.1 Job levels of men: all employees by ethnic group

Job Level	White %	West Indian %	Asian %	Indian %	Paki- stani %	Bangla- deshi %	African Asian %	Muslim %	Hindu %	Sikh %
Professional, Employer, Management	19	5	13	11	10	10	22	11	20	4
Other non- manual	23	10	13	13	8	7	21	8	26	8
Skilled manual and foreman	42	48	33	34	39	13	31	33	20	48
Semi-skilled manual	13	26	34	36	35	57	22	39	28	33
Unskilled manual	3	9	6	5	8	12	3	8	3	6

(**Source**: Colin Brown *Black and White Britain: The Third PSI Survey*, Gower, 1985)

It should also be noted that those from the ethnic minorities are more likely to be found doing shift work than Whites and to have much lower chances of promotion. Trade unions, too, have been guilty of failing to support Blacks against discrimination.

(b) Unemployment: Members of the ethnic minorities have much higher chances of unemployment than Whites, in general, as Table 8.2 shows.

Table 8.2 The rates of unemployment for black and white men and women

	Men			Women		
	White	West Indian	Asian	White	West Indian	Asian
Percentage of whole adult population who are registered unemployed	10	21	17	4	11	8
Percentage of population aged under 25 who are registered unemployed	20	33	19	13	21	19

(**Source**: adapted from Colin Brown *Black and White Britain: The Third PSI Survey*, Gower, 1985)

Unemployment rates vary according to region, and whether people live in the suburbs or inner cities. But the pattern that emerges is that the rates of unemployment of the ethnic minorities (particularly those from West Indian backgrounds) are consistently above the white figure no matter what the region or zone of the city.

The problem of unemployment is particularly acute for young people. For example, 50 per cent of 16–19-year-old girls from West Indian backgrounds are presently unemployed, compared to 23 per cent of white 16–19-year-old females.

Explanations for the differences in employment and unemployment patterns

A major national survey (*Black and White Britain* by Colin Brown) found that although there were some differences in language ability and in educational differences between the ethnic minorities and Whites, this simply could not explain the differences in the levels of jobs and the lack of promotion of Blacks and Asians. In the end the author concludes that discrimination against Blacks and Asians is still an important reason for their low job levels. Many sociologists have now suggested that Blacks and Asians form an **underclass**, which means a group of people blocked off from the better jobs who are forced into the worse paid employment (or into unemployment) and who have very much worse life chances than the majority of Whites.

2 Housing

The housing differences between ethnic groups is very marked indeed. Asian households have an extremely high level of home ownership. This is because they were unable to obtain council property, and Whites would not rent homes to them. The result was that they bought the cheapest houses available which were usually in the inner city areas from where most Whites wished to escape. A second reason for home purchase is the strong cultural stress amongst Asian families on home purchase.

Those in council property are found in the worst accommodation available from the councils – this is partially because they wish to live together in communities to escape racial harassment, even if this means living in poor accommodation.

West Indians have the highest rates of council housing. However, they live in the worst accommodation. They are most likely to be found in flats: more often flats at a higher level and with higher rates of overcrowding; they are less likely to have gardens; and the properties are more likely to be old.

8.7 Preventing Discrimination

In order to limit racial discrimination, a number of Acts have been passed. The **1965 Race Relations Act** made it illegal to discriminate in the provision of goods or services to the public, or in the areas of employment and housing. It became illegal to incite racial hatred.

The Community Relations Commission (CRC) was established to promote inter-racial harmony. The Race Relations Board (RRB) was established to investigate complaints of racial discrimination. The CRC and RRB were criticized for ineffectiveness. This resulted in:

1976 The Commission for Racial Equality (CRE) was established with greater powers than the RRB. The CRE can bring cases to court, whereas the RRB acted only in cases of **direct** discrimination (for example, when a person was denied employment because he or she was black); the CRE can bring institutions to court for **indirect** discrimination, which is really discriminating in intent but attempting to hide this in some way (for instance, if it is prohibited to wear any form of headgear apart from the official cap, this discriminates against Sikhs who must wear turbans).

Scapegoating...

Other ways to eliminate prejudice and discrimination include the teaching of Third World Studies or African history. These show that non-Whites were not uncivilized people without any culture until the white colonialists came, but had complex cultures already which were often deliberately destroyed. This helps to break down stereotypes held by young people.

How effective has the legislation been? A Home Office Report (*Ethnic Minorities*) in 1981 found that there had been a decline in discrimination suffered by Blacks and Asians. However, discrimination still exists and strongly affects the quality of Black and Asian people's lives. They have been affected more by the growth of unemployment since 1979; they pay more for housing and are more likely to have lower incomes than white people.

Passing laws can outlaw obvious discrimination but it cannot really alter people's racist attitudes if these are embedded in our culture. As long as our culture continues to reaffirm stereotyped views of people who are not white then prejudice will continue.

8.8 Summary

1 Although the term *race* is commonly used to describe people of different skin colour, there is no biological evidence to show that there are any important differences that can distinguish one so-called 'race' from another.

2 The term ethnic group is usually employed by sociologists to distinguish one form of cultural group from another.

3 In the late 1940s and early 1950s Commonwealth immigrants were welcomed into Britain because they were needed to fill job vacancies.

4 From the early 1960s onwards, as the number of jobs declined, so there were increasingly strong feelings against Blacks and Asians.

5 The numbers of Blacks and Asians coming into Britain since the 1960s has been very small, as there has been tight immigration control.

6 Less than 5 per cent of the population is Black or Asian in descent and the figure will increase only to 6.7 per cent in the year 2001. Thus only a tiny proportion of the population is Black or Asian.

7 Most immigrants went to the places where there was employment, and where there was a shortage of labour. They settled in inner city areas because that was where cheap housing was to be found.

8 People came to Britain for one of two reasons: the amount of work available or because of relatives already here.

9 Blacks and Asians face problems of prejudice, (which means to be disliked simply on the grounds of the colour of their skin) and of discrimination (to be treated differently because of the colour of their skin).

10 Explanations of prejudice include (a) the authoritarian personality, (b) stereotyping and (c) scapegoating.

11 Discrimination has been shown to exist in areas such as employment and housing.

12 There have been various government attempts to eliminate discrimination, such as the passing of the **Race Relations Act** in 1965. However, it is difficult to change attitudes held deep within the culture.

8.9 Keywords (*as they appear in the unit*)

race, ethnic group, legislation, New Commonwealth, push reasons for immigration, pull reasons for immigration, (racial) prejudice, discrimination, underclass, authoritarian personality, stereotyping, scapegoating, direct discrimination, indirect discrimination.

9 WORK

9.1 The Meaning of Work

Although it may seem easy to define work when asked, in fact it is very difficult, for no particular action can be described exclusively as *work*. What is considered as work varies, depending upon such things as time, place, society and individual preferences.

Examples:

1 *The task of planting seeds* If this is done by a farmer growing crops for sale, or for professional use in an agricultural society, then it is work. If it is done (even by the same people) as the leisure activity of growing flowers for pleasure in a garden, then it is not work.

2 *Playing a sport* If a professional plays football, then it is work; if a sociology student plays it is likely to be for pleasure.

The most common elements of work are that (a) it is paid, (b) it it not done primarily for pleasure, (c) most commonly, there is an employer who imposes his or her authority on the worker in exchange for wages, (d) usually work takes place in a special place put aside for that purpose—the office or factory, (e) usually there is some productive or useful outcome of the work—the building of a part of a car, the assessment of someone's insurance claim, etc. (f) the amount of time spent at work is clearly marked off from the hours of non-work.

Not all the above elements of work need be present, however, for an action to be considered work.

The division of a person's time between non-work and work is a relatively modern happening. Throughout history, the activities people engaged in to make a living and to survive have simply been a central part of their lives. There was no division into completely separate spheres. In agricultural or hunting societies, people simply lived their lives without any awareness that work could be divided from *leisure*. The two elements of life were closely integrated.

The division, as we know it now between work and leisure, developed during the Industrial Revolution, as the machinery in the factories needed to be started and stopped at precise times. Furthermore, the precise integration of all the jobs in a factory required a strict work discipline.

Before the Industrial Revolution most production had been carried out at home, and the family or kin was the economic unit.

9.2 Why Do People Work?

People work for two sets of reasons: **extrinsic** and **intrinsic**.

1 *Extrinsic* This means simply that a person works for a wage, and little else. This is typical of people in repetitive, manual occupations, such as a worker on the factory floor. This attitude to work is often connected to feelings of alienation at the place of employment.

2 *Intrinsic* This means that a person works for more than the wage. It may be for the interest and enjoyment of the job, such as in the case of many professional sportsmen.

However, this division, although important, glosses over the fact that work has a social aspect to it as well.

3 People work for the companionship they find among their workmates.

4 In the case of many women, it is to escape the restrictive role of housewife; indeed four out of five women questioned in a national survey in 1979 wanted to work irrespective of how much they earned.

5 Work gives people a sense of identity.

6 Work gives status.

9.3 The Occupational Structure

The occupational structure refers to the type of jobs performed by the working population.

Very broadly defined, there are two forms of labour:

1 Manual labour, work that involves physical labour of some kind such as a miner, bricklayer or a mechanic performs;

2 Non-manual (or white collar) labour, work that involves little physical labour but relies more on mental effort or force of personality. For example, shop assistant, clerk, or teacher.

There are three types of industry:
1 Primary, such as mining or agriculture, which involve exploiting our natural resources;
2 Secondary or manufacturing, such as industry, where objects are created to be sold;
3 Tertiary or service, involving providing a service of some kind, such as banking or transport.

Throughout this century, the following trends have been apparent in the British occupational structure.

1 A move away from manual work towards non-manual work

In 1911, non-manual workers formed only 19 per cent of the total workforce, today the figure is over 50 per cent.

It is important to note that within this trend:

(a) the growth of non-manual employment among women has been more rapid than among men. Now two out of every three female workers are in non-manual work, compared to less than half the men;

(b) the biggest growth area in employment has been in the professions and technical staff, which have more than doubled in the last 20 years.

2 A move away from primary and manufacturing industries towards service industries

As Table 9.1 illustrates, over the last 30 years there has been at least a halving of jobs in agriculture, and a loss of 3 million jobs in manufacturing (one third of the entire manufacturing workforce). Over this period, jobs in the service industries have increased by 5 million.

It should be noted that:

(a) The number of jobs in service industries has stopped increasing in the last few years, while the loss of manufacturing jobs continues;

(b) The statistics cover all jobs, including part-time employment. Therefore the true extent of the decline in manufacturing industry employment is not clear in these figures.

Table 9.1 Number of employees in different industries (figures in thousands)

	1961	1971	1981	1984	1990
Agriculture, Forestry, Fishing	710	432	352	340	298
Manufacturing	8540	8058	6221	5516	5151
Services	10 382	11 597	13 450	13 688	15 868

(**Sources:** 1961 and '71 *Social Trends*; 1981 and '84 *Annual Abstract of Statistics*, 1986; 1992 *Social Trends*)

3 An increase in the number of women in the workforce

In 1961, there were 7.7 million women in paid employment; by 1990 this had risen to 10.8 million. The number of male workers, however, has remained almost static.

(a) The increase in female employment has occurred through the growth in numbers of married women working. Today 70 per cent of married women work, over twice the proportion of 25 years ago;

(b) Much of female employment is part-time: 90 per cent of all part-time workers are women;

(c) Women are concentrated in the lower-paid jobs.

4 Growth in unemployment

Since the late 1970s there has been a considerable growth in the numbers of the unemployed. There is disagreement over the exact figure, but it is generally agreed that there are over 3 million unemployed.

CORE AND PERIPHERY SECTORS

There is a growing difference between (a) workers in safe, often well-paid work who have decent conditions of service, full holiday entitlements, and a degree of security – the **core** or **primary sector** and (b) workers who are in part-time, or low-paid work, including home workers who have little job security, poor working conditions and rights, and few holidays. The workers in this sector may well be temporary or on fixed contracts for a year and they then may or may not be re-employed. This is the **peripheral** or **secondary sector**.

One indication of the growth of the peripheral sector is the increase in part-time work; today almost 25 per cent of workers are part-time. They are therefore not entitled to many of the legal rights of full-time workers in terms of job security, holiday entitlement, etc.

GROWTH OF THE MULTINATIONALS

The British economy is increasingly moving to a situation where there are fewer and fewer companies who dominate. Linked to this is the growth of multinationals; companies whose main office and ownership is based abroad (usually in the United States) and who have factories or shops here. These vary from Ford Motors through to Macdonald Hamburgers.

This means that:

(a) as the headquarters are abroad, they are more likely to make any redundancies in times of stress in Britain rather than the 'home' country;

(b) employers can threaten to move their operations to another country unless workers accept their demands. There is no loyalty to Britain;

(c) companies can choose to set up factories in countries with weak labour laws, where they can impose their own work conditions;

(d) profits may go to the home country, and not be re-invested in Britain.

Although the differences between the groups are large, it should not obscure the fact that differences in working conditions occur **within** the manual/non-manual divisions:

(a) *Major divisions within the non-manual group*: owners, managers and professionals, clerks and routine white-collar workers.

(b) *Divisions within the manual group*: skilled, semi- and unskilled workers.

It is important to remember that these divisions are generalizations, and that situations will differ between workplaces.

9.4 Changing Technology

British society is based upon industry, that is the mass production by factories of objects for our use. Britain was the first country in the world to move from a society based upon agriculture and manufacture in the home to one based upon industry. It began to industrialize in the middle of the eighteenth century. The process of moving from agriculture to large-scale factory production is known as **industrialization**. Today most countries of the Western world including Europe, the USA and the USSR, and parts of South-East Asia, notably Japan, have industrialized.

The main characteristics of an industrialized society are:

1 Production is based upon complex machinery situated in factories (mechanization) as opposed to home working;

2 The majority of the population live in towns near the factories (urbanization), as opposed to being dispersed throughout the country;

3 The majority of the population work for an employer and receive fixed wages, rather than working for themselves;

4 In order to gain higher wages and better working conditions, workers have banded together in trade unions to argue their case against employers and industrial conflict is common;

5 Goods produced by the factories on such a large scale become cheap and available to the mass of the population who are able to achieve a much higher standard of living than before;

6 An ever-evolving technology with the movement from mechanization to automation;

7 A division of labour in society, such that people produce only one part of the complete finished product.

Some of these characteristics need examining in further detail.

1 The division of labour

The most efficient means of producing goods is by dividing the work into small, simple, repetitive tasks. The most famous example was the description given by eighteenth-century economist Adam Smith of production in a pin factory. If each person had worked to make a whole pin, then each of the ten people working there would only have made 20 pins, but dividing the labour they actually made 48 000 a day. Today the division of labour is regarded as the normal factory way of producing; televisions, cars, washing machines, etc. are all made in this way.

Advantages:
(a) More goods are produced at a lower price;

(b) More people can afford to purchase goods and so a higher standard of living is achieved;

(c) The low levels of skill required mean that many people who would be unable to cope with complex tasks find employment;

(d) Radical sociologists such as Henry Braverman suggst that the true advantage is that employers can earn greater profits from their workers by keeping control over the process of production. The workers in fact suffer.

Disadvantages:

(a) The work is boring and repetitive;

(b) The worker therefore obtains little or no satisfaction from his or her job;

(c) The boredom and dissatisfaction can cause industrial disputes as the workers seek consolation in higher wages;

(d) Traditional skills and pride of craftmanship are lost;

(e) Workers lose control over their work and the pace at which they work;

(f) Lack of pride in work leads to a lower quality of finished product.

2 Mechanization to automation

Mechanization and the consequent division of labour were the main changes brought about by industrialization, but since then technological advances have occurred. These include:

(a) *Assembly line production* In this process operatives work on a line of part-manufactured products, with the product moving along a conveyor belt of some kind from one worker to the next. Each worker performs some simple repetitive task which adds another part or stage to the product. As the product moves along the line it nears completion. This is how most mass-produced cars are made.

Research

Goldthorpe and Lockwood in *The Affluent Worker* studied car assembly workers at the Vauxhall factory in Luton. They found that workers were bored and frustrated in their work. The conditions of work (noise and monotony) prevented close friendships being made. The workers were mainly concerned about obtaining as high a wage as possible and spending this on family and leisure pursuits. Relationship with employers tended to be hostile.

(b) *Process production* This method of production involves a continuous process in which products such as chemicals or petroleum enter one end as raw material and are refined into the finished product. Two types of workers are required (a) those who control the machinery, this being skilled, moderately interesting work and (b) those who load and maintain the production process.

Research

Nichols and Beynon in *Living with Capitalism* found that the work in process production was very different for the two groups of workers. Whereas those in control had relatively pleasant, interesting work, those who maintained and loaded the processing plant were engaged in work not very different in lack of skill and amount of effort and unpleasantness from the production-line workers.

(c) *Automation* This is a general term to cover the use of machinery to perform tasks traditionally performed or at least controlled by workers. It varies from the very simplest form of automation where machines performing complex tasks are linked together by another machine which eliminates the need for unskilled labourers carrying and lifting objects. A simple example is the way that bread is passed from the oven to the slicing machine and finally passed on to a packing machine.

However, with the growth of the new **microchip** technology, automation has taken a huge step forward; now skilled jobs that involve measurement and close quality control can be undertaken by machinery. Indeed, Fiat manufactures most of its new cars almost entirely by computer-controlled machines. On a wider scale, microchips have radically changed service industries, so we have cash dispensers, word processors, pocket calculators, etc. This new form of technology has been called the **second industrial revolution**.

Advantages of automation

(a) Boring repetitive tasks can be eliminated.

(b) There is a demand for more highly educated workers to understand and control the machinery.

(c) The possibility exists of producing more goods for fewer hours of work. Therefore the working week could be shortened. There could be more opportunity for leisure.

(d) According to Blauner, automation brings the possibility of eliminating the divisions between production line workers and management. All could become involved in a team to solve work problems. This is because jobs would tend to be more responsible. They would involve responsibility for an area of production performed by machines.

(e) Work would become healthier and safer as the dangerous jobs would be eliminated.

Disadvantages

(a) The major disadvantage of microchips is their very advantage for employers. That is, they can perform a number of complex tasks which are the very essence of a person's skill. A simple example is the word processor, the use of which can be learned within a couple of hours and can give a perfectly typed letter or document. Previously it took a skilled typist. The word processor has also taken away all the skills of printers – what once took up to five years to learn can now be learned in a day with the help of a word processor. Henry Braverman has called this process **deskilling**, whereby workers lose their skills to machines. Employers use deskilling to cut the workforce and decrease wages.

(b) As a result of deskilling, a loss of pride and craftmanship in virtually every form of employment will occur.

(c) Unemployment will increase (this is discussed in greater detail on pp 87 – 92).

(d) Wages will decrease.

(e) A decline in interaction will take place, as people increasingly stay at home to work and to engage in leisure pursuits. This could alter the basis of our society which is dependent upon social mixing in shops, offices and factories.

9.5 Work Satisfaction

As work forms one of the main activities of our lives, the degree of satisfaction obtained from work influences our whole life.

Alienation

Karl Marx has suggested the term **alienation** to describe the situation of people who gain no enjoyment from their work. It has been suggested by Blauner that alienation includes the following elements:

(a) *Meaninglessness* A feeling that the job makes no sense. This occurs where the division of labour breaks work down into such small unrelated tasks that it becomes difficult to see what the point of the job really is;

(b) *Powerlessness* A belief that the worker has no power over the form his work takes, or the speed at which it is done. A car production line is a good example of this;

(c) *Normlessness* The worker feels that what his employer says he should feel about his job is not, in fact, how he himself sees it. It is difficult to feel pride and interest in the construction of a car if your job consists of putting on its wheels. This difference of opinion can lead to industrial conflict;

(d) *Isolation* Workers are cut off from each other by the noise and discomfort of the workplace; on a wider scale they are cut off by their work from feeling part of society. The work produces a desire only to better themselves and to forget the needs of others;

(e) *Self-estrangement* Ideally any job ought to use the abilities and intelligence of the worker, so that his work fulfils him. If the job fails to do this then the worker gradually loses his own personality and tries to express himself in his leisure activities.

What factors influence the degree of alienation and work satisfaction?

(a) *The division of labour* Extreme division of labour makes the individual's task irrelevant and small;

(b) *Repetition* This leads to boredom and monotony as a variety of tasks is needed to keep people interested;

(c) *Noisy, unpleasant work conditions* These cut off workers from communicating with each other;

(d) *Low levels of skill* According to Baldamus the greater the level of skill the greater the degree of work satisfaction;

(e) *Control over production* When workers have some degree of say in the pace and form of the production process, the degree of commitment increases.

As we can see, people engaged in non-routine work in pleasant conditions, such as professional, managerial and skilled manual workers, gain far more work satisfaction and are less alienated than those engaged in routine, unskilled work such as car assembly workers.

9.6 Attempts to Make Work More Fulfilling

There have been two types of attempts to make work more fulfilling: on the one hand the actions of the employers, and on the other the activities of workers.

Employers' attempts

(a) *Making a pleasant work environment* Modern factory machines are designed to be less noisy so that workers can talk. Cleanliness and safety are now encouraged in modern factories;

(b) *Increase in welfare provisions* Firms give subsidized canteens, welfare and recreational facilities;

(c) *Workers' representatives in the management* Elected representatives of workers sit on the board of the company and are consulted over pace of work etc.;

(d) *Workers complete the whole task, instead of the division of labour* Volvo in its Swedish plant divided its workers into groups to build complete cars. This encouraged workers into feeling responsible for the individual car they had built;

(e) *Higher wages or bonuses* Given to compensate for the boredom and difficulty of work.

Employees' attempts

Employees have devised their own 'unofficial' ways of resisting the conditions of work.

(a) *Limiting output* Workers agree on what they consider to be a reasonable amount of work and then impose informal sanctions on those who try to work too hard.

Research

In the 1920s Mayo studied a group of workers in 'The Hawthorne' studies. Any worker who tried too hard was brought back to the agreed output by sarcastic comments, practical jokes and, if all else failed, by being 'sent to Coventry'.

(b) *Daydreaming* In order to pass the boring time away workers (and students!) fantasize about life, particularly about what they will do in their leisure time.

Research

Ditton studied bakery workers and found that they regularly passed the time in a series of fantasies.

(c) *Playing tricks and practical jokes* Another way of passing the time is to play jokes on one another – this may be a way to ease the boredom, but it also serves to release tension by allowing disputes between individuals to be sorted out by practical jokes. Those who are most disliked are usually on the receiving end.

9.7 Industrial Relations

INDUSTRIAL CONFLICT

The nature of our society in which employers constantly strive to keep wage rates as low as possible, and employees seek the highest income possible, entails conflict. The level of conflict varies, and one way of measuring the degree of it is by the number of strikes.

Before we look at strikes in detail, however, we ought to note that they are only one form of industrial conflict. Sociologists have also identified two other forms of conflict:

(a) *Work to rule*, where workers stick rigidly to the letter of the rules of employment, which effectively slows down the production process;

(b) *Industrial sabotage*, where workers deliberately sabotage the machinery on which they are working in order to make their grievances known or to stop work for a rest.

These forms usually occur where the workforce is not strong enough to strike.

Types of strike

There are **two** types of strike:

(a) *Official* These are strikes officially recognized by the appropriate trade union.

(b) *Unofficial* These are strikes that are not formally recognized by the executives of the appropriate trade unions.

Hyman, in his book *Strikes,* suggests that most strikes are the result of an immediate response by workers to a particular problem which arises, and which is then solved locally by the factory-elected union representatives (shop stewards) without ever going through the official union channels to the point of being declared a strike. However, if the problem cannot be resolved by local negotiation it may take a number of days before it is declared **official** by the trade union. In both cases a number of days of **unofficial** strike occurs.

Causes of strikes

The causes of strikes can best be understood by dividing the explanations into two levels: the wider economic and political context; the immediate causes.

The wider context

(a) *Government action* The Conservative government of the early and mid-1980s was firmly opposed to the power of the trade unions. It therefore passed a number of measures to weaken their ability to strike. Their powers of picketing were limited; they could not strike without a prior ballot; they could be sued for damages in certain circumstances; and they could only strike against the company against whom they had a direct complaint. The result was a significant erosion of union power.

(b) *Economic depressions* If the economy is not particularly strong at any time, the numbers of the unemployed will rise, as people are made redundant. This has happened since 1979. The result is that the power of trade unions to strike is considerably weakened. They know that their members can be replaced by the unemployed and there is also the threat of large multi-national companies transferring production abroad. The result is a fear of striking (although other forms of industrial action, such as industrial sabotage, may well occur).

The immediate causes

(a) The main cause of strikes according to government statistics is wage disputes – in 1982, 43 per cent of stoppages and 66 per cent of days lost were due to wage disputes.

(b) Other reasons for strikes given in the official statistics included disputes over hours of work, redundancy, working conditions and disciplinary matters.

(c) Until 1982 a further cause of stoppages was **solidarity** actions by trade union in support of another group of workers; however, this form of action has been made illegal by the Conservative government.

We need to be cautious about the high proportion of strikes that are officially labelled as being over wage demands. It is clear that monotonous, alienating work (see p 79) can create conditions in which the workforce is generally discontented, and they may express their frustrations in the form of strike demands for higher wages, as they know they cannot fundamentally alter their jobs.

Research

1 Gouldner in *Wildcat Strike* studied a miners' strike in the United States. He found that new management changed the supervisory procedures, tightening them up considerably. The miners realized they had no right to demand lax supervision, so they expressed their frustration in higher wage demands.

2 Lane and Roberts in *Strike at Pilkington's* studied a strike at Pilkington's Glass Factory. Workers on unofficial strike for higher wages really resented their employers' way of treating them, and wanted to get back at them. (They also felt their union was not looking after their interests.)

3 Blauner in *Alienation and Freedom* argued that alienated workers in the car industry doing boring work were far more likely to strike than craftsmen engaged in interesting work in the print industry. So interest in work prevents strikes as well as high pay.

9.8 Representative Organizations

1 Employers' organizations

These organizations are formed by employers to watch over their mutual interests. The largest is the *Confederation of British Industry (CBI)*, which is an umbrella organization looking after the interests of all industrial concerns. It acts as a **pressure group** on their behalf.

There are also specific industrial organizations to represent the interests of a particular branch of industry or commerce.

Generally, these groups will lobby MPs or pay them a fee to look after their interests, and use specialist public relations companies to approach those departments of the government who are relevant to their interests.

2 Trade unions

Trade unions are groups of workers who band together in order to negotiate over pay and conditions with employers. They have a set of rules and officers who are elected to represent them in negotiations with employers.

There are four types of union:

1 *General unions* An amalgamation of many different types of worker in a variety of industries. Transport and General Workers Union now has a membership of 1¾ million.

2 *Industrial unions* These include all workers below management in a particular type of industry such as the railways.

3 *Craft unions* The original type of union, where men sharing a particular type of skill come together to protect their wages and skills. Often they control entry into the craft through a

long apprenticeship (they tend to be small in membership). They are increasingly under threat as modern technology, particularly the microchip-based machines, provide simpler **deskilled** ways of performing the same tasks. For example, the printing union, the National Graphical Association (NGA), is having its skills replaced by computer typesetting machines.

4 *White-collar unions* Unions of non-manual workers; the fastest-growing area of unionization. Originally formed from workers in particular industries such as the Civil and Public Servants Association (CPSA), they are now taking the form of white-collar General Unions, for example the Association of Scientific, Technical and Managerial Staffs (ASTMS), which recruits technical, lower managerial and professional employees from a range of industries.

Internal organization

Unions are democratic organizations based on local branches who elect representatives for area and national committees. These in turn usually elect an executive committee. At a national level unions have formed the Trades Union Congress (TUC) to coordinate their activities. They have to ballot their memberships to (a) call a strike; (b) give political funds to any organization.

Shop stewards

These are particularly important figures in the trade union movement. They are elected by the workers in a particular factory to look after their interests. These usually form a factory-based committee. The shop stewards are not paid union figures, but are directly drawn from the **shopfloor**. Their functions include:

(a) Representing the workers in the immediate day-to-day problems that arise in offices and factories;

(b) Liaising with the regional paid union officials to explain the view of shopfloor workers on individual matters;

(c) Encouraging union membership and activities;

The functions of a trade union

The chief function of a trade union is to safeguard the interests of its membership. In particular it:

(a) Seeks to improve wage rates;

(b) Seeks to improve working conditions, such as speed of the job and safety;

(c) Seeks to improve hours of work, such as shortening the working week, gaining longer holidays;

(d) Seeks to unite individual members so that they will have more bargaining power;

(e) Operates at a number of levels (i) directly on the employers and (ii) at the national political level influencing legislation relevant to its members.

However, some sociologists suggest that trade unions in reality perform rather different functions.

(a) Clarke and Clements (*Trade Unions under Capitalism*) argue that trade unions prevent any radical restructuring of the relationship between employers and employees by only ever focusing on wages and conditions, never on questions of ownership and control.

Changes in trade union membership

These have occurred throughout this century for a number of reasons:

(a) Union membership has increased overall this century from 2 million in 1900 to over 10 million today. However, membership has fluctuated. In particular, in periods of economic depression and high unemployment membership declines. The present level of membership reflects the present economic situation, as there appears to have been a 2 million drop in membership since 1981.

(b) There has been a clear shift towards fewer but bigger unions (usually of the general union type). In 1900 there were 1300 unions, but in 1980 the number had declined to 430. Average union membership in 1980 was approximately 30 000, but there were some dominant, extremely large unions such as the Transport and General Workers Union which had 1¾ million members.

(c) In the last 30 years the occupational structure has shifted away from manufacturing employment towards **service** industries such as banking, leisure, retail, etc. There has also been a large growth in clerical white-collar work. The result is that the traditional view of unions as representative of manual workers is now untrue.

Of the 10 million claimed union members almost 40 per cent are now drawn from white-collar employment and only this section of the union movement is increasing its membership.

This situation can be compared to 1950 when only 25 per cent were drawn from the non-manual sector.

(d) Reasons for the growth of white-collar unions are as follows:

(i) Growth of white-collar work and the decline of manual jobs means that there are more employees to join the white-collar unions. Also, many of these new employees would otherwise have gone into manual jobs and they bring the union-mindedness of manual workers to their job;

(ii) There has been a decline in the status and relative pay rates of white-collar work. This has made clerical workers more militant. So we have experienced strike action for instance in the Civil Service;

(iii) The **work situation** of clerical workers increasingly resembles that of manual workers in that large numbers of employers performing similar uninteresting tasks and paid similar wages are all working in close proximity to one another (especially with the growth of open plan offices). This promotes a sense of common purpose and solidarity;

(iv) Certain **aggressive** white-collar unions such as ASTMS have been successful in defending their membership. This has drawn new membership who can see the benefits;

(v) There has been a rapid increase in union membership among women, reflecting the fact that they now represent over 40 per cent of the workforce.

Professions

Millerson in *The Qualifying Associations* has suggested that professions have the following characteristics that distinguish them from trade unions:

1 A high level of skill involving theoretical knowledge. A mechanic may know how to repair a car while the engineer understands the theory behind the internal combustion engine;

2 An extensive education. The highest educational standards and training are needed;

3 The professional works for the general good of the public, not just to make money. The doctor is primarily a healer not a businessman or businesswoman;

4 A code of ethics which are of a high standard and regulate the behaviour of members of the profession;

5 Self-regulation – the profession has the legal right to control and discipline its own members;

6 Control of entry. Nobody can join a profession unless accepted by that profession's own governing body, who control the standard of entrants.

Millerson paints a rather rosy picture of professions; however, they have not gone uncriticized.

Criticism has come from Johnson (*Professions and Power*) who has suggested that professions are really middle class trade unions which are primarily concerned to look after their own interests; and factors such as control of entry do not primarily test competence, but instead restrict the inflow of new members, so keeping wages and fees high.

Professions have been so successful in attaining high fees and high status for their members that many other middle class workers have tried to have their employment known as a profession. Some, such as teachers and nurses, have not really succeeded and are **marginal professions**; some, such as architects, have succeeded. Groups such as estate agents are in the process of claiming professional status for themselves. The proof of success is the number of Millerson's characteristics which a group of workers can attain.

9.9 Work in Other Societies: A Comparative Approach

The difference between work in industrial and pre-industrial society

There are four main differences between work in a pre-industrial society and in an industrial one.

In pre-industrial societies:

1 *Working and social lives were unified*

(a) In most simple societies the maintenance of social ties between individuals was/is as important as work. Work was not just an economic activity which was paid for but also a cooperative, social activity that emphasized the bonds that held people together. If a person helped another then the receiver of aid would be obliged in turn to help the other when asked;

(b) In the much more advanced society of India when it was first colonized by the British, the Hindu religion regulated which tasks were to be performed by which particular group of people (for a discussion of the caste system, please see pp 40–1). People were born into castes which had specific economic roles and relationships to other castes;

(c) In the European feudal system of the Middle Ages, the use of land was given to a peasant by a member of the aristocracy in exchange not just for a fixed payment in terms of farm produce each year, but also for the swearing of personal loyalty. If the lord called upon the peasant for military service, for instance, the peasant was bound to go.

2 *Work roles were ascribed not achieved*

In most pre-industrial societies a person did not choose his/her job; it was passed on from the parent. This is known as **ascription** and was at its strictest in the Indian caste system.

This occurred because skills were relatively unchanging and could easily be passed on virtually unaltered across the generations. The rapid changes in the division of labour found in modern society do not allow this in industrial society. Most people choose their jobs within a range of possibilities open to them. This is known as **achievement**.

3 *The concept of work measured in time did not exist*

Industrialization introduced the idea of time into work. Before then what was important in people's lives was the time it took to undertake a particular task, and in the wider sense the seasons of the year. The requirement of factories with a high degree of division of labour was that all workers should start and finish the task together. Much of the early period of industrialization was taken up with the attempts to introduce time discipline into the workers. In modern society it is true to say that most workers sell their time – usually for eight hours a day, 48 weeks a year.

The Nuer of the Sudan work according to 'cattle time', that is to the demands of their herds.

Of course this means that putting special time aside for leisure was unknown in pre-industrial society – apart from ceremonial occasions.

The notion of the appropriate age for work was also less clear. Young children learned the skills of society and when they were able they began to help, their contribution to the tasks increasing with age and ability. Similarly there was no fixed age at which people finished working; they continued for as long as their abilities allowed.

4 *No separate workplace*

In industrial societies, there is generally a division between where workers are employed (the factory or office) and the home. This was not so in most pre-industrial societies, where the two were closely integrated. The division occurred as the machinery of industrial society had to be located in one place. Before that in simple societies, as 'work' was seen just as part of everyday life, there was no necessity to go to a separate place. In Britain just before the Industrial Revolution all the production of textiles took place in the home in what was called **domestic industry**.

9.10 The Growth of Industrialization in Japan

1 Before 1853 Japan existed in virtual isolation from the rest of the world.

2 There were laws against movement of people away from working on the land, and against changing occupation.

3 After a visit by an American naval squadron the Japanese signed a treaty in 1853 allowing entry to American and European traders. One result was the wiping out of the domestic handicraft industries of cotton and paper.

4 In the Meiji era the Imperial government set about creating industrialization in Japan. Freedom of movement off the land, of travel (useful for merchants) and freedom of trade were all created.

5 Primary education was introduced.

6 The government, not private individuals, began such things as banks, railways and factories; other small industries received massive state assistance – this is how Mitsubishi started (in shipbuilding).

7 Whereas in Britain a large number of small firms developed, in Japan a few very large firms emerged.

8 The values of pre-industrial Japan were partially carried over into the new factories. The attitude of employer to employee was **patriarchal** (acting like a father). In Japan employers look after the employees from their first employment through to their death. The employees are supposed to be entirely faithful to the company and to look after its interests like a member of a large family. (See p 23 for details of the Japanese family system, for a comparison.)

9 The concentration of capital in a few companies has meant that the Japanese are prepared to invest large sums in new technology. Workers rarely oppose the introduction of new technology as they are assured of their jobs – they know that they will not be made redundant.

10 Industrialization has created a process of urbanization in Japan, but there has not yet been a move towards suburbanization. Most of the labour force live and work in a few large conurbations.

9.11 The Influence of Work on Our Lives

Work influences our wider lives in a number of ways:

1 Family life

Family life is connected to the particular occupation. Those men who work away from home for much of their time (deep-sea fishermen), or who work in close-knit, all-male occupations (mining), have very different relationships with their wives and children than the typical commuter.

Research

When Tunstall studied deep-sea fishermen in Hull in the 1960s, he found that the men had a very particular relationship with their wives and children. As they spent most of their working lives out at sea, the wives and mothers remained very close. On his return home, the fisherman found himself as a bit of an outsider from his family. He therefore spent most of the time in the company of his friends.

2 Community life

This is connected to work. If one type of employment dominates an area, then this can influence the lifestyle of the whole community.

Research

(a) In the Bethnal Green studies by Young and Willmott in the early 1950s, the importance of the docks for the community life was quite clear. The docks provided local work, which meant that work and home were very close and so the experiences of most people in their daily lives were very similar. This helped to weld the community together. Fathers would get work for their sons as dockers and so a continuity was maintained.

(b) Phil Cohen studied certain aspects of life in Bethnal Green again in the late 1960s. He found that with the disappearance of dockwork, and the movement of population out of the inner city area, the community had lost much of its cohesiveness. The family, too, had been affected, as it was no longer the extended type—instead family members were widely scattered. The result was a fragmented community.

3 Work and health

Work is connected to health. Certain occupations are considerably more dangerous than others. For example, respiratory diseases (connected with breathing problems) are most common among those who work in industries where there is considerable dust in the air. Miners have 2½ times the average rate of death from these diseases. Workers in the metal industry are 1½ times more likely to die from lung and throat cancer than the national average. Cancer of the stomach is common among those employed in certain chemical industries and cancer of the lungs is common among those working with asbestos. Accident rates vary by industry. In 1984 there were 124 deaths at work in the construction industry, more than for all manufacturing industries in Britain that year.

4 Patterns of leisure

Leisure patterns are connected to work. Unit 11 deals with leisure in detail. There is some evidence to indicate that the particular form of employment of a person is connected to his/her particular pattern of leisure (see p 93).

5 Standards of living

Work influences income and therefore the standard of living, housing patterns and lifestyle of people.

9.12 Summary

1 No particular tasks can be described as **work** or **leisure**. Instead, the definition of what is work and leisure varies from one person/situation to another.

2 In pre-industrial societies, work and leisure were inextricably mixed together. It was not until industrialization came that the clear-cut division between time at work and time at leisure came about.

3 The occupational structure is the term used to describe the nature of all the jobs that people do and the way industry is organized.

4 The occupational structure of Britain has changed considerably over the last 30 years.

Changes include: (a) a move away from manual to non-manual work; (b) a move towards service industries; (c) an increase in the number of women working; (d) a growth in unemployment.

5 Different groups of people have very different chances of being successful in the occupational structure. There are significant differences between manual and non-manual workers, males and females, whites and the ethnic minorities, and different age groups.

6 Britain is an industrialized society and this means that the production of goods is carried out mainly by machines, and the bulk of the population live in towns and are paid employees, rather than working for themselves.

7 The division of labour is another characteristic of industrial society. Each person performs only a small task in the making of articles and the providing of services. This has very many drawbacks, the main one being that people find work less satisfying.

8 Industrialization has gone through a number of stages in the development of technology. The most important in terms of its social consequences is automation and, particularly, the development of the microchip.

9 Alienation is the state where people feel that their jobs and also their lives are pointless. It is influenced by the degree of freedom and power the person has in the workplace.

10 The number of strikes in Britain has declined greatly in the last five years – Britain has a very low level of strike action.

11 This has been due to government policy and to the world depression.

12 The main causes of strikes are wage demands and conditions of work, and they usually reflect a general dissatisfaction with work.

13 Employers and employees both form organizations to look after their interests.

14 Unions have been declining in size since 1981, although there has been a significant growth in white-collar unions.

15 Professional organizations look after the interests of the middle class workers. They seem to be the most effective means of protecting personal interests.

16 In pre-industrial societies, work was different from industrial societies in the following ways. Work and social lives were unified; work roles were ascribed or inherited; work as measured by time did not exist; there was no separate place for work.

17 Britain is unique in its process of industrialization. In Japan, for instance, the process of industrialization was greatly helped by the government and it was carefully built up. The differing cultures of the two nations has left considerable differences in the organization of work.

18 Work influences our lives outside in a considerable number of ways. It influences family life, the type of local community, leisure patterns and health.

9.13 Keywords (*as they appear in the unit*)

work, leisure, manual labour, non-manual labour, manufacturing industry, service industry, unemployment, core/primary sector, peripheral/secondary sector, skilled manual workers, non-skilled manual workers, industrialization, urbanization, trade unions, mechanization, division of labour, assembly line production, automation, process production, microchip technology, deskilling, alienation, industrial relations, work to rule, strikes (official/unofficial), industrial sabotage, pressure group, shop steward, white-collar work, professions.

10 UNEMPLOYMENT

10.1 The Extent of Unemployment

The exact numbers of unemployed is a matter of considerable debate. Estimates vary from the Government figure of around 2½ million to the Trades Union Congress (TUC) figure which is 1 million higher.

Figure 10.1 shows the changes in the numbers of unemployed over the last 20 years.

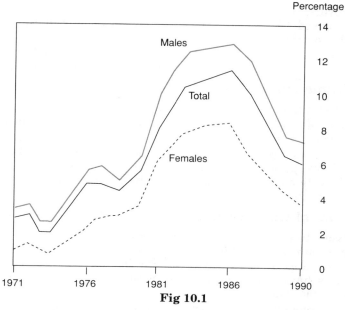

Fig 10.1

1 The number of unemployed were very low in the 1960s and early 1970s. In the mid-1970s they began to grow and leapt up considerably in 1981. In the 1980s numbers declined, but began to rise again at the beginning of the 1990s.

2 According to these statistics the proportion of females unemployed has regularly been only a third of the male unemployment figure.

3 Although not shown in the table, the length of time people are out of work has increased considerably.

Debate on the true extent of unemployment

The reasons for the differences in the government and the TUC figures for unemployment are:

1 That only people entitled to claim benefit are counted in the official statistics;

2 Many of those who are seeking work but cannot claim benefit are excluded. These include married women, for example, part-time workers and home workers. According to the TUC 250 000 people could be included on these grounds;

3 Those over the age of 60 claiming long-term supplementary benefit are not counted (because no one expects them to obtain any work);

4 All young people on special training programmes, such as YT, are excluded from the figures. According to the TUC 450 000 more people could be included.

10.2 The Duration of Unemployment

Until about 1980, most unemployment was short-term, lasting no more than a few months. However, since the beginning of the 1980s, the increase in the duration of unemployment has been startling. In 1986, around half the unemployed had been out of work for more than a year, and almost a third for two years.

This is important, for if the average duration of unemployment is short, it simply means that people are shifting from one job to another. When unemployment is of long-term duration, then it means that there are simply no jobs to go to and that eventually a solid group of long-term unemployed will develop. There are important implications for crime, political instability, the strength of the trade union movement and wage levels/job security, which are discussed in section 10.6 'Implications of unemployment for society'.

10.3 Differences in Unemployment between Groups

Not all groups of employees are likely to face the same risks of unemployment. The following groups are more likely to face unemployment.

1 The young and old

The two age groups on the extremes of the working age range have higher than average unemployment levels: 35 per cent of those under 24 have experienced at least one period of unemployment, for instance.

The reasons are (a) the older workers are usually the ones most likely to be laid off by employers, who prefer younger workers with experience; (b) the young are also likely to be unemployed, because there are few new vacancies and because they do not have the experience for the vacancies that do arise.

However, it appears that young people are likely to have shorter periods of unemployment than older workers who, once made unemployed, are likely to remain so.

2 Ethnic minorities

It appears that unemployment among the ethnic minorities is higher than among whites: 29 per cent of people from these groups have experienced some period of unemployment compared to 15 per cent of whites.

The reasons are (a) discrimination by employers; (b) the fact that in general the ethnic minorities perform less well in the education system; and (c) the fact that they are disproportionately represented in the younger age groups, which have higher rates of unemployment anyway.

3 Manual workers and the less skilled

Of every 10 workers registered unemployed, 7 are manual workers, although manual workers now account for only 50 per cent of the workforce. The less skilled manual workers have the highest rates of unemployment. For instance, 32 per cent of semi- and unskilled manual workers have experienced some period of unemployment, compared to only 5 per cent of professional employees.

The reasons are (i) that unskilled jobs are being lost to automation; (ii) that the shift in jobs generally is away from manufacturing towards white-collar and service industry employment; (iii) areas of production that use mainly unskilled workers are being shifted abroad where wages are much lower.

Table 10.1 illustrates the percentage of the groups mentioned above who have experienced some unemployment.

4000 men were interviewed in 1985 concerning unemployment: the results are shown here.

Table 10.1

Males aged	*with at least one period of unemployment in past year*
18–24	35%
25–39	16%
40–59	12%
60–64	17%
All males	17%
Colour	
White	17%
Coloured	29%
Socio-economic group	
Professionals and managers	6%
Junior non-manual	10%
All non-manual	8%
Skilled manual	17%
Semi and unskilled manual	32%
All manual	23%

(**Source**: *Social Trends* 1985 (adapted))

10.4 Unemployment by Region

Not all areas of the country have the same levels of unemployment (see Figure 10.2).

1 The highest levels of unemployment in mainland Britain are the North and the North-West.

2 The lowest rates of unemployment are in the South-East and East Anglia.

The reasons for variations in unemployment by region

1 The industries with the greatest levels of decline, such as heavy engineering, are mainly in the North;

2 The new light industries have developed near to the affluent markets of the South-East, around London;

Scotland
8.1–9.5%

Northern Ireland
11%

North
9.6–11%

Yorks and Humber
8.1–9.5%

North-West
9.6–11%

East Midlands
8%

Wales
8.1–9.5%

West Midlands
8.1–9.5%

East Anglia
8%

South-East
8%

South-West
8%

Official unemployment rates, 1991
(**Source:** *Social Trends* 1992)

Fig 10.2

3 There has been an overall move towards the South with the increase in trading with the countries of the European Economic Community;

4 The service industries grow to serve affluent areas. Their presence creates more jobs and so the area becomes more affluent, which leads to the development of more service industries. This is happening in the South-East and the reverse is happening in the North.

10.5 The Causes of Unemployment

1 A change from manufacturing industry to service industries. There has been a massive loss of jobs in British manufacturing industry in the last 25 years – with over 3 million jobs disappearing. The new manufacturing industries (sometimes called 'sunrise industries'), which are involved in electronics, need far fewer employees.

There has been a compensating increase in service jobs, but the people employed in this sector are not the same as those who are being made unemployed from the manufacturing sector.

2 There has been no real overall increase in fulltime employment sine 1980 (although there has been an increase in part-time work). At the same time, there is a constant inflow of new, young workers, seeking work.

3 Automation has been introduced into factories and increasingly into offices. In factories it has been used mainly to replace semi-skilled workers in such jobs as car assembly-line production. In offices it is being used to replace routine clerical work, such as recording accounts and sending out bills. Increasingly, microchip technology is allowing more skilled work to be done by machine.

4 Foreign competition in manufactured goods has made considerable inroads into traditional British markets, both in Britain itself and abroad. This has had the effect of making some British companies go out of business; others have laid off workers in order to reduce labour costs; and yet others have shifted their manufacturing operations to countries where wage rates are considerably lower.

10.6 The Implications of Unemployment for Society

There is an important distinction between high levels of short-term unemployment and high levels of long-term unemployment.

Short-term unemployment means that those who become unemployed have the definite prospect of another job. Long-term unemployment means that those without work are very unlikely to find any for a long time. We will examine the effects of unemployment for individuals later, but there are also implications for society as a whole.

1 Government money goes on unemployment benefit and social security, rather than on new hospitals and other forms of useful government expenditure.

2 Employers are able to threaten those in employment with the possibility of replacing them with the unemployed; this means that wages can be kept low and that conditions of work may deteriorate.

3 Large-scale unemployment weakens trade unions, as both they and the employers know that if workers withdraw their labour they can easily be replaced by the unemployed.

4 Nevertheless, there will still be a gap between the standard of living of the employed, particularly the professional and managerial workers, and of the unemployed. This could lead to a clear-cut division in society between the employed and unemployed – with the employed having consumer goods, decent food and housing, and money to spend on leisure activities.

5 Long-term unemployment and the possibility of living on social security means that there will be a great increase in poverty.

6 Those in poverty with no prospect of work may be tempted to turn to crime.

7 The political stability of Britain could also be threatened, as 'extremist' groups that reject the democratic system gain support. The unemployed turn to groups who claim to be able to solve the unemployment crisis. A similar thing happened in the 1920s and '30s with the rise to power of the fascists in Italy and Germany.

10.7 The Experience of Unemployment

The effects of unemployment are felt differently by different groups in society. Differences are noticeable between (a) the young, (b) the middle aged and the over 55s, (c) women.

1 The young

There has been some disagreement over how the young experience unemployment.

(a) Young people have no experience of work and do not see their **identity** in terms of their jobs as older people do.

(b) They do not have any major financial responsibilities, such as a family and mortgage, etc. Unemployment need not be as serious a problem to them as to the middle aged and older groups. They receive social security and help from the wider family.

(c) It seems that the young are caught in a period of *drift* between childhood and adulthood (as marked by full-time employment). There is a greater stress on the values and importance of the youth culture.

(d) There is relatively little stigma attached to being unemployed as half of all young people are in this situation.

(e) Spare time is spent with friends from school who are also unemployed.

Research

Simon Frith has argued that inner city youth have adapted themselves quite well to this period of unemployment and have developed various means of 'getting by', with short bouts of irregular employment and some petty theft etc. Unemployed youth are actually better off than when they were at school, as they receive social security. He sees a definite development of a new style of youth culture to cope with long-term unemployment.

A more **pessimistic** view of youth unemployment comes from Paul Willis in his research on unemployment in the Midlands. Willis argues that it is a normal part of a person's development in Britain to (a) get a job, (b) with the earnings buy smart clothes and consumer goods, such as a car, (c) to leave home, and (d) probably get married. Unemployment prevents many of these stages happening. Young people are stuck at home with little prospect of escape. This causes considerable tension.

According to Willis, the identities that older people gain through their jobs, and to a lesser extent through the things they own, are gained entirely through possession of status goods among the young. It is important to have a motorbike or car, the right clothes, to be able to afford to pay for drinks in pubs, etc. Unable to afford these things, the young person loses his/ her identity. Willis argues that this has, for example, led girls to become pregnant just to get a council flat.

Willis also points out that young people congregate in city centres where they can see and be seen. Their large numbers and high visibility, due to their styles of dress, make them a menace for the police who see them as potential threats to law and order. There develops therefore greater dislike and tension.

2 Middle age and unemployment

(a) The identity of the middle aged is closely bound up with their jobs. When asked 'what are you?', the reply is 'I am a teacher/nurse etc'. Loss of employment means partial loss of identity.

(b) It also brings financial problems, with payment of bills, such as gas, electricity, instalments on the consumer durables, etc., becoming very difficult. Gradually the luxuries are taken away and there is a shift to essentials.

(c) Apart from the discomfort this brings, it also means that the social life and the friends that went with it have to be abandoned. There is therefore a withdrawal from contact. This leads to a degree of loneliness.

(d) The reasons for unemployment are generally seen as personal, in that the unemployed persons ask what is wrong with them that they were made unemployed. This problem becomes worse as the period of unemployment lengthens. Indeed, it has been pointed out that the unemployed are more likely to become mentally ill and be depressed than the employed.

(e) The unemployed are likely to feel bored, useless and frustrated.

(f) Within the family, the presence of the depressed and frustrated father/mother at home all day can lead to family tension.

3 Women and unemployment

(a) Official statistics indicate that women have not been as badly hit by unemployment as men. There are a number of reasons for this: (i) women are more likely to be in part-time work (which men do not want); (ii) they are likely to be in low-pay work anyway, so employers are happy to keep them on; (iii) they are employed mainly in the service industries which have not had such a decline in employment.

(b) However, it is known that the unemployment statistics do not tell the full story and the number of women recorded as unemployed is below the true figure (see p 87).

(c) The effects upon women are not so very different from those on men, although there is a ready-made and socially acceptable role for unemployed women, as mothers and housewives, which is not open to men.

(d) However, as women go to work for two reasons – (i) because the money is needed in the home, and (ii) to make some form of social contact outside the home – the effects on them are generally just as severe as on men.

(e) There is considerable loss of income to the family and therefore financial problems arise, even where the husband is still working. This can lead to a similar pattern of social withdrawal by husband and wife from their circle of friends and a change in leisure patterns.

(f) The wife feels a loss of independence and must rely on her husband's salary.

(g) There is a feeling of isolation and a loss of the friendships provided by work.

(h) The traditional view of the female worker as someone who goes out to work for pin money fails to take into account single women, lone parents, the divorcees and those who are supporting elderly relatives. These are often in the lowest earning categories anyway.

Research

Angela Coyle in *Redundant Women* studied the effects of unemployment on two groups of women laid off in the early 1980s from the garments industry in Yorkshire. She concluded that unemployment was a particularly harsh blow for these women as they had seen their job as an escape from the routine of family life. The 'compensation' of the role of mother and housewife was not true for them.

10.8 Summary

1 There is some dispute over the true extent of unemployment. The official figures exclude certain categories of person.

2 In 1986 there were approximately 3½ million unemployed in Britain. This was the highest figure ever.

3 Since 1981, the length of time people are unemployed has lengthened.

4 Certain groups are more likely to be unemployed than others. In particular, the young and older workers, the ethnic minorities and the lower skilled.

5 Unemployment rates are much higher in the North of Britain than in the South.

6 Unemployment is caused not by personal defects in the unemployed, but mainly by automation and by foreign competition. The government's attitude to unemployment is also crucial.

7 There are a number of possible consequences for British society. This could include the weakening of trade unions' and employees' rights; a lowering of wages; a growing gap between the lives of the rich and the poor; an increase in crime and the growth of politically extreme groups.

8 Unemployment hits different groups in the population in different ways. Older people may find it affects their identities more, while younger people may be able to cope better. However, it has been argued that the effects are just as bad on young people.

9 Women appear to suffer just as much as men from the consequences of unemployment.

10.9 Keywords *(as they appear in the unit)*

short-term unemployment, long-term unemployment, automation, light industries, sunrise industries.

11 LEISURE

11.1 Defining Leisure

The first problem is to define leisure. On the surface, this seems very simple indeed, but it presents a difficult problem for sociologists.

Characteristics of work

1 It is paid.

2 It is generally constricting on the individual's freedom.

3 There are official obligations imposed.

4 Work involves acceptance of a hierarchy of power and prestige. We must follow another person's orders.

5 Most people gain relatively little pleasure from work.

Characteristics of leisure

1 It is unpaid.
2 Usually it involves a sense of freedom.
3 There is a large degree of choice.
4 All obligations are self-imposed and freely chosen.
5 Relationships are based on interest, not differences in power.
6 Usually there is a considerable degree of enjoyment.

11.2 The Growth of Leisure

Until relatively recently, the long hours of work, the few holidays and the poor pay of working class people prevented them from having much leisure as we understand it today. Until early in this century leisure was something for the aristocracy and the rich.

Veblen, writing a hundred years ago, suggested that there existed at that time what he called **the leisure classes**. These were people who worked very little and generally lived off inherited wealth. He suggested that the values that guided their lives were not of the importance of hard work, but of enjoyment, and all their energies were directed towards this end. Some sociologists have suggested that those leisure values characterize our society today.

After the end of the Second World War, there was a gradual increase in paid holidays and a shortening of working hours, so that leisure could become a reality for most of the population.

Although class differences do still exist in choices and possibilities of leisure activities, there has been a spread of leisure from the middle class to the working class. In the 1950s foreign travel was largely unknown among the lower middle and working classes, but the introduction of mass tourism in the 1960s soon altered this. The 'package' tour is now common to most social classes.

There has been a spread of sports, too, so that traditional middle class games like squash and golf are now more widespread.

11.3 Factors Affecting Leisure Activities

Factors that affect choices are:

1 Social class   **2** Age   **3** Gender   **4** Occupation

1 Social class

As we have seen from the tables earlier, clear differences emerge in leisure patterns of the working class. For instance, professional people tend to read more books and newspapers, to attend cinemas and theatres more often. The reasons for the differences include the following:

(a) Educational differences;

(b) Income differences;

(c) Amount of free time available for leisure;

(d) Exclusiveness of certain clubs associated with the middle class (such as golf clubs).

2 Age

(a) *Youth culture* A lot of uncommitted cash, spending on luxury items, records, clothes, etc. Search for excitement;

(b) *Young marrieds* Spending on the house and young children;

(c) *35–45 years* Increase in uncommitted income, spending on family and group activities;

(d) *45–64* Most affluent age, children leaving home, spending on luxury items;

(e) *Over 65* Decline in income, little cash for leisure activities therefore inexpensive pursuits followed. TV watching particularly important.

3 Gender

Cultural differences in our society prevent or discourage women from engaging in a number of activities (such as football), so leisure reflects the traditional roles of men and women in our society. Women tend to engage in yoga, keep fit and horse riding more often than men, but in general women are far less active in leisure than men.

4 Occupation

Stanley Parker (*The Future of Work and Leisure*) has suggested that the most important factor affecting leisure is occupation. He suggests three possible relationships.

(a) *Extension* This is when a person's leisure activities are a direct extension of his/her job, e.g. teachers who may enjoy reading about their subject in their spare time. In this relationship the job is interesting and fulfilling to the person. Leisure and occupation have been allowed to overlap. It usually occurs with people who have responsible, rewarding work. Typical leisure occupations include reading, theatre visits and active participation sports.

(b) *Opposition* This is the very opposite of the extension pattern. People who have work that is tough and exhausting seek to refresh themselves through their leisure activities. Miners, fishermen and many manual workers have this type of leisure pattern. They need the break away from the work which they seek to forget. Typical leisure activities include pub drinking or some **skilled** leisure such as model making or gardening. The skill and calmness of these help them to recuperate.

(c) *Neutrality* This refers to the increasing number of workers, notably in clerical occupations, who are not interested in their work, nor are they exhausted by it; instead they are bored. They seek to compensate for boredom in a number of ways, although no clear pattern of leisure emerges as in the other two types.

Conclusions

Leisure activities are not just a reflection of individuals' personalities; they are affected by a number of social and cultural factors. The most important of these factors is social class, but within social class the type of job performed in turn greatly influences the leisure patterns. Age and gender then further subdivide leisure into even more complex patterns.

11.4 The Future of Leisure

If leisure is strongly influenced by occupation, then the changes in the occupational structure will be reflected in leisure changes. The most important changes taking place today are:

(a) The growth of automation;
(b) The move towards white-collar work. There are two views of the future; let us call them the optimistic and the pessimistic.

The optimistic view

Writers such as Parker and Best suggest that:

(a) Machines will take over the boring, repetitive work that causes **alienation**. The remaining work will be interesting and could be fulfilling, indeed more like leisure than work. **Parker** actually sees a **fusion** of work and leisure;
(b) Less time need be spent at work and more on leisure;
(c) The affluence created by automation will lead to a greater stress on education and self-improvement;
(d) We will move towards a **leisure society** in which leisure becomes the central element in our lives, overcoming class and social occupational divisions.

The pessimistic view

Writers such as Wilensky are doubtful about the future:

(a) Machines may take over workers' jobs, but instead of escaping from boring work, the workers are made redundant;
(b) Unemployment in our society means a low level of income, from state benefits. This means that the unemployed are unable to afford most leisure pursuits. Unemployment does not lead to useful, enjoyable leisure, but poverty, boredom, frustration and a sense of failure;
(c) Leisure is increasingly dominated by large **leisure industries** which require payment for the services they offer. Decreasingly, leisure reflects our personalities, increasingly it reflects the manipulation of desires by the large companies.

11.5 Social Implications of Retirement

One form of enforced leisure is retirement, which occurs when a person's working life finishes. Retirement is viewed by many men, and to a lesser extent by women, as a dreadful state, as a person's perception of himself/herself is strongly influenced by his or her occupation. On retirement the identity provided by a job is removed. Of course, it can also be an escape for many from boring work.

1 In pre-industrial societies there was no fixed time of retirement – people continued to work as long as their abilities allowed it. However, there are now fixed ages of retirement.
2 As a result of the increase in life expectation, it is reasonable to expect at least 10 – 15 years of life after retirement, according to social class.

3 There has been a considerable increase in the elderly and this will continue to the end of the century.

4 This means that retired people form a considerable proportion of the population, for the first time in history, with about 10 million people over retirement age.

5 Retirement is an important *rite of passage* in society signifying the exit from work and the move into the final stage before death.

6 As a person's identity is linked to his/her employment (although this seems more important for males) there appears to be a considerable problem of loss of identity. Typically, people maintain their identity by prefixing their old job with the title 'retired' (e.g. a retired teacher).

7 As there has never been this number of elderly people in society before, there is not yet an acceptable role provided for them by society.

8 Leisure patterns appear to vary by gender and by social class for the retired (see p 42).

9 With high rates of unemployment and a desire of firms to continue to shed labour, it seems likely that there will be an increase in the numbers of 'younger retired people' – typically in the age range 55 onwards. These will be far more active (turn to p 101 for a full discussion of the problems of the elderly in society in general).

10 There are likely to be problems providing the resources for adequate pensions and so a likelihood of poverty among the retired, which will also affect their leisure patterns.

11 People often move on retirement to coastal resorts – this leads to problems of provision of hospital and social care facilities. It can also lead to loneliness for the couple who have moved from their friends.

11.6 Summary

1 There are no particular tasks that can be defined solely as leisure. The closest we can come to defining it is to say that it is the area in life giving the maximum amount of freedom, the maximum amount of pleasure, and that you are not paid for it.

2 There has been a considerable growth in leisure related to longer holidays, greater affluence and shorter working hours.

3 There has also been a spread of leisure across the classes. What was once considered possible only for the middle class, is now normal for all society.

4 However, leisure patterns are related to such things as class, gender, age and specific occupation.

11.7 Keywords *(as they appear in the unit)*

leisure, extension leisure, opposition, neutrality, leisure industries.

12 POPULATION

Definition

The study of population, more correctly known as demography, concentrates on studying changes in:

1 The size of the population;
2 The proportions in each age group;
3 The geographical distribution of the population;
4 The balance of the sexes.

12.1 Collecting Information

In order to get information sociologists have to collect statistics from a number of sources. The most important are:

The census This is a form consisting of questions (a questionnaire) which the Registrar-General's Department of the Civil Service delivers to every household in Britain. Each household must, by law, answer the questions, and the answers given are strictly confidential.

The census is taken every ten years and began in 1801. It includes questions on accommodation, amenities (number of rooms, bathrooms, etc), employment.

Registration of births, marriages and deaths Since 1836 in England and Wales, all births, marriages and deaths have had to be registered with the Registrar at the Local Council Offices.

Births must be registered within the first 42 days. Marriages are registered at the time of the ceremony: without a certificate a person is not legally married. Death certificates must be issued before a burial can take place. The accuracy of the information obtained from the census and the registration of births, marriages and deaths is very high indeed, as they are compulsory, and they give detailed information on the British population. The census tells us more about social conditions. The registration tells us more about changing patterns of births, marriages and deaths.

12.2 The Importance of Demography

The demographic information collected is extremely useful, as it gives the Government (a) a detailed picture of the British population at any one time; (b) a forecast of likely trends in the future. This allows the Government to plan future policies.

Here are just four examples of the uses of demographic information:

1 Education

It is important to know the numbers of children attending school in the future, so that schools can be expanded or closed, new teachers trained or excess teachers offered early retirement. It is also important to know in which area of the country they are likely to live, so the schools can be located in the right areas: it is no good building schools in Scotland if the growth of population is in the South-East of England! If the Government know the number of children born in a particular year, then they also know that five years later those children will enter primary school and 11 years later will enter secondary school.

2 Health

Knowledge of the age of the population and where they live, now and in the future, can help decide (a) the numbers of doctors and nurses needed; (b) the number and location of hospitals; and (c) the type of health care needed. For example, a young population would need a lot of maternity services, as they would be likely to have many babies; an ageing population would need geriatric hospitals, specially adapted to care for the needs of old people.

3 Housing and town planning

Long-term trends can be predicted so that just the right number of houses of the right type, in the right place, can be built, with appropriate roads and services.

4 Social services

Knowing the trends in the size and age of the population allows the correct social services to be provided. For example, the current growth in the numbers of old people means that more money is needed for pensions and welfare services for the old.

12.3 Population Size

The population of Britain rose steadily this century until 1971, but since then it has hardly grown at all. This is illustrated in Table 12.1.

Table 12.1 The change in Britain's population this century

Year	1901	1921	1951	1961	1971	1981	2001
Population in millions	38.2	44.0	50.3	52.8	55.6	56.3	57.5*

*This figure is a projection

The size of the population at any one time is the result of three causes:

1 The number of births;
2 The number of deaths;
3 The movement of people into, or out of, a country.

Changes in the number of births

The **(crude) birthrate** is the number of live births each year for every 1000 people in the population and is the measure usually employed by sociologists when they discuss changes in the size of population. The higher the birthrate the more children are being born in a particular year.

Sometimes sociologists use the term the **fertility rate,** which refers to the number of children born for every 1000 women of childbearing age each year. This is more accurate as it relates births to the proportion of the population who could have children.

In this century, there has been an overall fall in the birthrate and this has accelerated sharply since 1967. However, it has not been a constant decline as there have been three periods when the birthrate has risen: (a) 1919–21 (b) 1945–8 and (c) 1957–66.

Factors affecting the number of births

1 Knowledge of and use of contraceptives. There has been an increasing use of methods of birth control throughout this century.

2 The financial costs and benefits of having children. If children are useful, then it is likely that most people will try to have large families. At present children are seen as a burden, at least in economic terms.

3 Cultural stress on the correct number of children. Society's view of a *normal* size of family varies over time and people will tend to conform to the average.

4 Women's attitudes to childbearing. Women are increasingly rejecting the idea that they should spend most of their lives having children.

The patterns of births (and deaths) are illustrated in Figure 12.1.

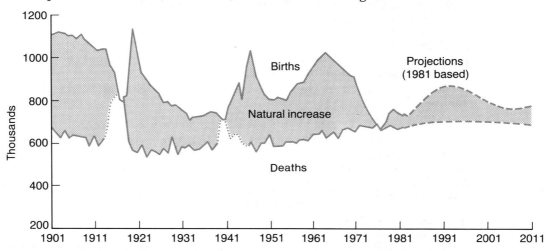

Fig. 12.1 Chart illustrating the birth and death rates in Britain this century

Note: The **natural increase** is the difference between the number of people born and the number of people who die in any particular period (Source: *Social Trends*).

A description and explanation about the changes this century

Before the beginning of the Industrial Revolution (1760) the British population grew very quickly. The improvements brought by industrialization led to a massive reduction in the death rate, while the high birth rate continued. This led to a population explosion which continued until the turn of the century.

From the turn of the century until 1919, the birthrate was falling rapidly. This was because:

1 Children had become an economic burden. This had happened as a result of the introduction of compulsory schooling in 1870, and the increasingly strict enforcement of it, which prevented children going out to work until 14. In previous times, the children's financial contribution to working class households had been considerable. This was also true for the better-off middle class, who found that the wages demanded by servants (and in particular nannies) were too high for them. The result was that they had to look after their own children and so restricted the size of their families.

2 Throughout most of this period, there were serious problems in the British economy, with low wages and high unemployment, so people were reluctant to have large families.

3 The numbers of children dying at or near birth had fallen dramatically in the 50 years prior to this period, therefore there was no need to have a large number of children in order to ensure that a few survived.

4 The beginnings of pension schemes were developed in this period, so people realized that it was no longer necessary to have large families to ensure there would be someone to care for them when they were old.

5 The restriction of family size was only possible because of the growing awareness of methods of birth control – at first among the middle class and later among the working class.

The average family size in this period was about 3.4 children.

From 1919 to the early 1920s, the birthrate rose steeply because of the return of soldiers after the First World War and their desire to start families.

From the early 1920s to the mid-1940s, the birthrate continued to decline because:

1 Mass unemployment and low wages meant that people could not afford to have children.

2 There was a growing belief in the virtues of small families, particularly among the middle class. This was linked to a change in attitudes to children, as people began to believe that children needed love and affection.

3 The use of contraceptives was gaining favour rapidly among the middle class.

The average family size in this period was about 2.5 children.

From 1945 to 1948, the birth rate rose steeply once again because of the return of soldiers at the end of the Second World War and their desire to start families.

From the late 1940s to the late 1950s, the birthrate continued its overall decline because:

1 There was by now widespread use of contraceptives among all social classes.

2 There was a strong emphasis on having fewer children and giving them far higher standards of care and affection than in the pre-war period.

3 Married couples were more interested in having a high standard of living than having large families.

The average family size in this period was about 2.4 children.

From the late 1950s to the mid-1960s, the birthrate rose because:

1 People were marrying younger and having children earlier.

2 This was a period of considerable affluence and people felt that they could have both a larger family and a high standard of living.

3 The children born in the 'baby boom' after the Second World War were having their children.

The average family size in this period was about 2.7 children.

From the mid-1960s until the present, the birth rate has declined, apart from a brief rise in the late 1970s, because:

1 There has been a change in the role of women in society. They are less likely to accept the role of 'housewife' and more likely to demand the right to a career of their own. This means that they wish to limit the number of children they have (ideally to two) and to have them when they are in their mid- to late twenties.

2 The 'pill' is widely used and highly reliable as a contraceptive, although a scare over the safety of the pill in the late 1970s led to women refusing to use it and a rise in the number of births.

3 The ideal family in British culture is now regarded as husband/wife and two children, with great affection and care lavished on the children.

There is likely to be a small rise in the late 1980s as the children of the early 1960s 'baby boom' have their children.

The average family size is now 1.9 children.

Social class and fertility

Historically, the poorer groups in society have always had larger families as a form of insurance against old age, and as a means of increasing the breadwinners in the family. The richer groups had less need for children and so tended to have smaller families. By the turn of the century, the middle class had begun to restrict the size of their families using contraceptive devices, because of the economic factors described above. The working class eventually followed the lead of the middle class about 20 years later. This time-lag was caused by:

(a) ignorance of contraception; (b) cultural patterns that emphasized the importance of large families; (c) the security that a large family provided. Over the century the patterns of contraceptive use and family sizes of the middle and working classes have become increasingly similar.

Changes in the number of deaths

The **death (or mortality) rate** is the number of deaths for every 1000 people in the population.

The patterns of deaths can be seen in Table 12.2.

Table 12.2 The death rates this century

Year	1901	1921	1931	1951	1961	1971	1981
Deaths per 1000 of the population	17.1	12.4	12.5	12.6	12.0	11.6	11.8

Overall the death rate has declined this century, although there has been no fall in the last 10 years. It rose sharply during the two world wars, 1914–18, and 1939–45.

The decline in the death rate has been explained by the following facts:

1 *Improvements in public hygiene and sanitation* Modern sewage and refuse collection systems have drastically improved the standards of public cleanliness, which has prevented many of the killer diseases such as typhoid and cholera.

2 *Advances in medicine* Medical advances, such as vaccinations against diseases, and improvements in medical care generally.

3 *Higher standards of living* This is probably the most important influence on the falling death rate. As people have generally become better off this century, so their diets, type of food and housing conditions have improved. The result is a much healthier population.

The infant mortality rate A most important element in the overall decline in the death rate has been the decline in the infant mortality rate, which is the number of deaths of infants under one year old for every 1000 babies born alive.

The infant mortality rate has been dropping sharply for the whole of the century, as can be seen in Table 12.3.

Table 12.3 The infant mortality rate over the last 100 years

Year	1891	1921	1951	1971	1981
Infant deaths for every 1000 live births	153	72	30	17	10

Factors affecting the infant mortality rate (which forms part of the death rate) are the same as for the death rate in general. However, the following additional points are important:

1 The NHS has provided an increasingly higher standard of health services for childbirth. These include highly trained midwives and clinics for advice and health care before and after the birth. These are free of course. In countries where these facilities are only for the better off, as they have to be paid for, the infant mortality rate is much higher, e.g. in Italy the infant mortality rate is 25, compared to our 10.

2 Boys have a higher infant mortality rate than girls. In 1981, for example the infant mortality rate for boys was 12.5 compared to only 9.6 for girls.

3 Class differences are still very noticeable, with the infant mortality rate for children of the poorest groups in society twice as high as those of the upper middle class. Working class mothers are also more likely to give birth to premature (and therefore weaker) babies. The causes of these class differences lie in lower standards of care, poorer diets and greater risks of accidents.

12.4 Changes in Migration

Immigration means the movement of people into a particular place or country. **Emigration** means the movement of people out of a particular place or country. Both words are based on the term *migration*, which in demography means the movement of people.

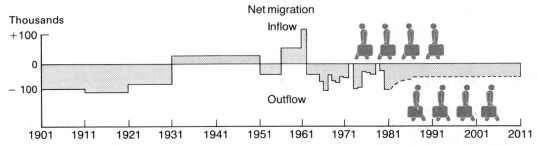

Fig. 12.2. Figure illustrating whether more people leave or enter Britain (Source *Social Trends*, 1984)

Britain has had a constant flow of emigration and immigration throughout its history. Figure 12.2 illustrates the general pattern of migration in this century. As you can see, in only two periods, 1931–51 and 1955–62, has immigration been greater than emigration.

Emigration

Throughout the last century and right up to 1930, the British Empire provided a place for those British people who wished to emigrate. The total number of people who emigrated from Britain in the 100 years up to 1930 totalled about 20 million people. During the 1950s and early 1960s, the levels of emigration were fairly low because of the number of jobs available in Britain. By the 1970s the lack of jobs in Britain had led to a significant increase in emigration. The level of emigration depends upon the availability of work in Britain compared to abroad and whether other countries are willing to accept our emigrants.

Immigration

The pattern of immigration to Britain resembles a series of waves. Usually the high point of a particular wave of immigrants reflects serious economic or political problems in their home country of emigrants.

In the last century Irish immigrants settled in Britain as a result of the dreadful economic conditions in Ireland. Today, the single largest group of immigrants are still those from the Irish Republic. Jewish refugees also came to escape persecution; they were still doing so in the 1930s to escape the Nazis.

In the early 1950s and '60s Commonwealth immigrants were recruited to come to Britain to fill job vacancies. In all 620 000 immigrants came from Asian and Caribbean countries between 1955 and 1967. Since then there has been a considerable decline in the numbers of immigrants (for discussion of this topic turn to p 69).

In 1983, 17 000 more people came into Britain than emigrated from it.

People come to Britain mainly to get work.

12.5 The Gender Balance

There are more males up to the age of 50 than females; there are then more females than males. This is partly because, although more males are born than females, they are more likely to die through sickness and injury.

Figure 12.3 below illustrates the proportions of males and females, by age.

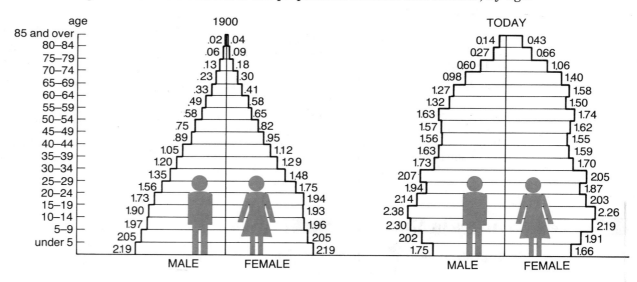

Numbers in millions

Fig. 12.3 Population pyramids of 1900 and today illustrating (i) the growth in proportion of old people and the decline in proportion of young people and (ii) the balance of the sexes. (Source: *The State of the Nation*, Fothergill & Vincent, Pluto Press. Original Statistics: *Annual Abstract of Statistics*, HMSO).

12.6 Changes in Population

People today live longer and healthier lives. In 1901, the average life expectancy (the typical length of life) at birth was about 48 for a man and 52 for a woman. Today it has risen to an average of 70 for a man and 76 for a woman. However, someone of retiring age can reasonably expect to live into his/her late seventies.

In 1902 only 6.2 per cent of the population was over 65; today the figure is 15 per cent, comprising 10 million people in all.

People live longer because of better housing conditions, healthier diets and higher standards of medical care (all the same reasons that the death rate has declined).

Gender differences Women are more likely to live longer than men and the vast majority of those over 75 years of age are women.

Women live longer because:

1 They are less likely to work in dangerous occupations such as mining or construction.

2 Most combatants in wars are males.

3 Men are more likely to smoke and drink heavily than women.

4 A greater proportion of young men are likely to be killed in motorcycle and car accidents.

Consequences of an ageing population

The consequences of an ageing population can be divided into two: **1** consequences for society; **2** consequences for individuals.

Consequences for society

1 The most important consequence is an increase in the *burden of dependency*—this means the proportion of the population who are too young or old to work compared to those of working age. At the moment the proportion of dependent people is very high at about 65 per cent. This means that 35 per cent of the population have to support the remaining 65 per cent. This can mean higher levels of taxation.

2 The elderly need more money spent on medical care than younger groups and therefore more has to be spent on geriatric wards in hospitals, on old people's homes and on increased medical care at home.

3 There needs to be an increase in social services for the elderly.

4 Government expenditure on the elderly in pensions and rent and rate rebates (provided by local government) must increase.

Consequences for individuals

1 As individuals grow older and receive only their pensions they experience poverty.

2 Families must care for the elderly if they are unable to cope. This places tremendous pressure on married daughters (on whom the burden usually falls) who must look after their own families plus their ageing parents. Often this means giving up paid employment.

3 As friends and partners die, the elderly may become increasingly isolated and lonely. This is particularly true for women, who generally live longer than men.

12.7 Consequences of Population Changes

An increase in population can lead to a number of problems, including the following:

1 Pressure on health services as more medical staff are needed.

2 Education—more teachers are needed and more schools need to be built.

3 Employment—there is an ever-increasing demand for the jobs and unless the economy can generate them a rise in unemployment takes place, with all the social problems related to it.

4 Housing – the numbers of houses must be constantly increased just to cope with the demand. At the same time, older houses may become unfit to live in and need to be replaced or modernized.

5 Environment – (a) the need for new houses, roads and services creates pressure on the countryside and developers will want to use the **green belt** (land set aside from building around cities in order to keep some countryside) and so **urban sprawl** (endless housing developments that link one town to another) may develop; (b) pollution increases with the increase in industry and waste disposal.

A *decrease in the population* can also lead to problems:

1 Ageing – normally a decreasing or stable population (like Britain today) goes hand in hand with an ageing population. The problems associated with an ageing population are discussed on p 67.

2 Lack of youthful ideas – there is likely to be a decline in new ideas and society will suffer from the lack of young, dynamic people.

3 Decline in consumer demand – the decline in the the number of people will mean a decline in the demand for consumer goods which could lead to unemployment.

4 Education – schools will have to close and teachers be made redundant.

12.8 Changes in the Distribution of the Population in Britain

The geographical distribution of the population refers to the way that the population is distributed in **1** different areas of Britain; and **2** in cities or the countryside. (See Figure 12.4.)

1 Areas

(a) There has been a shift in the population away from living in the North of England, Wales and Scotland to living in the South of England;

(b) The main growth area of all Britain is the South-East, particularly East Anglia.

2 Cities or countryside?

(a) Throughout the 100 years before 1950 there was a move away from the countryside to the towns and cities. This was known as **urbanization**.

(b) Since the 1950s there has been a move away from living in city centres to living in the suburbs. This is known as **suburbanization**.

(c) Since the 1950s there has also been a shift towards living in **new towns**, such as Milton Keynes. (See Unit 13 'Urbanization and Community' p 104 for a full discussion.)

Population change in England and Wales 1971–81

population, 1981 millions	population change, 1971–81 percentages
London 6.7	−9.9%
conurbations (large cities and their immediate surroundings) 11.2	−4.6%
other large urban areas 2.8	−5.1%
smaller urban areas 1.7	−3.2%
industrial towns 6.7	+3.0%
new towns 2.2	+15.1%
resorts and retirement areas 3.3	+4.9%
partly rural areas 9.5	+7.0%
rural areas 5.0	+10.3%

Fig. 12.4 Diagram illustrating the movement of population away from the big cities
(Source: *The State of the Nation*, Fothergill & Vincent, Pluto Press).

12.9 Changes in the World Population

The world population is over 4½ billion, an increase of 50 per cent over what it was 20 years ago. By the end of this century the world population is likely to be 6 billion, double its 1961 size.

The rate of increase is lowest in the technologically advanced nations of Europe and the United States. For instance, between 1977 and 1987, the British population only increased by about 1 per cent.

The fastest increases are taking place in the poorer nations of the world. For example, India had an increase of 30 per cent between 1971 and the early 1980s. The causes of the rapid population increase in the poorer Third World nations such as India are similar to the causes of rapid population rise in Britain in the nineteenth century.

1 A decrease in the death rate and in particular the child mortality rates due to medical and public health advances.

2 Lack of contraception either through non-availability of devices/pills or refusal to accept birth control programmes. This has meant a continuing high birthrate. In India in the late 1970s fewer than 5 per cent of fertile couples used contraceptives, although 12 per cent had undergone operations to make them sterile.

3 Children are still economically useful in most Third World countries.

4 The cultures and religions of many Third World nations stress the importance of having children.

Problems caused by the increase in the world population

1 Population increases cause most problems in societies which lack the technological and agricultural ability to provide adequate food, accommodation and material resources for their increasing populations.

2 It is mainly those countries lacking resources that are experiencing the birth explosion, such as India, Ethiopia and parts of South-East Asia. However, birthrates are declining in these countries – by as much as 15 per cent in the last 20 years.

3 Such massive population growth as has happened has led to problems of malnutrition and starvation, with 18 per cent of the world's population suffering from these problems.

4 Because of the lack of work in the countryside there has been a rapid rise in the numbers of town dwellers. This means problems of pollution, overcrowding and homelessness, similar to the conditions of early nineteenth-century Britain, are common throughout the world.

5 Food production in the Third World has not kept up with the population expansion. Each year food production lags behind the increase in the population. This means that food has to be imported from the richer nations and the cost is crippling to the poorer nations' economies.

12.10 Summary

1 Demography is the study of population patterns and changes.

2 It is important as it can help us to plan ahead.

3 Information on the population is found in the Census and the Registration of Births, Marriages and Deaths.

4 The size of the population is determined by the numbers of (a) births, (b) deaths and (c) the numbers of people who move in or out of the country.

5 The birthrate is the number of babies born for every 1000 people in the population.

6 The birthrate has been falling most of this century except for periods after the two world wars and from the late 1950s to the mid-1960s.

7 The fall in the birthrate is largely due to the increasing use of contraception, motivated by changing attitudes of women to their role and the increased costs of having children.

8 The death rate is the number of deaths for every 1000 people in the population.

9 The death rate fell in the early part of the century but has been steady for a number of years.

10 The infant mortality rate is the number of babies that die under one year old for every 1000 babies born alive.

11 The infant mortality rate has been falling throughout this century.

12 There are increasing numbers of elderly people in Britain, as life expectancy increases.

13 The increase in the elderly will cause a number of problems for society in providing adequate social services for them, and for individuals (usually the daughters) who will have to sacrifice part of their own lives to care for them. There may also be the problems of loneliness and poverty for the aged.

14 People are moving out of the cities to the suburbs, and smaller towns.

15 World population is growing rapidly and this is leading to desperate problems of poverty and starvation.

12.11 **Keywords** (*as they appear in the unit*)

demography, census, long-term trends, immigration, emigration, (crude) birthrate, fertility rate, birth control, natural increase, death rate, infant mortality rate, life expectancy, burden of dependency, urbanization, suburbanization.

13 URBANIZATION AND COMMUNITY

13.1 Urbanization and Industrialization

In 1801, about 17 per cent of the population of Britain lived in towns, by 1851 it had increased to 50 per cent, and 100 years later, in 1951, it reached its peak of 81 per cent. Since about 1960, however, there has been a change with people moving out of the big cities, and about 78 per cent of the population now live in large towns and cities.

1 The process whereby people move into cities from the countryside is known as **urbanization**. Urbanization occurred at its most rapid pace in Britain in the nineteenth century.

2 The process whereby people move out of the towns and cities to live is known as **de-urbanization**. This is happening now in Britain.

Urbanization

There is a very close link between the processes of urbanization and de-urbanization and industrialization.

1 The changes in agriculture, which included:

(a) the **enclosure movement**, in which the peasants were driven off the land;

(b) the introduction of new agricultural machinery which meant that far fewer workers were needed in agriculture.

2 Industrialization itself, which:

(a) switched manufacture away from isolated communities, to towns;

(b) introduced production by machine on a large scale, which meant that a large number of workers were needed in the factories.

3 The conditions of the workers in the towns were dreadful. Housing was of extremely poor quality. Houses were built in terraces, often also back to back.

4 The existence of large centres of population attracted traders and so shops developed on a large scale.

5 The growth in complexity of industry meant that administrative services were needed and this led to the development of offices, separate from factories.

6 As the towns developed, various areas became dominated by different social classes. The better areas of the town were taken by the middle class and the rich, while the workers lived next to the factories.

De-urbanization

During the twentieth century, changes have taken place that led to a gradual withdrawal of people from the cities. This became a 'flight from the cities' from the 1970s onwards.

1 The development of means of transport meant that people did not have to live next door to their workplace. At first it was mainly public transport and then later came the development and increasing ownership of private cars.

2 The result of the development of transport was that the middle class moved out to suburbs, or to 'commuter' towns near to the city, and would travel in to work. This development first took place in the 1930s.

3 This linked with the growth of large-scale housing schemes, both private (such as Stevenage in Hertfordshire) and public (such as West Derby in Liverpool).

4 Gradually the new developments and the transport links connected the large cities with surrounding towns. This led to a process of **metropolitanization**, in which large cities swallowed up smaller towns around them.

5 Local authorities in the 1950s engaged in massive redevelopments of the slum areas of the inner cities and moved much of the population out into large council estates, (for example Dagenham in London). In the 1960s, instead of large estates, people were moved to 'New Towns', such as Basildon in Essex.

6 Industry began to move out of the cities:

(a) rates were lower and so was the price of land;

(b) better communications, such as motorways and fast rail links, meant that the products could be quickly transported to the centres of population;

(c) this caused more people to move out of towns and cities.

7 The inner city districts have become problem areas, as the working class community has disappeared.

13.2 Community and Association

Sociologists have been interested in the way that the move from a rural-based society to an urban-based one has altered the way that people act towards each other.

The idea that the move from living in a rural situation to living in urban areas has influenced the nature of social life has been most thoroughly explored by (a) Tonnies and (b) Durkheim, both of whom were writing about one hundred years ago when the process of urbanization had just completed its most rapid phase.

Tonnies distinguished between two types of society, **Gemeinschaft** (community) and **Gesellschaft** (association). Sociologists use either the English or German words. Durkheim agreed with this distinction, using the terms **mechanical** (in Tonnies' terms **community**) and **organic** (in Tonnies' terms **association**).

What both writers were pointing out was that there are two fundamentally different ways in which people can organize their social life. One way stresses close, personal ties between people, the other, impersonal, formal relationships. They argue that these different forms of social networks are directly related to rural and urban society.

1 Community (mechanical society – found in rural areas)

(a) Relationships are very close between people and are based on personal acquaintance between them. This form of relationship is known as a **primary relationship**.

(b) People living in rural areas feel that they have interests in common and are united by these feelings.

(c) In rural society the social network is composed of fewer people, who are close-knit.

(d) People tend to play many different roles (e.g. father, shopkeeper, parish councillor, etc.).

(e) These roles sometimes come into conflict with each other, e.g. as a parish councillor advising on parking restrictions and as a shopkeeper who wants cars to be able to park outside his/her shop.

(f) A simple economy, usually based on agriculture.

(g) Little division of labour; workers cover a whole range of tasks, e.g. farm labourers.

(h) Mechanical society – most people are very alike in attitudes and behaviour.

(i) Ascribed status – the status of parents influences how people treat you.

(j) Locals – rural society is dominated by people who were born and bred there and reflect certain local values.

2 Association (organic society – found in urban areas)

(a) Relationships are generally impersonal and rather formal. It is rare that people are personally acquainted. Relationships tend to be rather shallow and transient. This form of social relationship is known as **secondary**.

(b) People living in urban areas feel little in common.

(c) The social network is large and dispersed. So urban dwellers meet many different people in daily life.

(d) People play fewer **multiple roles**, that is they generally play one role to one group of people, e.g. shopkeeper to his/her customers, but drinking companion in the pub with a different group of people.

(e) There is little role conflict because of point (d).

(f) The economy is complex, based on commerce, industry and personal services.

(g) Complex division of labour, with most people engaged in a specific task in a wide range of occupations.

(h) Organic society, with a great variety of types of people held together by mutual need.

(i) Achieved status – you are treated according to your personal merits, heavily influenced by your occupation and income.

(j) Cosmopolitans—the place is dominated by people who only stay for a short time and who have little commitment to that specific town.

Reasons for differences

Another sociologist, Wirth, has suggested three major differences between rural and urban societies which help to explain the differences between the community life in these areas.

Size

Towns and cities cover a large geographical area, unlike villages. This has many consequences, including the need for public transport and wide roads and the division of the town into areas often divided along class or race lines. Also the sheer size of the population prevents people from knowing each other.

Density of population

Towns have far more people per hectare than do rural areas. This concentration of people causes problems such as housing shortages and heavy traffic, as well as pollution. It also causes traders to provide many services, so there are shops, pubs, restaurants, etc.

Social heterogeneity

This means that people from many different backgrounds, divided for instance by race, class, and education, all live together. This creates tensions in some cases as the groups may be antagonistic to each other. It also accounts for the **cosmopolitan** nature of social life in cities, that is the exhilarating mixture of ideas and people that makes cities so lively.

Community in the city: association in the village

The idea that rural and urban life are so very different from each other has been strongly criticized by a number of sociologists. Studies of city and village life have not shown there to be such clear-cut differences between the social relationships.

Research

1 Pahl in *Patterns of Urban Life* studied Swansea and found that it was in fact divided into quite clear **neighbourhoods**. These formed separate communities, each having an individual identity in which the people exhibited a pattern of social relationships very similar to Tonnies' **community**—which it has been claimed could only be found in rural areas. Pahl explains that communities exist in Swansea because it grew in the nineteenth century as a tinplating town, attracting people from the surrounding rural areas to live and work. These new arrivals settled in specific neighbourhoods in the town depending upon their origins and associated themselves with that neighbourhood. The following generations retained these individual communities.

2 Young and Wilmott in *Family and Kinship in East London* conducted an in-depth study of East London in the early 1950s. They found a strong community in the city with strong family ties and a sense of identity grounded in the locality and the web of social relationships. When the area was redeveloped and many families were moved to new housing estates, it took a number of years for a new sense of community to develop among those rehoused.

3 In another study (*Urbs in Rure*) Pahl studied 'commuter villages' in Hertfordshire on the fringe of the London commuting area. He found that village life was not as described in the idea of 'community'. There were deep divisions among those who lived in villages. So the description of village life painted by researchers such as Tonnies was incorrect.

4 Raymond Williams in *The Country and the City* took an historical perspective and found that life in the medieval village, so often painted as idyllic, was just the opposite. The peasantry shared one important condition—they were exploited and oppressed by the landlords. He describes their situation as the *mutuality of the oppressed*.

Conclusion

The point to draw from these studies is that it is not the *place* in which a group of people live that necessarily determines their relationships, but other things such as **social class**, **affluence** and **ethnicity**, for example.

13.3 Housing Zones

In the 1920s and 1930s sociologists of the University of Chicago studied the housing and social patterns of the city. The results of the studies of Shaw and McKay suggested that levels of crime and of social problems in general were different in various parts of the city. They also noticed that people of similar social class and racial backgrounds settled in the same area of the city.

As a result of these observations, Burgess developed a theory (based on Chicago) that there were five **concentric zones** (that is zones in the shape of rings) in cities, as illustrated in Figure 13.1.

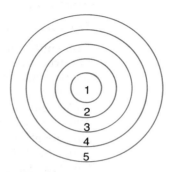

Figure 13.1 The concentric zone model

Zone 1 is the inner business district with the shops, civic buildings and commercial enterprises.

Zone 2 is the older residential area of large, once imposing houses. These were originally owned by affluent tradesmen, but they had long since moved away. The houses had fallen into disrepair, were divided and rented out to poorer people: in particular newly arrived immigrants, and those with irregular sources of income.

Zone 3 has a stable population of respectable working class people, with a sense of community.

Zone 4 is lived in by the middle class and is the typical suburban area.

Zone 5 is the wealthy district in which the rich live in expensive houses with large gardens.

These zones were called **natural areas** by Chicago sociologists as they were not deliberately created, but arose from the social patterns of migration.

Burgess's explanation, based upon the history of Chicago, for the pattern of concentric zones forming natural areas, was in terms of the waves of immigration that occur in cities as they grow. He argued that initially the rich people lived in exclusive areas in the inner cities, and the poorer groups lived further out. Gradually the richer people moved further out, leaving the inner city properties empty. The houses here were too expensive for the lower class groups to maintain, and they were prepared to let out rooms within the houses. When new poor immigrants moved into the city they rented properties in this increasingly run-down area. The more successful immigrants eventually moved out, and as they did so the next wave of immigrants arrived to take lodgings in the inner city areas. The history of the city was one of wave after wave of immigration with the few successful immigrants moving out. As all this took place in zone 2 it was called the **zone of transition**.

The constant changing of the population in the zone of transition and the poverty of the people led to numerous social problems such as delinquency, mental illness, prostitution and alcoholism. In Britain research has indicated that inner city areas do indeed have many more social problems than outer areas.

Research
Rex and Moore (*Race, Community and Conflict*) studied **Sparkbrook**, an inner city area of Birmingham. They found that the description of the zone of transition was appropriate. The area consisted of large dilapidated houses which were divided into rented accommodation. As this was one of the few areas in Birmingham in which immigrants could find and afford lodgings, it had a very high proportion of black and Irish families. These co-existed uneasily together and with the poorer local families who were unable to move out. They found that conflict over housing was one of the main reasons for different groups coming into conflict with each other and this prevented integration.

Criticism of this **concentric zone** pattern of city development has been on the grounds that it is true only for certain cities. In Britain a number of other factors have influenced the way that zones have developed.

1 Council overspill estates have been built at a considerable distance from the city centre; these are inhabited by working class people.

2 In recent years middle class people have been moving back into certain areas in the centre of big cities; for example, middle class people are now moving into the London dockland region. This is the opposite of the trends described by the Chicago sociologists. It is called **gentrification**.

13.4 Patterns of Life

Earlier we saw that one of the characteristics of the city is **social heterogeneity**, which means that there is a considerable number of different styles of life and groups within cities.

To illustrate this we can look at the different styles of life to be found in

1 the inner city, **2** the suburbs.

1 THE INNER CITY

(a) The diversity of the inner cities

The inner city areas have undergone major changes as the population has moved out to suburbs, overspill estates and new towns. Inner cities now have a wide variety of groups living there, replacing the traditional working class. Gans has suggested that the following groups can be found in the inner city areas:

(i) Bohemians – students and ex-students clinging to the student way of life. These move into the inner city area for the low rents and the nearness to the cultural life;

(ii) The ethnic minorities: these move here in the first place because it is the only area where they can find accommodation and because it is near to the available employment;

(iii) The deprived and the poor: usually these are people who are unable to work and have nowhere to go. They include the physically and mentally ill, tramps, the long-term unemployed;

(iv) The trapped: these are people who came before the decline in the inner city, but because of investments in a house or shop, or local loyalty, or because they have no alternative, remain in the inner city. These are the elderly and the poor generally.

(b) Problems of the inner cities

It can be seen, then, that to talk about the inner cities as if they contained one population would be wrong. However, the inner cities do have considerably greater problems than the rest of Britain.

A sociological study of the inner cities reported that they had:

(i) 7 per cent of the population, but 14 per cent of the unskilled workers;

(ii) 20 per cent of households with serious problems;

(iii) considerable racial tension;

(iv) at least twice the national rate of unemployment;

(v) up to 10 times the proportion of people living at below the supplementary benefit line;

(vi) four times the average number of overcrowded households;

(vii) twice the national average of one-parent families;

(viii) half the national rate of car ownership.

It should also be added that the inner city crime rate is the highest of any area in the country.

(c) The inner city riots

In 1981 and 1985 there were serious disturbances in inner city areas in Bristol, London, Manchester, and Liverpool.

The reasons why the riots exploded in each specific case were different. For instance, in Southall, London, in 1981 it was a battle between white skinheads and Asians who were defending their area, as they saw it, from racist attacks by the skinheads. In 1985 in Brixton it was young West Indians (and some Whites) who felt they were being pressured too greatly by the police. However, there are certain underlying causes that create the conditions and tensions leading to rioting:

(i) The extent of inner city deprivation;

(ii) The high rates of unemployment;

(iii) Racism;

(iv) Different policing tactics in the inner city areas.

All of these cause a feeling of hopelessness, a belief in the strength of racism and a sense of bitterness among the ethnic minorities in the inner city areas.

Research

Phil Cohen studied the changes that had taken place in East London during the 1960s. He found that the traditional working class East London community had been held together by:

1 The extended family structure: this has been fully described by Young and Willmott, and was the traditional working class extended family, which was based on the mother who kept all the members in regular contact with each other.

2 The density of population: a large number of people lived in the relatively small area of East London, in small terraced houses. People were thrown very much together. Because of the number of people to each house, much of the social life was outdoors in the streets.

3 All the jobs were local: most men worked on the docks and so homes and jobs were close to each other.

In the 1950s and '60s changes took place that effectively dismantled the local community. Most important of all was the rehousing of large numbers of people in the new towns and in overspill estates. The density of population declined and the extended family was broken up.

The second important change was the decline in the London docks so that men had to go elsewhere for work.

Thirdly, redevelopment drove out the traditional local traders and craftsmen who could no longer afford the high rents.

The result was the breakdown of the traditional working class East London community. As people were rehoused out of East London, there was an influx of Asian immigrants who now form a large part of the population of that area.

2 THE SUBURBS

The suburbs developed with the growth of transport in the early part of this century. They tend to be more affluent in character than the inner city areas, with more middle class people.

Life in the suburbs is less centred on the family, or the locality, but more on specific interests. People are friendly through activity at the local primary school parent/teacher association or the golf club. It appears that people are more likely to be measured on their possessions than their personalities. There is very little employment locally and so people who live in suburbs tend to commute to work.

In the last 20 years there has been a significant growth in home ownership among all groups of the population, so that the stereotype of the suburb as being necessarily middle class is now out of date. Affluence among the working class and a decline in rented property means that it is now normal for working class couples to move to the suburbs in search of housing.

Research

Willmott and Young (*Family and Class in a London Suburb*) studied life in the London suburb of Woodford. They found that family life was much looser than the close-knit kinship network they had found in their earlier study of the working class inner London area of Bethnal Green. Suburban people were 'on the whole friendly, neighbourly and helpful to each other. They attend clubs and churches together, they entertain friends and neighbours in their homes, they like (or at any rate prefer to like) their fellow-residents'. They suggest that middle class people have greater skill than working class people at **making friends**, as long as people conform to the middle class standards.

13.5 Summary

1 Urbanization is the process by which towns develop and the bulk of the population of a country come to live in the city.

2 De-urbanization describes the move away from living in cities. People move to small towns, distant suburbs and the countryside.

3 The process of urbanization began in the early nineteenth century and reached its peak in the 1950s, since when Britain has been de-urbanizing.

4 Urbanization and industrialization are closely linked. It was industrialization and the growth of factories that created towns and cities as we know them now in Britain.

5 There has been a distinction made between the form of life in rural areas and the form of life in urban areas. This distinction has often been described as *Gemeinschaft* (community) and *Gesellschaft* (association).

6 The main differences between *Gemeinschaft* (rural) and *Gesellschaft* (urban) forms of community life lie in the close personal ties to be found in the rural areas. In the city life is far more impersonal.

7 The differences have been put down to size, density of population and cultural mix of people.

8 There has been strong criticism of the idea that a place can influence the social relationships of people. Research has shown that there are close communities in the cities and there are major divisions in the villages and rural areas.

9 Cities have been divided into zones which have clear-cut social characteristics. In some of these areas, particularly in the zone of transition in the inner city, there are much higher crime rates.

10 The inner areas of the cities are suffering from a considerable number of problems, such as overcrowding, poverty, high crime rates and unemployment.

11 The new towns and overspill estates that were built in the 1950s have not fully re-created the traditional working class communities of the inner cities.

12 Increasingly, there has been a move out of the inner cities to the countryside. This has been mainly due to the growth in transport links – such as fast trains and motorways – and the move out of inner city areas of new employment opportunities. House prices, too, are lower out of the cities.

13.6 Keywords (*as they appear in the unit*)

urbanization, de-urbanization, industrialization, metropolitanization, community and association, *Gesellschaft* and *Gemeinschaft*, urban and rural, mechanical and organic society, housing zones, zone of transition, gentrification, inner cities, overspill estates, new towns, suburbs.

14 POVERTY

14.1 Defining Poverty

Any researcher trying to find out the extent and causes of poverty in Britain must first have a definition of it. At what point does a person become **poor**? Can we make a clear division between poor and **more affluent** people?

Definitions of poverty fall into two types: **1** absolute; **2** relative.

14.2 Absolute Poverty

One of the founders of sociological research into poverty was Seebohm Rowntree, who studied poverty in York in three different pieces of research published in 1899, 1936 and 1950. Rowntree believed that he could define a **poverty line** below which people were clearly in poverty, and above which they escaped from poverty. The line was drawn at the level of '**the minimum of provision needed to maintain health and working efficiency**'. Rowntree's initial aim was to shock people into awareness of the huge extent of poverty in Britain. In order to achieve this, he had to select an unambiguous poverty line which everybody would agree represented a true minimum level of existence.

Rowntree argued that there were three elements to a person's essential expenditure: (a) food, (b) clothing, (c) housing.

By finding the minimum possible costs of these three and adding them together, Rowntree believed he could construct the poverty line.

1 *Food* He asked a panel of doctors to work out a basic diet that would just keep a person healthy;

2 *Clothing* He calculated the minimum necessary clothing that a person needed to be reasonably warm and dry;

3 *Housing* Rowntree took the average rents paid by working class people for their housing. People had to pay the rents asked by landlords, so the average represented the minimum.

Rowntree then added the total amount needed and defined this as the poverty line.

Rowntree's definition has been influential and was actually used by the Beveridge Committee who created the basis of our present social security system:

There are criticisms of this **absolute** definition of poverty, however:

(a) How can the poor be expected to know what the best diet is?

(b) Rowntree assumed that they would always buy at the lowest possible prices, yet the lowest prices are usually obtained when buying in bulk, or at least the largest size packets and jars. Poor people cannot afford at any one time to pay out for the largest size containers. The poor therefore end up paying the highest prices.

(c) Rowntree did not allow for any **luxuries**, e.g. cigarettes or alcohol, however. It is unreasonable to exclude any spending on leisure or minor luxury items. (In the 1950 study he did allow a tiny amount for luxuries.)

(d) It is not possible to fix a line of poverty since what is considered to be poverty varies with time and society. This is the criticism that has led to the **relative** definition of poverty.

14.3 Relative Poverty

This definition of poverty is based on the argument that you cannot isolate what is considered as poverty (or wealth) from the expectations and general living standards of a society.

Expectations change over time in a particular society, and also vary from one society to another. For example, in the early 1950s in Britain those who could afford black-and-white televisions were regarded as affluent; by the 1970s those who could only afford a black-and-white television and not a colour one would be seen as poor. Today, it is seen as a sign of affluence to have a video recorder; in ten years it will probably be regarded as normal to have one of these. So spending patterns and expectations are always changing. The easiest example is that of clothes: according to Rowntree if the clothes keep you warm and dry then they are adequate. But what about fashion changes in clothing styles? Obviously taste and fashion are often as important as keeping warm and dry, particularly in modern Western society.

The person who has put forward this view of relative poverty is Peter Townsend, who argues that people are poor when they have inadequate means to 'obtain the types of diets, participate in the activities, and have living conditions and amenities which are customary, or at least widely encouraged and approved, in the societies to which they belong'.

When it comes to actually creating some **measure** of relative poverty, three different methods have been put forward:

1 supplementary benefits + 40 per cent; 2 relative income; 3 index of deprivation.

1 *Supplementary benefits + 40 per cent* This measurement was first proposed by Abel-Smith and Townsend in 1965. It is based on the supplementary benefit payments plus an additional 40 per cent. The additional 40 per cent was added because people are allowed to earn a small amount above their supplementary benefits level and many need to receive additional state aid on top of their supplementary benefit payments.

The reason that this is a good measure of poverty is that it is the lowest level of income a government considers adequate for a person to avoid destitution. It is relative because the Government regularly reviews social security rates and adjusts them roughly in line with the general standard of living. (Although it is always well below the average income.)

Criticism A government that increases social security payments would actually increase the numbers of those living in poverty according to this definition! This is because it would include many lowly paid people in employment whose wages would fall under the level of social security payments + 40 per cent. In fact governments have never shown any inclination to raise supplementary benefit levels above the minimum possible.

2 *Relative income* An alternative definition of poverty is to take a certain proportion of the average wage and to say that anybody below that figure is poor. Researchers have used 50 per cent and 80 per cent average incomes. This effectively links poverty in a clear way to average income and expenditure, and the income level of poverty line can be adjusted with the annual changes in average earnings.

Criticisms (a) Townsend argues that the figure of 50 per cent or 80 per cent is arbitrary and simply depends upon the viewpoint of the research – why not 60 per cent or 30 per cent? (b) Townsend also points out that some people who have similar incomes have different **resources**. One couple may get 80 per cent of the average income but may own their house, have a helpful family, etc., while another couple may have the same income but fewer resources. Are they really in the same category?

3 *Index of deprivation* This measure of poverty originates from the criticism just made. It is not just income that creates a person's life style but a whole range of resources. For instance, people also have extra assets (such as owning homes), or different work conditions (such as longer/shorter paid holidays) or different levels of social services available (cheap bus fares, local government crèche facilities, good doctor's services, etc.) or income in kind (vegetables from an allotment, gifts and help from friends and family). The point is that we can only measure the extent of a person's poverty if we know what he or she is **deprived of**. Income is the most important, but not the only, guide to this.

14.4 The Significance of Definitions of Poverty

The variety of definitions of poverty given here is at first rather confusing and possibly appears to be pointless.

1 Different definitions, however, give substantially different estimates of the numbers living in poverty. For instance, an **absolute** definition would suggest that there are very few people in poverty in Britain. Any of the **relative** ones would put the estimate at a minimum of 5 million people in poverty.

2 Different definitions draw the line of poverty so that whole groups of people are placed in or out of poverty depending on the definition. For example, if the definition of poverty is everybody with an income below that of social security payments, then all those in receipt of social security are out of poverty; raise the definition to 140 per cent of social security and millions of people immediately become 'poor'.

3 The different definitions will then have important implications for Government policy. If the definition suggests that large numbers of people are in poverty, then clearly the Government needs to act, for instance, by raising social security benefits.

14.5 The Poverty Line

All the definitions discussed so far have aimed at producing a line of poverty that can distinguish the poor from the rest of the population. However, we must be cautious in stating that these are poor people who are somehow distinct from the rest of the population. It is more accurate to say that at certain periods in their lives (such as in the periods of dependent children and old age) and under certain conditions (such as illness, temporary unemployment) people may decline into poverty. At other periods they may move out of poverty. So we should see people moving in and out of poverty, rather than a clear group of poor people.

14.6 Research on Poverty: A Summary

1899, 1936 and 1950 Seebohm Rowntree studied York (*Poverty: A Study of Town Life*). In 1899, he found that 20 032 people, about half of the working class population, lived in poverty. The main causes of poverty were low wages, large families and unemployment. He later carried out two more surveys in 1936 and 1950 in which he found a considerable decline in poverty, measured in absolute terms.

After the creation of the Welfare State in 1948, and the period of affluence in the 1950s, it was commonly believed that poverty had disappeared. However, a series of Government reports in the early 1960s on London housing (*Milner-Holland Report*), primary school education (*Plowden Report*) and the personal social services all pointed out that there were still great problems.

1965 Abel-Smith and Townsend (*The Poor and the Poorest*) wrote the most influential book since Rowntree's much earlier studies. They found that if a relative definition of poverty was used, that is 140 per cent of supplementary benefit, then the numbers of people living in poverty had actually increased in the 1950s. Their research method was to re-analyse information collected by the Ministry of Labour (now the Department of Employment) in two surveys – one in 1953/4 of 13 000 households and one in 1960 of 3500 households. Their conclusion was that in 1953 10 per cent of the population earned just above the supplementary benefit level (then called National Assistance level) and by 1960 this had increased to 18 per cent.

1970 Coats and Silburn (*Poverty: The Forgotten Englishman*) studied the St Anne's area of Nottingham. This was an inner city slum district which was then being redeveloped. They compared life here to that in a council estate, known locally as 'The Island'. They found a high degree of deprivation and despair among the poor of St Anne's. When they returned to St Anne's in 1976 to re-study the area, they found it completely changed, with new housing and tower blocks. Much of the original sample had moved from the area. However, they still found poverty and deprivation at a similar level as in their earlier study.

1979 Townsend (*Poverty in the United Kingdom*). Although this book was published in 1979, most of the research was undertaken 10 years earlier. The complexity of the statistics led to this massive delay. Townsend constructed an **index of deprivation** (see p 111), which measured the amount or lack of resources his respondents had. The respondents completed a questionnaire by ticking the resources they had. For instance, had they had at least one cooked meal in the last two days? Did they have adequate footwear for both wet and fine weather? As a result Townsend suggested that as many as 12½ million were truly deprived of what would be regarded as normal amenities.

1983 Mack and Lansley (*Poor Britain*) This was a national poll of the whole country which asked people what they regarded as necessities in modern Britain. From the results of this survey the researchers made a list of what are regarded as basic necessities. They then went out and asked people if they had these necessities. Those who did not have three of the basic necessities were regarded as poor. Necessities included such things as: heating, indoor toilet, damp-free home, bath, beds for all members of the family, warm waterproof coat, three meals a day for children. In all there were 26 necessities.

Some conclusions of the study were that:
Three million people cannot afford to heat the living areas of their homes; six million go without an essential item of clothing – such as a warm coat – because of lack of money; 1½ million children go without toys or leisure equipment of some kind because of lack of money; 3 million people cannot afford celebrations at Christmas or presents for the family once a year; at least 5½ million people cannot afford meat or fish every other day, a roast joint once a week, or two hot meals a day.

14.7 The Extent of Poverty

Clearly the extent of poverty is related to the definition of it.

1 Taking the supplementary benefit level as the lowest income level to which the Government will allow people to fall, in 1986, there were 11.7 million people estimated to be in poverty (by the House of Commons statistical division). This includes almost 3 million people with incomes below the supplementary benefit level (which ought to be impossible).

This has increased from 8.8 million in 1983.

2 Taking the estimates based on lack of necessities used in the *Poor Britain* survey by Mack and Lansley, the figures of people living in poverty are 5 million adults, 2.5 million children, which is a total of one in seven of the population.

14.8 Who are the Poor?

According to Mack and Lansley, the following groups comprise the poor:

(a) the low paid;

(b) the unemployed;

(c) the elderly;

(d) the sick and disabled;

(e) single parents.

They also found that there was far more poverty in the North of Britain.

(a) **The low paid** Of all families in poverty, 40 per cent have a head of household in full-time employment. This affects about 2.75 million people;

The lowest-paid section of the workforce has not improved its income relative to the national average since the beginning of the century. The bottom 10 per cent of male earners receive little more than 60 per cent of average pay;

In 1983, 680 000 workers in full-time employment earned less than the supplementary benefit levels.

This certainly disproves the idea that the poor are lazy.

(b) **The unemployed** About 33 per cent of those in poverty are unemployed. According to Mack and Lansley, there are about 2½ million people in poverty as a result of unemployment.

There are at present (1992) about 2½ million people unemployed.

In 1983, 65 per cent of all families with one or more members unemployed had an income level below supplementary benefit level + 40 per cent.

(c) **The elderly** One of the most important demographic changes in this century has been the increase in the numbers of the elderly. There are now about 10 million people of pensionable age, an increase of 30 per cent compared to 1951.

The problems of low income for retired couples is made worse by the fact that in staying at home all day, they have higher household bills for heating and lighting.

The estimates for the numbers of the elderly living in poverty vary considerably. Mack and Lansley argue that the figure is 1.5 million, accounting for about 20 per cent of the poor.

(d) **The sick and disabled** Of the poor, 30 per cent (or about 1.5 million people) are sick or disabled. Most disabled people are poor because they are unable to work, or to find suitable employment. If they do find work, it is very often low paid.

(e) **Single-parent families** These are usually headed by a woman, as a result of illegitimate births or divorce. Today, one-parent families constitute 12 per cent of all households, and are increasing significantly in number each year. Mack and Lansley have suggested that about 20 per cent of children in poverty are from one-parent families.

Over half of families with only one parent are in poverty.

Northern poverty

Poverty is far more often found among the large cities of the North than in the South; 40 per cent of the poor live in the conurbations (such as Merseyside) of the North of Britain.

14.9 Causes of Poverty

The following explanations have been put forward for the continuing existence of poverty:

1 the cycle of deprivation   2 the culture of poverty
3 functions provided by the poor   4 the structure of society

Before we examine the different explanations for poverty we ought to discuss one myth, that the poor are in that condition because they are lazy or workshy. From the information we have examined so far on the groups in poverty, we have seen that old people and those in full-time employment receiving a low wage are the two biggest groups living in poverty. In no way can these be labelled lazy.

1 THE CYCLE OF DEPRIVATION

This approach was put forward by Sir Keith Joseph when Secretary of State for Social Services; he argued that poor families with backgrounds of social problems tend to intermarry and reproduce the cycle of deprivation all over again. They bring up their children in an inadequate manner failing to give them the opportunities most children have. These people are unable or unwilling to find work and therefore have a low income.

Research

Rutter and Madge (*Cycle of Disadvantage*) studied a group of families with multiple problems who would be typical of the type of families to fall into the cycle of deprivation. They found that the cycle of deprivation really did occur when at least three of the following were present: (a) intellectual backwardness (b) family instability (c) poorly educated children (d) inadequate, poorly kept home (e) large family.

Criticism

Criticism of this view has come from Jordan (*Poor Parents*), who argues that there are just as many problems among middle class families, such as divorce, suicide and alcoholism. Thus problems are not the cause of poverty, although poverty may in its turn cause or exacerbate problems that poorer families have. The problems that they have are a response to the sort of society in which they live, which gives them little chance of success in life.

2 THE CULTURE OF POVERTY

This explanation was first suggested by Oscar Lewis (*Children of Sanchez*) who argued that certain groups who live in abject poverty develop their own set of values (a **subculture**) which allows them to cope with their poverty. However, the result of this subculture is to keep them in poverty. For instance, poor people believe that it is best to accept life as it is and to have some fun now, not worrying about the future. This is a reasonable response to the insecurity and uncertainty of the life of the poor. However, the result is that it prevents the poor from trying to break out of their poverty. Their values trap them. Lewis says 'By the time slum children are aged six or seven they have usually absorbed the basic values . . . and are not psychologically geared to take full advantage of . . . opportunities which may occur in their lifetime.' This explanation and the cycle of deprivation explanation led the Government to introduce **Community Development Projects** (see p 116).

Criticism

Charles Valentine has pointed out that this explanation does not give the reasons *why* the poor are in poverty in the first place. It explains cultural adaptation to poverty, not the cause of poverty.

3 FUNCTIONS PROVIDED BY THE POOR

Gans (*More Equality*) argues that the poor are in that state because it benefits the more affluent members of society to keep them like that. The poor do not have enough power to challenge their treatment. Among the functions performed by the poor for the rich are:

(a) the poor provide cheap services for the affluent, e.g. as waitresses, shop assistants, etc.;

(b) the poor provide work for incompetent professionals whom the affluent do not want e.g. the worst doctors and dentists.

Differences in power

In essence this argument is really saying that the poor do not have the **power** that the rich have and so they will remain poor. The only way out would be politically to challenge the advantage of the better off, possibly through strong unions.

4 THE STRUCTURE OF SOCIETY

This approach, which is taken by Marxist sociologists among others, stresses the fact that the very nature of our society leads to poverty for certain groups. **Westergaard**, for instance, argues that our society is based upon the creation of profit by industry and in order to do this it pays people the lowest amount it can. Employers can do this because they are more powerful than workers. In response workers form trade unions and thus we have industrial conflict.

However, people in strong trade unions usually have adequate wages. The poorest groups are working-class people who are unable or unwilling to join unions. Thus, workers in the service industries which by their nature split up workers into small groups (e.g. shops or restaurants) find unionization difficult and have low wage rates. There is no way to change this, as our society is actually based on a few people making a profit out of the rest of the people and this will always lead to poverty. According to Marxists, unemployment is inevitable in capitalist society as this provides employers with a pool of cheap labour.

They argue that the existence of the poor is very helpful to employers, for if those in employment demand higher wages, then the employers can threaten to replace the employed by the unemployed. According to Marxists, society is really a battle ground between those who work and those who employ. The wealth of the rich depends upon taking the maximum from the workers.

14.10 Policy Implications of the Different Explanations of Poverty

1 *The cycle of deprivation* suggests that a determined effort must be made by the Government to place greater resources in the hands of social workers and local authorities in order to help the children to break out of the trap they are in. Most important here would be the role of a social worker. The Government did try CDPs (see p 116).

2 *The culture of poverty* The main thrust of policy here would be to put greater effort into the education of the children. The Government tried Educational Priority Areas, with limited success. The idea was to compensate the children for the values and ideas they took from their home.

3 *Functions provided by the poor* Here the policy implications would be to get workers to organize themselves into trade unions in order to get more power and therefore higher wages.

4 *The structure of society* The policy implication of Marxism is a revolution! Only in a society where everybody owned the factories and offices would there be a lack of exploitation of the workers and an end to poverty.

14.11 Living in Poverty: The Poverty Trap

People who are poor not only suffer from a small income, but often face other problems as well.

1 There are fewer doctors' surgeries in the poorer inner city areas, so that medical help may be harder to find.

2 The poor are less likely to seek help from doctors, and studies indicate that the health service is proportionately more used by the middle class.

3 The children of the poor do less well at school. They are less likely therefore to get jobs and to escape from poverty.

4 They are less likely to know their rights to state benefits. Field points out that there are over 500 000 unemployed people (and therefore their families) who are eligible for supplementary benefit but who are not claiming it.

5 Standards of living in the deprived inner city areas are lower than the suburbs. The poor in these areas are likely to have worse housing conditions, lack of community facilities, higher crime rates, and to suffer from pollution of the environment.

6 Increasingly the supermarkets are moving out to the suburbs and to out-of-town locations. A car is needed to reach them. The poor are therefore forced to shop locally at the smaller and more expensive shops. In those shops, they cannot afford to buy the larger-sized economy packs and therefore have to pay proportionately more for the small packs and jars.

14.12 The Welfare State and Poverty – the Role of Government

WELFARE PROVISIONS

The Government has undertaken a series of measures to try to eliminate poverty in Britain. First among these are the major provisions incorporated into the **Welfare State**.

1 free education   **2** free health service
3 unemployment benefit and supplementary benefit   **4** pensions
5 FIS (Family Income Supplement)   **6** allowances   **7** housing benefits

1 Education

The British State education system is free up to the age of 18. The aim is to allow any child to benefit from education irrespective of the home background. After the 1967 *Plowden Report*, which showed that deprived home backgrounds influenced educational achievement, the

Government introduced **Educational Priority Areas**, which were areas of inner cities with particularly bad social problems. Schools in these areas received additional resources to compensate for home deprivation. This is also known as compensatory education.

2 Free health services

The National Health Service was created in 1948 to give free health care. The principle has been eroded since then, particularly with the continuing increase in prescription charges. In recent years there has been a considerable growth in the private sector, so that many argue there is now a two-tier system of health care.

3 Benefit

(a) *Unemployment benefit*, which is paid to those who have been working, but have lost their job. It is paid for one year and then the person switches to:

(b) *Supplementary benefit*, which is a payment calculated on the difference between a person's lost income and his/her requirements as laid down in a scale the DHSS considers is the correct amount of money for those requirements.

4 Pensions

Retirement pensions are paid to women over 60 and men over 65. These were introduced as long ago as 1908 in one form.

5 Family credit

If a person's wage is below a minimum figure set by the Government he or she can claim an allowance.

6 Allowances

There are a number of these, but the main ones are:

(a) *Child benefit,* which is paid for each child in the family.

(b) *Sickness benefit/invalidity benefit*, which is payment for those incapable of working as a result of illness.

7 Housing benefits

Those with low incomes can obtain rate/rent rebates from their local authorities.

There are a number of criticisms of these measures:

(a) The rates of payment are inadequate; one million claimants need extra payments because the supplementary benefit is inadequate. In 1977 even the Chairman of the Supplementary Benefits Commission criticized the rates as being too low.

(b) Benefits are difficult to obtain. This occurs through lack of publicity and the complexity of claims procedures: in 1980 there were 118 different social security leaflets.

(c) There is a stigma attached to claiming benefits so people often prefer not to claim. Every year £500 million of Supplementary Benefit remains unclaimed. The take-up rate for Supplementary Benefit is 74 per cent. An estimated 760 000 retirement pensioners fail to claim Supplementary Benefit.

(d) The poverty trap – because most payments are only given up to a certain level of earnings and because these benefits are not closely related to taxation, people can be in the position of actually taking home less money when they increase their earnings.

In 1988, major changes in welfare benefits come into operation.

Taxation

The introduction of **progressive taxation** (the more you earn the greater your payment) should have eliminated gross inequalities. However, it has failed to do so. The method of measuring is complex, but Kincaid has argued that the lower income groups pay a higher proportion of their income in various forms of taxation than do the more affluent.

Community development projects (CDPs)

Influenced by the explanations of poverty based upon the cycle of deprivation and culture of poverty approaches, the Government introduced 12 Community Development Projects in 1969. These were projects in which small teams of social workers entered particularly deprived inner city areas and attempted to organize the local people into combating their own problems. By the mid-1970s the projects had folded with little achieved. In the 1980s, the central government and local authorities have cooperated in 'INNER CITY PARTNERSHIPS', to renew housing in the inner city and to try to redevelop a sense of community.

14.13 Summary

1 There are basically two competing definitions of poverty: (a) an absolute definition based on the minimum amount needed to keep someone clothed, fed and housed; and (b) a relative one based on the idea that poverty varies with the normal expectations of society.

2 Most modern studies are based on the relative definition.

3 It is not true to say that the poor consist only of one separate group of people in poverty the whole of their lives. Many people move in and out of poverty at different periods of their lives. Poverty is therefore a very dynamic, changing thing.

4 There is a minimum of 7½ million people in poverty.

5 The groups in poverty are the low paid, the unemployed, the elderly, the single-parent families, the sick and disabled.

6 There is greater poverty in the North than the South of Britain.

7 The reasons that have been suggested for the existence of poverty are:

(a) the cycle of deprivation; (b) the culture of poverty; (c) lack of power; and (d) the very structure of society itself.

8 Once people are in poverty they are often trapped there with little means of escape.

9 Poor people suffer not just from lack of money but from such things as lack of educational provision, health care and decent housing.

10 British governments have intervened to try to limit poverty. There is now an educational system that is free up to 16, a health service, supplementary benefits and pensions, various allowances and a progressive taxation system.

14.14 Keywords (*as they appear in the unit*)

absolute poverty, relative poverty, supplementary benefits, relative income, index of deprivation, poverty line, cycle of deprivation, culture of poverty, community development projects, structure of society, poverty trap, welfare state.

15 THE WELFARE STATE

The term Welfare State refers to a society in which the State actively intervenes to ensure that its citizens have adequate standards of income, housing, education and health services.

15.1 Development of the Welfare State

The origins of the Welfare State go back to the Liberal Government of 1908. Booth's writings, and Rowntree's research on poverty in York, influenced the Liberal Government to introduce old age pensions. The most important measure was the introduction of **National Insurance** in 1911. This is a scheme in which employers, employees and the state all make contributions to a fund to provide insurance against illness and disablement. By 1914 there were 14 million people contributing to the scheme.

Between 1906 and 1919 the Liberals introduced new services in the fields of social security, health, education, housing, employment, and the treatment of offenders. Many of these services were then cut back between 1921 and 1939.

In 1945–50 the Labour Government committed itself to a far wider and more radical reform than the Liberals had attempted. Nobody was to be allowed to live in poverty and everybody was to have proper health care and education regardless of their income. The difference between the Labour version of the Welfare State and the Liberal welfare provisions was that the Welfare State was to be for everybody.

Most of the provisions of the Welfare State were based on the recommendations of a committee headed by Lord Beveridge. The scheme introduced the **Social Security** system, the comprehensive **National Health Service**, a **free secondary school** system, special **help for**

the handicapped and disabled, provision for **decent housing**, state intervention to maintain **full employment**, and a system of **family allowances**.

Although changes have been introduced in the system since it was initiated between 1945–50, it remains fundamentally the same. However, since 1979 the Conservative Government has shown that it would like to see the system partially dismantled in favour of a two-tier scheme. For instance, in the sphere of medicine, it would like to see most people paying for **private** health care whilst only those who could not afford to pay would go to the National Health Service.

The reasons why the Labour Government introduced a Welfare State have to be seen against:

1 The background of 20 years of mass unemployment before the Second World War, when there was little help given to alleviate poverty;

2 The previous measures introduced by the Liberal Government were found to be totally inadequate;

3 The wartime destruction of British cities gave the impetus for the construction of new, better-built houses in well-planned environments;

4 There was an overwhelming desire shared by the mass of the British people never to return to the pre-war conditions.

15.2 The Debate on the Welfare State

1 Advantages of the Welfare State:

(a) It has eliminated the worst excesses of poverty;

(b) It helps people who through no fault of their own (such as physical handicap) are unable to work, and without financial aid would have been reduced to begging or voluntary charity;

(c) It has given everybody access to decent medical treatment;

(d) Before the Second World War it was mainly the children of more affluent parents who could receive a secondary school education, as fees were charged. Today education is freely available;

(e) It has led to the elimination of the worst forms of slum housing that existed in Britain;

(f) It has provided elderly people with an income that allows them to live with some degree of dignity in their old age.

2 Disadvantages

In recent years there has been a growth in criticism of the Welfare State.

(a) One group of critics argues that it does not provide enough help for the poor, disabled, and elderly. They argue for an extension and a raising of the standards of the Welfare State;

(b) However, other groups argue that the Welfare State has gone too far and ought to be partially dismantled. They argue that the Welfare State:

(i) Is wasteful: because the Welfare State is universal, that is it gives certain benefits to everybody, for example Child Benefit, many who do not actually need financial help receive it. This is seen as a waste of money. These people argue for more **selective** provision, that is giving only to those who can prove they are in need;

(ii) Because of the enormous financial cost of the Welfare State the level of benefits is too low. They argue that by concentrating selectively, the same money could provide better services for fewer people;

(iii) The Welfare State is too bureaucratic and impersonal and increasingly controls our lives;

(iv) The provision of benefits to all robs individuals of their desire to look after themselves. They do not have to worry about the future, or try very hard to get employment, as they know that the Welfare State will always look after them. This criticism seems rather weak if one looks at the levels of benefit given for unemployed people for instance: they are so low that few people can truly wish to live permanently on them;

(v) The provision of benefits and health care weakens the family, by taking away its functions. If there was less provision by the state, families would have to cope and this would strengthen the institution of the family.

Conclusion

The critics of the Welfare State may have some valid points, but a glance back to life for the working class in Britain before its existence shows a dreadful level of poverty, disease and misery, which the Welfare State has undoubtedly relieved.

15.3 National Benefits

The Welfare State operates in five main areas:
Education; social security; community care; health; housing.

The services provided by the Welfare State are divided into those looked after nationally by the central government and those looked after at a local level by local authorities.

At the national level the Government is responsible for:

1 The National Health Service

The NHS costs about £20 billion per year to run. Most of the money is spent on hospitals, but there are many other services provided by the NHS. These include: family doctors; dentists; opticians; health centres; ante- and post-natal clinics; health visitors; health education; day centres for the mentally and physically handicapped; ambulance services and immunization services.

The result of the creation of the NHS has been a considerable decline in the number of diseases; for instance, in 1950 16 000 people each year died of TB, but by 1970 this had been reduced to only 1500. The general rise in the standards of health also means that we can all expect to live longer. Everybody has the right to use the medical services, and the most commonly used part of the NHS is the family practitioner service (your family doctor). Each person registers with a doctor and if health care is needed this is provided free of charge. Doctors are paid a fixed allowance by the Government for each patient and they usually have around 3000 per practice.

2 National Insurance

When people are working they must pay contributions to the National Insurance scheme. Contributions are also made by the employer and the Government. The contributions are recorded weekly and if you become unable to work for whatever reason then you are entitled to claim a payment from the insurance scheme. You can only claim if you have paid an adequate number of contributions, but you are entitled to claim money as a right. It is not a form of charity. National Insurance includes the following benefits:

(a) *Unemployment benefit* Payable for a year after the beginning of unemployment, if the claimant is registered for work at the local Department of Employment Office. If a person leaves work through his own fault or decision, he must wait six weeks before he can claim;

(b) *Sickness benefit* Paid when somebody is unable to work through illness;

(c) *Retirement pensions*

(d) *Child benefit* A monthly payment for each child up to the school/college leaving age.

3 Social Security

This covers a wide range of payments, mainly to people who do not qualify for National Insurance payments:

(a) *Supplementary benefit* Anybody without work and with inadequate income can apply. The amount paid depends upon a person's circumstances. The main social groups claiming supplementary benefits are: single parents; long-term unemployed; pensioners whose pension is too low;

(b) *Family Credit* Payable to people in full-time work whose earnings are below a certain level. For instance, in 1983 the level for FIS was £82.50 for a couple with one child.

15.4 Local Benefits

The local government authority is responsible for:

1 housing;
2 social services;
3 education: the provision of schools, colleges, adult education, youth services;
4 public health;
5 planning; local road building and maintenance, local redevelopment.

1 Housing

Approximately 30 per cent of British homes are publicly owned. The local authorities initially became involved in housing because of the overcrowding and poor standards of privately rented accommodation. The local authorities are also responsible for maintaining the housing. Local authorities are obliged by law to provide accommodation and ensure that nobody is homeless. They also pay **housing benefits** which consist of rent or rate subsidy for those on low incomes, or the direct payment of rent and rates for those on supplementary benefit.

2 Social services

In every town there are people with social problems. The local authorities provide a number of services to help certain groups in the population who may not be able to look after themselves.

3 Education

The local authority is responsible for the provision of education: schools, colleges, adult education institutes and youth clubs are all provided.

4 Public Health

The local authority must ensure that the level of pollution is acceptably low and that infectious diseases are contained. This is done particularly by checking premises in which food is prepared and sold. The person in charge of these duties is the *District Community Physician*. The local authority is also responsible for refuse disposal.

5 Planning

The local authorities must devise development plans indicating how they intend to cope with changing demands for housing, roads, shops, etc. The idea is that growth should take place in an orderly and controlled manner. Local authorities have the power compulsorily to purchase certain properties if they stand in the way of redevelopment.

15.5 Voluntary Organizations

Apart from the welfare services provided by the state, there is a whole host of voluntary agencies which provide assistance. These have grown to complement the state services and fall into two main groupings.

1 Formally organized groups and charities

Their object is to help others in need. Examples of these include:

(a) *Marriage guidance* Counsel and help with sexual and marital problems. Counsellors are unpaid but highly trained;

(b) *Mencap* Helps mentally handicapped people;

(c) *Community Service Volunteers* CSV takes volunteers between 16 and 35 to perform one year of full-time service. They receive board and lodging and some small payment;

(d) *Shelter* This organization is primarily concerned with housing issues and tries to help the ill-housed and homeless;

(e) *War on Want* This collects money for international help.

2 Self-help groups

These are organized to protect or promote their own interests. They include such organizations as:

(a) *Gingerbread* This is an organization looking after the interests of single parents;

(b) *Alcoholics Anonymous* People who have alcohol problems and so meet regularly to help themselves over their difficulties.

Voluntary services still exist in the Welfare State because:

(i) Small voluntary agencies are often better able to cope with specific problems which the state bureaucracy may find difficult to handle. The work of **Release** with drug addicts is a good example, as there is little state provision to help people with drug problems;

(ii) Volunteers are far more flexible in the hours they are prepared to work, so the Samaritans, who provide advice and friendship over the phone, have somebody on call 24 hours a day;

(iii) Volunteers have often had similar problems themselves and can bring a degree of personal experience into their work. Alcoholics Anonymous is an example of this;

(iv) Volunteers may help groups that are not generally popular. **PROP** is an organization that looks after the rights of prisoners;

(v) Volunteer agencies sometimes exist to attack the state's complacency over certain problems. For instance, the Child Poverty Action Group actively criticizes the Government for leaving millions of children in poverty.

15.6 Summary

1 The Welfare State was created at the end of the Second World War.

2 Its aims were to wipe out poverty, poor housing, low-standard education, and inadequate health care for the masses.

3 The Welfare State has only partially been successful in its aims.

4 There has been a vigorous debate between those who argue for a cut-back in the Welfare State, claiming that it is no longer needed and that it is a waste of resources, and those who defend it – pointing out that it is still desperately needed and that the alternative would be to turn the clock back to the 1930s, when health care depended on ability to pay, not degree of illness.

5 The Welfare State operates at two levels, national and local. The national level pays out mainly pensions, supplementary benefit and unemployment allowances. The local government level pays out housing benefits, provides education and social workers.

6 The role of the voluntary services remains crucial to the running of welfare services in Britain, as the state is not able to provide everything.

15.7 Keywords *(as they appear in the unit)*

universal benefits, selective benefits, national health service, national insurance, insurance, social security, social services, public health, voluntary organizations.

16 POLITICS AND POWER

16.1 Power and Authority

Max Weber distinguished between 'power' and 'authority'.

Power is the situation when a person forces his/her will on others so that they do as they are ordered. The people may not agree with what they are told to do but they obey. Power is usually enforced by threats of one kind or another. This is the method by which many non-democratic societies are controlled.

Authority is when the people who are told to do something willingly obey. There is no threat. There are three types of authority:

1 *Charismatic* A person is obeyed because of the sheer force of personality – as, for example, Jesus Christ.

2 *Traditional* A person is obeyed because of his/her position. The person in that position has always been obeyed and it is customary to do so, e.g. tribal chiefs, parents.

3 *Bureaucratic* In modern societies most places of work and most organizations have a bureaucracy, which consists of people doing different tasks with some having more important positions than others, and being able to tell others what to do.

Authority here is related to the 'job' a person does, not the personality of the individual. Whoever fills the role in the organization has the right to demand obedience. However, outside the specific requirements and rights of the job, the person has no authority: e.g. a teacher in school can tell pupils what to do. In the shopping centre on Saturday, however, the teacher has no such rights.

In reality, of course, the three types of authority get mixed together. However, the distinction between those who have power (based on threat) and those who have authority (based on agreement) is clear cut.

Most political systems spend a great deal of time and effort trying to persuade their people that they are fortunate to live in a society with a good political system, which they should obey willingly – this is termed **political socialization**.

16.2 Different Political Systems

The study of politics concerns itself with the ways that societies are governed. In particular it is concerned with the way that power is divided among people and how it is used by them.

POWER IN SIMPLE SOCIETIES

1 In the simplest societies there are no special political organizations or government in our sense, nor are there people who specialize in political activities. In the smallest societies, which subsist by hunting, the struggle to survive reduces conflict within groups. Quite simply, to survive, the group needs to cooperate. Furthermore, the tribe often splits into groups of 20–30 whose small size dampens down any really serious divisions. Control of individual members is by informal social sanctions. For example, the hunter who does not share out his meat fairly is ignored by the rest of the group. This is a serious punishment in a type of society where cooperation with others is vital for survival.

2 Slightly more complex, agricultural societies have well-defined customs and obligations as to correct behaviour and appropriate punishment. Usually control is exercised through the family, as in the Tonga of Zambia. Families are exceptionally important, not just because they exercise control but because intermarriage links different families, so keeping harmony.

3 Traditionally, in certain East African tribes, such as the Turkana, people are bound together by **age groups**. All those initiated into adulthood at the same time are linked by a common bond of mutual obligations. This binds them together.

4 Finally, order is also maintained by common customs, languages and religions. When groups come together as a result of religious ceremonies, their common identity is reinforced. This was first pointed out by Durkheim (see the discussion on Social Control p 145).

MODERN POLITICAL SYSTEMS

Most political systems fall within the two extremes of democracy and totalitarianism.

Democracy

This comes from the Greek words *demos* (people) and *kratia* (power, rule). It therefore means that the people make their own decisions. In Ancient Greece, in the period around 5 BC when there was only a small population, the citizens of each city met to discuss all important decisions affecting the society. The Greeks, however, did not let women or slaves have any say in decision making.

Modern, complex and densely populated societies could not be governed by all the people meeting to discuss and vote. Instead, in Britain we have **representative democracy**. Individuals (almost always representing political parties) are elected by those over 18 who are not insane, serving a prison sentence, or a member of the nobility. Each representative (*Member of Parliament*) represents an area containing approximately 60 000 people. We also elect representatives (*councillors*) to represent us in local government.

Apart from voting for a Member of Parliament, people can influence decision making by joining pressure groups (see p 128). These are basically people with similar interests who join together to try to persuade political parties that their aims are for the good of society and should be made into law. The third important influence on power in a democracy is a **free press**, which generally means that the Government does not control the newspapers or television, and that these are critical of the actions of the Government if they think it has been mistaken.

The aim of democracy is to ensure as far as practicable that individuals can influence political decisions. In modern democracies this is carried out in two ways: through voting and through the activities of pressure groups.

Examples of democracies include: the United Kingdom and all the countries of the European Economic Community such as France, West Germany and Italy.

Totalitarianism

This refers to political systems where power rests entirely in the hands of a small group (an **élite**), or one person only (a **dictatorship**). The majority of people in society have no way of influencing political decisions, as there are no elections. The newspapers, television and radio are always government controlled and are never critical of its actions.

Examples of totalitarian regimes include: Germany from 1933 to 1945 under Hitler; Chile since 1973, when an elected government was overthrown by the army under its leader Pinochet, who is still in power today.

The major differences between totalitarian and democratic societies are:

Democracy

1 A wide variety of views openly expressed;

2 An independent judiciary (judges and magistrates) and legal system;

3 Civil liberties (the right to protest, to demonstrate, not to be arrested at will or on whim by the police);

4 A free press, radio and television;

5 Elections to choose between genuinely different parties.

Totalitarianism

1 Only one viewpoint (that of the government) allowed;

2 The judges and the law are controlled by the government;

3 No civil liberties – the power of the police and state is complete and absolute;

4 The press is government controlled;

5 No true, free elections.

16.3 British Political Parties

1 Socialism: the Labour Party

This is one of the major political parties of Britain. It believes in a fairer distribution of wealth than exists at present in our society and thinks that the state ought to take ownership of the largest companies. It is a very strong defender of the **Welfare State** and is closely linked to and financed by the trade unions. It is totally committed to the democratic system.

It began in 1900 as the Labour Representative Committee and became the Labour Party in 1906. Since 1924, when it formed its first government, it has vied with the Conservative Party as the biggest party in Parliament. After the 1992 election Mr Neil Kinnock stood down as leader of the Party and the leadership was contested by Mr Brian Gould and Mr John Smith.

2 Social Democracy: the Social Democratic Party

This is a party formed in 1981 by people who left the Labour Party because they were unhappy with its policies. They believe that the Labour Party is too left wing.

3 Liberalism: the Liberal Democrats

The Liberal Party was formed in 1860. It originally argued for the least amount of Government intervention in the economy – a position now taken by the Conservative Party. It was a major political party from 1868 to 1914, when it began to lose much of its support to the Labour Party. There is currently a resurgence in support of liberalism with the emergence of the new third party in British politics – the Liberal Democrats. Its leader is Mr Paddy Ashdown.

4 Conservatism: the Conservative Party

This derived from the Tory Party in about 1870 and originally supported the interests of the rich landowners. Its policy is based on conserving what it considers the best of the past while allowing very slow change. It is generally considered to look after the interests of the better off in society, as it supports the continuing inequalities of wealth in British society and receives great financial support from big business. Under Mrs Thatcher the party has argued strongly that business interests should be free from Government control. It is easily the richest of the British political parties. Its leader is Mr John Major.

16.4 Voting Behaviour

The main influences on the way people vote are:
1 Social class
2 Party images
3 Family
4 Geographical location
5 Age
6 Gender
7 Religion
8 Ethnic group

1 VOTING AND SOCIAL CLASS

(a) How the classes traditionally divide

Undoubtedly class is a most important factor influencing voting behaviour, although it has declined in its importance over the last 15 years. Most of the other influences we have mentioned above are in some way related to social class.

The Labour Party normally takes the majority of the working class votes in elections and the Conservative Party takes the majority of the middle class votes. The Liberal Democrat party has no **class base**, but takes its votes fairly equally from all social classes. When questioned, it seems that the working class have traditionally see the Labour Party as representing their interests best, because it stands for greater help for the poorer sections of the society. On the other hand, the middle class believe more in self-reliance and generally want to see lower taxes and less government 'interference'.

Other points that explain the traditional support for the Labour Party by the working class are: (i) the Labour Party has developed out of the Trade Union movement, which exists to further the interests of workers; (ii) voting sympathies are passed on through the family along with a whole range of other attitudes. Working class parents therefore bring up their children with Labour sympathies.

(b) Working class Conservative voting

Earlier it was stated that most of the working class voted Labour. Those who vote for the Conservative Party, do so for the following reasons:

(i) *Deference* Some people believe that those from the upper middle class are 'born to rule'. As Conservative politicians are more likely to come from this background and to represent traditional values, they receive the support of these **deferential voters**.

(ii) *Dominant values* Parkin (in *Working Class Conservatives: a theory of political deviance*) has suggested that the mass media and the basic values of British society are essentially conservative and so socialist parties (such as Labour), have to compete with 'accepted' values in order to obtain votes. Labour are most likely to be successful where there is a large, tight-knit working-class community.

(c) Middle class Labour voting

There is a considerable number of people from the middle class who vote Labour. Two explanations have been given: (i) that these are people in the 'caring professions', such as social work and teaching, who through the problems they encounter in everyday life are sympathetic to the problems of the working class; (ii) these middle class Labour voters are from working class families originally and still retain the early class loyalty they learned from their parents.

(d) Voting and the changing class structure

A very important recent influence on voting has been the change in the sorts of jobs people do; as a result there are far fewer workers in factories and far more people employed in offices. Not only this, but those people still working in factories are now more likely to be skilled than in the past.

The result of all this is that there has been a split in the working class between the 'new' and the 'traditional' working class. The 'new' working class is made up of those who own their own houses, live in the South and have a high standard of living, and are usually employed in newer light industries. The 'traditional' working class is composed of those who live in council housing, work in older, heavier industries (such as coal) and live in the North and Scotland. The 'new' working class is far less likely to vote Labour than the 'traditional' working class. Many of the new working class no longer see themselves as being working class and so this lessens their loyalty to the Labour Party.

This move away from supporting the Labour Party has been called **class de-alignment**.

(e) The future of voting and social class

The changing nature of jobs in Britain will continue, with ever-decreasing numbers of jobs in the traditional manufacturing industries. This means that the pool of votes that is automatically given to the Labour Party will continue to decline.

(f) Class, voting and the Liberal Democrats

The Liberal Democrats have taken their votes from right across the range of social class and can claim to be truly a non-class party.

2 PARTY IMAGES

Few people actually know the exact policies that a political party intends to introduce if elected. Instead people have general 'images' of what a party stands for: for example, the Labour Party is generally seen as the party that has the interests of the working class at heart. People then vote for the party whose image they like best. In an election campaign, all parties spend large amounts of money on mounting effective advertising campaigns as a way of improving their images and raising their public profiles.

3 FAMILY

People are strongly influenced by the voting preferences of their parents. This is because political attitudes are learned in the home as part of the general socialization process.

4 GEOGRAPHICAL LOCATION

(a) The North of England, Scotland and Wales tend to vote Labour. The further South, the stronger the Conservative vote. This reflects the greater poverty and the existence of traditional industries (e.g. mining, heavy engineering) in the North and the greater proportion of working class people there. Alliance support is spread more evenly across the country.

(b) The outer suburbs of towns tend to support Conservatives, and to a lesser extent the Alliance, while the inner areas are more likely to support the Labour Party. This reflects the social class patterns of housing, with the better off living in the suburbs. House owners of any class are more likely to vote Conservative or Liberal Democrat. This is quite important, as there has been a doubling of house ownership since the 1950s.

5 AGE

There is no clear evidence to support the belief that people are more likely to vote Conservative as they get older, as many people claim. Butler and Stokes argue that voting preferences are partly influenced by important political events in people's **politically formative years** (when they first become interested in politics). For example, a young person who was 18 in 1968 during the height of student radicalism is likely to retain his/her leftist allegiance in some form throughout his/her life.

6 GENDER

Traditionally women have been more likely to support the Conservative Party, but in recent elections this has not been true.

7 RELIGION

This is no longer an important guide to voting behaviour, except in Northern Ireland. However, as Catholics are more likely to be found among the working class, they are more likely to vote Labour. Anglicans are more likely to vote Conservative.

8 ETHNIC GROUP

The ethnic minorities tend to support Labour, which is seen as more sympathetic to them.

Voting behaviour: Conclusions

Changes in the occupational structure of Britain and the changing perceptions of class are influencing voting behaviour. Although people still vote along class lines, there has been a shift towards white-collar work, and a decline in heavy industries which employed the traditional Labour-voting working class. In future the Labour Party will have to vie with the Liberal Democrats and the Conservatives for the increasing numbers of the 'new' working class.

16.5 Political Socialization

The discussion on voting behaviour is closely related to the idea of political socialization. Political socialization is where people learn the values of and beliefs sympathetic to one political party or one political system.

Important agencies of political socialization include:

1 The family – how your parents vote crucially influences your own political sympathies (see p 125).
2 Social class – the values and ideas linked to social class include sets of attitudes concerning politics (see p 124).
3 The media – the values that are constantly repeated in the newspapers and television over a long period of time can influence the attitudes of people to events (see p 154).
4 Religion – the values stressed by the churches can reaffirm the values of particular political parties and conflict with others.

Political socialization should not be seen as separate from socialization as a whole, but as part of the whole process.

TYPES OF VOTER
The loyal voter

This type of voter stays with a particular party most of his/her life; most often he/she is a working class Labour supporter or a middle class Conservative supporter.

Non-voters

In general elections approximately 27 per cent of the electorate do not vote. It appears that (i) poorer people, (ii) older people, (iii) women, (iv) younger voters, and (v) the least educated tend to abstain (not vote) more often than the national average.

People abstain for either positive or negative reasons:

1 *Positive reasons*

(a) No candidate standing for the party the person would normally choose;
(b) The candidate standing for the party of his/her normal choice may be objectionable to the person;
(c) There may be an aspect of his normal party's policy with which he disagrees, but he cannot bring himself to vote for another;
(d) The person may regard the result as so obvious (a safe seat) that he may not bother to vote;
(e) The individual disagrees with the political system or with all of the political parties providing candidates.

2 *Negative reasons*

(a) Apathy (cannot be bothered to vote);
(b) Illness;
(c) Does not have any faith in politicians;
(d) Fails to understand the policies of the parties.

Abstaining from voting is important because it can influence the result of an election, especially in a seat with a very small majority for the sitting Member of Parliament (a marginal seat).

Floating voters

Floating voters are people who regularly switch votes. This group is the main target for political propaganda. As class de-alignment increases, floating voters become more important.

Tactical voting

When people realize that the candidate of their first choice has absolutely no chance of winning, they may switch to a second choice candidate of another party in order to defeat the likely winner whom they deeply dislike. It has been suggested that the Liberal Democrats receive many of its votes through tactical voting, as Conservative voters switch to the Democrats in safe Labour seats and Labour supporters do the same in safe Conservative seats.

16.6 Voting and Opinion Polls

Opinion polls are surveys that find out the voting intentions or political opinions of the electors. Gallup Poll Ltd were the first to use them in Britain as long ago as 1938. Since 1974 they have predicted accurately (within 2 per cent) the voting figures for the general elections. Before then, however, they were slightly erratic; indeed in the 1970 election all the polls except one (4 out of 5) predicted a Labour victory, yet the result was a win for the Conservatives.

The accuracy of the polls depends upon:

1 The accuracy of the sample – it must be a true 'mirror' of those voting.

2 The quality of the questions asked – poorly framed questions can lead the person questioned to misunderstand the meaning of the question and so give a wrong, or inappropriate, answer.

3 The nearer the election, the more accurate the results as people will have made up their minds by then.

4 Polls should avoid asking questions on voting intentions after sensational political events as people may temporarily change their views.

(Opinion polls are a form of sociological survey. The discussion on pp 7 – 10 considers the problems of surveys in detail.)

The influence of opinion polls on voters

In some European countries, for example West Germany, the publication of polls near elections is banned because it is felt that they could influence voting patterns. They could do this in two ways:

1 If the polls predict a substantial win for one party, its supporters may be lulled into a false sense of security and they may not bother voting, as they think victory is certain. The numbers of people who do this may be so great that their party actually loses.

2 A party may be appearing to win by such a large margin that people who are undecided may vote for the 'weaker' of the two (or more) parties, just to make sure that no one party has too great a majority and introduces 'radical' policies. This may have happened in the 1986 French elections when the right-wing parties were predicted to win by a large majority, but in the end they only just scraped home with a small majority. Possibly, people switched votes to ensure just this outcome.

The influence of opinion polls on politicians

Polls are also used to test public opinion on certain issues and may be used by pressure groups to influence politicians (see p 128). Obviously a government following very unpopular policies would be silly not to take notice of opinion polls telling them so. However, most senior politicians argue that it is the job of Government to *lead opinion* not just to *follow it*.

16.7 Politics and the Mass Media

Newpapers in Britain are generally more sympathetic to the Conservatives than they are to Labour or the Liberal Democrats. The only newspaper that regularly supports the Labour Party is *The Mirror*. *The Guardian* also presents the Labour case sympathetically, although it generally takes a more centrist stance. Patterns of ownership and attitudes of a newspaper's journalists will often influence decisions as to what line to take on a particular political issue.

Broadcasting (radio and television) is legally obliged to present political debate *impartially*, which means the programmes cannot be biased against one party or another. Both the BBC and ITV have been accused of sympathy to the Establishment, by always presenting the views supporting the authorities (employers, the police) far more sympathetically than those critical of them, although in 1986 the Conservative Party accused the BBC of bias against them in news reports. Research evidence on change in political attitudes as a result of exposure to the media's influence suggests that they do not change existing attitudes but **reinforce attitudes** already held. This is because readers and viewers select the message which they want and which fits the attitudes they already hold.

However, it is important to remember, as Stuart Hall points out, that newspapers **set the agenda** in defining what is regarded as important. If stories are not prominently covered by the media, they are not noticed or discussed. Only information and stories regarded as newsworthy by journalists appear. If journalists consistently, if unintentionally, present only one side of the story, then in the long run they will influence political attitudes.

16.8 Pressure Groups (Interest Groups)

Political parties try to persuade electors to vote for them, so that they can form a government. They usually have policies on a wide range of issues.

Pressure groups (often also called interest groups) differ in that they are groups formed to defend or promote one specific cause only. They do not try to win seats in Parliament, but instead attempt to influence the policies of political parties.

An example of a political party is the Labour Party. An example of a pressure group is the Campaign for Nuclear Disarmament (CND).

There are two types of pressure group:

1 Promotional pressure groups

These put forward a particular viewpoint which they believe is socially or morally for the good of the community. An example of this type of pressure group is **Friends of the Earth**, which tries to oppose the destruction of the environment by governments (French nuclear bombs in the Pacific) and by industry (the dumping of nuclear waste in the Irish Sea).

2 Defensive pressure groups

These attempt to defend the specific interests of their members. An example of this sort of group is a trade union, which concerns itself with the wages and conditions of work of its members. The division between promotional and protective groups is not hard and fast. Very often groups are both protective and promotional. For example, the RAC and AA look after the interests of their members and promote the interests of car owners in general.

THE IMPORTANCE OF PRESSURE GROUPS IN DEMOCRACY

Pressure groups are absolutely essential in a democracy. Whereas political parties deal with broad areas of policy, pressure groups represent particular causes. Political parties are constantly being approached by different groups seeking support. It is through this that political parties are able to keep in touch with people and can respond to their wishes. A vote every five years is not an adequate enough way for people to tell politicians what specific policies they ought to follow in certain areas. In effect, pressure groups prevent the political parties from becoming too remote from the electors, by constantly channelling opinions to them. This approach has been called **pluralism** (the term comes from the word 'plural', meaning 'more than one', so it indicates 'more than one centre of power').

Criticism

It ought to be remembered that not all groups of people have the same ability to influence decisions. Which group has more power, the unemployed or the employers' organization – the CBI? Richer, better-organized groups are more likely to influence the Government than poorer ones – even if these poorer groups are more representative of public opinion.

THE METHODS USED BY PRESSURE GROUPS TO INFLUENCE DECISIONS

1 Consultantships

Many Conservative MPs are paid by industries or individual companies to keep an eye on possible parliamentary actions that might influence their activities.

2 Sponsorship

MPs have either secretarial or electoral expenses paid for by trade unions and in return they speak for those unions in Parliament.

3 Block votes

A pressure group encourages its members to support a political party which agrees to support its aims.

4 Publicity

Pressure groups try to influence what appears in the newspapers and on television. They try to gain a large amount of media attention and to be portrayed sympathetically if possible. The anti-seal culling groups have been very successful in this, having television news film shown of the slaughter of seals in horrifying detail.

A less successful method of gaining publicity is to hand out leaflets and hold street protests, marches, etc.

5 Specialized knowledge

If a decision involves complex technical knowledge, then the decision makers turn to the experts. So, influencing the experts can eventually influence the final decision. Large construction companies and National Power maintain close contact with nuclear power experts. In the debate on nuclear versus non-nuclear forms of power generating they have the sympathy of many of the experts.

6 Key positions

In order to execute certain government policies, politicians may need the cooperation of the group actually carrying them out. If the group has a monopoly over the task it can influence the decision. The British Medical Association (BMA) has been very successful in looking after the interests of doctors.

7 Civil disobedience

If all else fails then pressure groups turn to civil disobedience. They may block roads or stage illegal protests. An example of this is the activities of the Greenham Common protestors against American cruise missiles. In the extreme, some groups turn to criminal activities. An example of this is the Animal Liberation Movement, which breaks into factory farms and experimental laboratories and frees the animals.

EXAMPLE OF PRESSURE GROUP ACTION

In 1986 there was great pressure group activity concerning the opening of shops on Sundays. On one side was the 'Open Shop' pressure group which, with Government support, sought to change the law so that shops could open on Sundays. Opposing it was the 'Lord's Day Observance Society' with the support of unions and the Church. Through publicity, public protests and the influence of the churches, the Bill was defeated.

16.9 The Role of the State

The state is the political organization that dominates and controls society; it consists of the elected parliament, the legal system and the Civil Service. In democratic societies the state ought to reflect the beliefs of the population in general and ultimately be under their control. In a totalitarian society it generally reflects the will of only a few rich and powerful people who control it.

CONTROL OF THE STATE: THE THEORIES

Sociologists have disagreed on the extent to which the state in Britain really does reflect the will of the people. Indeed, some writers, influenced mainly by the writings of Karl Marx, have argued that the state in Britain really operates to the benefit of a small number of rich and powerful people comprising less than 5 per cent of the population.

Two clear views have therefore been expressed:

1 That the state represents the interests of the people and that power is widely spread among the people. This is known as the **pluralist model**.

2 That only a small group of people rules. This is known as a **ruling class model**.

Pluralism

This is the model of the political system that sees the state firmly under the control of the people. They are in control in two ways: first through elections. Every five years the electors choose the political party they prefer. Second, in between elections the political parties are kept informed by pressure groups which arise from specific concerns of the people.

The strength and amount of activity of pressure groups reflect their following in the population as a whole. By responding to pressure groups the politicians are responding to the popular will.

This has been criticized by those who argue that the power of pressure groups reflects how much money and how many political connections they have rather than popular support. (For more detail on pressure group activity turn to p 128.)

Ruling class model

Marxists argue that a small, unrepresentative group rules. The basis of its power is the ownership of the major manufacturing and commercial institutions. The rich ensure that they retain their wealth by creating a political system that effectively rules out any fundamental change, and by funding political parties that look after their interests. Marxist writers point out that 70 per cent of Conservative and 10 per cent of Labour MPs went to public schools, the hallmark of the **Establishment** in Britain. Over half of Conservative MPs are company directors. They further point out that only 10 per cent of the British population own almost 70 per cent of the wealth.

This approach can be criticized as it fails to realize the extent to which ordinary people can engage in pressure group activity and influence government decisions.

THE CIVIL SERVICE

This is the **executive** of the Government, carrying out its policies. Like the **legislature** (that is the Houses of Parliament and the Government itself), it has been the centre of tremendous debate over the nature of its power. It is supposed to carry out the decisions of the legislature. However, many sociologists see it as being a power in its own right.

Its senior staff are recruited overwhelmingly from public schools and the Universities of Oxford and Cambridge. For instance, in 1984 of 102 new entrants to the highest grades of the Civil Service, 72 had attended the 'élite' universities of Oxford or Cambridge. Furthermore, most of the top civil servants come from the highest social classes in British society – particularly those working in the Foreign Office. Those who do not are socialized into a special 'civil service culture', which gives them a particular set of values. Left-wing politicians who have gained power have all commented on how efficient the Civil Service is, but also how it obstructs any radical left-wing changes. It is basically a conservative force therefore. In recent years, fears have been expressed about the very close relationship that has developed between top civil servants and industry. It has now become common for top civil servants to 'retire' into high positions in industries related to their Civil Service experience. For instance, a top Ministry of Defence civil servant recently left the Civil Service to a senior post with United Scientific Holdings, a major weapons producer.

16.10 Summary

1 Democracy is a political system that reflects the opinions and wishes of the community as much as possible. Its main features are (a) freedom of speech, (b) civil liberty, (c) the right to vote, (d) the existence of pressure groups reflecting popular opinion, (e) an independent legal system.

2 A totalitarian society, such as a dictatorship, is a society where a small group rules for its own benefit. Its main features are (a) government control of the media, (b) Government control of the legal system, (c) no right to vote or express an opinion.

3 In Britain the main political parties are Conservative, Labour and the Liberal Democrats.

4 The way people vote is mainly influenced by their social class. But other influences include (a) party images, (b) geographical location, (c) family socialization, (d) age, (e) gender and (f) religion.

5 The changes in the class structure have been very great in recent years and this has meant that class is slowly weakening as a predictor of voting preferences. This is known as **class dealignment.**

6 Tactical voting is when people prefer to switch their vote to a party other than the one of their first choice in order to prevent the candidate of another party winning.

7 Opinion polls are surveys to find out the political preferences of the electorate, in particular to predict how they will vote in an election. It is sometimes argued that the opinion polls can influence the outcome of elections by providing enough information for people to engage in tactical voting.

8 The mass media do not seem to have any powerful effect on how people choose to vote; however, in general the media are sympathetic to the Conservative Party and create a 'climate of opinion' favourable to them.

9 Pressure (or interest) groups are organizations that try to persuade those in power to act in particular ways which they see as beneficial to themselves or the community. Their members do not seek political office themselves. They influence MPs in a number of ways, including (a) consultantships and sponsorships, (b) block votes, (c) publicity, (d) providing or influencing those with specialized knowledge, (e) withholding cooperation if they are in key positions, (f) public demonstrations and civil disobedience.

10 The state refers to the Government, its Civil Service and its legal system. There are two views of the state: (a) the pluralist model which sees the British state as reflecting the will of the people, (b) the ruling class model, which sees the state operating in the interests of a small minority.

16.11 Keywords (*as they appear in the unit*)

power, authority, charismatic, traditional, bureaucratic, democracy, totalitarianism, socialism, social democracy, liberalism, conservatism, dominant values, new working class, traditional working class, floating votes, tactical voters, set the agenda, pressure groups, promotional pressure groups, defensive groups, pluralism, ruling class, the Establishment.

17 SOCIAL CONTROL

17.1 Meaning of Social Control

Through your study of sociology you will have discovered that in order for society to exist there must be order and predictability. Any group of people living together must have common expectations if they are to engage in any form of social life. If I cannot predict how you are going to act, how is it possible for us to act jointly? Indeed, those who act in an unpredictable way are defined as **eccentric** or even **mad**. People in society need to share a common set of **values** and **beliefs** about social behaviour. These commonly held beliefs, however, are only very general guides to action, they are not specific in telling us how to behave. Sociologists suggest that there are specific guides to action which we call **norms**. 'Norms' simply means normal ways of behaving. Sometimes these are referred to as **mores**.

In order to persuade people to follow these norms, societies have developed two methods of ensuring conformity: informal and formal control.

17.2 Informal Control

This is the most common form of control and is based upon the socialization process, which we experience as we grow up. Socialization and social control are mixed together, so it is difficult to distinguish one clearly from the other. However, at its simplest, we can say that socialization consists of **learning** the values of society, while social control consists of **reinforcing** those values once learned.

1 Primary socialization

This is the process of learning the values of society directly from contact with people around us who are very close to us, such as our family and friends. This occurs first in the family, where we are taught the expected patterns of behaviour. If we conform we are praised, but if we behave against the accepted values then we are punished – punishment may take various forms, from being smacked through to our parents simply telling us off. Most importantly, however, we learn to believe that certain behaviour is correct or preferable. This **internalized** guide to behaviour is what we commonly call our **conscience**. This process of learning the rules and values is reinforced by our friends. As a person moves from childhood through to adulthood, the **peer group** becomes particularly important, modifying the values of childhood and preparing the youth for adulthood.

2 Secondary socialization

This is the process by which the fundamental patterns of behaviour learned in childhood in the family and from friends are strengthened by institutions such as the school, the mass media and the church.

These institutions constantly put forward a set of values which support the society as it is, guiding our behaviour towards conformity.

The result of informal control through primary and secondary socialization is to **create** within people's minds an acceptance of the correctness, normality and 'naturalness' of society as it is. Sometime sociologists refer to this process as one of **ideological control**.

CHANGES IN INFORMAL CONTROL

Informal control has changed over time. Since the end of the last century the power of religion has declined and that of the education system and the mass media have increased.

Up until the last century, the simplest way of making people conform was to stress the existence of a god, who would punish people after their death if they acted against the values of society. As no one comes back after death to talk about their experiences, then there is no way to contradict this threat. However, with the growth of secularization, the use of a threat of a punishing god declined. The education system and the mass media developed effectively to replace religion.

The education system operates at two levels. First there is the choice of material that is taught in the schools – this usually reinforces the values of society. For example, in most schools Orwell's book *Animal Farm* is studied and is generally used as a warning against the evils of totalitarianism and communism. The choice of the book in effect strengthens the claim that our form of society is the best: it is extremely unlikely that Orwell is studied in Soviet schools.

Second, there are the comments and expectations of the teachers, the so-called **hidden curriculum**. Teachers often have expectations of pupils based on their own values: the appropriate behaviour for girls, for instance. If the children do not conform, the teachers may not punish them, but show disapproval.

The mass media portray a version of events in the world which strongly supports accepted values, while criticizing the activities of criminals and political 'extremists'.

THE VARIETY OF VALUES WITHIN THE MAIN CULTURE

Although we learn to share a common set of values, beliefs and norms called the culture, we also learn alternative variations of this culture (which, however, still exist *within* the dominant culture). These are known as **subcultures**, which usually vary with such things as age, social class and ethnic group.

17.3 Formal Control

Informal control is based on rewards and encouragement for correct behaviour and sanctions such as ridicule, gossip and comment for incorrect behaviour.

Formal control refers to the public, legal forms of controlling the population. Certain activities are regarded as dangerous to society, by those who hold power, and are therefore forbidden.

Formal social controls are enforced by special agents appointed for that purpose, the most formal are the police, courts and prisons who catch, judge and punish anyone who breaks the law; they attempt to deter others from doing the same thing.

When the normal mechanisms of social control break down, then the army may be called in, as occurred in Northern Ireland.

Although they appear to be the strongest forms of social control, formal controls and the legal rules they underpin are in fact much weaker than the informal controls based upon commonly held values and internalized in individuals' consciences.

17.4 The Nature of Social Control

Few dispute the fact that some form of social control is necesssary in order to ensure that people conform to the rules of society. However, there is a major dispute about *who benefits* from the rules of society.

There are two views on this: **1** the pluralist position and **2** the Marxist-influenced approach.

1 The pluralist position

This approach stresses that rules generally reflect the true feelings of the population of any society. The law, the media, the education system all reflect the needs and the wishes of the people. (The term 'pluralist' comes from the word 'plural' and simply means that decision making is in the hands of many people.)

2 The Marxist-influenced approach

This approach states that social control in most of its forms (especially the formal ones) is part of a system in which the ruling class composed of the rich and the powerful maintains its own power and influence.

Force is used only in the last resort, for it is far more effective to control the population by persuading them to accept the society as it is.

EXAMPLES OF SOCIAL CONTROL

Throughout this book, social control has been dealt with in some detail as it relates to particular topics.

Social control and the family: p 13;   Social control and religion: p 144;
Social control and education: p 28;   Social control and politics: p 121;
Social control at work: p 75;   Social control and the media: p 150.
Social control and gender: p 54;

17.5 Social Control in Other Societies

In simple, tribal societies there are no such things as agencies of formal control. All social control is informal. Among the Bushmen of the Kalahari Desert in Africa, for example, there is no chief or leader. The group travels the desert in search of food, and decisions are made more by common sense and by custom rather than any person taking the active role of leader. Clearly there are some in the group whose opinion is considered of more worth than others, but that is all.

Social order is maintained very much by informal methods, such as gossip, publicly voiced complaints against someone in order to bring shame upon him or her, people refusing to talk to someone else. In very serious cases of dispute, then the offender may be rejected by the tribe, or if an offender has harmed another member of the tribe, it may be that a relative of the dead or injured person has the right to take revenge.

However, it is important to realize that conflict and deviance such as we know them were extremely rare in simple societies. Some of the reasons why include:

1 *Small groups*

The groups in simple societies were very small, as food was in such short supply that rarely could more than a few dozen find enough food in one area to survive. Social harmony is easier to create in small groups.

2 *The uncertainty*

In simple societies, there was only ever just enough food to go around. No one could be sure of finding food, or remaining well enough to go out to look for themselves. By cooperating with others and stressing this cooperation, there was a greater chance of survival. Hunters cooperated in finding food and the kill was brought back and divided among the whole group. Even if one person failed to obtain food on a particular day, he/she would still eat.

3 *The gift relationship*

One of the most important methods of maintaining cooperation in simple societies was the giving of gifts. If a person needed help to build a shelter, for example, then another would offer to help. The individual was obliged to accept the offer of help and was obliged to offer some form of thanks, either by giving help or a gift on another occasion.

4 *Intermarriage*

Because of the small size of the societies, there was considerable intermarriage, so that most people were related. These kinship ties also helped to pull people together.

5 *Age ties*

In a number of simple societies, such as the Turkana of the Sudan, there are ties among all those of the same age. These go through the **rites of passage** of entry from childhood into adulthood together and swear allegiance to others of the same age. In this way, when the tribe fragments into smaller bands, separately herding their cattle, the bonds formed by the age ties cross over the suspicions and differences that emerge over time.

5 *Religion*

This is possibly the most important of the forms of social control. Among the Turkana, for instance, murder is virtually unknown as their religion tells them that murder prevents rain. As they live in semi-desert conditions, this is obviously an extremely important rule.

Usually, the basic values of society are contained in the religion of the society and failure to observe religious instructions is believed to lead to some form of natural disaster.

17.6 Summary

1 Social control consists of the forms of pressure that are put on people to conform to the accepted patterns of behaviour in society.

2 Formal control consists of the official rules and laws of society that are enforced by specially created agencies, such as the police, the judiciary and the prisons.

3 Informal control relates to the many expectations of behaviour made by society which are not enforced by the law. The agencies that enforce these unofficial rules of society are the family, peer group, the media, etc.

4 Without social control society would not exist, for order and predictability are absolutely necessary for every society.

5 However, every industrial society has a number of different sets of values within it which provide a slightly different form of social control. These varieties are known as subcultures.

6 There are two views on the nature of social control. The first is that social rules are applied for the benefit of everyone and that the law is a reflection of the feelings of the people.

The alternative approach is that the laws reflect the interests of the most powerful groups in society and that they have also managed to impose their way of thinking on the population through the agencies of social control.

7 In simpler societies there are no agencies of formal control. However, informal control is much more important and much stricter.

17.7 Keywords *(as they appear in the unit)*

beliefs, norms, mores, informal control, primary socialization, internalized, peer group, secondary socialization, ideological control, formal control, hidden curriculum, subcultures.

18 CRIME AND DEVIANCE

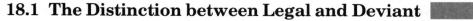

18.1 The Distinction between Legal and Deviant

In the distinction between formal and informal social control, discussed in the previous unit, it can clearly be seen that **illegal** acts and **socially incorrect** acts may not be the same thing. For instance, it may be viewed as morally bad by certain groups in the community to be homosexual, but it is not necessarily illegal. As sociologists study social rules and social actions, the more important distinction for them is not between legal and illegal acts, but rather the difference between **socially acceptable** acts and **socially stigmatized** acts. Acts that are regarded in some way as socially wrong are labelled by sociologists as **deviant**. Deviant acts, therefore, are all acts that are regarded as rule (norm) breaking whether they are legal or illegal.

Variations in the definition of deviance

What is regarded as deviant, according to Howard Becker, varies: (a) across time, (b) across society, and (c) by who commits the act. For instance, rules of dress vary according to time, society, person and place. Women in most traditional African societies would not consider it normal or necessary to cover their breasts. In contemporary British society it would be considered deviant behaviour for a woman to walk in the streets in summer with her breasts uncovered. Yet it is now generally considered that women can go topless on the beach, whereas 15 years ago even this was not permissable. A man, however, with no covering on his chest excites no comment whatsoever. It can be seen that it is not the nakedness as such that is deviant, but how it is defined by other people. As Becker puts it: 'Deviant behaviour is behaviour that people so label'.

Why definitions of deviance vary

It is difficult to explain exactly why an act is deviant in one situation, but not in another; or when performed by one person, but not when committed by another. Sociologists suggest that acts are more likely to be defined as deviant in the following instances:

1 The person performing the act has low status.
2 The person performing the act has little power.
3 The act clashes with generally held values, which change over time.
4 As society is comprised of many subcultures making up the main culture, people acting according to the norms of one subculture may be acting against the values of the main culture or another subculture, and therefore may be defined by others (but not themselves) as deviant.

These points can help explain why in certain circumstances an act is considered acceptable and in other circumstances not:

(a) When performed by one group and not when performed by another, e.g. university students being rowdy during rag week and skinheads being rowdy after a football match;
(b) When performed in one subculture but not another, e.g. toughness and violence is considered good in the army, but bad in civilian life;
(c) When performed at one time, but not another, e.g. today it is considered normal to regard women as equal to men and to listen to their contributions in discussion. A hundred years ago women were regarded as stupid and inferior; in fact they had the same legal rights as lunatics!

18.2 Reasons why some Deviant Acts are Criminal

Why are some deviant acts **illegal** and others not? The following explanations have been suggested:
(a) reflects majority view that a particular act is extremely deviant;
(b) moral crusades;
(c) suits the interests of the powerful.

(a) Reflects the majority view

This explanation sees certain deviant acts as being so extreme that the majority of the population agree to ban them and so a law is passed. Durkheim is associated with this approach.

(b) Moral crusade

This approach stresses the activities of a particular pressure group, who manage to have a law passed making particular acts which they disapprove of (for moral reasons or for their own gain) illegal.

An example of a moral crusade is the activities of the National Viewers and Listeners Association which is trying to have much stricter controls placed on the level of sex and violence on television.

(c) The interests of the powerful

Marxist-influenced writers argue that the law reflects the interest of powerful groups in society and it benefits them. They point to the way that white-collar 'crime' – that is, theft by middle class people, such as tax evasion, is seldom prosecuted; and how the law basically protects the property of the better off.

18.3 Patterns of Crime

TYPES OF OFFENCE

Table 18.1 Crime and deviance

Notifiable offences recorded (000s)	*England & Wales*			
	1971	1981	1984	1990
Violence against the person	47	100	114	184.7
Sexual offences	23	19	20	32.4
Burglary	451	732	897	1006.8
Robbery	7	20	25	36.2
Theft and handling stolen goods	1004	1603	1808	2868
Fraud and forgery	100	107	126	147.9
Criminal damage	27	387	498	553.5

(**Source**: Adapted from *Social Trends* 1992)

As can be seen from Table 18.1:

1 The offences that receive the highest amount of publicity and appear to cause the greatest public concern, such as violence, sexual offences and murder, in fact form a relatively small proportion of the total number of more serious (*indictable*) crimes.

2 The most common offence is theft and handling stolen goods: it represents roughly half of all criminal offences.

3 Burglary accounted for about a quarter of all offences.

4 Of all offences committed, about 1 in 20 was against the person, that is violence against the person, robbery and sexual offences.

In the last 10 years, the rate of violence against the person has almost doubled and there has been an increase in all types of crime.

TYPES OF OFFENDERS
Table 18.2 Offenders by (1) sex and (2) age

	1977	*1978*	*1979*	*1980*	*1981*	*1982*	*1983*	*1984*
Males								
				(Thousands)				
14–21	*149*	*152*	*150*	*170*	*176*	*179*	*170*	*167*
over 21	*188*	*180*	*183*	*200*	*207*	*215*	*216*	*210*
all ages	*357*	*350*	*349*	*387*	*398*	*408*	*397*	*387*
Females								
14–21	*21*	*20*	*21*	*21*	*22*	*21*	*20*	*—*
over 21	*45*	*43*	*40*	*43*	*42*	*42*	*41*	*39*
all ages	*68*	*65*	*63*	*68*	*65*	*66*	*63*	*60*

The evidence from the official statistics (see Table 18.2) shows that most crime is committed by males:

under the age of 25;
living in urban areas;
from working class backgrounds.

There is also discussion concerning the relationship between race and crime.

1 Gender and crime

There are far fewer crimes committed by females compared to males. For example, the conviction rate (found guilty) of male to female offenders is approximately 7 to 1.
  The explanations for this include:

(a) That the behaviour expected of males, to be 'tough and dominant' for instance, is more likely to lead to criminal behaviour;

(b) As there is a dual standard of morality in Britain with regard to the sexual behaviour of males and females, whereas delinquency can serve as a protest for males, for females, much the same protest can be made through sexual activity.

Criticism

The official statistics, on which these statements of different levels of crime are based, have some flaws. In particular it has been argued that the police are far more likely merely to caution females, under the belief that they were 'led astray' by male companions. Approximately 70 per cent of females are cautioned to about 50 per cent of males.

Research

A. McRobbie and J. Garber (*Girls and Subculture*) wanted to find out why delinquency was mainly male. McRobbie studied 56 girls who went to the same school, lived on the same council estate and attended the same youth club, in the *Mill Lane Girls*. The main conclusion was that the girls' teenage activities reflected the cultural expectations of them as female. Most of their time was spent in appropriately **feminine pursuits** which are stressed in our culture. They were concerned with being *attractive, sexy* and *getting a boy*, while at the same time romanticizing the future **ideal** of a husband and their own home.

2 Age and crime

The period at which a person is most likely to commit a crime is after 14 and before 25. About half of those convicted of indictable offences are under 21, for instance, although under-21-year-olds only account for a fifth of the population.
  Young people are the ones least likely to be tied down with a job and a family to support – they are therefore more open to social experiments, seeking excitement and new experiences. Matza has called youth a period of *drift*, when young people do not feel totally committed to society.

3 Crime and geographical location

There appear to be considerably higher rates of crime in large urban areas than in the rural areas. Explanations include:

(a) There is greater opportunity for criminal activity, with the presence of shops, warehouses, etc.;

(b) In the large cities there is far less informal social control. People do not know each other and are therefore less likely to be inhibited in stealing from one another locally;

(c) The inner cities have the highest rates of deprivation, and social problems in general.

Criticism

It has been suggested that the difference in the numbers of crimes in the city compared to the countryside is not as great as the official statistics suggest. Policing methods in the smaller towns and the suburbs are different from policing methods in the inner city areas. In the rural area, policemen are less likely to arrest offenders, preferring merely to warn them.

4 Social class and crime

Although official statistics do not provide information on the social background of offenders, it has been estimated that the sons of manual workers are four times more likely to be convicted of offences than the sons of professionals and businessmen.

(a) Working class youths are more generally worse off than middle class youths;

(b) It has been suggested that **subcultures** exist among the working class which justify a certain level of crime;

(c) Working class youths may feel more frustrated and bitter against society, as they have far worse prospects than middle class youths;

(d) The home backgrounds of certain working class youths may not be as stable as for the middle class youth.

(These ideas are developed more fully in Sociological Explanations of Crime and Delinquency on p 139.)

Criticism

1 There is a greater police presence in working class areas and therefore greater likelihood of persons being seen and arrested by the police when committing an offence.

2 Working class youths tend to spend more of their spare time out of doors on the streets where they come to the attention of the police.

3 Police have stereotyped definitions of which sort of groups are likely to be troublemakers, in particular working class youth, and therefore they are more likely to be the focus of police attention.

Howard Parker (*View from the Boys*) studied a group of Liverpool youths who lived in the Roundhouse, a central Liverpool tenement renowned locally for the high levels of juvenile delinquency. He used an observational method of research *hanging around* with the *boys*, and eventually joined in many of their activities. The *boys* earned the little money they had from breaking into cars and stealing radios. Parker suggests that any simple explanation for their actions is mistaken. They act the way they do to *have a laugh* and to earn a bit of money. They are not really rebels and they eventually move away from criminal acts as police activity threatens them and as they gain new responsibilities. Their attempts to brighten their lives need to be set against the certainty of dead-end jobs and essentially routine lives.

5 Ethnic group and crime

From the Home Office statistics, and a study by Stevens and Willis (*Race, Crime and Arrests*), it is true to say that the **arrest rate** for those of West Indian origin is higher than for other groups in the population.

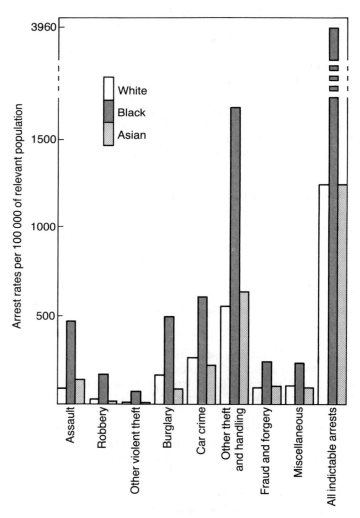

Fig. 18.1 Source: *What is to be done about law and order?* Penguin

There is, however, considerable debate concerning the interpretation of these figures.

(a) Youth of West Indian origin do have significantly greater rates of disadvantage than most white youth, compounded by racism directed towards them, which might lead to criminality;

(b) The object of the bulk of crime committed by those of West Indian origin or parentage is people from the same ethnic group. The amount of crime against whites is actually below what is statistically expected;

(c) It is argued that the activities of the police contribute to the large proportion of those of West Indian origin who are arrested. This is because the police (i) believe that there is much more crime committed by Blacks, this leads them to stop and search Blacks and consequently this increases the possibility of arrest, (ii) areas of high Black population are heavily policed – increasing the likelihood of arrest, (iii) it has been suggested that racism is common among the Metropolitan and other city police forces and therefore certain police officers welcome the chance of arresting Blacks;

(d) Asian youth, however, have the lowest crime rate of all groups.

18.4 Sociological Explanations of Crime and Delinquency

Sociologists have suggested a number of possible explanations for criminal behaviour. These include:

1 The subcultural approach;   2 Anomie;   3 The Marxist approach.

1 The subcultural approach

This approach has a number of variations, some of which are mentioned below. However, they all share the basic belief that those who commit crime share a set of values which is different from the values of society as a whole. That is, they have a **subculture** (see p 4). Generally, the explanation is that they were brought up by their parents to have values sympathetic to crime.

(a) *Lower working class values*

Walter Miller widened the scope of subcultural theory. He argued that the values of the working class could often lead to crime. For example, it is a central working class value for men to exhibit their 'masculinity' by being 'tough'. This could easily lead to fighting and violence.

(b) *Status frustration*

Albert Cohen put forward a different version of subcultural theory in his study of delinquent boys. He suggested that boys who fail at school feel frustrated and lack any status. They therefore engage in delinquent acts to *get back at* the society that condemned them. This approach is known as the **status frustration explanation**.

Criticism of the subcultural approach

Matza has strongly criticized the subcultural approach. He argues that there is no clearly distinct subculture of deviance. Indeed, most delinquents and criminals are generally law abiding and support the law in general. In other words, criminals are little different from any law-abiding person. Instead Matza suggests that all of us are deviant at certain times and we usually make excuses for our behaviour: for instance (a) we might say we 'were drunk' (so it is not our fault, but the alcohol's) or that (b) the person we hurt 'deserved it anyway' (because they were homosexual or fans of another football team), or that (c) there was 'no real harm done anyway' (stealing a book from a large bookstore).

All that happens is that criminals *extend* the excuses that are normally made. Matza goes on to point out that most crime is committed by young people who are at their most uncertain as to their own personality and might therefore be less restrictive in their uses of 'excuses' (Matza calls these excuses **techniques of neutralization**).

Research

David Downes (*The Delinquent Solution*) studied a group of youths in East London. He could find no evidence of a distinctive set of values which could be called a subculture. Instead he found that the youths passed their time, trying to get as much fun out of life as possible. Sometimes this brought them into conflict with the law.

2 Anomie

Robert Merton has suggested that all societies, in order to motivate people, provide them with some aim which they can achieve through hard work. However, in certain times the aim (which is usually to be financially well off) becomes impossible for the majority of the population, and especially for the working class, to attain, e.g. in periods of high unemployment. Merton argues that this leads to an increase in the level of crime, as people turn to illegal means to achieve financial success. Merton calls this situation when the goals of society are not possible by conventional means **anomie**.

3 The Marxist approach

Sociologists following the tradition of Karl Marx have suggested that the true causes of crime lie in the type of society we have in Britain. In our *capitalist* society, the ownership of most industry and commerce is in the hands of a few people – at most 10 per cent of the population. (This is an economic explanation of crime.) According to Marxists, (a) **the values** and (b) **the laws** of society are heavily influenced by the wishes of this powerful group.

(a) *The values*

Capitalism is based upon *materialism and competition*. The more goods you possess the more successful you are in life. We are constantly told by the media, for example, to buy more to own more. If we do not have such things as a good home, a new car and fashionable clothes, then we are failures. To obtain these things we need to compete against each other. Marxists argue that this constant stress on possessions, and the need to compete in order to own, drives people into trying to obtain things in any way they can. In short, capitalism is based upon greed and once greed is unleashed it is difficult to hold back.

(b) *The laws*

Laws largely reflect the wishes of the powerful, according to Marxists. Thus the criminal law looks after *their* interests, stressing as it does the importance of private property, for example, of which they have the most. The laws therefore make the activities of other groups criminal, and justify the activities of the powerful.

The groups whose behaviour is made criminal therefore are those who have less power.

18.5 Alternative Explanations for Crime and Deviancy

Sociologists have not been alone in seeking to explain the causes of crime and deviant behaviour.

The physiological approach

Early attempts to explain deviant behaviour centred on the physical or biological differences between 'normal' people and criminals.

Lombroso Writing at the end of the nineteenth century he argued that deviants were in some way physically marked and this indicated a natural drive to deviant behaviour. He pointed to things like jug-shaped ears, large eyes, hairy hands, etc. This may seem absurd today, but the idea was extremely influential a century ago.

Extra 'Y' chromosome theory In the 1960s the theory was proposed that criminals differed from others in that their chromosomes (the form of the genes that determines your biological make-up) were abnormal. The argument was that this chromosomal abnormality drove people to commit crime. Evidence to prove this came from a study in Sheffield of secure wards of a mental hospital where the most dangerous mental patients were kept. It was found that there was an above average number of inmates with chromosomal abnormalities.

The psychological approach

Psychological approaches to deviance have stressed that as well as some possible natural desire in some people to commit deviant acts, there is also an element of their upbringing, or socialization, that influences them to commit deviant acts.

The best-known approach is that of the psychologist Hans Eysenck. Eysenck argues that there are two extreme types of personalities, which people are born with: *extrovert* and *introvert*. Most people are born with a personality biased to one or the other.

The extrovert is fun-loving and outward-going. The introvert is quiet and reserved. Eysenck argues that the extrovert character is harder to socialize into the values of society and is more likely to deviate. Most criminals are therefore people of extrovert character who have been badly socialized.

Criticism

The physiological and the psychological approaches to crime and deviance are flawed in that they ignore the fact that the law (which really *creates* crime) is made by society, or at least the powerful in society – it is not *natural*. What is crime in one society at one time is the heroic act of the same society at another time. For instance, to kill when at war is possibly the action of a hero(ine). So a natural ability to be violent is good in the armed forces and bad outside.

In short, it is how actions are **defined** that is important, not the actions themselves. If this is so, then it is impossible for anybody to be born a deviant or criminal – it just depends upon how their society defines what is normal and abnormal behaviour.

18.6 Labelling

In order to simplify and make sense of the world, we *classify* objects and people. For example we talk about 'flowers', meaning a whole variety of plants, or 'houses', a term that covers hundreds of different styles of dwellings. When it comes to people, we also clarify or apply labels, such as a 'troublemaker', a 'homosexual', a 'fool', or a 'saint'. Each label carries with it a complete package of images and prejudices. The result is that we treat people differently according to the label. (The reasons why certain acts are labelled as deviant and why certain groups/people are more likely to be labelled as deviant than others is discussed on p 135.)

The consequences of labelling can be very great for a person – altering his/her whole life. The results of labelling have been called **a deviant career** by sociologists, meaning that if a person is given the label of being a deviant, then he/she will find him/herself treated very differently by others and this, in turn, will influence his/her own behaviour. For example, let us take the example of two people, both of whom steal some money.

Person A This person is caught and labelled a thief, friends desert her, others gossip and comment about her, and if she is arrested and sent to prison she loses her job. On release from prison, she will find it difficult to obtain other employment and so may have to resort to crime in order to survive.

Person A's perception of herself is also changed as she may now view herself as a thief and a criminal.

Person B This person is not caught and life continues as before.

It can be seen then that it is not the committing of a deviant act that is important, but the labelling of someone as having committed the act.

18.7 Labelling and Deviancy Amplification

It has been argued that in certain circumstances the labelling of some groups as deviant by agencies such as the media and the police can actually generate more deviance. This idea is known as **deviancy amplification**. We will examine two examples of deviancy amplification here: the role of the mass media and the role of the police.

The mass media

The mass media are very powerful in their ability to label certain groups as deviant. As most people may never meet the labelled groups themselves, the description of the group of individuals given by the media will be the image they hold of them. As the media tend to sensationalize issues in order to attract readers and viewers, it is likely that the labels attached to groups will be exaggerated in order to generate interest.

It has been suggested that newspapers and television create **folk devils** – that is people who are supposedly the source of tremendous disruption to society. The interest created by the media in these folk devils makes good news, but also causes **moral panics**. A moral panic is the situation where a group of folk devils (such as football hooligans or drug addicts) is presented so often in the media as evil and troublesome, that the public and the police become obsessed with eliminating it. Greater police resources are allocated to the control of this group and as a consequence more arrests are made.

The point is that the creation of the labels by the media and the moral panic that follows are based on great exaggeration of the true amount of trouble caused by the labelled group.

The police

The activities of the police are guided by ideas of which groups constitute the most likely to cause trouble to society, and how they ought to be handled. In particular working class and black youths are seen to be potential troublemakers. The police therefore tend to stop and search working class and black youths far more often that any other group in the population. The result is that they are more likely to uncover crime among this group. And this, of course, proves to them that they are right to pick on this group in the first place. The police therefore will put greater resources into controlling this group and there is a corresponding rise in criminality which is uncovered.

Research

Jock Young (*The Drugtakers*) studied the activities of the police in Notting Hill, London. He found that when the police decided to crack down on drug taking, they did so by having an intensive period of stopping and searching people who they thought looked 'the drug-taking type'. They uncovered an amount of drugs and this encouraged them to crack down harder on the same type of person.

As a result of the police activities and prosecutions of those who sold drugs on a casual basis, the supply of drugs declined. In stepped professional criminals who were prepared to take the risks, but who demanded much higher prices. They were also prepared to add other ingredients into the drugs to cheat on the weight, which could cause serious illness or even death. To pay for the drugs, the drug takers were tempted into crime. Furthermore, the isolation of drug takers into small, secretive groups had the effect of making these people define themselves as drug takers and experiment with stronger, physically addictive drugs. So police activity actually made the situation worse.

18.8 Understanding Criminal Statistics

Official statistics need to be treated with considerable caution. The following points need to be taken into account:

THE DARK FIGURE

Table 18.3 Crimes reported to the police

Percentage of British Crime Survey Offences reported to the police	
Household offences	*% reported to the police*
Vandalism	22
Theft from motor vehicles	30
Burglary	66
Theft of motor vehicle	95
Bicycle theft	64
Theft in a dwelling	18
Personal offences	
Theft from the person	31
Wounding	39
Robbery	47
Sexual offences	28

Table 18.3 above shows the percentage of crimes committed that were actually reported to the police, according to *The British Crime Survey*. To arrive at this estimate, the researchers interviewed 11 000 people, asked them what crimes had occurred to them, asked if they had reported the crime to the police, and finally worked out from the differences between what happened and what was reported an estimate of the number of crimes committed.

As you can see the difference between recorded and unrecorded levels of crime is truly remarkable. For example, only 22 per cent of acts of vandalism were recorded, and 30 per cent of thefts from motor vehicles. On the other hand nearly 100 per cent of thefts of cars were recorded (because cars are insured against theft). The table indicates that official police figures of the extent of crime ought to be treated with caution.

Sociologists call the difference between the actual number of crimes committed and the number appearing in criminal statistics **the dark figure**. Two factors affect the dark figure, firstly failure to report crime to the police, and secondly the possible failure of the police to record crime.

1 Failure to report crimes to the police
The British Crime Survey revealed that people failed to report crime to the police because:

(a) They regarded the matter as too trivial, e.g. only a small amount of money stolen;

(b) They felt the police would be unable to do anything about the offence, e.g. a theft from a busy shop which could have been committed by anyone;

(c) They felt it was a private matter they could deal with themselves, e.g. theft between friends;

(d) They feared or disliked the police, e.g. drug user who has been tricked into parting with his money for a 'bad deal';

(e) We can add to these that in the case of sexual offences, women who have been sexually assaulted often feel too embarrassed and humiliated to report it to the police.

2 Failure of police to record crime
Police may not record crime where:

(a) They regard the complainant of too low a status or too unreliable to take seriously, e.g. a complaint by a tramp or a drunk;

(b) They may regard the crime as too trivial to waste their time on, e.g. theft of a few pence;

(c) They may regard the matter as having nothing to do with them, even though it is technically an illegal act, e.g. less serious marital violence as a result of a quarrel between husband and wife.

The decision to define an act as illegal and to respond to it as such is dependent on the policeman's or policewoman's **discretion**.

POLICE ACTIVITY

According to Stanley Cohen, police may become **sensitized** (strongly aware) towards certain types of crime or category of offender. In this case they will take notice of this offence. As a consequence the figures for this crime rise. A good example is **mugging** which, according to Stuart Hall, increased dramatically after 1974 as a result of the media coverage of the phenomenon, which in turn led policemen to crack down on the phenomenon.

Also, certain police forces tend to pursue certain crimes more than others. Jarvis points out that Nottinghamshire has particularly high rates of motoring offences, not because of bad driving, but because of strong police emphasis on motoring law in that county.

Distribution of police

According to Box, more policemen are sent to patrol working class areas of cities than middle class suburbs, therefore crime rates in the working class areas are higher, simply because there are more police to **notice** criminal acts.

Increase in police

Between 1970 and 1987 the police force in Britain increased by one third. There may be more crime observed and recorded as a result of this.

Changes in the law

Categories of crime are sometimes changed as a result of changes in the law. For instance, the figures of crime before and after 1977 are not strictly comparable because of a change in the categorization of crimes that year.

Categorization of crimes by the police

Different police forces categorize crimes differently, and this leads to complications in giving national figures.

18.9 Summary

1 Deviant acts are acts that are considered wrong by the majority of the population.

2 The actions that are defined as deviant vary according to time, society and who it is that commits the act.

3 The reasons why an act is deviant in one situation, but not in another are related to (a) the power and status of the person committing the act, (b) the values that deviance is measured against, which change over time, and (c) the different sets of values that exist at the same time in one society (so that one person's acts may be defined as deviant by others from a different subculture).

4 Deviant acts can be distinguished from illegal acts. Only some deviant acts are classified as illegal.

5 Deviant acts are illegal in one situation but not in another, because (a) they reflect a generally held view that these particular acts are very bad, (b) there is a 'moral crusade' to make an act illegal and (c) those with power influence the creation of the law and they wish certain acts to be illegal.

6 There are certain groups in the population which, according to the official statistics, commit higher than average levels of crime.

Males commit more crime than females – about 7 to 1 in proportion.

Younger people are most likely to commit crime: about half of all crime is committed by those under 21.

Levels of crime are much higher in the inner city areas.

Working class youth have higher rates of crime than middle class youth – about 4 to 1.

7 There is a debate on the proportion of crimes committed by those of West Indian origin. The official statistics show their levels of crime to be higher – however, the statistics are hotly disputed.

8 It has been suggested that part of the reason for the higher levels of crime among the groups mentioned above compared to the population in general is related to (a) the different attitudes of the police and (b) defects in the official statistics.

9 There have been a number of explanations for crime and delinquency. They include:

(a) the subcultural approach, which is based on the idea that the person who commits crime has different values from the rest of the population. There have been three versions of this:

(i) the ecological approach, (ii) working class values, (iii) status frustration. The whole subcultural approach has been criticized for overstressing the differences in values between the middle and working classes.

(b) Anomie – where people feel that they want the material possessions of society and are encouraged to possess them by advertising and the whole culture. When they cannot get them legally, then they turn to illegal methods.

(c) The Marxist approach – this, too, stresses the importance of the desire to possess and suggests this is a natural outcome of 'capitalist' society. Marxists also point to the ability of the powerful to have the acts they want defined as crime.

10 There have been a number of alternative explanations for crime, stressing the psychological and physical differences between criminals and the majority of the population.

11 Labelling means to place particular people in a category and then to act towards them in a particular way. For instance, if a person is labelled as a hero(ine) then he or she is treated with great respect; if labelled a coward he or she is treated equally with disrespect.

12 Labelling is very important in its consequences for people. Those who are labelled as deviant (even if they are not) are treated very differently, and this can affect their whole lives.

13 The activities of the police and the mass media are very important in their ability to label people.

14 Sometimes the media can create the idea that society is under threat from certain groups (such as 'football hooligans') and a 'moral panic' occurs which actually raises the level of the crime. This process is known as deviancy amplification.

15 The official statistics on crime need to be treated with great caution. It appears that many people do not report crimes to the police and that the police sometimes do not record acts which have been reported to them as crimes.

16 People are most likely to report crime when they can benefit themselves by it – for example, by reporting burglary and car theft because they have insurance. They are least likely to report it when they may be harmed themselves or regard the matter as private.

18.10 Keywords (*as they appear in the unit*)

deviant, moral crusade, white-collar crime, indictable offences, subculture, the ecological approach, status frustration, techniques of neutralization, anomie, materialism, physiological, psychological, labelling, deviancy amplification, folk devils, moral panics, the dark figure, discretion, sensitized, egoistic, altruistic, social cohesion.

19 RELIGION

We live in a world of extraordinary complexity. Events occur, most expected, but many totally unexpected. It is necessary to have some form of explanation for these events. Science and common sense provide us with many, but not all, of the answers. Some questions are unanswerable, e.g. why am I here? Is there a meaning to life? It is to these questions that religion addresses itself. It is a way of helping us to make sense of the world. It is because a religion consists of a set of answers, or **beliefs**, to these questions, that sociologists often refer to religion as **belief systems**. Belief systems include any set of beliefs which purport to explain our position in the world and the purpose of our existence, therefore Marxist-Leninism is a belief system, too, although religion is distinct in that it believes in God (or gods). Belief systems take many forms and are generally related to the economic, social and cultural situation of groups. This explains why religion takes the form of Judaism, Buddhism, Hinduism, Rastafarianism, and Muslim belief systems, as well as the Western Christian belief system.

A distinction can be made between churches, sects and denominations.

1 *Churches* generally tend to be large in membership and to hold values which are in line with the general values of society. Often churches are closely related to the State and like the Church of England may be recognized as the State religion; in such circumstances the Church is known as the **Established Church**.

2 *Sects* are usually fairly small in membership and are very exclusive in their acceptance of members. They place great stress on obedience and strict conformity to the rules of the sect. They believe that only they know the correct way to Heaven. Examples of sects are the Moonies or Jehovah's Witnesses.

3 A *denomination* is a general description of sects that have become respectable in the eyes of middle class society. Membership is usually democratic with all members having a say in the affairs of the denomination. There is no claim that clergy have supernatural powers. A denomination lies between a church and a sect, e.g. Presbyterians, Baptists, Methodists.

19.1 Religion and Social Control

Society consists of a group of individuals with their own thoughts, desires and feelings. Society can only exist if all these conflicting thoughts and desires are somehow controlled and channelled. One way of controlling and channelling the thoughts and sections of the people in society is to make laws which they must obey under threat of punishment. A second way is to socialize people in such a way that they will come to regard the values of the society as the best possible way of living. This second method of controlling people and channelling behaviour is the task of religion in society.

There are three approaches to religion and social control, which roughly follow the writing of Durkheim, Marx and Weber, all writing in the second half of the nineteenth century.

DURKHEIM: THE FUNCTIONALIST APPROACH

Durkheim, writing at the end of the nineteenth century, was one of the first sociologists to study religion. His work stressed that religion performs a number of beneficial **functions** for society including:

1 *Social cohesion* Religion strengthens the basic beliefs and values of a society, giving them a degree of sacredness that places them above any possible questioning or doubt. This is the function of social cohesion stressed by Durkheim. Each time a religious ceremony takes place, the fundamental values are publicly reaffirmed.

2 *Sense of belonging* Religion provides an individual with a sense of belonging. As a church member he/she feels bound to society and this will motivate the person to continue as a conforming, contented member of that society.

3 *Sense of purpose and meaning* Religion helps to explain the purpose of life, (Why are we here?) and helps to make sense of the uncertainty of life. In primitive societies it provides explanations for the failure of the crop or the lack or rain.

4 *Moral guidelines* Religious values give each individual a set of guidelines to measure behaviour by.

The functions are useful for:

(a) The society, because they hold it together by reaffirming basic values, and motivating and guiding individuals to act in such a way as to ensure social conformity or, as some sociologists prefer to call it, **social control**;

(b) The individual, who is motivated to carry on and given a sense of belonging and meaning in life.

MARX AND SOCIAL CONTROL: A CRITICISM OF DURKHEIM

The functions we have just examined strongly stress the benefits of religion to the individual and to society. However, Karl Marx, writing in the nineteenth century, preferred to emphasize the negative aspects of religion. Indeed, he called it the **opium of the people**.

Marx argued that life for the mass of people consisted of working for others and being exploited by them. Most working people are used by the rich and powerful and pass their lives working to increase the wealth of the rich.

The main purpose of religion is to *control* the working class, to prevent them from refusing to be exploited. Marxists see religion as an **agency of social control**, keeping the working class as a docile workforce. How does religion perform this role?

1 By promising a better, fairer life after death. People can bear their troubles on earth if they know that they will be rewarded in Heaven. This ensures that the working class will not rebel as they believe their reward awaits them after death. Indeed religion generally makes suffering in this life a virtue.

2 Religion makes people believe that society was created by God; to change it is to go against the work of God. Therefore there are **naturally** the rich and powerful, and **naturally** the poor and powerless.

Criticism

Marxism stresses that religion always helps to control the working class, so that they can be subordinated. However, the church has played a leading role in attacking repressive governments in some countries, particularly in South Africa. In South America, in Nicaragua and El Salvador, the local Catholic church has also been very active in defending human rights (although it has been strongly criticized by the Vatican for this, as Marx would have predicted).

RELIGION AND SOCIAL CHANGE

Durkheim stressed the importance of religion to society in maintaining order and stability. Marx argued that order was really social control for the benefit of the few. Weber took up the second element of Durkheim's work, stability. Weber argued that religion, as well as maintaining stability, also helped to bring about social change.

In *The Protestant Ethic and the Spirit of Capitalism* Weber looked at the role of the strict version of Protestantism known as **Calvinism**, in bringing about industrialization. In the eighteenth century the values of Calvinism stressed working hard, saving money and not engaging in frivolous pursuits. When new machinery was being invented in the eighteenth century, the Calvinists were some of the few people who had spare **capital savings** to finance the building of machines and factories. As a result of their thrift, industrialization based on **capitalism** first occurred in Britain. If the values of Calvinism had not led to there being spare capital available, industrialization may not have occurred. So, for Weber, religion can bring about social and economic change.

In recent years the role of the Islamic faith in the Middle East—notably Iran and Lebanon—has been of a revolutionary nature, and has been the motivation behind political revolutionary action.

Social control: conclusions

1 Durkheim stressed the positive functions of religion (a) for society in that it performs the function of social control, holding society together for the benefit of all, and (b) also providing a sense of belonging and purpose for individuals.

2 Marx stressed the negative functions of religion in that it helps the rich to control the working class and exploit them.

3 Weber argued that religion can help bring about social change.

19.2　Secularization: The Declining Importance of Religion

Secularization means that the importance and influence of religion is in decline, and people are less religious in their attitudes and behaviour.

There is a debate among sociologists concerning the extent of secularization in British society.

THE ARGUMENT FOR SECULARIZATION

1 In 1986 18 per cent of the adult population **belonged to** a Christian church, while only 10 per cent actually attended. This can be compared to the 1851 **English Census of Religion** which showed that 40 per cent of the population were churchgoers.

2 Between 1961 and 1980, in the Church of England, confirmations declined by over 50 per cent and Roman Catholic confirmations declined by 33 per cent.

3 Between 1966 and 1980, the number of marriages solemnized in register offices rose from 33 per cent to 51 per cent, indicating a lower proportion marrying in church.

4 The Church has lost any significant power to influence political decisions. Indeed most major religious appointments of the Church of England are decided by politicians.

5 Although all schools must teach religious knowledge, the central importance of religion in education has declined. Before 1870 most elementary education was provided by the churches. Today, the majority of schools are provided by the state through the local authorities.

6 People no longer necessarily take their moral lead from the Churches. Examples of this are the increase in divorce, the passing of the abortion law in 1969 and the widespread use of contraception among Catholics. Wilson argues that it is sometimes Churches that follow the changes in morals of the general population, for instance the Church of England's acceptance of divorce.

7 The clergy are not the central figures in the community that they once were. They have lost both status and an adequate income to maintain themselves at a comparative level to other professions.

8 Fewer people believe in God and many regard the Churches as irrelevant to modern life, except for the traditional ceremonies associated with birth (baptism), marriage and death (burial service).

Reasons for decline

Wilson suggests that the following are the main causes of secularization:

1 The growth of science and rational thought. Science seeks to explain the relationships between various physical phenomena, for instance, the relationships between tidal movements and the gravitational pull of the moon. Religious explanations of the natural (and social) world have been consistently challenged by science. As a result of science, society generally is characterized by rational thought, which tends to reject supernatural explanations of the world.

2 The weakening of traditional values which stressed that church attendance was necessary in order to be **respectable**.

3 The weakening of the family, so that children are less likely to attend church with their parents and to be socialized into church attendance.

4 The influence of new political and social philosophies which criticize the importance and role of the Church.

5 Religion has been weakened by the growth of material values. Religion stresses the importance of good behaviour, and that a person ought to be measured by how good he or she is. Today, people are measured far more by what they possess.

CRITICISMS OF THE SECULARIZATION ARGUMENT

1 The meaning of the statistics: evidence for the declining importance of religion should not be taken as proven from the statistics of church attendance and membership. Statistics do not show the amount of private prayer, or visiting of churches. According to a 1982 survey only 7 percent of people do not identify with a church.

2 People no longer attend church because it is **the thing to do**, as in Victorian Britain, instead they attend through a much stronger sense of commitment.

3 The majority of the population still believe in some form of god. Over 70 per cent of the population believe in God.

4 In recent years there has been a proliferation of new **sects**, such as Elim, Pentacostal, Rastafarian, usually attractive to the deprived groups. These tend to appeal to groups traditionally ignored by the older-established churches.

5 The older traditional churches have failed to appeal to the working class and poor, although middle class attendance is significantly higher. This is the main reason for the decline in church attendance and for the compensating growth of sects.

Table 19.1 Church membership: estimates, 1975 and 1990

Trinitarian churches	Adult members (millions) 1975	Adult members (millions) 1990	**Non-Trinitarian churches**	Adult members (millions) 1975	Adult members (millions) 1990
Anglican	2.27	1.84	Mormons	0.10	0.15
Presbyterian	1.65	1.29	Jehovah's Witnesses	0.08	0.12
Methodist	0.61	0.48	Spiritualists	0.06	0.06
Baptist	0.27	0.24	Other non-Trinitarian	0.09	0.13
Other Protestant churches	0.53	0.70	*Total*	0.33	0.46
Roman Catholic	2.53	1.95	**Other religions**		
Orthodox	0.20	0.27	Muslims	0.40	0.99
Total	8.06	6.77	Sikhs	0.12	0.39
			Hindus	0.10	0.14
			Jews	0.11	0.11
			Others	0.08	0.23
			Total	0.81	1.86

(**Source**: *Social Trends* 1992)

6 There may be a decline in certain Christian denominations, but there has been a massive increase in non-Christian religions. For example, the number of Muslims has doubled in the last 10 years.

THE CHANGING FACE OF RELIGION

What appears to have happened over the last twenty years is:

1 A decline in the more traditional churches.

2 A large growth in sects, which draw their membership from those who feel the traditional churches no longer look after their interests. There are two very different types of member:

(a) 'rejecters' who reject society and seek a new lifestyle, who join sects such as the Moonies;

(b) the 'rejected', the poor and deprived who turn to the sects for comfort.

3 The rapid growth of non-Christian religions.

19.3 The Significance of Non-Christian Religions in Britain

Although the majority of people in Britain are Christians, there has been a significant growth in the last twenty years in other non-Christian religions, in addition to the already established Jewish religion.

The three major religions that have established themselves recently in Britain are:

1 Islam
2 Hinduism
3 the Sikh religion

1 Islam

Followers of Islam are known as Muslims and in Britain normally come from the Bangladeshi and Pakistani community. There are about 900 000 Muslims in Britain.

The religion derives from the Middle East and is based on the preachings of Muhammed, born in about AD 570. Islam is the second largest religion in the world after Christianity. The holy book of Muslims is the Koran and it contains the beliefs and duties of Islam. Muslims believe in one God, whom they call Allah, and they believe in the same prophets as Christians. However, they do not accept that Jesus was the Son of God, merely another in a line of prophets which finished with Mohammed.

Muslims demand strict obedience to the Koran, unlike the rather loose guidance that modern Christians seem to take from the New Testament.

In Britain Islam is the fastest-growing religion. Its numbers have doubled since 1970. It is the religion of most of the Pakistani and Bangladeshi immigrants and reflects the growth in the numbers of their descendants. It imposes strict rules of behaviour on its members, and women in particular are expected to be extremely modest. It is considered unseemly for women to expose any of their body to men and in its most rigorous forms, women are expected to cover their faces with a veil. It has become the unifying factor among immigrants in Britain from these countries and so not only reflects religious belief, but provides a sense of identity.

2 Hinduism

Hinduism derives from India and dates back at least as far as 650 BC. It is based upon the principle of rebirth (reincarnation). How a person behaves in this lifetime determines what form he or she takes in the next. Hindus are divided into various castes (see pp 40–1 for details) which are ranked according to their holiness. They believe that their God or Brahma is present everywhere in everything. Hindus believe in three main incarnations of God: Brahma, as creator; Vishnu, as preserver; Shiva, as destroyer.

In Britain Hindus are mainly immigrants, or descendants of immigrants, from India and the ex-colonies of Britain in Africa. They tend to be educated and mainly middle class. Like the Muslims, the religion has provided a focal point for Indian immigrants from a wide variety of backgrounds. It is not as strict a religion as Islam, although it stresses the importance of modesty among women, the dominance of men and the importance of the family. There are almost 140 000 Hindus in Britain.

It appears that the caste system has declined in importance in Britain.

3 Sikhism

The Sikhs (or 'learners') derived their religion from Hinduism. Their founder was Nanak (1469–1538) who lived in the Punjab, Northern India, which is the centre of Sikh religion. The Sikh religion emerged as a response to the fatalism of Hinduism which stressed the acceptance of everything that happened, but more importantly it rejected the caste system. Under the leadership of Gobind Rai in the seventeenth century, the Sikhs developed into renowned warriors and even now are obliged always to carry a sword. Practising Sikh men do not cut their hair or shave – hence the turbans.

In Britain The Sikhs are found in relatively small numbers and the community, although originally from India itself, is quite distinct from, and often hostile to, the larger Hindu community. This is to do with the demands of Sikhs in India for a separate homeland. Sikh temples are unusual in that there are no statues to worship. Congregations gather for readings of the holy book, the Granth, and to listen to sermons from it. Sikh men are highly visible because of their turbans. There are about 175 000 Sikhs in Britain.

19.4 The Significance of Religion in a Simple Society

All known simple societies have some form of religion or magic. In these societies, people as a rule believe that all the activities are under the control of a god or gods.

1 In simple societies, magic and religion are closely connected. Religious or magical ceremonies help to explain not just the purpose of life, but also the relationships between natural phenomena. An excellent example of this was given by the anthropologist Malinowski in his study of the Trobriand Islanders of the South Pacific, before the Second World War. For these islanders, the major method of obtaining food was through fishing. The Trobriand Islanders fished either in the open sea, which was dangerous and unpredictable, or in a lagoon which was simple and relatively safe. Interestingly Malinowski noticed that there were a number of important magic rituals that the fishermen performed before going fishing in the sea, but that there were no rituals for fishing in the lagoon.

Malinowski explained the difference in the need for rituals in one situation and the lack of them in the other, by referring to the unpredictability and danger attached to sea fishing. The magic rituals gave the fishermen a feeling that they could obtain some predictability over the weather and the currents, thus lessening the danger. The magic rituals, if performed correctly, were supposed to guarantee safe fishing. If the weather or the sea caused loss of life, then the Islanders explained this by saying that the rituals had not been performed correctly. Magic therefore helped to overcome the unpredictability of the world. Of course, we now know the real cause of the storms, so we rely upon science for our ability to predict the weather.

2 Not only does religion then help to overcome the problems of uncertainty facing people in their lives, but also, rituals and ceremonies mark important stages in individual lives – birth, transition to adulthood, marriage, death. There are other rituals, too, which serve to mark key phases in the calendar of a community. For example in an agricultural society, there are ceremonies to mark the arrival of rains or the harvest. So in traditional European societies there were the summer harvest festivals and among the Trobriand Islanders the yam festival (yam is a large vegetable).

19.5 Summary

1 The Christian religion is represented by a number of different denominations, ranging from large churches of ancient establishment to small recent sects.

2 Religion plays a crucial role in social control, helping to maintain stability in society. It does so by implanting a certain set of values as coming from God and which are therefore unquestionable.

3 In recent years the importance of religion as a means of control has declined. It has been replaced by the schools and the media.

4 Religion has also had considerable influence on social change. Weber has argued that the Industrial Revolution first occurred in Britain because of the growth of strict forms of Protestantism.

5 There is a debate on the extent to which the importance of religion has declined in Britain. One view is that a process of secularization has taken place. The other view is that although church attendance has declined, people are as religious as they ever were.

6 Secularization is supposed to be proved by the decline in church membership and attendance and the decrease in those who marry in church, as well as the decline in influence in society in general of the clergy.

7 The opponents of the secularization theory argue that once church membership was a social necessity, whereas nowadays people go to church because they believe in God. They also argue that many people who believe in religion and the church do not necessarily attend, but follow the general teaching of the churches.

8 Increasingly there has been a growth of non-Christian religions in Britain, such as Islam, Hinduism and the Sikh religion. These powerfully influence the way of life of those from immigrant backgrounds.

9 In simple societies religion is the focus that holds society together.

19.6 Keywords (*as they appear in the unit*)

churches, denominations, sects, social control, social cohesion, rites of passage, opium of the people, Calvinism, secularization, Islam, Hinduism, Sikh religion, rituals.

20 MEDIA

20.1 Types and Characteristics of the Media

The media is the term used to cover the following forms of communication: TV, radio, newspapers, magazines, books, films and recordings.

1 All these are one-way systems of communication from a single source to a large number of people (a 'mass' of people).

2 The audience receiving the information has little or no chance of responding to the source.

3 Mass media always involve the technology of broadcasting, or print and distribution.

4 The mass media are usually operated for profit (although not the BBC and many other national broadcasting systems).

5 The mass media are usually run by full-time professionals whose job it is to communicate the ideas thought important by the owners and controllers of that medium.

6 The mass media present information or entertainment in a specific format. Television, for example, has many half-hour programmes divided into categories such as 'news' or 'light entertainment'.

Two-way communication

This is in contrast to two-way, face-to-face communication where two people exchange ideas or messages, such as in a conversation.

1 The communication is highly personal.

2 Either of the people may interrupt the other and present an alternative viewpoint.

3 The communication is started and finished according to the desires of people to communicate, not a fixed schedule.

4 Much personal communication is conducted without any technology being involved – although, of course, telephones and CB radio are used.

By contrast, mass communication is based on the use of technology. Generally, the words or images are broadcast or printed and distributed.

20.2 Socialization, Social Control and the Media

(For detailed discussion of socialization see p 1; for social control see p 131.)

The mass media play an extremely important role in **secondary socialization**, which is the form of socialization that reinforces the basic **primary socialization** learned in childhood. They are able to do this in a number of ways:

1 They are the most important source of information about the wider world, beyond the personal experience of most people. We only know about politics, crimes and sporting events through the media, unless we are actually present.

2 Attitudes and opinions about the world are therefore formed by the media.

3 How the media present information is crucial. They do not simply show the facts or the situation as they are, but put an interpretation on them.

4 This interpretation consists of stressing the basic values of society in their contents, emphasizing the difference between the normal and the deviant.

5 This emphasis is achieved in two ways: (a) by *selection* of material. A typical news story consists of a 'shocking' event, such as a violent crime which highlights what society disapproves of – normal everyday behaviour is not regarded as news; (b) by *presentation*, reporting deviant events in a way that shows they are not approved of – newspapers generally present their news on criminals, drugtakers, etc. in such a way as to show their disapproval.

6 Once formed, people's views of the world are constantly *reinforced* by the media.

There is considerable dispute between those who argue (a) that the media are owned and controlled by a few of the rich and powerful who then impose their values on the population and (b) those who argue that the media reflect the views and attitudes of most of the population, and if they did not, they would not survive in a fiercely competitive market. They also point out the role of the press in uncovering corruption and wrong-doing among the powerful.

20.3 The Media and Social Control

WOMEN AND THE MEDIA

The media help to perpetuate the division of roles between males and females. Daily Newspapers, for example, include photographs of semi-naked women. The contents of specialist magazines for women reaffirm that the accepted role for women is to make themselves attractive, to be good mothers and housewives. Different magazines may cater for different age groups and interests, but these themes remain, merely being adjusted in tune with the age groups. Female youth magazines, for instance, stress the need to get a boyfriend and the importance of romance in girls' lives.

Male magazines on the other hand tend to be concerned with specialist hobbies, such as cars, motorbikes or windsurfing. There are some that consist almost entirely of female nudes.

On the wider issues of the images of males and females presented in the media, research has shown that the roles of the main heroes and the other dominant characters in most plays, films and television programmes are written for men, with women playing their assistants. It is the man's role to provide excitement and the woman's to provide attractiveness.

The process by which the media reinforce and maintain the gender divisions in society begins as soon as a person can read. The first reading books tend to have very clear-cut male and females roles. Virtually all books, until a few years ago, automatically used male examples (e.g. if a student studies hard, *he* will pass the sociology exam).

Research

1 Marjorie Ferguson in *Forever Feminine* studied the three best-selling women's magazines between 1949 and 1974: *Woman, Woman's Own* and *Woman's Weekly*. She found certain themes running through all those years. They included: women's need for emotion; feminine unpredictability; the importance of being young; love and marriage; and the theme of self-improvement. When she came to study the magazines for 1979–80, Ferguson found a change in that there was a greater stress on women being independent and not just being housewives – showing that women's magazines are changing to reflect the changing role of women. Nevertheless, she still found that the key message of the magazines is that women are different from men and have different needs.

2 Angela McRobbie in *Jackie, an Ideology of Adolescent Feminity* examined the stories in the girls' magazine *Jackie*. She found that the main message of the stories was that a girl was someone to be looked at and appreciated, rather than someone who went out and about doing things. The main theme of the magazines was romance and love. McRobbie argues that the magazines encourage girls to be passive and to regard only romance as truly important in their lives.

3 Suzanne Czaplinski's *Sexism in Award-Winning Picture Books* is an American study of children's illustrated books. She found that (a) there was very strict division of roles between males and females – even though the roles were often outdated; (b) there were far more male than female characters; (c) the roles that women were given were as mothers and aunts, rather than as the main characters of the story.

The **stereotype** of what are female characteristics is constantly reinforced by the media. In terms of **social control** women who challenge the stereotype are regarded as being odd in some way, or deviant.

RACE AND THE MEDIA

The British population is 95 per cent white. Blacks and Asians are a small minority, over half of whom were born here. The impression given by the media, however, is that there is still an immigration problem and that there are far more Blacks and Asians than actually exist. The stress of media coverage is on the conflict caused by so many immigrants in Britain, rather than on Blacks' and Asians' difficulties in the fields of work, housing and education.

The differences between Blacks and Whites are constantly referred to and thus in reality reinforced.

Research

Troyna in *Public Awareness and the Media: A Study of Reporting Race* found that between 1976 and 1978 the reporting of race in the media was based upon the theme of the outsiders who were living among us. The second biggest topic of race was the issue of immigration – even though there has been a very sharp decline in the numbers of Black and Asian immigrants in the last 20 years.

In a survey he carried out, he concluded that the media did encourage people to believe that Black people were a source of trouble.

Criticism

The argument that the media actually encourage racial prejudice has been criticized by Braham, who argues that the British press merely reflect racist feeling already held by the population.

The result of the media treatment of Blacks is, however, to strengthen a stereotype of them.

CRIMINALS AND THE MEDIA

The media are commercial institutions trying to earn profits from attracting as many viewers, listeners or readers as possible (and the BBC has to work in this commercial environment). The result is that some crimes which are of greater 'human interest' are grossly over-reported compared to others. For example, crimes of violence are over-reported by 36 times their actual occurrence and crimes of indecency by 34 times. The result is that people receive a highly distorted view of the sorts of crimes taking place, and thereby people's fears are greatly increased.

The media creates a stereotype of the 'typical' sort of crime, and creates public fear about it — which can lead to moral panic. When this occurs people get so worried about certain crimes as a result of the media coverage that all the forces of law and order are thrown against the stereotyped deviants, while other forms of crime are left alone.

Research

Stuart Hall, in *Policing the Crisis*, argued that in the early 1970s there was a sudden upsurge in the reporting of a crime dubbed as 'mugging', in which a person or small group was attacked and robbed in the streets. The coverage in the media was intense, even though the actual number of muggings formed a small proportion of all crimes. As a response to press coverage, a huge number of police were drafted into Brixton, the area regarded as the centre of mugging in London. A stereotype of the mugger became the Black youth. The police, who had been looking for a justification of heavy policing of Brixton, used the mugging crisis as the reason for swamping the district. The **stereotype** criminal becomes the inner city delinquent and the **social control** element is that the factors causing the problems of inner city youth are ignored and the spotlight taken off the multi-million pound swindles in the City of London.

20.4 The Media, Labelling and Moral Panics

The media are the providers of information on deviance for most people, including politicians and, to some extent, the police. The image projected about deviance and crime by newspapers and television can affect the activities of the police and the attitudes of the public.

Labelling or stereotyping is when a person or group is described as having certain characteristics, and then responded to in a way that seems appropriate for people with these particular characteristics. For example, if a person is described as 'mad' then, *whether it is true or not*, he/she will be treated as mad, even if his/her behaviour is perfectly normal.

The media have the power to label certain groups and their actions in this way and sometimes to create great public concern about them.

Research

In the mid-1960s Stanley Cohen, in *Folk Devils and Moral Panics*, studied the way that the media helped to create an image concerning the original mods and rockers.

In 1964, at the Easter bank holiday, there was little news and as a result some papers printed stories about trouble between mods and rockers at various seaside resorts, even though nothing out of the ordinary had happened. As a result of the press coverage, many young people began to identify themselves as mods or rockers. The next bank holiday, drawn by the media, thousands of mods and rockers converged on seaside towns. But so did the media looking for stories, and the police concerned about possible mass fighting.

The press, eager to make a good story, grossly exaggerated; the police, over-responding to the large number of young people, arrested numbers of them for very minor offences. A huge public panic began and at each bank holiday for some years the police effectively swamped seaside towns, eager to search out and stop any trouble.

According to Cohen the results of the media's activities were:

(a) *The label* For young people a certain style of dress came to symbolize being a mod — and the behaviour expected of mods was to go to seaside resorts on bank holidays and to look for trouble with the rockers. The police and public, too, saw a style of dress signifying 'trouble'. So *anybody* dressed like this was a possible troublemaker.

(b) *A moral panic* The activities of the media created such irrational fear among the police, the public and the politicians that there was effectively a panic to introduce measures against the perceived troublemakers.

(c) *The amplification of deviance* The result was a greater increase in actual deviance as a result of the media's activities than there would have been without them.

The example given earlier of Stuart Hall's study of 'mugging' is a second example of stereotyping by the media.

Hall argues that in the 1970s there was a breakdown in social control in the inner cities as a result of increasing unemployment and social problems, and an excuse was sought for heavier policing. The media's mugging 'campaign' provided the justification.

20.5 Explanation of Media Influence on Behaviour

It is generally believed that the mass media influence behaviour, and much of the discussion on socialization in this unit rests upon this assumption. However, sociologists are not in agreement on the *extent* to which the media influence our behaviour and *how* they influence our behaviour.

1 The behaviour (or hypodermic syringe) model

The first attempts to explain the influence of the media were based on the commonsense approach that if it was true that the media influence our behaviour, then watching a violent or sexually stimulating film would alter a person's behaviour.

Research

In the 1960s Bandura showed a film of children being violent to dolls to another group of children, who were then given dolls themselves. He found that the children tended to imitate the violence on the screen.

Criticism

The idea that people watch a television programme or film, and are so influenced by it that they abandon their normal behaviour and go out to attack people, seems too naïve. It treats people as if they had no minds or views of their own.

2 Audience selection

The model just described has been replaced by a greater understanding that people choose what programmes they wish to watch and which newspapers they buy. Instead of being passive, the audience in this approach is seen as actively interpreting the information given.

In order for something to influence our behaviour we must first have a receptive attitude towards it. An **attitude** is a firmly held belief which causes a person to respond in a particular way to a stimulus or event. Attitudes are necessary in order for us to make sense of our world. They form a **code** (or cultural **map**) which allows us to respond with consistency to similar types of situation. The mass media can **reinforce** attitudes already held, but it is difficult for them fundamentally to change people's attitudes. This is because people tend to **select** the information they want to hear or read. Thus:

(a) People select the type of newspaper they wish to read, usually one that confirms their political attitudes;

(b) People view events through their particular bias and select the elements of the **facts** that reinforce their existing attitudes;

(c) People remember information that confirms their opinions and forget the rest.

The effect of the information upon our attitudes is also influenced by (i) the origins of the information: a prestigious source is more likely to be believed than an unknown one; (ii) the situation in which the information is received – whether it **fits** in and helps to make sense of the situation in which the audience find themselves.

Research

David Morley, in *The Nationwide Audience*, studied the responses of different groups of people to a popular BBC 6 o' clock 'magazine' show that appeared in the 1970s. He found that the different groups approached the material presented in the programme in different ways, reflecting the particular background and values they held. For instance, bank managers saw the programme's treatment of the 1977 budget in the very different light from a group of shop stewards.

3 The cultural approach

This approach derives from the **audience selection** approach, but sees the influence of the media as being more powerful, *over a long time*, in that they create a culture or climate of thought, within which people hold opinions. In other words, the media define the range of acceptable opinions on any matter. The first two approaches, then, stress that the media have an influence after a short time. The third approach stresses less the direct effect, rather the creation of a climate of opinion.

20.6 Violence and the Media

Much research has centred on the role of the media (particularly television) in encouraging violence. But the research has not been conclusive.

Research

1 In *Violence on Television* (1972), a report prepared for the BBC by Katz *et al*, a questionnaire was completed by a minimum of 600 households on 12 evenings of television viewing. Further

to this, individuals and 50 families were also interviewed. The results indicated that as most violence seen was so obviously fictitious and unrelated to real life, it had little influence on the viewers. The authors found that the viewers were, however, becoming **desensitized** by so much violence, so that they were becoming less alarmed by it in real life. However, violence on television did not incite people to violent acts in real life.

2 In *Television Violence and the Adolescent Boy* (1978), which is based upon interviews of over 1500 boys aged 12–17 in London, Belson found that **high exposure** to violence on television does increase the amount of serious violence in adolescent boys.

3 Halloran, who was heavily involved in a study commissioned by the Independent Broadcasting Authority, *The Portrayal of Violence on TV* (1978), argues that it is a mistake to try to form a **direct** link between violence and television viewing. Although the study found that violence on television could **reinforce** existing aggressive attitudes, it also argued that television is only one of many influences on people's behaviour. So violent adolescents may be drawn to watching violence on television, but television is not the **cause** of the tendency to violence.

We can see that the answer to the different survey results lies in the fact that the mass media's influence on our behaviour must be balanced against the importance of family socialization, the strength of the legal system and the wider cultural values of our society, all of which abhor violence.

20.7 Mass Media and Political Opinion

Sociologists are generally of the opinion that in the short term the mass media do little to change people's voting intentions. However, exposure over a long period of time to a political message can change people's opinions towards it. Therefore, party political broadcasts and the mass media's election coverage may influence only the **floating** voter; the rest have already made up their minds who they are going to vote for. Over a number of years the mass media's coverage of certain political events (e.g. the Common Market, industrial disputes) can cause a change in attitude. Butler and Stokes found in a study they conducted that between 1964 and 1966, 73 per cent of their respondents had altered their opinions towards the political party supported by the newspapers they read, while 27 per cent actually changed party allegiance to that of their newspapers. This brings us on the next point.

The findings of Butler and Stokes are important because the vast majority of national daily and Sunday newspapers support the Conservative Party. This can be seen in the chart below.

Newspapers supporting the Conservative Party		*Labour Party*	*Other*
The Times	Sunday Express	Daily Mirror	The Guardian
Sunday Times	The Sun	Sunday People	Observer
Daily Telegraph	News of the World		The Independent
Daily Mail	Daily Star		Today
Mail on Sunday			
Daily Express			

Most people read a particular paper for reasons other than its political slant – for example for its arts or sports coverage. However, for whatever reason a particular newspaper is bought, the fact remains that it is supporting the policies of one or other political party. This party is usually, but not always, the one favoured by the paper's proprietor.

Interestingly, television is seen as being independent and providing more reliable news than newspapers. The BBC is a public corporation, while the **independent** channels are controlled by the Independent Broadcasting Authority who combined to form the Independent Television Authority. The television companies are therefore seen to be less influenced by any one person. However, as the next section will show, television's presentation of news and information can be as misleading as that of the newspapers.

Whereas a newspaper owner may deliberately influence the paper's support of certain policies, journalists are often guilty of **unwitting bias**. What becomes news, both in newspapers and on radio and television, is shaped not only by commercial pressures and the constraint to act within the law, but also by organizational pressures from within the mass media. Golding and Elliott have pointed out that the content of news portrays a very particular, one-sided view of the world. This is not the result of a **conspiracy**, however, but is a necessary consequence of how events are regarded as news in the first place, and are then selected and presented to the audience. Journalists emphasize the more interesting, colourful areas of social life at the expense of the more mundane. A result of this is that those in powerful and privileged positions are more often consulted for information and opinion. Howard Becker has called this the **hierarchy of credibility**, whereby those in powerful positions in society are more likely to be believed than the man in the street.

(Further discussion on politics and the media can be found in the sections Ownership and Control p 156 and Social Control p 131.)

20.8 Contents of the Media

1 Newspapers

The **contents** vary according to readership.

(a) 'popular' papers such as the *Sun* concentrate on:

(i) human interest stories, such as the lives of TV celebrities, pop stars and royalty;
(ii) mainstream sport, such as football, snooker and cricket; (iii) 'sexy' or 'spicy' stories;
(iv) sensational happenings, usually in Britain.

(b) The 'quality' newspapers usually concentrate on:

(i) political events; (ii) economic problems; (iii) in-depth coverage of a particular topic, possibly on a weekly rota basis (for instance, every Tuesday *The Guardian* has a section devoted to education); (iv) sport.

The **presentation** varies with the type of newspaper.

(a) popular papers: (i) have very short articles; (ii) they are written in extremely simple English; (iii) the information given is very simple and viewpoints (if included at all) are presented in black-and-white; (iv) there is great sensationalism – with every attempt to excite the reader; (v) great use is made of photographs – particularly of attractive women.

(b) The quality papers: (i) have much longer articles; (ii) they are written in depth; (iii) the information is usually fairly complex and there is some attempt to give different viewpoints – although most of the papers are biased towards a conservative viewpoint; (iv) the presentation is usually fairly dull, with less exaggeration; (v) fewer photographs are used.

2 Television

In the past the BBC was far less sensational than ITV. However, the need to keep audiences high has led to adoption of the ITV style of broadcasting, which is to attract the biggest audience possible.

Both BBC and ITV have specialist channels where the programmes for minority tastes are shown: BBC 2 and Channel 4. In some ways this division reflects the popular/quality divisions in newspapers.

3 The record industry

The record industry is dominated by a very few large companies. It is in their interest to stabilize the market for records. The greater the diversity of music, of groups and of styles, the more complex the selling of records becomes. The result is that record companies (as well as radio stations) push a relatively small number of musicians whose music is 'mainstream'. The wider diversity of styles is ignored. After a while, however, if this sound gets stale, the public will usually become attracted to another style of music of another group. At first these pose a threat to the established order, but gradually the new style is taken on by the record companies, polished, and becomes the new mainstream. This pattern of stagnation is particularly strong in the United States.

20.9 Reasons for the Style of the Media's Contents

1 Profitability

The media, like other commercial institutions, need to be profitable in order to survive. The exception is the BBC, which is funded by the government, who levy an annual licence fee on the use of television sets. However, the BBC exists in a commercial environment and has to compete against the private television stations in order to prove its popularity and its right to exist.

For broadcasting (i.e. television and radio) and newspapers, profitability involves:

(a) Having the maximum number of viewers/listeners or the maximum possible number of sales;

(b) Advertising – having large sales or viewing figures is not enough, what is also needed is advertising revenue. This is attracted by having large circulation/viewing figures of the right target group for advertisers. The better-off the audience, the smaller the numbers of people viewing/ reading is necessary for the newspaper or television station to exist.

The biggest-selling newspapers today, the *Sun* and the *Daily Mirror*, have mainly a working class readership. The smallest-selling, *The Times* and *The Guardian*, have a middle class readership.

For the commercial television stations, the sheer size of the audience means that they are attractive to most types of advertisers.

2 Differences in audience/readership

Newspapers deliberately aim their contents to attract a particular sort of reader. The 'popular' dailies, such as the *Daily Mirror*, which are aimed at a largely working class audience, tend to concentrate on what they regard the working class as wanting: which is basically sensational 'stories' with dollops of sex. The quality papers consider that their middle class audience wish to read about politics and money.

3 The ownership of the papers

As you can see below, in the section on ownership and control, newspaper owners are relatively few in number in Britain. Rupert Murdoch, owner of *The Times* and the *Sun*, and Robert Maxwell, owner, among other papers, of the *Daily Mirror*, are best known. There is clear evidence from journalists that both impose their views on the editors to ensure that the papers reflect their ideas.

4 The activities of journalists

Undoubtedly, journalists' activities are the most important influence on the content and presentation of the news. Journalists work with a concept of **newsworthiness**. Among the elements guiding journalists in the way they select and present their material are:

(a) *Frequency* Things that happen quickly, and which are easily understood, fit into frequency of publication of daily papers – a big bank robbery, for example. Events that take a long time to unfold are not regarded as news. Until the intervention of Bob Geldof, there was very little interest in the famines in Africa.

(b) *Threshold of importance* The assumed importance of an event. Something at local level will not be regarded as important enough for national news. The assumed importance affects the amount of coverage. A local car accident is not worthy of inclusion in national news, but a 50-car pile-up on the M1 is. This also applies to people; some are more important than others.

(c) *Clarity* The simpler and clearer an event is – or at least the clearer that it can be presented – affects its inclusion in news. Problems with the economy are difficult to present, but a strike is easy and clear.

(d) *Meaningfulness* Events have to be culturally meaningful to the journalist and to his/her audience. So events in non-Western countries receive little coverage.

(e) *Unexpectedness* Things that happen every day or are entirely predictable are not news worthy – there needs to be an element of surprise. However, the news must also be culturally meaningful.

(f) *Composition* There is a belief that there ought to be a balance of types of news items. For example, there ought to be a mix of exciting and topical stories, balanced with 'human interest' items.

(g) *Personalization* The stress is always on personalities, not on the political, economic, or social background from which they are drawn.

20.10 Patterns of Ownership and Control

OWNERSHIP

The debate between **pluralist** and **radical** writers in the Social Control section is closely related to the patterns of media ownership. The more widespread the ownership of the media, the greater the diversity of views. On the other hand, concentration of ownership in a few hands tends to strengthen the radical writers' argument.

Table 20.2, adapted from Golding's *The Mass Media*, shows the degree of concentration of the market. It illustrates the proportion of the total market taken by the top five companies in each field in the early 1970s.

Table 20.2 Proportion of total market accounted for by the five leading companies in each medium

National morning newspaper	86%
National Sunday newspaper	88
Commercial Television – % of homes served	73
Paperback books – % domestic production	86
Cinema – % of box office takings	80

Newspapers:	Mirror Group, Beaverbrook, News International, Associated Newspapers, Thompson.
TV:	London Weekend, Thames, Central, Granada, Yorkshire.
Paperback Books:	Pearson Longman, Granada Publishing, HarperCollins, Thompson, Pan.
Cinema:	EMI – MGM, Fox Rank, Columbia, Warner.

1 Concentration of control

We can say from the evidence of the table that the first characteristic of the mass media is **concentration of control**. Since the table was compiled in 1972 there have been a number of changes within the top five companies of each sector, not affecting the overall pattern but shifting the proportion of concentration from one large company to another.

One of the more successful companies in the newspaper business, for example, has been Rupert Murdoch's News International Company which now owns *The Times, The Sunday Times,* the *Sun* and the *News of the World*; these four account for 41 per cent of all daily and 45 per cent of all Sunday newspaper sales.

2 Diversification

The second important characteristic of the mass media is **diversification**.

(a) Large commercial concerns with no previous experience of mass media ownership are now diversifying their interests and acquiring ownership of a range of media outlets. This has produced a tangled web of interlocking interests.

(b) Owners of a particular medium are buying into another to minimize the financial risks of specializing in one medium where they may be stranded if there is a shift of popularity (e.g. from the cinema to the video). This means that new media reflect the format and values of the existing media.

3 Multi-nationalization

The third characteristic is **multi-nationalization** which means that the media have increasingly become international, e.g. Murdoch's *News International* is an important force in Australia and the United States as well as in Britain.

CONTROL

1 The power of the owners

We can see from the evidence above that the ownership of the media rests in the hands of a few companies. The biggest-selling group of newspapers in Britain – that producing the *Sun* and the *Daily Star* – is owned by one man: Rupert Murdoch, renowned for imposing his values on the contents of his newspapers.

Indeed, Harold Evans a former editor of *The Times,* alleges was forced to resign because of his refusal to write editorials according to the wishes of its owner Mr Murdoch. Within the restraints of good taste and the need to be commercially successful, a newspaper's owner has a tremendous amount of power to shape its political direction. The day-to-day decisions are left to an editor who knows what his/her employers expect of him/her.

2 Influences running against the control of the owners alone

It is important to realize that the owners are not the only influence on the contents of the media, as we saw earlier. The following also influence the contents:

(a) Journalists' sense of news values (discussed on p 156). Journalists have certain ideas of what constitutes news – although the views of the owners will profoundly affect the content and the viewpoint of the newspapers, there does exist a professional sense of what constitutes news values.

The freedom of the journalists to decide on the content varies with the newspaper group.

(b) The need to be commercial. For a newspaper or television station, there is the need to have high readership or viewing figures. Clearly, contents that are too far from public opinion and taste are therefore excluded.

(c) The need to attract advertising. Advertising revenue is crucial to the success of any newspaper or television/radio station (other than the BBC). The contents of the media must therefore (i) attract the right sort of audience to interest advertisers, and (ii) not offend the interests of advertisers.

3 Control and broadcasting

Control of radio and television is different from that of newspapers and the recording industry.

(a) The BBC is state owned and run with state subsidies;

(b) Commercial radio and television, although privately owned, are under the authority of the Independent Broadcasting Authority, which has considerable controlling powers.

However, this means that control still remains in the hands of very few people, who are usually chosen for their pro-Establishment views.

4 The Government's influence on the media

(a) *Licence fees* This is the means by which the BBC is financed. The licence fee is paid by the viewer to the Government who passes it on to the BBC. The BBC is, by law, totally independent of the Government. The Government could not withdraw its finance because it did not agree with the content of the BBC's broadcasting.

(b) *Government subsidies* This is a different type of support from licence fees; subsidies are not provided for by law and can be easily withdrawn from media too critical of the established political and social order. Government support in this country is not so structured as in other nations. It is rather an informal system of aid and takes the following forms:

(i) for the BBC the Government makes up the shortfall between the revenue from licence fees and the actual amount required. The BBC also receives a grant for its external services;

(ii) for commercial television there is a reduction in the levy on advertising revenue. In 1971 the levy was substantially reduced and in 1973 was altered to apply to profits rather than revenue;

(iii) Britain has no direct system for aid for newspapers, but government advertising is a significant form of indirect support. Like private advertising, however, its distribution is uneven, favouring the more popular papers.

CONCLUSION: PATTERNS OF OWNERSHIP AND CONTROL

1 The mass media are dominated by a few companies, plus the BBC. On the surface this points to a close control of media output by their owners who can use it to express their own opinions.

2 However, other factors heavily influence the content of the media. Hartley points out that the mass media operate in a competitive commercial environment and therefore need to be economically viable. This entails (a) attracting advertising revenue, (b) maintaining a large audience.

3 Commercial factors probably influence the decisions and attitudes of the owners of the media, rather than personal political preferences.

4 In the actual **news-making** and **leisure-producing** activities of those employed in the media the **informal methods of control** operate to limit the breadth of values and views expressed in the media.

20.11 Summary

1 The term **mass media** refers to the following forms of communication: television, radio, books and magazines, newspapers, recordings and films.

2 All these share the characteristic that one source of information communicates with a large number of people, who have no means of communicating back.

3 The development of the media has been linked to the changes in technology and the growth of an affluent audience.

4 We are at the beginning of a revolution in mass communications with the introduction of word-processors and satellites.

5 The media are an important part of the process of **secondary socialization** (this includes other agencies such as the school and the church), which reinforces the activities of the family in its role of **primary socialization**. They reinforce the values learned in the family which allow people to become full, participating members of society.

6 The media perform an important role in society control, by helping to create attitudes to certain forms of behaviour and groups of people.

7 There is a dispute among sociologists as to whether the media, as agents of social control, benefit the rich and powerful, or the whole society.

8 There are certain images and stereotypes that are constantly being presented in the media. A stereotype is a simplified image of a supposedly typical member of a particular group, which distorts reality.

9 One example of this is the presentation of women in the media, which creates a particular image of women through the use of photographs and language.

10 The effect of the media on crime is important. The amount and type of coverage of an event can create an increase in crime, known as an **amplification of deviance**.

11 It has been argued that the media have been used to distort the extent of crimes in inner cities in order to justify extra policing.

12 Explanations of the influence of the media fall into three groups: those that stress the powerful immediate response of people to stimulating material—the **behaviourist model**; secondly, those that stress that audiences choose the information they want from what is presented to them—the **audience selection model**, (therefore, for instance, only those already attracted to violence would be affected by a violent film); and thirdly, the **cultural approach**, which stresses that the influence of the media is much more long term, creating an agenda of appropriate attitudes.

13 Violence and the media: the evidence of the studies is contradictory, but would suggest that high exposure to violent films and TV programmes can reinforce violent values already held.

14 The effect of the media on political opinion is extremely complex. They do not appear to influence voting patterns directly as people tend to choose the facts they want. However, it can have a general socializing affect by creating the general climate of opinion.

15 The contents and presentation of the media vary according to the type of audience that is aimed at. Newspapers do not simply report 'facts' that have happened, but choose what they consider to be interesting pieces of information for the particular readership they serve.

16 Their choice of material depends mainly upon the journalists' idea of what constitutes **newsworthy** material.

17 The media in Britain are owned and controlled by a very small number of people.

18 Over a period of time three trends can be found: concentration; diversification and multi-nationalization.

19 The owners' power to influence the contents is great, but other factors such as advertising and the need for a large audience are just as powerful.

20 Advertising has considerable influence on the contents of the media — as the advertisers are important economically to the media.

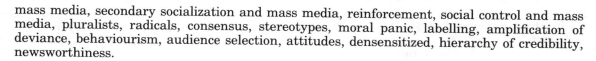

20.12 **Keywords** (*as they appear in the unit*)

mass media, secondary socialization and mass media, reinforcement, social control and mass media, pluralists, radicals, consensus, stereotypes, moral panic, labelling, amplification of deviance, behaviourism, audience selection, attitudes, densensitized, hierarchy of credibility, newsworthiness.

SELF-TEST UNITS

Socialization

1 How do sociologists explain the way people behave in society? Is it through natural biological drives or is it through learning from others?

2 What do sociologists mean by the term 'socialization'?

3 Give an example of a society where the behaviour of women is different from what we regard as 'normal'. How would sociologists explain this?

4 What happens when people are not socialized? Give one example.

5 What do sociologists mean when they write about (a) primary socialization and (b) secondary socialization?

6 Give three examples of groups that help to socialize us, explaining how they do so.

7 Explain how socialization varies by social class.

8 What does the term 'culture' mean?

9 What are the major differences between norms and beliefs?

10 What does the term 'role conflict' mean? Give one example.

ANSWERS

1 Sociologists argue that learned behaviour is far more important than natural biological drives.

2 Socialization means the process by which people are taught the values and behaviour expected of them in society.

3 One of the following:

In the Tchambuli tribe of New Guinea the women are the ones who do all the work and who have short hair and wear no jewellery or make-up.

In the Kgatla tribe the women do all the work outside the home.

In the Manus tribe the women do not bring up the children; this is the role of the men.

Sociologists would explain these differences quite simply by pointing to the different patterns of socialization in these societies compared to our own. This suggests that behaviour which we regard as 'normal' is not. It is only 'normal' in our society.

4 If people are not socialized adequately, then they can hardly be described as human beings as we know the term. They do not understand appropriate behaviour, they usually cannot speak and they behave 'oddly'. In order to become a full member of any society, people need to be taught the values and expectations of that society.

Examples of people who have not been adequately socialized include:

(a) Anna who was isolated from people up to the age of 5 and who could not eat properly, speak or understand what she was told.

(b) Isabell, who was isolated with her deaf-mute mother up to the age of 6½. She could not talk and could hardly walk.

(c) Shamdev was found in Northern India and had been brought up by wolves. He acted just like them, as he had learned how to behave from them.

You should have given one of the above.

5 Primary socialization: this is the process by which people first learn the values and behaviour expected of them from people who are very close to them and important in their development. These people would include the family and the peer group.

Secondary socialization is the process by which we learn the values and ideas of the wider society, which build upon our previous socialization in the family. Typical institutions that influence us are the school and the mass media.

6 Three of the following: the family, the peer group, schools, the mass media, the workplace.

In each of your three examples you ought to note that behaviour is modified in some way and that people are rewarded for acting in certain ways and punished for acting in other ways.

In the family, people first learn how to behave and they are also given adult roles to copy. Very importantly they also learn gender roles.

In the peer group, wider roles are learned from friends and so the child moves slightly away from the influence of the family. Play is extremely important as children learn to play a wide variety of adult roles, and to learn to put themselves in the places of other people through learning team games.

In schools the common expectations of the wider society are imposed upon all children. Those from certain class and ethnic backgrounds are introduced to the dominant values of society. Discipline is also taught and there is the first introduction to the constraints of work.

The mass media convey messages concerning society's attitudes to a wide range of issues. People's attitudes are formed.

The workplace socializes people into very specific attitudes and forms of behaviour in order for them to cope with their day's work and to get on with colleagues.

7 Socialization varies by social class as our society is divided along class lines, with the middle and working classes holding very different values and beliefs. Middle class people are brought up with a belief in looking after themselves and to have relatively little sympathy for the unemployed. The working class by contrast are brought up to feel greater loyalty to their fellow workers. The socialization differences are not just over values like these, but cover such things as differences in dress, behaviour, accent and leisure patterns.

8 Culture means the whole range of the knowledge, ideas and habits of society which are transmitted from one generation to the next.

9 Norms are specific expectations of behaviour in particular situations. On the other hand beliefs are simply general values held by the people in a society about the world. They do not actually tell a person how to behave. So the differences boil down to the degree to which they guide behaviour.

10 Role conflict is when the different roles that people play in life can come into conflict with each other. The example given in the text concerns a person who is a policeman catching a friend who is speeding – does the policeman book his friend or let him/her go?

Research Methods

QUESTIONS

1 Explain why research techniques are important to sociologists.

2 Some sociologists use scientific methods similar to those used by scientists, carrying out research in a number of stages. Briefly describe the five stages used.

3 Explain what is meant by the following types of study:
(a) cross-sectional study (b) case studies (c) longitudinal studies.

4 What is meant by the term 'sample' when used in sociological research?

5 Explain the meaning of the term 'sample frame'?
What sample frame would you use to find information from everybody over 18 in a particular town?

6 What are the two main types of sampling methods? Briefly explain the main differences.

7 What are secondary sources? In what ways are they useful to sociologists?

8 In what circumstances would a sociologist choose to use (a) a mail questionnaire and (b) participant observation?

9 What are the advantages of using observational methods? Are there any drawbacks?

10 What is meant by the following terms:
(a) open-ended questions (b) interviewer bias (c) experiment?

11 How can a sociologist's values influence the research process?

ANSWERS

1 Research techniques are important to sociologists because they need to discover information about society, in order to understand social life and to make accurate explanations of behaviour in society. The more accurate and exact the methods used, the more accurate the knowledge they will have.

2 The five stages are:
(a) observation, where the social scientist notices some feature about society that he/she thinks is an important thing to study;
(b) hypothesis, where a possible explanation is given for the feature of social life that has been observed;
(c) research planning – the social scientist needs to decide just which research methods will be most useful and how the research will be organized;
(d) collecting the information – the social scientist now does the actual job of collecting all the information he/she needs;
(e) drawing conclusions – having collected all the information, the social scientist studies it carefully and compares it with the original hypothesis.

3 (a) Cross-sectional studies are surveys of the population at a particular time – a good example would be an opinion poll.
(b) Case studies are in-depth studies of a particular place or event which help us to understand it. The information, however, is not necessarily helpful in understanding other situations.
(c) Longitudinal studies are those carried out on a particular group of people over a long period of time. Typically, this involves following a group of children through their lives.

4 Because sociologists cannot interview or collect detailed information about the whole British population, they have to choose a small, representative group drawn from the population. Any information obtained from this group should reflect the views, behaviour and attitudes of the population as a whole. The small representative group chosen is called a 'sample'.

5 A sample frame is any list from which a sample can be selected that will allow sociological research to be carried out.
The sampling frame that contains the names of all those of age 18 years and above is the *electoral list* of a particular area. These lists are kept in the public library and contain the names of everyone who is legally allowed to vote.

6 The two main types of sampling are random and quota, although there are many other subtypes, such as snowball and cluster sampling.
Random sampling is when a researcher might choose the

sample by, for example, picking every tenth name in a telephone directory. By choosing a random sample in this way, people who are to be used in the research are selected just like in a lottery.
Sometimes the population is first divided into groups by age, class, etc. and then chosen at random.
Quota sampling is generally used in commercial market research. The population is first divided into proportionately sized groups by age, class, ethnic group, etc. and then each interviewer is told to go out and question a specific number (a quota) from each group.

7 Secondary sources consist of information that are collected by people other than sociologists for various purposes. These include a wide variety of sources such as official statistics as in the Census, personal diaries and newspaper reports. They are useful to the sociologist as they generally provide information that he/she is unable to find out for him/herself. They provide background information and help to confirm the research of the sociologist. They are always used where the sociologist has to delve into the past when there is no one available to question.

8 The sociologist would use a mail questionnaire in order to ask questions of a large number of people, who would probably be scattered over a wide area. The sociologist would use participant observation when he/she wanted to study a group of people in depth in order to understand their motives and behaviour in action. Generally the group under study would be in one place and would not be the sort of group to which a questionnaire or formal interview could be given, for example, a group of delinquents.

9 In order fully to understand a group of people it may not be adequate just to ask them questions. It may also be important to observe them as they behave in normal circumstances. These people may not be able or willing to fill in questionnaires. By joining them, and in some cases actually becoming one of them, the sociologist can truly understand them.
The main problems of observational methods are that the researcher may become too influenced by the group and therefore may fail to analyse the information in an objective manner. Alternatively the researcher may influence the group and so disturb the 'natural' activities of the group.

10 (a) Open-ended questions are those questions that do not require a specific choice of reply, such as 'yes' or 'no'. They allow the respondent free choice to express him or her/self in his/her own words. Open-ended questions are generally used when discussing complex issues and the researcher is seeking some depth of reply.
(b) Interviewer bias occurs when the values of the interviewer influence the replies of the person interviewed. The interviewer may irritate the person interviewed so that he/she responds in an abrupt or misleading way. The interviewee may want to please the interviewer and so says what he/she thinks the interviewer wishes to hear. The interviewer may induce the person interviewed to reply in a certain way by asking 'leading' questions, or by altering the tone of voice to show disapproval.
(c) Experiments: these are when people are placed in carefully controlled situations where their responses can be closely observed. Sociologists do not use them too often as the situations are artificial and do not reflect real situations and therefore real responses.

11 A sociologist's values can affect the research process in a number of ways. Firstly, the very areas of research chosen are a reflection of what is considered important by the sociologist – for example, until recently feminism was regarded as an unimportant area of study.
Secondly, the researcher may bring in his/her values into the interview with a particular person and so produce a biased interview, by asking leading questions, for example.
Thirdly, when analysing the information, the researcher may prefer to overlook information that contradicts his/her point of view.

The Family

QUESTIONS

1 Why is the family thought to be the most important influence on our lives?

2 What is meant by the terms 'nuclear family' and 'extended family'?

3 Why is the extended family considered to be the normal type of family in pre-industrial societies?

4 Bearing in mind the possible differences between the middle and working classes, explain how the coming of industrialization in Britain had a major impact on the family.

5 List the five functions of the family.

6 According to sociologists how have the functions performed by the family changed in recent times?

7 Why is the assumption that the family is beneficial for its members criticized by some sociologists?

8 How have the roles of men and women changed within the family since the beginning of the century?

9 According to research evidence, what differences were observed between the family relationships of working and middle class people in the middle of this century? How has this situation changed more recently?

10 Define the term 'symmetrical family' and say how widespread this type of family has now become.

11 How has the position of children changed within the family during this century?

12 What useful part do old people play in the modern family?

13 Why is the image of the typical British family consisting of a wife and husband plus two or three young children not a wholly accurate one?

14 What does it mean to say that the family is a 'dynamic institution'?

15 What characteristics of ethnic minority families distinguish them from typical families?

16 Explain briefly how *kibbutzim* traditionally differ in character from the typical British family unit.

17 How does the family in modern Japan differ from the typical British family unit?

18 In what ways does marriage mark a crucial change in a person's status in society?

19 Define the term 'serial monogamy'.

20 Explain why a decline in first marriage has occurred.

21 Why might divorce statistics not accurately reflect the true extent of marital breakdown?

22 List five reasons for the rise in the divorce rate.

23 Why might it be argued that 'in recent years we are witnessing the end of marriage as we know it'?

ANSWERS

1 (a) The care received by a child determines its physical health throughout life; (b) parental effects on a child's educational success; (c) the family teaches the child the values and beliefs of society; (d) the family determines the social class position of the children born into it.

2 *Nuclear* family – consists of two generations (parents and children) living together, This type of family usually found in modern industrial societies such as Britain today.

Extended family – consists of three generations (grandparents, parents and children) living close together. This type of family is usually found in pre-industrial societies such as the Bedouin of the Negev desert.

3 The extended family has advantages in that it provides a large number of workers within the family and the larger the family the greater the security, since sick and old members can be supported (but see Laslett's findings on England before the Industrial Revolution).

4 As families moved to the towns to live near the new factories there developed a local working class community based upon the kinship or extended family network which provided aid and support for its members. Women married earlier and had children earlier – in the second part of the nineteenth century the average life span lengthened. See the research of M. Anderson, which emphasized the increase in the extended or three-generation family among the working class in Preston. Among the middle and upper classes the extended family continued much as before.

5 (a) The regulation of sexual behaviour (b) reproduction (c) socialization (d) economic (e) emotional support.

6 According to some sociologists (e.g. Talcott Parsons, McIver and Page), the family has now lost many of its functions, especially since the state provides so many services and the family is no longer an economic unit in the sense of all producing and working together. Other sociologists (e.g. Fletcher) have argued that many of the original functions remain, although perhaps in a changed form; and it can also be said that the modern family looks after its members to a higher standard than ever before.

7 It is argued that the family can be emotionally intense, involve the repression of women, and lead to violence and psychological disorders. Marxists see the family as a purveyor of very conservative values and as a convenient unit in perpetuating the capitalist economic system.

8 At the beginning of this century the family was male dominated with the father being the 'breadwinner' and 'head of the household'. Women were regarded as inferior and spent their lives looking after their children, their husbands and their homes. The legal position of women reflected this.

More recently greater equality has been established between husbands and wives. Domestic tasks are shared, women are more likely to go out to work and contribute to the family budget. The husband and wife tend to spend their leisure time together.

9 Traditionally (see research of Dennis Henriques and Slaughter in Ashton, and Young and Willmott) in working class families women and men lived separate lives; (a) friendships were always of the same sex; (b) leisure activities were separate; (c) husbands and wives had few emotional bonds between them; (d) the woman's life was home-centred, caring for husband and children; (e) wives had close relationships with their mothers, even more than with husbands. By the same period middle class marriages had become more of a partnership in the terms of decision making, the sharing of household tasks, leisure activities, etc.

Since the 1950s these middle class characteristics have been increasingly observed in working class families.

10 Young and Willmott described the modern family as symmetrical, meaning simply that the modern family gives equality in all areas to husband and wife. Undoubtedly there are many couples in both the middle and working class who do not share tasks and still lead relatively separate lives (see Elizabeth Bott *Family and Social Network*). Feminists also argue that women benefit far less from marriage than men, shouldering the major proportion of housework, taking the responsibility for children and cooking, etc.

11 Children are now treated more as responsible individuals and have more freedom than previously. At the same time, parents provide greater care of children and closer emotional bonds are formed. Treatment of boys and girls is much nearer to being equal, but differences still remain.

12 Depending upon their health, old people can play a useful part in family life. They can help to bring up children, especially when mothers go out to work, and often provide financial assistance.

13 Such families only represent about 30 per cent of households in Britain, 27 per cent are married couples with no children, 27 per cent of the population do not live in a family, 8 per cent are couples living with grown-up children while the remainder are one-parent families.

14 Families are changing all the time as awareness of the concept, the family life cycle, indicates. Over a period of time the family goes through various stages, as the parents pass from young through middle to old age.

15 Research on Asian families indicates that they tend to be extended in form, male-dominated and the lives of women are relatively confined. Marriages are arranged and the family unit is much closer than is usual in Britain, perhaps with members working together in business.

Other ethnic minorities exhibited some of these characteristics; Driver emphasized the importance of the mother-centred family among West Indians.

16 Like other communes *kibbutzim* traditionally stress the importance of the community over the individual or his or her family; children are brought up by the community and only spend part of the day with their parents. Marriages are simply and easily entered into and ended.

17 Many of the values of the traditional family are still common in modern industrial **Japan**. The male still dominates and women tend to stay at home, look after the children and do the housework. Relatively few married women go out to work in Japan, although this is changing. Children are expected to be obedient to their parents.

18 Marriage is usually seen as characteristic of adulthood and the first stage in creating a family. It makes a decision to maintain sexual relations exclusively with one person. In terms of the social order, marriage gives us identity and status.

19 In addition to first marriage there are now second, third and even fourth marriages. This tendency to marry, divorce, remarry is known as serial monogamy.

20 The decline in first marriage is the result of such factors as changing values in respect of cohabitation, the smaller proportion of the population in the 20–30 age group and the growing tendency for people to marry later in life, although the number of marriages should pick up again once this particular trend has stabilized.

21 Divorce is not the only form of marital breakdown; there are also cases of separation and desertion, and unhappy marriages. For some of these categories, especially the last two, there are no reliable figures.

22 (a) legal changes; (b) changes in attitude; (c) expectation of marriage; (d) specific historical factors; (e) increasing independence of women.

23 The number of people marrying has declined by 15 per cent since the 1970s. Divorces have increased by 30 per cent in the last ten years and 1 child in 8 is now born outside marriage despite the wider availibility of means of controlling unwanted pregnancies. The number of one-parent families is increasing and people are more likely to exercise their right to separate if they are unhappy in marriage.

Education

1 Clearly explain the difference between formal learning and informal learning.

2 Why was there no need for a formal education system in 'simpler', agricultural societies?

3 (a) Explain the meaning of the term the 'hidden curriculum'.
(b) Give two examples of the things that the hidden curriculum teaches us.

4 Explain the meaning of the following (a) labelling (b) social control (c) equality of opportunity.

5 What are restricted and elaborated codes?

6 Name four functions of the education system.

7 In what ways do the functions of the education system relate to the needs of society?

8 The idea that education performs functions for society has been criticized by Marxists. What is their criticism?

9 Explain the term the 'tripartite system of education'.

10 (a) What are the main advantages of comprehensives? (b) What are the main disadvantages?

11 Name three ways in which a child's home background can influence his/her education.

12 How can it be said that the neighbourhood a person comes from can influence educational achievement?

13 (a) What is a peer group? (b) How important is it in influencing a child's approach to school?

14 Explain the terms (a) 'compensatory education' (b) 'cultural deprivation'.

15 Describe any two social effects of streaming.

16 Explain the term IQ. Why are sociologists unhappy with it?

17 Give two examples of the differences in educational patterns between males and females.

18 How can it be said that the school influences the different educational attainment of males and females?

19 Why do children from the ethnic minorities generally perform poorly at school?

20 (a) Do all children of the ethnic minorities do badly at school?
(b) Give two reasons why some children of immigrant origins do better than others.

21 Give two ways in which racism can be combated at school.

ANSWERS

1 Formal education takes place in a special institution such as a school or college, whereas informal education normally takes place in casual interaction between the members of families or between friends etc.

Formal education usually consists of a specific, clearly defined skill or set of skills such as is taught in the school curriculum.

Informal education cannot be clearly defined in its aim except that the child learns the values, beliefs and daily knowledge necessary to act in a normal way.

Formal education usually only occurs for a set period of people's lives, whereas informal education continues throughout our lives.

Formal education usually only takes place in modern industrialized societies, whereas informal education occurs in both simple and technologically advanced societies.

2 There was no need because the skills of one generation were adequate for the next. In simple societies based on agriculture there is little technological or social change. In modern societies, with the rapid changes in ideas and technology, the skills of one generation are redundant in the next. Schools and colleges teach the relevant skills.

3 (a) The hidden curriculum means the ideas and values that the pupils learn in the school from teachers and other pupils, which are not officially part of the lessons.
(b) Two of the following:
(i) Gender roles are learnt at school, through the comments of teachers, the contents of books and the attitudes of the peer group.
(ii) Racial differences: through jokes, attitudes and book contents.
(iii) Class differences: these are also learned through comments on accents, differences in spending patterns, comments about parents' jobs and teachers' expectations.
(iv) Streaming and examinations not only grade children by ability, but also teach children to expect to be treated according to ability. This will later be reflected in different standards of pay and status in employment.
(v) Language: only middle class English is seen as correct.
(vi) Social control: children are taught to be obedient. By learning to obey teachers they are also learning to obey their foremen/women and bosses later.

4 (a) Labelling: when a teacher believes the pupil to be a particular type of child and adjusts his responses accordingly. For instance, he may label a boy as a troublemaker and be excessively harsh in his dealings with that boy. The boy then responds in some way to that label, perhaps even becoming a troublemaker out of resentment. It does not matter if the original label is correct or not as long as the teacher believes it to be so, and this belief influences the future behaviour of the boy.

(b) Social control: every society needs to control its members. If it does not do so then people will act any way that they wish. This can lead to chaos. In our society there are a number of agencies of control, among them the school. Social control is taught both formally in the rules and discipline of the school, and informally in the ways that pupils learn from other pupils and the teachers the normal response to most social situations;

(c) Equality of opportunity: Before 1944 in Britain the quality of a person's education depended upon the ability to pay. This resulted in the rich having an unequal chance of being educated. Many intelligent working class children were denied an adequate opportunity. Since 1944, the educational system has tried to provide every child with an identical chance of a good education. The height of this is the comprehensive system. However, public schools still provide the children of the rich with major advantages.

5 Restricted code: a simple form of speech that uses short colloquial sentences and relies upon the fact that the listener is fully aware of the background to the speech. It is generally used in conversation between friends/family members. It is not the form of speech or writing required in the education system. It is difficult to express new ideas in restricted code;

Elaborated code: a code of language that uses more complex grammar and a wider vocabulary. It is the type of speech used in formal situations and in academic work. It usually assumes that the listener does not share the same assumptions as the speaker. Facility in this is necessary in the education system.

Everybody uses both codes of speech, but only some people are adept at the elaborated code necessary in academic work. The ability to use both codes depends upon a child's upbringing. Parents who explain things to their children and use the elaborated code help their children considerably in their later academic work.

6 The transmission of culture; social control; economic training; social selection.

7 Modern societies are extremely complex, both culturally and technologically. It is impossible for the necessary values and skills to be passed on from one generation to the next by the family as in more simple societies.

The education system ensures that the basic needs of society are catered for. First it is necessary for a degree of order to exist, both culturally and politically. Without some order society would collapse in chaos. The first two functions of the education system ensure that a core set of beliefs and values are passed on from one generation to the next. This is the transmission of culture. The second function, of social control, ensures that people obey the norms of society and the laws.

The third and fourth functions are mainly concerned with the need of society to produce the food and products necessary for our survival. Economic training ensures that skills are taught so all jobs can be performed, at every level. This is particularly important in rapidly changing societies such as our own, where skills useful in one generation are obsolete in the next. Social selection by schools ensures that the most able children are chosen to perform the most difficult tasks. Examinations therefore sort out and grade children.

8 The Marxists criticize the functionalists because they claim the functionalist view gives the false impression that the education system is good for everybody in society. This, the Marxists say, is not true. What really happens, according to them, is that the powerful impose their values on the majority of the population through the school (and the media). People come to accept society as it is, while learning the skills necessary to keep the offices, shops and factories running.

9 The tripartite system was a way of dividing children into secondary schools on the basis of a test administered at the age of 11, which was supposed to distinguish between children of different abilities. On the basis of this test children were allocated to one of three types of schools: grammar for the academic, secondary modern for the less able and secondary technical for those of more technical and vocational abilities.

10 The advantages and disadvantages of comprehensive schools.

(a) Advantages
(i) Children are allowed to develop at their own pace instead of being selected at 11;
(ii) There is a greater possibility of breaking down social class divisions;
(iii) Larger schools allow the introduction of more and better facilities;
(iv) Less able children are no longer thrown on the educational scrap heap at 11, and may benefit from the contact with more intelligent children.

Sociological evidence supports the argument that although an improvement, comprehensive schools have not achieved any great change in the educational achievement of working or middle class children. This is because education merely reflects the wider society. The existing social differences cannot be eliminated by changing the type of school.

(b) Disadvantages
(i) The more intelligent children may be slowed down;
(ii) The schools are too large and thus the child is not treated as an individual;
(iii) Class barriers remain as they have always done.

11 Three of the following:
(a) Parental values and the degree of interest shown by them in their child's education can crucially influence the child's interest and attitude towards education. Douglas found this to be the single most important factor;
(b) The language used in the home and taught to the child. Bernstein suggested that two codes of language exist, restricted and elaborated. The ability of the child to use elaborated code will significantly aid him or her in the educational system;
(c) The physical condition of the home. Children who live in poor conditions and suffer from poor diets are more often unwell and develop lower academic capacities. According to Wedge and Prosser more than 1 in every 16 children in Britain suffer from multiple deprivation in their own circumstances;
(d) Cultural deprivation occurs when the home and the neighbourhood from which the child comes do not offer a normal introduction to the values, and knowledge of our society. The child feels lost and isolated in the normal society. This often happens to the children of very poor, and to some immigrant children.

12 The neighbourhood can influence educational achievement in a number of ways. Most importantly the values of the neighbourhood can create in the pupil an attitude favourable or unfavourable to study. Sugarman for instance argues that the values of working class neighbourhoods are generally against studying and emphasized more an attitude of enjoyment now.

Other sociologists have pointed to the existence of the culture of poverty and the existence of what they see as cultural deprivation, where the poorest groups in society actually lack the mainstream culture of society and are unable to compete at school.

Of course the poverty of certain inner city environments must not be forgotten with the lack of facilities available in schools and libraries, the poor homes, etc.

13 (a) A peer group is a group of people of similar age and circumstances. What this means in terms of the peer group at school is other pupils in the same year with whom one is friendly. (b) The peer group is very important indeed in influencing the pupil's attitudes towards studying and the teachers. Hargreaves showed how pupils polarized into two groups, those who supported school and the teachers and those who loathed them. The very different attitudes were strengthened by making friends with those of similar attitudes. In an extreme case, Willis's study showed how those pupils who hated school clustered together in a strong protective group, constantly trying to outdo each other in showing how far they could go in defying the school.

(It is important in your answer to point out that there is a strong relationship with social class in the pupils' attitudes to school.)

14 (a) Compensatory education derives from the Plowden Report of 1969 which claimed that there were certain children from poor and immigrant homes who suffered at school because their home environment did not provide them with the cultural 'tools' (such as books, use of English, etc.) which would have given them the essential background to their school studies. To remedy this the Plowden Report recommended that extra resources should be pumped into schools in certain poor areas (educational areas) to compensate for the poor environment. This is compensatory education.

(b) Cultural deprivation is an idea that first developed in the United States and was then used first in Britain in the Plowden Report. As explained above, it is a term used to describe a situation where certain very poor or immigrant groups were thought to be lacking in the culture of the mainstream society. This lack of the mainstream culture seriously interfered with the pupils' school progress, as they lacked ability in such things as English language.

15 Two of the following:
Once in a class, pupils adjust themselves to the general academic and behaviour standards of that class.

Pupils in lower streams feel failures compared to higher stream pupils. This can lead to feelings of frustration and so to rebellious behaviour against the school. The attitudes of teachers alter with the stream they are teaching. The lower the stream the less the teacher expects and this in turn can influence the motivation and self-respect of the pupils.

16 IQ stands for intelligence quotient and it is supposed to be a measure of a person's natural intelligence. It is based on the average figure of 100: if a person's IQ is above 100 then he/she is above the average intelligence.

Sociologists are very critical of the idea of IQ, as it suggests that intelligence is something which is inherited from parents. Sociologists argue that most intelligence is developed by our upbringing. Also what is defined as intelligence varies from one society to another. Finally who decides what is intelligence and what is not?

17 Two of the following: (a) Girls are more successful than boys at O Level.
(b) They choose different subjects from boys, mainly preferring arts and social science to maths and physical sciences.
(c) Fewer girls take A Levels and again the differences in subject preferences appear.
(d) Fewer women than men choose to go on to university.
(e) Women are more likely to take caring and secretarial courses in further education than males, who choose the technical and scientific subjects.

18 Apart from the powerful influences of the home and the wider culture, the school is very important indeed. In particular it operates in two ways. First, the choice of subjects offered to males and females is different. By the time the GCSE subject choices have been made, it is quite normal for the 'male' subjects of CDT to be on the timetable at the same time as the domestic science and the office skills subjects.

Secondly, the attitude of teachers is often one that encourages boys at the expense of girls. Teachers generally have greater expectations of males than females and they are more likely to encourage males into science and maths subjects. The content of books, too, generally stresses male heroes and place women in less important roles.

The peer group is also very important for girls, as they learn that looking good and attracting boys earns them far more status than being clever at school.

19 They perform less well at school for similar reasons to those explaining the under achievement of the working class in general. But on top of these reasons, they also have to face direct racism sometimes from teachers and fellow pupils. It has also been shown that even where teachers are not racist they do believe that Black and Asian children are less intelligent.

The hidden curriculum of the school also plays an important part in lowering the self-respect of children from the ethnic minorities. Their use of English may be looked down upon in the school and the content of the schoolbooks may ignore their culture, stressing only white European culture.

20 (a) No, the children of certain Asian grops, noticeably those of African Asians, do particularly well. The children of West Indians and Bangladeshis appear to perform worst of all.
(b) The explanations for the variations in performance appear to be linked to:
(i) family background – that is levels of education and amount of encouragement/expectations; (ii) the ability to reject racism – it seems that the cultural strength of Asian backgrounds helps them to reject the racism they experience; (iii) if the Asian or West Indian children are from middle class backgrounds, then they do particularly well in the education system.

21 Two from: (a) retraining of teachers to appreciate the cultural backgrounds of pupils; (b) language lessons for the children of the ethnic minorities; (c) elimination of racism in teaching materials; (d) more teachers to be recruited from the ethnic minorities; (e) positive discrimination with more resources going to schools with high proportions of pupils from the ethnic minorities.

Social Stratification
QUESTIONS

1 What is meant by 'social stratification'?

2 Class is one example of social stratification. Give three other examples.

3 Explain how social class is different from these other forms of social stratification.

4 Explain the terms 'objective' and 'subjective' effects of social class.

5 What are a person's 'life chances'?

6 Briefly describe the basis of social class according to Marx and suggest reasons why his ideas are criticized by some sociologists.

7 Explain how divisions between people in society are very complex according to Max Weber.

8 Briefly describe the functionalist approach to social class and say how this explanation of social divisions may be criticized.

9 Why are simple measurements of social class often based on occupational differences and why are there problems in using such an approach?

10 What are the main differences between the Registrar-General's classification and that developed by Hope and Goldthorpe?

11 Why is the simple division between manual and non-manual workers said to be increasingly unsatisfactory?

12 List the changes that have taken place in British society over the last 30 years which help us to understand the changes in the nature of social class in Britain.

13 (a) Explain the term 'embourgeoisement'.
(b) Why was it agreed that 'embourgeoisement' developed in Britain in the 1950s?

14 How was the embourgeoisement theory criticized by sociologists in the 1960s?

15 Explain the term 'decomposition of labour'.

16 Identify TWO major changes that have occurred in the middle class in Britain.

17 For what reasons is it argued that clerical workers now form a marginal group which straddles the borderline between the working and middle classes?

18 Account for the growth of the professions.

19 Explain how the middle class has begun to show divisions between 'traditional' professions and 'newer' professions.

20 Define the term 'wealth' and explain briefly why wealth is said to be divided unequally in Britain.

21 To what extent has there been a redistribution of wealth during the course of this century?

22 Account for the very marked differences in income that still exist in Britain.

23 Define 'social mobility' and explain why it is difficult to measure accurately.

24 To what extent may it be said that upward social mobility has increased in Britain?

25 Explain the difference between the functionalist and Marxist views on social mobility.

ANSWERS

1 Definition: social stratification is the way in which people are divided into different social groups. They are then awarded unequal amounts of prestige, economic rewards and power according to their membership of these groups.

2 Caste, estates (feudalism), slavery.

3 Social class is less rigid and more open than the other forms of social stratification mentioned and social mobility is more possible. The separate steps in the hierarchy of social classes are less clearly defined than in the caste system, for example, and intermarriage is possible in a social class system. People are divided into social classes because of economic differences: these divisions are not defined legally.

4 The objective effects of belonging to a particular social class include health, expectation of life, family size, housing, education, income, job security, ownership of material possessions and leisure activities; whereas subjective effects include ideas and values, as expressed in voting behaviour, views on social issues, attitudes to work, etc.

5 Life chances are a person's chances of success or failure in life, which sociologists believe are strongly influenced in Britain by the social class into which we are born.

6 According to Marx, society is divided into TWO classes — those who own wealth and property and those who have to live by working for a wage. The former, who own the wealth, will exploit the latter, who work for wages.

Those who criticize Marx usually argue that the class structure is much more complicated than he suggested, and that there is a wide variety of groups existing in society and not just two. His argument that revolution must occur in industrial society because of the conflicts between the two classes has also been denied.

7 Weber argued that people could be divided by more than their ownership of wealth: economic factors such as wealth and income, status, and power needed to be added together in order to indicate a person's life chances. As people do not necessarily enjoy equal amounts of all these elements, society represents a complicated variety of divisions.

8 Functionalists claim that differences in status, power and prestige reflect differences in the importance of certain jobs in society; society needs certain jobs to be performed in order to survive and hence rewards those who do such jobs.

Critics argue, however, that it is difficult to grade jobs in this way and that levels of income are determined by other factors apart from the usefulness of certain jobs; comparison of some obvious jobs may be said to demonstrate this weakness in the functionalist approach.

9 Occupation is often related to a range of other factors such as:
differences in income; differences in prestige; differences in education; differences in life style, speech, dress, etc.

Problems involved in using this approach include the fact that some people in similar occupations may have very different backgrounds and resources, and in any case the same job title may mean very different things in different circumstances. Occupational classifications also ignore the unemployed.

10 The chief difference is that the Hope and Goldthorpe classification is a more refined version of that devised by the Registrar-General: it contains eight divisions instead of five, distinguishes between the self-employed and those employed by others, and arranges the eight divisions into three classes which reflect more accurately the changing occupational structure of Britain.

11 As the nature of industry and commerce is changing there are less people involved in what we formerly described as manual occupations; routine white-collar jobs are increasing, however. Increasingly the real divisions are those between the higher-paid managers and professional workers and the rest.

12 (a) Greater affluence and the wider availability of consumer goods. (b) There are now at least 3½ million unemployed and a real division is occurring between those in secure employment and the rest of the workforce. (c) More people now own their own homes and are moving from inner cities to outer city suburbs and new towns. (d) Greater opportunities exist within the educational system. (e) The occupational structure is changing considerably with the decline of manual occupations, also connected with the impact of new technology. There has also been a growth in professional and junior management job opportunities and more openings for people of working class origins. (f) The number of women in employment has been increasing consistently.

13 (a) Embourgeoisement means to become middle class.
(b) As working class people in Britain became more affluent in the 1950s it was believed that the better-off sections of the working class were joining the middle class.

14 Following the research of Goldthorpe and Lockwood, based on studies of Luton car workers in the 1960s, it was argued that although these workers were earning high wages they had not broken away significantly from the traditional working class in terms of political loyalties, values, etc. They still received lower incomes than non-manual workers, found little satisfaction from their work and retained their beliefs and life styles which were different from the middle class. Goldthorpe and Lockwood did, however, acknowledge that more stress was now laid on the nuclear family rather than the extended family.

15 The 'decomposition of labour' represents a new argument put forward that the working class is now divided into two groups, the traditional working class and the new working class. The work of Paul concluded that there was a growing gap between the families in these two groups.

16 (a) The proletarianization of clerical workers.
(b) The growth of the professions.

17 There is evidence that clerical workers have suffered a decline in wages and job opportunities and are aware of themselves as a distinctive group from management (the middle class). On the other hand, they still enjoy some clear advantages over manual workers in terms of working conditions and fringe benefits, and see themselves as a distinct group from the working class.

18 There are two main reasons:
(a) There has been a decline in the number of people working in the manufacturing industries and an increasing number employed in service industries.
(b) The growth of employment by the state has provided a big expansion in such areas as education, health and welfare.

19 Those people engaged in 'traditional' professions, such as solicitors and doctors, receive better incomes and greater status than those engaged in the 'newer' professions, such as teachers and social workers.

20 Wealth means the ownership of such assets as property and stocks and shares. Much wealth is owned by a relatively small proportion of the population of Britain, the top 1 per cent of the British population own 23 per cent of marketable wealth.

21 There is some evidence that the proportion of wealth owned by the top 10 per cent has declined in this century and attempts have been made to redistribute wealth by the introduction of such legislation as Capital Gains and Capital Transfer Taxes. There is much evidence, however, to show that relatively little change has occurred: 50 per cent of the British population only owns 6 per cent of all wealth between them and wealthy people have discovered ways of avoiding the effects of government legislation.

22 According to the evidence (e.g. Westergaard and Resler) progressive taxes and the Welfare State have had relatively little effect on the distribution of incomes. The highest earners have lost a higher proportion of their incomes in direct taxation, but have regained it through the existence of various tax concessions for mortgages, pensions, etc. They also enjoy fringe benefits from employers which are not subject to tax.

23 (a) Social mobility means the movement of people up and down the social scale. The two types of social mobility are 'intragenerational' and 'intergenerational'.
(b) Measurement of social mobility is difficult because occupational categories are not easy to define accurately and over time the status and significance of jobs tends to change, making comparisons complicated. Furthermore, at what point in a person's career do you measure his/her social mobility?

24 Research, such as the Oxford Mobility Study, has demonstrated that upward mobility has certainly increased. Evidence shows that the chances of going into higher occupational groups, e.g. the service class, has increased and that the class structure was more open in the middle of this century than at the beginning.

It was also recognized, however, that there were significant differences in the relative chances of different social groups and that the changing occupational structure had given rise to a greater proportion of higher categories of employment, and this created more room at the top. It should also be noted that there have been few studies of the patterns of social mobility of women. Finally, there is much evidence to show that the top positions in society are still held by the elite (or ruling class).

25 The functionalist view argues that there is a meritocracy or open society in which those who have ability and work hard can move upwards and achieve greater rewards, while the less able and less industrious sink down.

The Marxist view states that the ownership of significant wealth remains concentrated in the hands of a relatively small group. Even though people may progress upwards in the occupational structure they have relatively little chance of joining the ranks of those who own the wealth. Social mobility therefore operates only within a fairly small range of incomes.

Gender

QUESTIONS

1 What do we mean by the term 'gender role'? Give one example each of a male role and a female role.
2 How do women learn the behaviour expected of them?
3 What was the status of women in pre-industrial Britain?
4 What explanation has been suggested for the decline in women's status 150 years ago?
5 Briefly describe the political, legal and social position of a woman in the middle of the last century.
6 What recent legislation has there been to improve the position of women in society?
7 What reasons have been suggested for the increasing status of women in society?
8 Why is it possible to say that although women have achieved legal equality with men, this does not mean that they have full equality today?
9 (a) To what extent has there been a growth in women working this century?
(b) How does this compare with changes in the numbers of men in employment?
10 What reasons are there for the increase in women working?
11 Why do so many women work part-time?
12 In which areas of work are women most likely to be involved?
13 Why are women likely to be employed in low-status, low-paid work?
14 Despite the passing of the Equal Pay Act, women still earn less than men. How can this be?
15 What are the main characteristics of housework? Is housework really work?

ANSWERS

1 Gender role refers to the expectations of behaviour which we have of males and females. Typical gender roles are labourer (male) and housewife (female).
2 Women learn the behaviour expected of them through their socialization. This starts in the family at a very early age, is confirmed at school and strengthened through the media. They are taught to behave in different ways from boys and to have different expectations – usually these centre around the home and having children.
3 The status of women in pre-industrial Britain was similar to that of men. They were regarded as partners in the marriage and were expected to do similar work to men.
4 Oakley has argued that the decline in status occurred because women were gradually shut out of the workforce and forced into staying at home to care for children. She argues that the decline in economic power led to a decline in status and independence.
5 Women had a very low position socially at this time. A women had no right to any possessions – if she was married then they became the property of her husband. She was not able to divorce her husband, and his adultery was not grounds for divorce – though hers was! Women had no vote. They were generally denied any education, too. It was almost inconceivable that a women should want a career and impossible to achieve.
6 The most recent legislation has been (a) the 1970 Equal Pay Act, which came into force in 1975 and made it illegal to pay women less money; (b) The 1975 Employment Protection Act, which gave women the right to paid maternity leave; (c) the 1975 Sex Discrimination Act which made it illegal to discriminate against women on the grounds of their sex.
7 The increasing status has come about (a) mainly through the growth in the economic power of women, the sense of independence and power this has given them has enabled them to demand changes;

(b) increased educational opportunities have allowed them to challenge men for better jobs;
(c) legal changes which strengthen further their position;
(d) the expansion of the social services which support women in crucial periods, particularly childbirth. This helped women to be free from dependence on men;
(e) the activities of feminist groups and their success in raising the awareness of women to their position in society;
(f) decrease in size of family has freed women from a lifetime raising children.

8 Legal equality and equal treatment in social life, employment and education are very different things. The attitudes that society holds towards women still mean that they are expected to do things, like rearing children and being good housewives, that effectively prevent them having a successful career. It is not by chance that women are trapped in low-paid, part-time and low-status work. Men's attitudes have to be changed towards women if they are to achieve equality.

9 (a) There has been a considerable growth in the numbers of women working this century. In 1901 they formed only 29 per cent of the workforce, by 1961 it had risen to 32 per cent and now it is well over 40 per cent. Predictions are that within the next ten years women will form half the workforce. In 1983 there were 10.7 million women working.
(b) The numbers of women in the workforce continue to rise, but the number of men is actually falling. For instance, in 1981 there were 16 million men working; today the figure has dropped by more than half a million.

10 Reasons for the growth of women working include:
(a) there has been a shift away from the male-dominated 'heavy' industries to the 'light' industries of electronics and the service industries, both of which tend to employ more women;
(b) there was a labour shortage for much of the period between 1950 and 1970 which encouraged the entry of women into the labour force;
(c) women often work for lower wages than men and are therefore more attractive to employers;
(d) women are prepared to (or have to) work part-time and are therefore a more flexible form of labour;
(e) as women have benefited from educational opportunities that are more nearly equal they are more able to compete with men for jobs;
(f) smaller families have freed women from having to stay at home most of their lives looking after young children.

11 Women usually work part-time because of family commitments. They are expected to look after the children and therefore have to arrange their work hours around the times of school. In the 1971 General Household Survey, 90 per cent of women questioned who would have liked to work, but did not, said they were prevented from doing so by their commitments to their children.

12 Women are primarily involved in clerical occupations, service occupations and low-level technical and professional occupations. Women are usually employed in the lower grades and earn less money than men.

13 Mainly because they are encouraged to see themselves primarily as mothers and housewives rather than as career women. Research among female school students found that the girls' main ambition was usually to get married and have children. It is argued that this is because they are constantly encouraged to do so by the educational system, the family and the media.

14 Women earn less than men because the women are concentrated in lowly paid, low-status work and have little opportunity for doing overtime. The lowest paid workers in Britain, 'homeworkers', are generally women.

15 The main characteristics of housework are (a) that it is unpaid and supposedly done 'for love'; (b) that it is low status and not regarded as real work; (c) it is monotonous and boring like factory work; (d) housewives are very isolated, as they spend most of their day with young children and may only come into contact with other adults at the shops for instance.

Housework is certainly work, merely performed at home and unpaid.

Age

QUESTIONS

1 Why is age a topic of interest to sociologists?
2 Give a brief account of how 'childhood' is viewed in Britain today.
3 How does the experience of childhood in Britain today differ from the experience of childhood over 300 years ago in this country?
4 In Britain today how are children brought up by their parents differently according to class?
5 How, according to Colin Turnbull, were children regarded by the Ik tribe of North-East Africa?
6 How are the old commonly regarded in modern British society?
7 Give a brief account of the position of old people in simple societies such as the Aborigines of Australia.
8 Why were the old so much respected in pre-industrial Japanese society?

ANSWERS

1 Sociologists are interested in age because people are treated differently according to their age and are expected to act differently from others of a different age. Expectations of behaviour vary according to society and are not directly linked to biological age.

2 Generally children are protected from the 'realities' of life because childhood is seen as a period of great innocence. Children are not allowed to partake in the same activities as adults (e.g. work activities, voting, drinking alcohol). It is believed that children are not sufficiently mature to make sensible choices. They must be moulded into the appropriate values through socialization.

3 The tendency to treat the child as someone in need of care and protection only derives from the eighteenth century. Before this time children over the age of 5 were treated as little adults. Children worked with adults and did not have separated games, lengthy education, etc.

4 According to the Newsons, working class parents are more liable to give commands to their children whereas middle class parents explain their wishes. Children in middle class families are more likely to be asked their views. Working class parents are more erratic in their punishment of children than their middle class counterparts.

5 In a very harsh physical environment the Ik were very harsh in their attitude to children, regarding them as a curse. They were treated very harshly in early life and thrown out of home at the age of three, when they were expected to look after themselves. Childhood contained none of the ideas of purity and innocence usual in our society.

6 Old people in Britain have low status and are regarded as having little to contribute to society. Because old people have retired this creates problems of self-identity, since a person's employment often gives him/her identity.

7 In simpler societies old people enjoy positions of power and status. As the rate of change in such societies is slower, the knowledge of one generation is generally useful to the next and the old therefore have high status. Old people are more likely to withdraw gradually from active work and do not undergo the process of disengagement experienced in modern British society.

8 In Japanese households the male head of house owned everything and allotted tasks to family members. Whatever they received for their work was dependent on him, as there was no such thing as a wage. Elderly women were treated with respect, although effectively power was in the hands of the men.

Race and Ethnicity

QUESTIONS

1 What is the difference between 'race' and 'ethnic group'?

2 Explain the meaning of the terms (a) scapegoating and (b) authoritarian personality.

3 What is a zone of transition? Why do ethnic minorities live there?

4 Give a brief description of the three phases of immigration into Britain since 1950.

5 In which areas of Britain have immigrants settled? What reasons can you suggest for this pattern?

6 Give three reasons why immigrants came to Britain after 1950.

7 What are the main causes of racial prejudice?

8 Give brief accounts of the discrimination which Blacks and Asians face in (a) employment and (b) housing.

9 What steps have been taken in recent years to reduce the amount of racial discrimination in Britain?

10 How effective has government legislation been in reducing racial discrimination?

ANSWERS

1 Race is taken to mean a group that shares certain biological characteristics. It is extremely difficult to divide people into clear racial groups as there are great overlaps. Ethnic groups are groups of people who share a common culture, often different from that of the majority of that society.

2 Scapegoating is the process by which certain 'out' groups are blamed for the problems of the whole society. This occurs because it enables blame to be shifted from the society in general to a small, easily distinguishable group and provides a simple explanation for society's problems. Examples of scapegoating are the persecution of the Jews in Nazi Germany and the unfair blaming of Blacks or Asians in Britain today for causing unemployment or housing shortages.

Authoritarian personality is the type of personality found in people who are very rigid in their beliefs, intolerant of weakness and change. A sociologist, Adorno, has argued that these sorts of people are more likely to be racially prejudiced.

3 A 'zone of transition' is an area of the inner city which is in decline and which has a high proportion of immigrants. Originally the area was inhabited by rich people but when they moved out the large houses fell into disrepair and were divided into separate apartments. These formed cheap housing for the worse-off groups in society, including immigrants, and the area subsequently became a centre for transient, poorer people who needed cheap accommodation.

Immigrants generally live in 'zones of transition' because they suffer from the prejudice of people who do not want to rent them property. They were forced into living in the only areas of cities that would accept them, namely the zones of transition. Often immigrants bought these houses and then sublet them in order to pay for the costs of purchase. Because they had to pay back a large amount of money, they took in considerable numbers of immigrant tenants causing overcrowding. Often the more successful families move out of the zones when they can afford it.

4 1951–61 was a period when there was a sharp increase in immigration of people from West Indian and Asian backgrounds. The non-Whites in the population increased from 75 000 to 200 000.

1962–71 saw a decrease in the numbers entering Britain,

but wives and children came in to join the first waves of non-white immigrants of the 1950s.

1972–84 saw a continuing decrease in immigration. Today, about 50 per cent of all immigrants come from the New Commonwealth and Pakistan and almost all of these are dependants of people already living here.

5 Most immigrants moved to West Yorkshire and the East of Lancashire, the West Midlands, and the South-East, especially London. Within these areas they settled in inner-city districts of places such as Birmingham or London.

Immigrants moved to these areas because there were job vacancies in industries in which British workers were not interested, mainly in low-paid, unpleasant work in declining industries. It has been argued that without immigrant labour many of the traditional British industries would have collapsed.

6 The reasons why immigrants came to Britain after 1950 are (three of the following) firstly, because of poverty and unemployment at home, thus they were forced to look for work elsewhere. Secondly, because of persecution where the dominant groups in their 'home' society were persecuting the minority group, forcing them to flee to another country which would accept them. This happened in Uganda. Thirdly, immigrants are attracted by the possibility of work. This often involves active recruitment from the 'host' country. In the case of Britain in the 1950s the limits of the British working population had been reached and so workers were encouraged to come from abroad to fill vacancies. The final reason for immigration in Britain concerns the fact that once a member of the family has come to Britain, the rest of the family may wish to come to Britain in order to be re-united with the original immigrant. The original workers to come to Britain, especially among Indian, Pakistani and Bangladeshi people, were men, and they later sent for their wives and children. The system of arranged marriages also means that fiancées are brought over from the original homelands.

7 Among the main causes of prejudice are:

(a) the tendency of people who are intolerant of others' beliefs and customs to be prejudiced against the minority groups;

(b) stereotyping, which means that many people regard other racial groups as being inferior. Stereotypes of black people are often a result of our colonial past and many continue to believe that black people are inferior, less intelligent and less dependable than Whites. All Blacks are regarded as having these same weaknesses;

(c) scapegoating, which means that in periods of economic decline or social tension certain groups are blamed for the problems which exist. In Britain people are sometimes blamed for unemployment, inner-city problems and crime.

8 Discrimination in employment: all the immigrant groups tend to be over-represented in jobs requiring fairly low levels of skill. In particular, black people face discrimination in obtaining work and unemployment among black people, especially youths, is much higher than the national average. Black people who have jobs are likely to experience poorer working conditions than Whites and have far fewer chances of promotion.

Discrimination in housing: although reasonably high proportions of Blacks and Asians own their own houses a much smaller proportion are council tenants and research shows that they tend to wait longer on housing lists than white people. Generally they can face discrimination in renting private accommodation or when trying to buy property. They also tend to live in older, poorer quality housing, often with inadequate facilities.

9 Legislation has been passed to reduce racial discrimination. The Race Relations Act makes it illegal to discriminate in the provision of goods or services to the public, or in the areas of employment and housing. It it also illegal to incite racial hatred.

In 1976 the Commission for Racial Equality was established with the power to bring cases of discrimination to court and to encourage greater awareness of the need for racial harmony.

There have also been moves to introduce changes in the British education system to cater for the needs of our multi-racial society. This has included the introduction of teaching programmes dealing with other cultures.

10 Although there are indications that the degree of prejudice and discrimination against black people and other ethnic minorities has declined, there is still much discrimination in our society. Given the growth of unemployment and other economic problems this is likely to continue.

The evidence shows that passing laws is not enough since what is really needed is a change in people's attitudes.

Work

QUESTIONS

1 Why can it be said that it is very difficult to define work?

2 What are the most common characteristics of work?

3 Jobs performed by the working population can be divided into two very broad forms of labour – manual and non-manual.

What is the difference between 'manual' and 'non-manual' work?

4 List the trends that have been apparent in the British occupational structure throughout this century.

5 What are the differences between the 'core' and 'periphery' sectors of employment?

6 What are the main characteristics of industrialized societies?

7 What is meant by the 'second industrial revolution'?

8 What further changes in society are likely to result from this 'second industrial revolution'?

9 Define the term 'alienation' and mention the elements associated with it.

10 What attempts have been made to make work more fulfilling?

11 What is meant by 'industrial conflict'?

12 Unofficial strikes account for 90 per cent of all strikes in any year. (a) What is an unofficial strike? (b) What reasons are there for unofficial strikes?

13 Why do strikes occur?

14 What are the aims of employers' organizations?

15 Name four types of trade unions and give one example of each type.

16 How has union membership changed during the course of this century?

17 Distinguish between a professional association and a trade union.

18 Give a brief account of the four major differences between work in industrial and pre-industrial society.

19 Identify the main points of comparison between the process of industrialization in Japan and that in Britain.

20 Give four ways in which work influences our lives outside work.

21 Give brief accounts of how studies of fishermen and miners have illustrated the impact of work on family life.

22 How did the disappearance of dockwork in Bethnal Green in the late 1960s affect community life in the area?

ANSWERS

1 It is difficult to define work because what is thought of as work varies according to such things as time, place, society and individual preferences: e.g. if a professional takes part in a sport it is work, but if an office worker plays a game of football it is likely to be seen as pleasure.

2 Work is usually paid, not done mainly for pleasure, done under the authority of an employer, takes place in a special

place, such as an office or factory, has a productive outcome and is done at particular times.

3 Manual work: physical labour of the kind done by miners, bricklayers and mechanics, for example.

Non-manual: white-collar work which requires little physical effort; work done by teachers and office workers for example.

4 (a) a move away from manual towards non-manual work; (b) a move away from primary and manufacturing industries towards service industries; (c) an increase in the numbers of women in the workforce; (d) the growth in unemployment.

5 Workers in the 'core' sector have good working conditions and secure jobs paying better incomes and offering decent conditions of service, whereas workers in the 'peripheral' sector enjoy few benefits, little job security, poor working conditions and low pay; workers in this sector are often part-time. The gap between the two sectors is said to be growing and labour involved in the 'peripheral' sector is increasing as a proportion of the work force.

6 (a) production is mechanized and located in factories; (b) the majority of the population live in towns near factories; (c) most people work for employers paying fixed wages; (d) workers have joined trade unions and conflict with employers is common; (e) cheaper goods are produced in large quantities and the mass of the population can achieve a higher standard of living; (f) technology is continuously evolving – growth of automation; (g) a division of labour is established.

7 The term 'second industrial revolution' describes the growth of the new microchip technology, because of which automation has taken a huge step forward. In manufacturing industry this technology performs and monitors the majority of tasks in the production process. Microchips have also radically changed service industries with the introduction of cash dispensers, word processors, etc.

8 Apart from the general benefits of automation, the use of the new microchip technology will result in changes such as the following:
(a) people will be able to order goods and services from their own homes; (b) more people may work from home, using computer keyboards linked to an office or factory; (c) better-quality goods of consistently high standard are likely to be produced; (d) information will be more easily stored and available for recall.

There will also be disadvantages, as deskilling and lack of job satisfaction will occur, unemployment will increase while wages decrease, and social mixing will be reduced.

9 Marx defined alienation as a situation where people gained no enjoyment from their work. Its elements include a feeling that a person's work is meaningless, a belief that a worker has no control over his work, increasing conflict between workers and employers since they do not share the same interest in the work, a sense of isolation from others in society, and a loss of personality on the part of the worker.

10 (a) Employers have attempted to make work more fulfilling by creating a more pleasant work environment, introducing fringe benefits for workers, giving workers a share in management, moving away from the division of labour and paying higher wages and bonuses. (b) Workers have in their turn reacted against the conditions of work by limiting output, paying little attention to their work, and by playing tricks and practical jokes to relieve boredom.

11 Industrial conflict usually involves poor relations between workers and management and shows itself in the number of strikes and cases of 'working to rule' and 'industrial sabotage', where workers deliberately set out to damage a firm's output.

12 (a) An unofficial strike is a strike that is not formally recognized by the executive of the appropriate trade union. (b) Many unofficial strikes are (according to Hyman) short-term responses to immediate problems which are solved locally before official union channels become involved. However, Cameron and Eldridge in *Unofficial Strikes* suggested that unions did not declare strikes official in order to avoid having to pay strike pay, or in other cases tended to wait to see how successfully a strike developed before deciding to call it official.

13 The tendency to strike may be related either to the wider economic and political context (e.g. government action, or general economic circumstances may affect the tendency of unions to strike) or to more immediate causes related to wage disputes or disputes over hours of work, working conditions and level of job satisfaction in particular industries.

14 Employers' Organizations (e.g. the CBI) exist to protect the interests of employers and act as a pressure group in promoting these interests in Parliament and elsewhere.

15 General unions: Transport and General Workers' Union. Industrial unions: National Union of Railwaymen. Craft unions: National Graphical Association. White-collar unions: Association of Scientific, Technical and Managerial Staff.

16 Changes in union membership this century:
(a) There has been a general increase in membership but this has declined in periods of economic depression and high unemployment (see the substantial drop in recent years);
(b) There has been a shift towards fewer, but larger unions, usually of the general union type;
(c) There has been a substantial growth of unions among white-collar workers, who amount to approximately 40 per cent of all union members.

17 According to Millerson (*The Qualifying Associations*) professional associations are likely to have the following characteristics: (a) a high level of skill involving theoretical knowledge; (b) an extensive education; (c) professionals seek to serve the public and not just make money; (d) have a code of ethics; (e) be self-regulative (control themselves); (f) control and limit entry.

18 In pre-industrial societies:
(a) Work was not just an economic activity but a social activity, too, emphasizing the bonds that held people together – working and social lives are unified.
(b) People are likely to have their jobs passed on to them from their parents, a process known as ascription. In industrial societies people choose their occupations.
(c) The concept of work measured in time did not exist. There was less of a tendency to measure work in strict terms and at the same time the notion of there being an appropriate time to go into employment was also less clear.
(d) Work was less likely to be done in a separate workplace away from the home.

19 Some points of difference between Japan and Britain:
(a) Until the mid-nineteenth century Japan was virtually isolated from the rest of the world and society was rigidly controlled to prevent changes to the economy.
(b) After American involvement and the arrival of US warships the local economy was wiped out and the government inspired a number of radical changes in a relatively short period.
(c) Large firms were developed rather than the small firms characteristic of the British process of industrialization.
(d) The values of pre-industrial Japan were carried over into the new factories.
(e) The concentration of capital in relatively few hands provided plenty of scope for massive investment in technological development.

20 Work influences family life, community life, health and leisure activities.

21 (a) Turnstall's work among Hull fishermen illustrated that long periods away at sea made a man something of an outsider in his own family and had significant effects on his relationships with his wife and children.
(b) The work of Dennis, Henriques and Slaughter concerns a Yorkshire mining community; it was established that the nature of the men's work tended to strengthen their social cohesiveness outside work while women tended to remain apart in their own groups.

22 The research of P. Cohen in the 1960s should be compared with the earlier research of Young and Willmott in the early 1950s. Cohen found that the disappearance of dockwork and the movement of population out of the area led to a loss of cohesion in the community and a scattering of the members of the formerly extended families. The result was a fragmented community.

Unemployment

QUESTIONS

1 Why are official statistics thought to be less than the true extent of unemployment?

2 How has the duration of unemployment altered during the 1980s?

3 Which groups are more likely to suffer unemployment than others?

4 How does unemployment vary according to region?

5 How can some of these variations of unemployment according to region be explained?

6 In general what are the causes of unemployment?

7 Give a brief summary of the effects of unemployment for British society.

8 What effects of unemployment are felt by young people in society?

9 How are the middle-aged affected by unemployment?

10 In what ways are women likely to be affected by unemployment?

ANSWERS

1 Official statistics include only those people entitled to claim state benefits, not those who are over 60 claiming long-term supplementary benefit or young people on special training schemes such as YTS. Others looking for work, but not entitled to benefits, are also excluded.

2 During the 1980s the duration of unemployment has increased considerably. By 1986 half the unemployed had been out of work for more than a year – it is feared that eventually a solid group of long-term unemployed will develop.

3 Groups more likely to suffer unemployment include: (a) the young and old; (b) members of ethnic minorities; (c) manual workers and the less skilled.

4 The highest rates of unemployment in mainland Britain are the North with 18 per cent, followed by Wales and 16 per cent. The South-East (9.5 per cent) and East Anglia (10 per cent) have much lower rates.

5 The changing nature of industry has mean that those areas of the country with the greatest concentrations of heavy industry, now in decline, are likely to suffer most unemployment. Due to membership of the EEC there has been a general move to the South where trading links with Continental Europe are most easily established.

Service industries grow more readily in affluent areas where there is most demand for such services.

6 (a) The decline in manufacturing industry generally and the wider use of new technology in new manufacturing industries. Service industries have increased, but do not of course supply employment opportunities equal to those lost in manufacturing;
(b) Lack of increase in full-time employment during the 1980s;
(c) The effects of automation, new technology, etc.;
(d) Increasing foreign competition.

7 Some of the effects of unemployment include:
(a) Government expenditure is diverted from useful projects to employment and other state benefits;
(b) Employers might exploit the situation to pay lower wages and provide poorer conditions for those in work;
(c) Trade unions are weakened;
(d) There is an increasing gap in standards of living between the unemployed and those in work;
(e) Increasing poverty in society;
(f) Increasing crime rates;
(g) The possibility of political instability as people feel less confident in the democratic system.

8 To some extent unemployment might not have such damaging effects on young people as it has on other age groups, for young people do not have large financial responsibilities and feel relatively little stigma, since half of all young people are in the same situation.

On the other hand, it is argued that young people feel resentment at not being able to obtain consumer goods etc., or leave home and get married – hence considerable tension results (possibly leading to criminal activity etc.).

9 Loss of employment causes partial loss of identity for the middle aged and brings serious financial problems. Loneliness results from loss of contact with former workmates and the unemployed feel depressed, bored, useless and frustrated. Family tensions also result from all these factors.

10 Despite the fact that official statistics indicate that women have not been as badly hit by unemployment, the effects upon women are not that different to that of men. Loss of income affects family finances and loneliness and frustration result, as in the case of men. Research indicates that the roles of mother and housewife are not adequate compensation for the loss of work.

Leisure

QUESTIONS

1 What do we mean by leisure?

2 What evidence is there that there has been a significant growth in leisure since the Second World War?

3 Name the factors that affect the type of leisure activities people choose.

4 Give brief explanations of the three possible relationships between leisure and occupation, according to Stanley Parker.

5 Contrast the optimistic and pessimistic views of the future of leisure in an age of automation.

ANSWERS

1 Leisure is difficult to define, but it might be said to have certain features – it is time free from employment; it is time spent in enjoyment and pleasure; it is time spent in ways we choose; it is not paid.

2 It can be agreed that since the Second World War the values of the majority of society have laid less stress on the importance of hard work and more on the enjoyment of leisure. In the period referred to there has been a gradual increase in paid holidays and shortening of working hours, so that leisure has become a reality for most of the population. Leisure activities formerly exclusive to the higher social classes are now more widely available.

3 Factors which affect the type of leisure activities chosen include a person's (a) social class (b) age (c) gender (d) occupation.

4 The three possible relationships between leisure and occupation are:
(a) Extension: where a person's leisure activities and work tend to overlap. This is typically found in a responsible and rewarding occupation.
(b) Opposition: where a person's occupation is so tough and exhausting that he/she seeks leisure activities that are entirely the opposite and thus a complete break from work.

(c) Neutrality: where an occupation is so boring that leisure activities are sought as compensation, although no clear pattern of leisure emerges as in the other two types.

5 The *optimistic* view sees automation as eliminating the more boring types of work and leaving more time for participation in leisure activities which will become the central element in our lives, overcoming class and occupational divisions. The *pessimistic* view sees automation as causing massive unemployment which, given poor state benefits, will lead to the majority of people unable to afford leisure activities. Increasingly large companies will provide leisure activities requiring payment for the services they offer, and manipulating the public.

Population

QUESTIONS

1 What does the term 'demography' mean?

2 How does the census and the registration of births, marriages and deaths assist the student of demography?

3 What sort of question does the census ask?

4 Why is all this demographic information of such importance to the Government?

5 What is the birthrate?

6 What changes have taken place in the last 40 years?

7 What factors affect the birthrate at any time?

8 What is the deathrate?

9 What has happened to the death rate over the last 150 years?

10 What factors have influenced the changes in the death rate?

11 What does 'infant mortality' mean?

12 What changes have taken place in it over the century?

13 What three factors influence the size of the population?

14 Explain the meaning of the term 'natural increase'.

15 Explain the relationship between social class and fertility.

16 What does the term 'an ageing population' mean?

17 What problems does it cause?

18 Why do women live longer than men?

19 Distinguish between 'emigration' and 'immigration'.

20 Describe the main patterns of immigration and emigration this century.

ANSWERS

1 It is the study of population, concentrating on changes in its size, the proportions in each age group, geographical distribution and balance of the sexes.

2 The census gives valuable information on where people live, how many of them there are, and in what circumstances they live.

The Registrar records all births, marriages and deaths in an area and so a picture can be built up of the changes in the population.

3 It asks questions about such things as the jobs people have, about their amenities and their marital status.

4 The information collected helps the Government to plan its future policies by saying how many schools, hospitals, roads and social services are needed. Without the information the Government would simply have to guess the extent of needs.

5 The birth rate is the number of live births each year for every 1000 of the population. It gives us a guide to the increase or decrease in the number of children born every year.

6 In the 1950s, the birth rate was high, but declining. In the late 1950s to the mid-1960s it rose, and since then it has been declining.

7 The factors that affect the birth rate are:
(a) the use of contraceptives, which allow parents to plan and limit families. Effective birth control methods have been known for about 100 years, but it is much easier to obtain contraceptive advice today than it was even 30 years ago.
(b) The financial benefits or costs of having children; if children are seen as an economic asset then there will be a tendency to have large families. Children are useful when there are few social services provided by the state and when there are no pensions. In Britain the provision of pensions to old people and the compulsory attendance of children at school has led to children being regarded as more an economic liability than an asset.
(c) Cultural stress on the 'correct' number of children to have. In each period there are certain attitudes that develop concerning the normal size of family. In Britain at the moment it is two children.
(d) Women's attitudes to childrearing: women's attitudes to the roles of wife and mother have changed in this century. Many women prefer to work than to stay at home as housewives. With the availability of contraception they have chosen to limit the number of children they have.

8 The death rate is the number of deaths for every 1000 of the population. It gives a measure of the changes in the number of deaths each year.

9 The death rate fell until the 1950s, but in recent years it has remained fairly static. At the turn of this century, for example, it was 17 per 1000 and today it has fallen to less than 12.

10 Changes in the death rate have been caused by:
(a) Improvements in sanitation and public hygiene. The result of effective sewers and rubbish disposal has been to eliminate many diseases which previously caused death. Clean water, for example, has eliminated cholera.
(b) Medical advances have ensured that diseases which would have killed a hundred years ago are now controlled by medicine. In particular, vaccination gives us much greater defence against 'killer diseases'.
(c) The rise in the standard of living in Britain has meant that people have better diets and greater home comforts. This has led to better health and a population that is physically stronger.

11 Infant mortality means the deaths of infants under one year of age. The infant mortality rate is the number of deaths of infants for every 1000 live births.

12 The main reasons for the decrease in the infant mortality rate have been the same as for the death rate in general: i.e. vaccination, rise in the standard of public hygiene, healthy diets, decent housing. On top of this has been the high standard of health care provided by the National Health Service, especially the antenatal and postnatal clinics.

13 The three factors are the birth rate, the death rate and the level of migration.

14 Natural increase means the increase in the population of a country caused by the greater number of births over deaths.

15 Traditionally, the working class have always had more children than the middle class. It was generally agreed that the difference was caused by the fact that the working class traditionally saw children as an economic asset and, secondly, that they were less likely to understand, or wish to use, contraceptives. In recent years the differences between the working and middle classes have disappeared. A typical family now has just two children in both social classes.

16 An ageing population means that the numbers of old people are increasing in proportion to the rest of the population.

17 The consequences for society are that:
(a) There is an increase in the 'burden of dependency', which means that the working population has to support an increasing number of non-workers.

(b) There has to be an increase in the provision of medical services for the elderly.
(c) There has to be an increase in the provision of social services.
(d) For individuals there is increasing loneliness.
(e) The elderly may become an increasing burden on the family.

18 Women on average live longer that men because they are less likely to work in dangerous occupations, less likely to be combatants in wars, less likely to drink or smoke heavily, and because far more men than women are killed in motor vehicle accidents.

19 Emigration is when people leave a country or area permanently to live elsewhere.
   Immigration is when people move into a country or area permanently from a different country or area.

20 Emigration: up to the Second World War many people emigrated to the British Commonwealth and Empire. For 20 years after the Second World War the numbers of emigrants declined as there were so many opportunities in Britain. In the 1970s the numbers increased again.
   Immigration: levels were low before the Second World War, then they increased significantly in the 1950s and '60s. There has been a marked decline in the 1970s and '80s.

Urbanization and Community
QUESTIONS

1 What do the terms 'urban' and 'rural' mean?

2 Explain what is meant by the terms (a) 'urbanization' (b) 'de-urbanization'.

3 Briefly explain the relationship between industrialization and urbanization.

4 Explain the difference between 'community' and 'association'.

5 What three reasons have been suggested to explain the differences between rural and urban life?

6 Why are simple contrasts between life in rural and urban societies sometimes misleading?

7 How, according to the sociologists of Chicago University, was the city divided into five concentric zones? How did this help to explain why crime and social problems were concentrated in certain parts of the city?

8 Why is the concentric zone pattern not true for all cities?

9 What groups of people tend to live in the inner cities?

ANSWERS

1 Urban means towns and cities. Rural means areas in the countryside.

2 Urbanization is the movement of people from living in rural areas to living in urban areas. De-urbanization means the movement of people out of the cities to live in outer suburbs and in the countryside. They may still be working in the city, however.

3 Industrialization led to the growth of towns and cities as we know them in Britain. The development of factories led to the need for large numbers of employees in one place, so that people were drawn to a few industrial centres. Houses were needed and with them shops. Offices developed with the growing complexity of industry (which attracted yet more people).
   De-urbanization began to occur partly because the factories declined and the employment patterns changed, with the move of offices and the new industries out to the New Towns and countryside. The workers followed.

4 Tonnies distinguished between two types of social life: community and association. Community refers to a society in which people are bound closely together, knowing each other. Generally the society is fairly small. People are judged not just on their behaviour, but also on who their parents are and how great their status is. People living in a community tend to identify with it, feeling proud of it and exhibiting a reluctance to move.

An association consists of a society of much more formal relationships, usually called 'secondary relationships' by sociologists. A person is measured much more by what he/she does than who he/she is, and there is little identification with the neighbourhood.

Community is generally connected with life in a rural area and association with city life.

5 The three reasons for the differences in size of the housing developments, the sheer numbers of people, and the wider variety of backgrounds of people.

6 Simple contrasts between life in rural and urban societies are sometimes misleading because:
(a) Some neighbourhoods in towns have strong community links and people have a great sense of belonging, especially if there are many family ties in the area.
(b) Life in the 'commuter villages' studied by Pahl, which ought to have had a community life, were deeply divided and had little sense of community. Williams, too, has pointed out the myth of the tranquil, happy rural life in his historical studies. The sense of belonging came from what he called the *mutuality of the oppressed.*

7 According to the sociologists the city was divided into five zones. Moving out from the centre, they were as follows:
(a) The inner business district, with shops, large city buildings and commercial offices.
(b) An older residential area of larger houses, now fallen into disrepair and divided up into flats for poorer people.
(c) An area occupied by better-off working class people.
(d) A typical middle class suburban area.
(e) A wealthy district where rich people live in expensive houses, with large gardens.

The division of a city showed that as people became more prosperous they tended to move out from the centre, leaving the poorest and least successful in the inner city areas (especially zone 2). This inner city area was the one in which new arrivals to the city always settled. As each new group settled then the more successful would move out to the suburbs, leaving the least successful behind. Over time the constant inflow of new arrivals and the constant outflow of the successful created a cultural area where there was a great mixture of values and ideas, many of them contradictory to the values of the older society. The result was the development of subcultures which allowed crime deviance. Other social problems developed, too, such as prostitution, alcoholism and mental illness.

8 The concentric zone pattern does not apply to all cities because many local authorities in Britain have built council developments away from the inner cities. Redevelopment has taken place in the inner city areas with new offices and roads, replacing the run-down inner city housing. Also, affluent middle class couples have moved into the decaying areas and improved the older houses.

9 Groups living in the inner cities include the 'bohemians', the ethnic minorities, the deprived, the poor and the elderly who are trapped there.

Poverty

QUESTIONS

1 What is the difference between 'absolute' and 'relative' poverty?

2 Why are different definitions of poverty significant for their implications on government policy in Britain?

3 Explain what is meant by the term 'the poverty line'.

4 How might it be said that poverty was rediscovered in the 1960s?

5 Which groups are most commonly found among the poor?

6 Give brief accounts of four explanations for the continuing existence of poverty.

7 What are the implications for government policy arising from these explanations?

8 Apart from the problems directly caused by having small incomes, what other problems are often faced by the poor?

9 Why does poverty continue to exist in Britain despite the introduction of the Welfare State?

10 To what extent has progressive taxation eliminated inequalities in society?

ANSWERS

1 *Absolute poverty* is a term used by those who argue that it is possible to establish a line representing the minimum income people need to keep themselves in a satisfactory standard of health and efficiency. At this standard a person would have a level of food, clothing, and housing which could just be regarded as satisfactory. Anyone with an income below this level would be regarded as being in a state of absolute poverty.

Relative poverty – many sociologists, regarding the definition of poverty already given as being inadequate, argue that it is not possible to fix a 'line of poverty', as what is considered poverty varies from time to time and from place to place. It is argued, therefore, that poverty is relative.

2 Different definitions draw lines of poverty by which whole groups of people are placed in or out of poverty depending on the definition chosen. If a definition of poverty is accepted which suggests that large numbers of people are living in poverty, then clearly the Government needs to take action.

3 This line represents the minimum income required to support a person in a satisfactory state of health. It has to be calculated by estimating the minimum costs of food, clothes, housing, etc. required for a person to survive. This line cuts off the poor, who are below it, from the rest of the population.

4 Although it was commonly believed that the creation of the Welfare State had led to the disappearance of poverty, research findings in the 1960s, and after, clearly established the facts of its continued existence. Government reports, the research of Titmuss (1962), Abel-Smith and Townsend (1965), Coats and Silburn (1970), etc. provide plenty of evidence.

5 The low paid, the unemployed, the elderly, the sick and disabled, single parents, people living in certain regions of the country (e.g. North of England and Scotland).

6 (a) *The cycle of deprivation* It is argued that poor families with backgrounds of social problems tend to intermarry and reproduce the cycle of deprivation all over again. Rutter and Madge claim that this cycle occurred when at least three of the following were present: (i) intellectual backwardness; (ii) family instability; (iii) poorly educated children; (iv) inadequate, poorly kept home; (v) large family.
(b) *The culture of poverty* It is argued that certain groups in poverty develop their own set of values, which enable them to cope with their poverty, but also trap them in it.
(c) *Functions provided by the poor* This claims that the affluent members of society keep sections of the population in poverty for the benefit of the better off, e.g. for cheap labour.

7 In general such explanations might be found to indicate:
(a) More effort on the part of social workers and local authorities to help children to break out of their present condition.
(b) More expenditure on education.
(c) More effort to raise wages and encourage unionization among lower-paid workers.

8 The poor tend to have fewer medical facilities provided for them and the NHS is proportionately more used by the middle class. The children of the poor often do less well at school. Living in deprived inner city areas the poor often have poorer housing conditions, fewer community facilities and more problems to cope with than in the suburbs. They also have less chance to shop economically. They are less likely to be aware of the state benefits to which they are entitled.

9 Poverty continues to exist despite the Welfare State because:

(a) Rates of benefits are too low.

(b) Benefits are difficult to claim because the system is so complicated.

(c) Some people are too ashamed to claim benefits because they feel that there is a stigma attached.

(d) The existence of the 'poverty trap'. People on relatively low pay can actually end up taking home less money because of the way the system works.

10 It is generally argued that it has failed to do so. According to Kincaid, lower income groups actually pay a higher proportion of their income in various forms of taxation than do the more affluent.

The Welfare State
QUESTIONS

1 Give a defintion of the term 'the Welfare State'.

2 Why did the Labour Party introduce the Welfare State at the end of the Second World War?

3 In what ways did the Conservative governments after 1979 try to change the Welfare State?

4 In which areas of the social services does the Welfare State operate?

5 Name any three advantages and three disadvantages of the Welfare State.

6 Give examples of the kinds of services provided by voluntary organizations.

7 Why are voluntary organizations still important despite the growth of the Welfare State?

ANSWERS

1 The Welfare State means that the state has taken on the responsibility of ensuring that every one of its citizens has the right to adequate standards of income, housing, education and health.

2 The Labour Party introduced a Welfare State because there had been over 20 years of mass unemployment. The existing provision of services introduced earlier by the Liberal government was not doing enough to combat the dreadful poverty. The destruction of the cities during the Second World War had meant that new houses had to be provided for the population. Finally, public opinion was very strong in its desire never to return to the pre-war conditions.

3 Generally, the Conservatives argue that those who can provide for themselves should have to do so and only those who cannot should be helped by the Welfare State. According to this view, money is wasted giving assistance to everybody. As a result the governments after 1979 tried to cut back the Welfare State and to encourage the development of private alternatives, for example by encouraging the development of private health care.

4 The Welfare State operates in five main areas: education; social security; community care; health; housing.

5 Advantages of the Welfare State include the following: firstly, it has eliminated the greatest excesses of poverty and deprivation in Britain. Secondly, it aids many people who through no fault of their own would have been reduced to begging. Thirdly, it allows everybody, not just the affluent, to have medical treatment. Fourthly, it gives all children the opportunity to use their talents to the full, because it gives free secondary and higher education. Fifthly, it has allowed people to live in adequate homes, through the development of massive housing developments. Finally, it allows old people some dignity and independence in their retirement by providing a pension.

The disadvantages of the Welfare State, it is claimed, are that it is wasteful of resources and should restrict its benefits to the very poor and the seriously disabled, while the rest of society ought to make provision for themselves. Secondly, the Welfare State is seen as being too bureaucratic and as having gained too much control over our lives – this takes away people's initiative and also makes the Welfare State too complacent and unaware of our needs. Thirdly, the family is weakened, as the state takes over its functions.

6 There is a wide range of services provided by voluntary organizations. These include: (a) marriage guidance counselling; (b) help for those who are physically or mentally handicapped; (c) help for the homeless and the inadequately housed; (d) services for single parents; (e) help for those with drug and alcohol problems. Basically, they fill in the gaps in what the Welfare State provides.

7 The voluntary organizations are important because the state simply cannot cope with all the problems in society.

The voluntary services respond quickly and flexibly.

Volunteers are prepared to work more flexible hours.

Volunteers are often people who have experienced the very problems that they are helping others to overcome.

The voluntary services often act as a 'thorn in the side' of the Welfare State, trying to persuade it to do more and to act more effectively.

Politics and Power
QUESTIONS

1 Explain the differences between:

(a) democracy and totalitarianism;

(b) fascism and communism.

2 Give two other characteristics of a democracy other than the right to vote.

3 What is a pressure group?

4 How is a pressure group different from a political party?

5 Name two pressure groups.

6 Explain how pressure groups go about achieving their aims.

7 Is it true to say that the more members a pressure group has, the greater its influence? If not, why not?

8 Explain the meaning of the following terms:

(a) floating voter; (b) opinion poll.

9 How could opinion polls possibly influence the outcome of an election?

10 Explain the part played by the mass media in influencing how people vote.

11 Give two reasons why people may not vote in elections.

12 Explain the relationship between class and voting behaviour.

13 What is the relationship between geographical location and voting behaviour?

14 Explain the term 'pluralism'.

15 What is the typical social class background of (a) MPs (b) civil servants?

16 What comments have Marxists made about the disruption of power in society?

ANSWERS

1 (a) Democracy is the political system where the government of a country is controlled as far as possible by the people themselves. People vote the government into power in regular elections, have a free press and legal system, and the right openly to criticize the government.

Totalitarianism is the political system in which the views of the people are not represented in the creation of the government or it decisions. A small group or individual rules, making all the major decisions and imposing them on the majority.

(b) Fascism refers to a political 'ideology' which is based upon totalitarian rule and is usually racist in nature. Certain groups, such as Jews or Blacks, are used as scapegoats for the problems of a country.

Communism is the political ideology associated with Karl Marx. It is based upon the principles of social and economic equality. Marxists believe that capitalist countries are controlled by a small ruling class who own the most important commercial and manufacturing concerns. They argue, for example, that this group rules Britain for its own benefit. Communists argue that these industrial concerns ought to be run by the people and profits ought to be shared among them.

2 Two of the following: a free press, civil liberties, an independent judiciary, the right to criticize the government.

3 An organization formed to promote or protect certain interests. Its members aim to persuade political parties or those in power to adopt their views.

The two types of pressure groups are: protective, which try to defend their own interests; and promotional, which try to put forward ideas for the benefit of society as they see it. In practice, the two groups overlap and there is no clear dictinction between them.

4 The main difference is that a political party tries to gain power in elections; also a political party is concerned with a broad range of issues, the pressure group with only one. Sometimes pressure groups develop into political parties, as the Labour Party developed from the trade union movement.

5 The ones mentioned in the chapter are: CND, Friends of the Earth, TUC, CBI, ALRA, RAC, AA, SPUC, Animal Liberation, Open Shop, Lord's Day Observance Society.

6 Consultantships, block votes, publicity, specialized knowledge, key positions, civil disobedience.

7 No. Size of membership is not the most important thing. Power, wealth, connections to government are all more important. For example, the CBI has been far more successful than the Campaign for Nuclear Disarmament.

8 (a) A person who changes vote from one election to another.
(b) Opinion polls are a type of survey carried out to find people's political preferences and voting choices. They are most commonly carried out at election time. However, an opinion poll does not have to be about politics – it could be about any subject on which people have differing views.

9 They could persuade people to switch votes in order to block the election of a party they particularly disliked, if the party of their first choice was coming last in the polls. Alternatively, they could make voters feel so certain that their party was going to win that they might not go out to vote at all – so many people could feel the same way, that they could alter the outcome of the election.

10 The mass media do not seem to have a direct influence on voting, as most people select the information they want from the papers. Over periods of time, however, they may create images about certain parties.

11 They may not be interested. They may not like the candidate standing for the party of their choice. They may be sure their party is going to win or lose so that there is little point in voting. They may disagree with one aspect of the policy of the party they generally support, but do not want to vote for another party.

12 Class is the single most important influence on the way people vote. Most other factors influencing voting are connected to class. Basically, working class people are more likely to vote Labour and middle class to vote Conservative. However, a large minority in both classes do vote for the party of 'the other class', i.e. working class Conservative voters and middle class Labour voters. The SDP and Liberals are able to draw their votes from all social classes.

13 Geographical location is also linked to voting behaviour. The further North the stronger the allegiance to Labour, with some exceptions. People in inner city areas are more likely to support Labour. The South and the suburbs are Conservative territory, with some exceptions. The SDP's main strengths are the suburbs and small towns. The Liberals are strong in Scotland and the South-West.

14 Pluralism is the approach to the study of government which believes that power is not centralized in Britain, but divided in the hands of many groups. It sees pressure groups and political parties reflecting the will of the people and government decisons are simply the outcome of their activities.

15 For both groups it is middle class and a large proportion of them are public school educated.

16 They argue that power is held by the well off and people under their control. The Government is dominated by the upper middle class, as is the Civil Service. They ensure that the interests of the rich are looked after. They claim that most pressure groups representing ordinary people have little influence.

▨ Social Control ▨

QUESTIONS

1 What do sociologists mean when they use the term 'social control'?

2 What is the difference between 'formal' and 'informal' control?

3 What is the distinction between socialization and social control?

4 What do we mean by the term 'ideological control'?

5 How does the education system help the process of social control?

6 Give two examples of 'agencies' that enforce social control.

7 There is some dispute over the nature of social control between those who are called 'pluralists' and those who are influenced by Marxist ideas. Explain what the differences between these groups are.

8 How can there be such a thing as social control in the workplace?

9 It has been suggested that religion plays a part in social control. Briefly explain this.

10 Do 'simple' societies have any form of formal control? Explain the reasons for your answer.

ANSWERS

1 In order for societies to exist there must be order and predictability. Social control ensures that people act in similar ways that are acceptable to society in general.

2 Formal social control is when there are specific organizations set up to ensure that people are behaving correctly – such as the police and the courts. Informal social control is simply the control that is placed upon people by others around them, which is not organized but spontaneous. A person behaving rudely at the table is stared at by others, and comments are made.

3 Socialization and social control are tied closely together. However, it could be argued that socialization consists of learning the values of society and social control consists of reinforcing those values and patterns of behaviour.

4 Ideological control is the term used when a society (or group of people within society) succeed in making people believe that a certain pattern of behaviour is natural and normal.

5 The education system operates at two levels to impose social control. Firstly teachers teach the values and the accepted knowledge of society in their lessons as part of the curriculum (the subjects taught). Secondly, the teacher and the other pupils impose their values and expectations on each other. The teacher, for example, might not teach in the lesson that there are different patterns of behaviour associated with being male or female, but he/she might treat pupils differently according to sex and so reinforce gender roles.

6 There are many of these. Any from: the family, the peer group, religion, the media, the police, the courts.

7 Pluralists argue that the rules and values of society reflect the general feelings of the people in that society. On the other hand, the Marxists argue that the rules and values of society reflect the interests of the rich and powerful, who are able to impose those ideas on the rest of the population.

8 The social control enforced in the workplace refers to the fact that there are certain expectations of behaviour which apply to people at work. Colleagues and employers then apply pressure to ensure that people behave accordingly. For example, the manager who does not wear a tie will soon be told by his employer to dress more formally or be sacked. On the other hand, the expectations of colleagues are also important. In factories the worker who works too enthusiastically, although praised by management, may be the subject of practical jokes, barbed comments and may even be 'sent to Coventry', in order to make him/her slow down.

9 Religion plays an important role in social control, although it has declined in recent years. The basic values of British society are founded in the Christian religion. In the past the power of religion was much greater and people were frightened of going to Hell, so they would be very likely to obey the clergy. This gave the preachings of the church great weight.

There is some dispute, however, as to whether the preachings of the churches and their interpretations of the New Testament are linked to the interests of the rich and powerful. Marxists argue that the teachings of the churches are used to support the society as it is now and to prevent change.

10 Simple societies rarely have any formal agencies of control like a police force. They rely much more on informal social control, with pressure being brought to bear to enforce conformity, by comments and reactions from others. This can work very well because simple societies generally have few members and so everything that happens is clear to others, and it is difficult to avoid public comment on any deviation from the rules. Also there is the need to rely on others' cooperation in order to survive – if a person is rejected by the others then death is almost certain. To strengthen this, people are held together by very tight bonds of marriage, of age groups and of the 'gift relationships'.

Crime and Deviance

QUESTIONS

1 Explain the differences between deviant acts and illegal acts.

2 Are deviant acts always defined the same in every society?

3 Why are some deviant acts defined as criminal?

4 Explain the meanings of the following terms: (a) moral crusades (b) dark figure.

5 Examine Table 18.1 on page 136.
(a) What was the number of recorded offences of burglary in 1984?
(b) Which offences have increased by the greatest amount between 1971 and 1984?

6 Look at Table 18.2 on page 136. Do females commit more indictable offences than males? Can you offer any explanation for this?

7 Explain the relationship between social class and crime.

8 What sociological explanations have been suggested for crime and delinquency?

9 What does the term 'labelling' mean?

10 What are moral panics?

11 Why do official statistics of crime need to be treated cautiously?

ANSWERS

1 Illegal acts are actions that break the law and are punished by the legal system. Illegal acts are formally codified in the law. Anybody accused of breaking the law is judged in the courts.

Deviant acts are any acts that are regarded in some way as socially wrong. They may be classified as illegal in certain cases, but this is not necessarily so. A deviant act may be one that is relatively unimportant and usually punished by some informal sanction by other people, not in a court.

2 No, deviant acts are not always defined the same way in every society. They vary according to (a) time (b) the society and (c) who committed the act. Behaviour that was regarded as normal one hundred years ago might be regarded as deviant today, just as acceptable behaviour in one society may not be acceptable in another. Even within a society, the behaviour of minority groups might be considered deviant by the majority.

3 Various acts come to be defined as criminal because:
(a) The majority of people might regard certain deviant acts as being so dangerous or extreme that they must be banned.
(b) Particular pressure groups may influence society to ban certain activities of which they disapprove.
(c) It is argued by Marxists that those who have power in society can make laws to suit their own interests.

4 (a) Moral crusades are activities by organized groups to have a law passed making acts of which they disapprove illegal. An example of a moral crusade is the activities of the National Viewers and Listeners Association which is campaigning for stricter controls on the level of sex and violence on television.
(b) The dark figure refers to the number of crimes committed which are unknown to the police. It is caused by the fact that many people do not report offences to the police.

5 (a) 297 000
(b) Criminal damage.

6 No. Females commit considerably fewer offences according to the official statistics.

Explanations for this include: (a) the male gender role can encourage males into criminal activity; (b) females may express anti-social feelings through sexual activity; (c) the official statistics on crime may not reflect the true level of female crime.

7 There appears to be a much higher level of criminal activity among working class youths than among middle class ones. Reasons include the fact that they have different values which may encourage them into delinquent activity; they may feel bitter against society; they may simply have less than middle class youths and therefore are more likely to steal; they may be picked on by the police who believe that they are more likely to uncover illegal activity among the working class youth; they may simply be 'having a laugh' but are more likely to attract police attention.

8 There is a wider number of explanations for criminal activity. These can be summarized into (a) the subcultural approach; (b) anomie; (c) the Marxist approach.

(a) The subcultural approach has a number of variations, but all of them share the basic idea that delinquents are brought up differently or develop a different set of values from the majority of society, which encourages them to commit crime.
(b) Anomie stresses the fact that those who are unable to attain success in life legally may turn to illegal routes to achieve the aim of money and possessions.
(c) The Marxist approach stresses the fact that our society encourages people to be greedy and competitive, not caring about others. In this situation crime seems a 'natural' outcome. Also, the laws are created to be biased against the

working class and to look after the interests of the rich. Hence all the laws on property.

9 Labelling is the process whereby we place 'labels' on people, classifying them in certain ways: for example, 'clever', 'thief', 'mad'. As a result of this labelling people are treated differently by others – even if the label is not accurate. The important point is that it is not committing a deviant act that is significant, but being labelled by others as having committed one and therefore to be treated differently.

10 Moral panics are situations in which the police, media and public get extremely concerned with the behaviour of a particular group and over-react, usually clamping down very tightly, imposing the full force of law and order on them. This is part of the process of 'deviancy amplification'. Often the group are treated as if they were folk devils.

11 Official statistics only include crimes that are reported to the police. There is much evidence to suggest that many crimes go unreported because people may regard some crimes as insufficiently important or may not want to get involved with the police for various reasons. The police may also be unwilling to treat certain reports of crime seriously enough to record them. The distribution of police, too, can affect the numbers of crimes recorded and the way that they categorize activities influences the final crime figures.

▨ **Religion** ▨

QUESTIONS

1 To what sort of questions does religion address itself?

2 What are 'belief systems'?

3 In what way does religion play a crucial role in holding society together?

4 Why do sociologists describe religion as a form of social control?

5 Give a brief account of the functionalist approach to religion as defined by Durkheim.

6 Why did Karl Marx and others consider religion to be against the interests of the majority of the population?

7 How, according to Weber, did religion help to bring about social and economic change?

8 Give a definition of 'secularization'.

9 Why is it argued that Britain has become more of a secular society?

10 Why has the importance of religion declined in society?

11 What are the main arguments of those who claim that the extent of secularization in British society has been exaggerated?

12 Name three major religions that have established themselves recently in Britain.

13 What particular value do religious ceremonies have in simple societies?

ANSWERS

1 Although science and common sense provide us with many answers to questions in the world today, they do not provide all the answers. Religion addresses itself to the questions that seem to be unanswerable, e.g. Why am I here?

2 Belief systems include any set of beliefs that claim to explain our position in the world and the purpose of our existence – therefore Marxist-Leninism is a belief system just as much as religion.

3 First of all, religion usually binds society together by stressing the basic beliefs and values that should influence people's actions. Religion also stresses the importance of traditions, and gives people a strong sense of belonging with a group of other people in society.

People also find that religion helps them to cope with the uncertainties of life and that it gives them emotional support in times of stress and personal hardships.

Finally, religion tends to encourage those who have done wrong to find a way back into society, and religious values give people a set of guidelines against which to measure their conduct.

4 Sociologists claim that religion acts as a form of social control and is part of the socialization process, which helps to ensure conformity to society's rules and contributes to social order.

5 Durkheim concluded that religion played a crucial role in holding society together, a form of social glue. Functionalists identify a number of functions which religion performs in society e.g. the establishing of moral guidelines, and argue that they hold society together by reaffirming basic values, and motivating and guiding individuals to act in such a way as to ensure social conformity.

6 Karl Marx described religion as the 'opiate of the people' because he believed that religion's purpose was to control people who were being exploited in society and to stop them from protesting against their exploitation.

Religion taught people to suffer in this life because they would eventually be rewarded after death, and to accept the present division of wealth and power in society because God had intended that it should be so.

7 According to Weber, religion encouraged people to be thrifty and to work hard. As a result industrial society came about partly due to religous influences.

8 According to Wilson (*Religion in a Secular Society*), secularization is 'the process whereby religious thinking, practices and institutions lose social significance'.

9 The most obvious argument would be that attendance at religious services has declined rapidly. More people are now married in registry offices, too.

The church is also less influential in politics and education, there has been a considerable increase in the number of divorces, clergymen and women have lost their social prestige and most people seem to believe that the churches are irrelevant as far as modern life is concerned.

10 The main reasons for the decline in the importance of religion are:
(a) People have found that science is increasingly able to answer questions for which only supernatural explanations were previously available.
(b) Traditional values have been weakened and it is no longer necessary to attend church in order to be considered respectable.
(c) Family ties have weakened to some extent and children are less likely to attend church with their parents.
(d) New political and social attitudes criticize the church.

11 See Martin (*The Religious and the Secular*). Briefly, secularization has been exaggerated because:
(a) Statistics of church attendance should not be taken as the only proof of interest in religion.
(b) Those who attend church today are the genuinely committed; less attendance is due nowadays to regard for social conventions.
(c) Research shows that many people do believe in God and supernatural forces.
(d) Christianity still provides the basic values in our society, and the major events in our personal lives (birth etc.) and the life of the nation (Coronations etc.) are still marked by religious ceremonies.
(e) Recent church reforms are making religion more attractive to people.
(f) There has been a substantial growth of support for new religious sects outside the traditional churches.
(g) There has been a massive increase in non-Christian religions.

12 Islam, Hinduism, the Sikh religion.

13 In simple societies, magical or religious ceremonies are particularly important in overcoming the unpredictability of the natural world. People believe that they give protection against natural forces such as bad weather.

The Media

QUESTIONS

1 What are the distinctive characteristics of the mass media as composed to other forms of communication?

2 What changes have occurred in the nature of media organizations in recent years?

3 In what ways are the media controlled in Britain?

4 In what ways do the media play a role in the process of socialization?

5 Explain the difference between the pluralist and radical approaches to the question of the relationship between the media and social control.

6 Give two examples of how the media create stereotypes in the ways they portray certain groups in society.

7 Why are such stereotypes important as examples of social control?

8 With the help of examples, show how research has demonstrated the media's importance in perpetuating the division of roles between males and females.

9 What characteristics are commonly found in the way the media deal with race?

10 How can the media give a distorted impression of the types of criminal activity found in Britain today?

11 Define the term 'labelling'.

12 How do the media's activities result in the 'amplification of deviance'?

13 Distinguish between the 'behaviourist model' and 'audience selection' as two explanations of the way the media influence behaviour.

14 It is often said that the media (especially television) encourage violence: what evidence is there for this?

15 What, according to the pluralists, are the functions of the mass media in a democratic society?

16 To what extent do the media influence people's voting behaviour?

17 How does the presentation of 'popular' papers differ from that of 'quality' papers?

18 What factors are chiefly responsible for the style of the contents of the media?

19 Briefly summarize the elements guiding journalists in the way they select and present their material.

20 With reference to ownership of the media, what are the three principal characteristics that should be noted?

21 How far are newspapers and other media influenced by the views of their owners?

ANSWERS

1 The mass media are one-way systems of communication from a single source to a large number of people who have little or no chance of responding. The mass media involve considerable use of technology and are operated by professionals who communicate the ideas thought important by the owners and controllers of the various media; a profit motive is usually involved. The information and entertainment is organized according to a fixed schedule.

2 Media organizations have grown substantially in size and complexity, especially as production costs have become very considerable, thus requiring heavy investment. Ownership of media organizations is now concentrated in relatively few hands.

3 Broadcasting is controlled by the BBC and the IBA and newspapers are supervised, somewhat less strictly, by the Press Council. The Government also has the power to issue 'D' notices to restrict the publication of certain information in the national interest.

4 The media play an important role in secondary socialization, reinforcing the basic primary socialization learned in childhood. They do this because they are the most important source of information about things beyond our personal experience, thus forming our attitudes and opinions about these matters. The media interpret this information, influencing our view of what is normal and what is deviant. Once formed, our views are constantly reinforced by the media.

5 Pluralists argue that the media fulfil a number of useful functions in society, reflecting the attitudes and desires of its audiences, allowing the free discussion of viewpoints and encouraging greater awareness. They do recognize that the media can have harmful effects and argue the need for controls to be maintained to restrict such possibilities.

The radical approach, influenced by Marxism, claims that the media are used by one group of people – the rich – to control society by manipulating the mass of the people into accepting unfairness and inequalities.

6 Two examples of stereotypes in the media:
(a) Women are often shown as being mainly concerned about love, marriage and recipes.
(b) Strikers are usually shown to be lazy people who do not really want to work and are 'holding the country to ransom'.

7 It is argued that stereotyping or applying labels to certain groups helps to keep them in their place, e.g. feminists who disagree with the images of women in the media are made to appear as odd troublemakers deviating from the norm.

8 M. Ferguson (*Forever Feminine*) studied popular women's magazines and found that, although their treatment of women has changed in the years since the 1940s, women's and men's needs are readily accepted as being different. A. McRobbie showed the main theme of girl's magazines to be romance and love.

The study of children's books emphasized the dominance of male characters in the stories and the subordinate roles assigned to females.

9 The media perpetuate the public belief that there is still an immigration problem and give the impression that there are far more Blacks and Asians in Britain than there actually are. They also associate 'immigrants' with conflicts in society, and the differences between Blacks and Whites are constantly referred to and thus in reality reinforced.

It has also been argued, however, that the media merely reflect racist feelings already held.

10 Some crimes are thought to be of greater 'human interest' than others and are grossly over-reported compared to other crimes. Emphasis in the media on stories of crimes of violence, muggings, cases of indecency, etc. give the public a highly distorted view of the sorts of crimes taking place. This distorted view also affects the law and order policies operating in society.

11 Labelling occurs when a person or group is described as having certain characteristics and then treated in a way that seems appropriate to someone with these particular characteristics. (See the media creation of the images of mods and rockers.)

12 The media label certain individuals and encourage expectations of certain kinds of behaviour from such individuals. This can lead to a panic to introduce measures to deal with such troublesome behaviour and an increase in the amount of actual deviance. (See the media's role in the troubles in certain seaside towns.)

13 According to the 'behaviourist model' the watching of a film or any other exposure to the media can alter a person's behaviour in a significant and immediate way. The 'audience selection' explanation argues, however, that people select the information which they want to hear or read, thus the media can only reinforce attitudes already held.

14 Research has produced rather mixed results. Some suggests that the media have little impact in directly encouraging violence, but exposure to violence in the media does make people less likely to be concerned by violence in everyday life; and where other factors encourage aggressive tendencies in individuals, the media can reinforce and further encourage them.

15 The media provide most people with their principal link with the affairs of government, and with most of their information about politics. They also give them an opportunity to voice criticism of government policies.

16 In the short term the mass media may only influence the 'floating' voters, but over a long period they may actually bring about a change in party loyalty or cause a change in a person's attitude to certain political issues or events.

17 Compared to quality papers, popular papers have short articles written in extremely simple English.

The information given is very simple and sensationalized, with viewpoints offered in black-and-white. There are plenty of photographs, particularly of attractive women.

18 The media are usually influenced by commercial considerations in determining the style of their contents. In particular, advertising revenue is of vital importance and has great influence on media organizations, which therefore need to attract large audiences. The media also set out to win certain types of audience for their publications.

There is evidence that owners have influence over what is contained in the media and journalists themselves also play a significant role.

19 Journalists are influenced by the following:
(a) a preference for immediate events rather than long-term developments; (b) events having more than local significance; (c) events and issues that are easy and clear; (d) events that are not too unfamiliar culturally; (e) the public interest in the unexpected rather than the commonplace; (f) the need to provide a balance of items in the news; (g) an awareness that some people and countries are regarded as more important than others; (h) the public's interest in personalities; (i) the need to assume that there is a basic consensus in society.

20 Concerning the question of ownership there are three principal characteristics: concentration of control, diversification and multi-nationalization.

21 As the activities of Rupert Murdoch and Robert Maxwell show, owners have considerable influence, but see also the importance of journalists' views, the need for publications to be commercial and the need to attract advertising.

TYPES OF EXAMINATION QUESTIONS

Each of the Examination Groups has devised a different form of examination, which mixes different types of questions.

First I will list the type of questions that each examination group gives, and then I will go through each type of examination question, suggesting the best way to answer it.

Check the sort of examination question listed under your Examination Group, and then turn to the appropriate example.

1 London East Anglian Group

(a) Multiple-stimulus response (b) Structured response (c) Essay.

2 Midland Examining Group

(a) Multiple-stimulus response (b) Stimulus response.

3 Northern Examination Association

(a) Short-answer questions (b) Structured response (c) Guided essay.

4 Southern Examining Group

(a) Stimulus response.

5 Welsh Joint Education Committee

(a) Short-answer (b) Structured response (c) Guided essays.

Advice on Answering Examination Questions

When answering examination questions remember that although the *style* may be stimulus response, structured response or whatever, the actual question will be one of only three types, each of which is trying to get you to reply in a particular manner.

Factual questions: those that ask you some points of fact which you have learned in your sociology course, or that are given you in stimulus material. Here all that is required is that you give the exact information asked for.

Explanatory questions: these usually ask you to explain a particular point or sociological argument you have studied.

Questions of interpretation: these are ones that ask you to give your evaluation of a particular piece of information, usually given to you in stimulus material.

1 When answering a question always look at the number of marks available for it, which will be in brackets beside it.

2 The greater the marks, the greater the weight and amount of effort you ought to put into answering it.

3 Clearly, if a question is only worth 1 mark, it is pointless writing half a page. Usually there are one or two points to be made, and that is all you need to do. On the other hand, a question that is worth 7 or 9 marks, for instance, requires greater effort and a full development of a discussion.

4 Typically, factual questions are worth less than 4 marks, while explanatory and interpretation questions are worth between 4 and 9.

5 Always read the question very carefully, and then answer exactly what the examiner is asking you, not what you would like him/her to ask you.

6 No marks are ever taken away for mistakes, or irrelevant information. Examiners will award you marks on what you produce which is relevant to the question. So you can only gain marks, never lose them.

7 Try to remain calm and collected in the exam. Work your way at a careful pace through the material. Do not rush: you will have adequate time to write all you wish. The best thing to do is to check the total amount of time available for the complete examination and then divide by the number of questions. You will know then approximately how long you have to spend on each question. It is better to spend an extra half hour and get a higher grade than rush through the examination just because you see others leaving the examination room early.

8 If you have worked your way through this book and you have thought about the ideas in it, then I am sure that you will do very well indeed. So be confident!

1 MULTIPLE-STIMULUS RESPONSE

These questions have a number of different pieces of information which you must read carefully. There follows a series of questions which are based on the 'stimulus' (the information) provided. Each question refers to a specific source or sources, except for the last question which usually requires you to draw together information you have learned in the course with the information provided in the extracts overall.

Advice on answering the multiple-stimulus questions

(a) These questions appear very difficult, but in reality are the same as the ordinary stimulus response. It is just that two or more normal stimulus response questions have been put together.

(b) Read through all the information provided at a reasonable pace, getting the general idea of the information provided.

(c) Check through all the sub-questions, working out whether they are of the factual, explanatory or interpretative type.

(d) Examine the number of marks awarded for each question. Remember the higher the mark awarded the greater the depth or the difficulty of the sub-question. Therefore, give greater weight to the sub-questions awarding the higher marks.

(e) Time the pace of your answer to fit the time allowed, making sure that you finish at about the time allowed. Do not rush and do not go too slowly.

The following multiple stimulus response question is from the London East Anglian Group:

SOURCE MATERIAL

Source A

'Love is now considered important to marriage in most parts of the world. But only in societies like ours is the ideal of romantic love all powerful. From early childhood we are socialized into falling in love – not just by parents and friends but by popular songs, films, TV programmes, magazines and the other mass media. This influence is so strong that young people may be led to expect too much from marriage, and be bitterly disappointed when the passion of courtship is cooled by the daily routines of married life.'
From R. J. Cootes The Family (Longman Group UK Ltd)

Source B

Margaret Mead spent a lot of time with Manus people in New Guinea in the 1920s before the impact of modernized societies like America and Australia had much influence on their way of life. In Manus societies marriages were arranged and the relatives lived together in extended family groups.

'The relationship between husband and wife is usually strained and cold. The blood-ties with their parents are stronger than their relationship to each other, and there are more factors to pull them apart than to draw them together.

The bridegroom has no attitude of tenderness or affection for the girl whom he has never seen before the wedding. She fears her first sex experience as all the women of her people have feared and hated it. No foundation is laid for happiness on the wedding night, only one for shame and hostility. The next day the bride goes about the village with her mother-in-law to fetch wood, and water. She has not yet said one word to her husband.

This sense that husband and wife belong to different groups persists throughout the marriage, weakening after the marriage has endured for many years, never vanishing entirely.'
From J. L. Thompson, Examining Sociology 1980 (Hutchinson)

Source C

Average age at first marriage: UK 1911-71

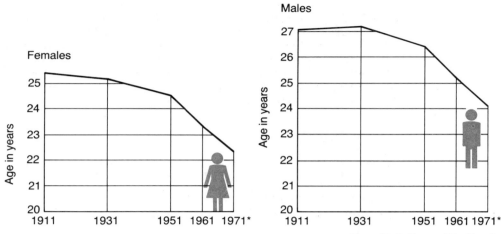

Females

Males

*Figures for 1972-6 show no significant change, thus suggesting that the downward trend has stopped.

From R. J. Cootes *The Family* (Longman Group UK Ltd)

Source D

Percentage of women who had lived with their husbands before their marriage

---

Great Britain	Percentage	
	1971–3 Year of marriage	1977–9

First marriage for both partners: Age of woman at marriage		
Under 20	4	16
20–24	8	17
25 and over	10	34
All ages (percentages)	7	19

Second or subsequent marriage for one or both partners: All women (percentages)	43	59

Adapted from *Social Trends 12* (HMSO)

Source E

Divorce

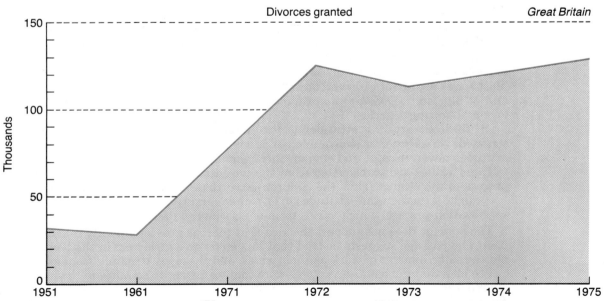

Divorces granted

Great Britain

From: R. Whitburn *Investigating Society – Talking to People* (Macmillan)

Source F

'Though the 1980s' couple go into marriage on technically equal footing, true equality within marriage is still something of an ideal. The idea of the 'househusband' is still fairly rare, as Ann Oakley found when she looked at the domestic division of labour in *The Sociology of Housework* (1974). She asked 20 working class and 20 middle class housewives how far their husbands helped out with the housework and looking after the children. Fewer than a quarter of the husbands gave the kind of help that could be described as doing an equal share of the work – and these tended to be middle class.'   From *Society Today* 13/11/80

QUESTIONS

Answer all the questions; they may be attempted in any order.
The marks shown should be taken as guides to the lengths of answers expected.

1 State four ways in which 'we are socialized into falling in love'.   [2 marks]

2 (a) What was the average age of marriage in 1911 for females? (Source C)   [1 mark]

(b) What has been the trend, for each sex, of the 'average age at first marriage' during this century? (Source C)   [1 mark]

3 What does Source E show about divorce?   [3 marks]

4 Does the concept of 'romantic love' apply to marriages in all societies? Explain your answer, with reference to Sources A and B.   [4 marks]

5 Some sociologists argue that there is now greater equality in marriage. To what extent does Source F support or oppose this view?   [4 marks]

6 What can be learned from the Sources about the ways in which marriage in Britain has changed during this century?   [6 marks]

7 Source B deals with an example of a society very different from our own. Why are sociologists concerned to look at such examples?   [9 marks]

ANSWERS

1 Parents and friends   Popular songs   Films   TV Programmes
(Magazines and 'other mass media' were also mentioned)

2 (a) 25½

(b) The trend has been for the age of marriage to fall, but particularly sharply since 1951.

3 Source E indicates that the number of divorces has risen overall between 1951 and 1975. In 1951 there were approximately 30 000 divorces and this remained stable until 1961. There was a sharp rise up to 1972, when the numbers rose to over 120 000. There was then a slight decline in the number of divorces the following year. However, after 1973, the numbers started to rise again. In 1975 they had reached about 130 000.

4 The concept of 'romantic love' does not appear to apply to marriages in all societies.

In Britain, people are socialized into falling in love. This occurs as part of the normal pattern of socialization in society, through which we learn the accepted behaviour and accepted values and beliefs. From early childhood we are socialized into the belief that we will fall in love. This socialization is carried out firstly by our parents with their attitudes to each other and their explanations of why they married. This is then continued by the influence of the mass media. Most songs are about girls and boys falling in love. The theme of much of published literature, and of film and television programmes, stresses the normality and desirability of falling in love and getting married.

On the contrary, the attitudes of the husband and wife among the Manus are cold and strained. No affection is shown and sex is something to be feared and hated by women. These attitudes never change, and remain throughout married life.

These values are transmitted from the parents to the children as part of the socialization process of the Manus. Thus the children learn that this is the true nature of marriage.

It can be seen then that attitudes to love and marriage are not natural, but the product of the socialization process, which varies from one society to another.

5 The passage does not support the idea that there is greater equality in marriage than in the past. The passage suggests instead that husbands give little help in the home – only a quarter did the same amount of work as their wives, and these were mainly from middle class homes.

The idea that husbands and wives were coming nearer to equality in the home and that they shared their tasks first came from Young and Willmott in their study *The Symmetrical Family*. Their study of families in London and the South-East showed that there was a greater tendency for the husbands to stay at home and share tasks with their wives. Oakley's study, on the other hand, indicated quite firmly that husbands saw it as their role to 'help' their wives in their home, but the main burden remained hers.

6 The sources tell us a lot about the changing nature of marriage this century.

The first point that emerges is that the age of the marriage had fallen quite noticeably from over 25 years for a female and 27 for a male to 22½ and 24½ respectively by 1971. However, since the table was published evidence shows that the age of marriage has increased again and that it is now back to the levels of 1911. This delay in marriage can be linked with Source D, where the table shows that there has been a significant increase in the number of people living together before marriage. It would seem now that it is increasingly common for a couple to live together before they marry – only if they feel that they want to marry do they do so. This would suggests a decline in marriages that occur because the woman is pregnant.

The information on the increase in divorce and the statistics on the numbers of second marriages show that increasingly people are divorcing if they are not satisfied with marriage – although they do appear to be marrying again afterwards, so it is not the institution of marriage they are rejecting but their partner. This could be linked to the stress on love and self-fulfilment, which is discussed in Source A.

An important background point to these changes is the changing position of women. Increasingly women are rejecting the role of the housebound mother who must stay at home looking after the children, and the husband when he returns from work. They now wish to return to work and seek out the companionship of their workmates. Although there has been a change in the attitudes of men towards the home, the research by Oakley suggests that it has not yet gone far enough for the relationship of marriage to be described as equal.

One final point: we must be wary of placing total reliance on the official statistics. For example, the increase in divorces does not just mean that people are more likely to divorce because they have high expectations; the statistics reflect just as much the easier availability of divorce.

7 Sociologists are interested in looking at societies different from our own for a number of reasons.

By examining the habits and customs of other societies, we learn that ideas, values and traditions that we regard as normal or natural are simply one of a large number of ways of organizing social life. The traits in mankind that we dislike, but which we believe are inevitable and therefore can do nothing about, can be shown to be merely a product of our culture and therefore it is possible to change. A good example of this is the way that some people believed that the role of women was determined by their biology. They were born to be mothers and to look after the house. Comparisons with other societies have shown that the role of women varies across societies and so cannot be natural. Sometimes, too, by examining the practices of other societies, we can gain insights into our own society. For example, we can see the uses of religion as a means of social control in a simple society and so this helps us to understand one of the uses of religion in Britain today.

By comparing the practices and customs of different societies we can often explain the causes of certain problems in our own society. For example, when Durkheim studied suicide, he compared suicide rates in different societies and he grouped the societies according to the degree of 'social solidarity'. What he found was that suicide was closely linked to social solidarity. This helps us to understand the rate and types of suicide in Britain today.

Also, by comparing societies, we can see the consequences of changing certain aspects of our own society. For example, when the family, as we understand it, was abolished in the USSR for a period after the revolution there was an element of social chaos, partially resulting from the family's abolition.

So comparing societies is a useful exercise.

Please note that these are my own answers written in the time allowed by the examination board. They are not the only answers possible.

STIMULUS-RESPONSE QUESTIONS

Stimulus-response questions are ones in which you are given a piece of information (the stimulus) which may be in the form of a written extract, or a photograph, or a diagram, or a statistical table. You are then given a series of questions (about five or six) which generally get progressively harder. The final question or questions usually require more knowledge of sociology than is given in the stimulus.

Advice on answering stimulus response questions

(a) You normally have a choice of which questions to answer. Go through the questions and examine the sub-questions that give the highest marks (usually the last two). Base your decision on which stimulus response questions to answer on whether or not you can answer the sub-questions that award the high marks. (Students often look at the stimulus information and the first couple of sub-questions, which are worth only a few marks. They then decide to do that particular stimulus-response question on the basis of whether or not they can do the low mark sub-questions. When they reach the high mark sub-questions at the end they find they cannot do them.)

(b) Remember that if the sub-question is worth only 1 or 2 marks, then long explanations are not necessary.

(c) Conversely, the greater the number of marks the greater the difficulty and the more time you must spend on it.

The following example is taken from the Southern Examining Group.

2 During the early years of this century a group of workers are having their lunch break. The conversation moves around to poverty.

> 'Poverty', continued Jack after a short silence, 'consists in a shortage of the necessities of life. When things are so scarce or so dear that people are unable to obtain sufficient of them to satisfy their basic needs. Linden is poor. His family are actually starving. There is no food in the house and the children are crying for something to eat. All last week they have been going to school hungry for they had nothing but dry bread and tea every day and this week they don't have that.'
>
> For Owen, poverty was more than this. 'Yes, Linden is poor,' he replied, 'but poverty should not be counted only as those who are starving. People are poor when they are not able to secure for themselves all the benefits of civilization – not just the necessities but the comforts, pleasures and refinements of life, leisure, books, theatres, pictures, music, holidays, travel, good and beautiful homes, good clothes, good and pleasant food.'
>
> From *The Ragged Trousered Philanthropist*, R. Tressell

(a) From the above information, name two things which Owen says all people should be able to enjoy. [1 mark]

(b) According to the above passage, is Linden's family situation getting better or worse? Give a reason for your answer. [1 mark]

(c) The poverty described by Jack and that described by Owen are different. What two terms might sociologists use to describe them? Briefly explain these terms in your own words. [4 marks]

(d) Explain how people can be caught in a poverty trap in Britain today. [6 marks]

(e) Britain has many Welfare State services, but some poverty still exists. Discuss why this is so. [8 marks]

ANSWERS

(a) Leisure, books (you could have answered any of the others mentioned such as theatres, pictures, music, holidays, travel, good and beautiful homes, good clothes, good and pleasant food).

(b) The situation is getting worse. Last week they had bread and tea, but this week they do not even have that.

(c) The two types of poverty are first *absolute* as described by Jack and secondly *relative* as described by Owen.

Absolute poverty is when people are so poor that they cannot afford the basic necessities of life, such as food, housing or clothes.

Relative poverty is when the person is unable to afford what the society generally regards as a reasonable standard of living. This definition varies according to the standards of society.

(d) The poverty trap is the situation when a person is caught in poverty and is unable to climb out on his/her own. There are a number of reasons why this is so.

Firstly, this occurs because the poorest groups often find that they actually have to spend more than the better-off to live. Not having a car they are unable to go to the large supermarkets in the out-of-town locations, where the prices are lowest. This means shopping in local shops where prices are higher. In the shop they are only able to afford the smallest units on sale (for example, of washing powder), whereas the purchase of the larger economy pack is actually cheaper in the long run.

Larger items and clothing are usually bought on credit, often in mail order catalogues. Clearly credit is more expensive than cash purchases. The poor will therefore have only a basic set of clothes. When it comes to interviews this apparent scruffiness may go against them. It may be difficult too for poorer people to be able to afford to attend interviews.

The poor are often those who are unaware of their rights and so large amounts of money which are available to claimants goes unclaimed each year. This is particularly true for old age pensioners.

Lack of nutritious food and inadequate heating can often cause illness and so prevent a person from working.

The children of the poor are trapped, too, as all these factors can harm their education, so that they are unsuccessful at school and in turn fail to obtain a decent job.

(e) When the Welfare State was set up at the end of the Second World War, it was expected to eliminate all poverty. The belief was that there would be jobs for everybody and that National Insurance payments would pay for adequate pensions, National Health Services, and social security payments.

Unfortunately this has not been the case. Firstly, because the definition of poverty that the Welfare State was based upon was really an absolute one. Certainly starvation and dreadful housing conditions have largely been eliminated, but the rising expectations of society in general have meant that this is inadequate. The originators of the Welfare State did not foresee that there would be so many people in full employment on such low wages that they are considered to be in poverty, nor the huge rise in the numbers of the unemployed. It is also true that many of those entitled to payments do not claim, presumably because they are unaware of their rights.

Poverty also continues to exist in Britain because the causes of poverty have not really been tackled by the Welfare State.

The following causes have been suggested for poverty:

Firstly that there is a cycle of poverty where one generation of the poor are trapped in poverty and through their style of upbringing, through lack of resources in the home and through the deprivation of the environment in which they live, they trap their children in the same poverty.

Secondly, there is the culture of poverty, in which certain values among the poorer groups in society – particularly feelings of hopelessness and the pointlessness of trying to break out of poverty – actually trap the poor in their situation. This was first pointed out by Oscar Lewis.

Thirdly, Gans has suggested that the real reason why poverty continues is that the poor lack power compared to the more affluent in society – without the power to force the better off to give them better wages, pensions and social security benefits, they will never be better off themselves.

Finally, it has been argued by writers influenced by Marx that poverty continues because it is in the very nature of our society. In order for there to be rich people, there have to be poor people. In capitalist society the owners of the commercial institutions try to obtain the highest profit and in order to do this, they try to keep wages to the lowest possible. Furthermore in times of crisis, workers who would cost money and who provide no profit are laid off and made unemployed. The unemployed are very useful for they serve as a threat to those who are in employment that they can easily be replaced and so wages are kept down.

Please note that these are my answers written in the time allowed by the examination board. They are not the only answers possible.

SHORT ANSWER/STRUCTURED RESPONSE

Short-answer questions

These are simply questions that require a fairly limited answer, based on your knowledge of sociology. They are mainly factual in content and generally require no discussion.

Structured-response questions

These are identical to the stimulus-response style questions, without the stimulus. They follow one theme and build up in difficulty. The last sub-questions usually require some discussion.

Advice on answering these questions

(a) Look at the number of marks awarded for the question and base the length and depth of your answer on this.

(b) Read the question carefully and answer exactly what you have been asked.

Short answer

These are taken from the Northern Examination Association.

1 What do we call a family that includes only father, mother and children?
Answer: A nuclear family   [1 mark]
2 Name one form of polygamous marriage.
Answer: Polyandry   [1 mark]
3 The roles of men and women are changing. What does 'role' mean?
Answer: It is the pattern of expected behaviour which is attached to certain statuses in society, and which guides our actions.   [1 mark]
4 Why are church attendance figures not always a good guide as to how many people are religious?
Answer: The figures only show how many people attend church, not how many people believe in God or the influence of religous faith upon our lives.   [1 mark]
5 What is the difference between 'sex' and 'gender'?
Answer: 'Sex' is the term used to describe the biological division of humans into groups – male and female.
'Gender' is the division based upon sex which describes the socially constructed expectations linked to each sex in our society.
So sex is biological and gender is sociological.   [2 marks]

6 Describe the differences between 'caste' and 'class'.

Answer: Caste is based upon 'ascription', which means that you are born into a caste and cannot change it.

Class is based upon achievement, which means that through social mobility you can change your class.

The basis for caste is religious.

The basis of class is solely economic. [4 marks]

Structured response

The following question is taken from the London East Anglian Group.

(a) Explain the difference in meaning between the terms 'birth rate' and 'fertility rate'.

[4 marks]

(b) What changes have occurred in the birth rate in Britain since 1900? [5 marks]

(c) Account for the changes in the birth rate in Britain since 1900. [6 marks]

ANSWERS

(a) The birth rate is the number of babies born each year per 1000 members of the population.

The fertility rate is the number of babies born each year per 1000 women of childbearing age.

The fertility rate is regarded as a more accurate indicator of the changing patterns of birth as it is related to the number of women who could have children.

(b) The birth rate has been declining overall this century, although the decline has not been constant or even. In 1919 through into the early 1920s, in the late 1940s and early 1960s the birth rate rose. The mid-1960s to the late 1970s saw a further sharp fall in the birth rate, to a point where the society was not reproducing itself in similar numbers. In the 1980s there has been a stabilization of the birth rate. The average number of children in a family in 1900 was about 3.5, while today it is about 2.

(c) The explanation for the overall decline in the birth rate in this century can be linked to the increasing use of contraceptives. This usage has come about mainly because new forms of contraceptive have been introduced, such as the 'pill', and these have become socially acceptable. Furthermore, attitudes to children are such that it is considered most important to give them the highest possible standards, and this can only be achieved for the majority of people by restricting the number of children.

The attitudes of women, too, have changed over this century, as they now feel that they wish to be liberated from the constant burden of bearing children, preferring instead to go out to work.

Rises in the birthrate can be linked to the ending of the two world wars in 1918 and 1945. During these periods of war spouses had been separated and marriages delayed. The ending of war meant that the reunited couples wished to complete or start their families at the earliest opportunity. The early 1960s, rise in the birthrate is linked to the decline in the age of marriage at this period, when it became fashionable to marry young and to have children. It has been suggested that the early marriage was related to the growth of affluence in the late 1950s and the ability of people to set up a home of their own at a very young age.

ESSAY-STYLE QUESTIONS

The final style of question is the essay. There are two types:

The open essay

This is the traditional type of essay question. This asks a relatively open question which you are required to answer with your own ideas and within your own structure.

The guided essay

This is an open question, but the examiners give suggestions as to the subject matter which you ought to include. You can add additional relevant information of your own, for which you will be awarded extra marks.

Advice on answering essay style questions

(a) Read the question carefully.

(b) In the open essay, make a very brief plan of what you intend to write.

(c) All the plan need contain is a number of keywords that remind you of the central points you wish to make.

(d) In the guided essay there is a form of plan already made for you. Use this, but where possible fit in any additional points you think are useful.

(e) Even if you disagree with the plan, cover the points suggested by the examiner. (For example, in the guided essay below I would have written it differently if there had been no guidelines given.)

(f) Keep an eye on the time. Make sure that you use all the time you have available and that you finish all you want to do in the time allowed.

(g) The sociology examination is not a test in English essay writing, but is does help if your work is organized, clear and well written.

An open essay question

This question is taken from the London East Anglian Group.

How far is it true to say that a distinct youth culture exists in Britain?

ANSWER

In most traditional societies there are various ceremonies called rites of passage which clearly mark the changeover from being a child to becoming an adult. There was therefore no intermediate period. In modern Britain, however, there exists no clear-cut age at which people move from childhood to adulthood. Instead there has developed an intermediate period known as youth culture. This fills in the gap between childhood and adulthood. The idea of it being a 'culture' means that it is supposedly a period in which the values and ideas of youth are different from those of their parents. Correctly speaking it ought to be called a youth subculture, as it is still part of the wider culture of modern society. It has been suggested that the main reasons for the growth of youth culture were, firstly, that there has been rapid social change in this century and so the values of the older generation are not appropriate for the younger generation. Consequently they have to develop their own values and ideas. Secondly, there has been an extension in the amount of time that young people spend in education, away from the world of work. Allied to this in recent years has been the growth in unemployment, which has also prevented young people from going into jobs, where they would be subjected to the discipline of work. Originally, in the 1950s, the degree of affluence of youth influenced various media organizations and fashion houses to concentrate on the youth market, because it was one that had a lot of income which, unlike that of the older generation, was not committed to household expenses.

All this evidence was used to describe the growth of a distinctive youth culture. Sociologists such as Talcott Parsons suggested that the youth culture gave young people the confidence to pass through the uncertain transitional period from childhood to adulthood and to cope with the changes involved. Evidence to prove the existence of the distinct youth culture seemed very clear – starting with the teddy boys of the 1950s, and on through the mods and rockers to skinheads, and later casuals. Riots among youths, distinctive clothes, the growth of pop music and the availability of magazines written especially for young people, all underlined the definite existence of a separate youth culture. However, in the 1970s a number of sociologists began to dispute this explanation of youth culture. What they argued was that there was not one youth culture but a number of youth cultures and that these youth cultures were related to the social class, ethnic and gender backgrounds of people. The divisions between people were not so much based upon age in this account.

Researchers such as Phil Cohen found that young people were responding to the particular problems of their social class and their neighbourhood. He found that by adopting the traditional working class styles of boots and braces the skinheads were somehow rediscovering their roots, which helped them to cope with the disruption of the inner cities caused by the redevelopment in the 1960s. On the other hand young West Indians found a way out of their problems by turning back to the religion of Rastafarianism. This gave them a feeling of pride in their culture. Female youth culture is very much based on the feminine roles found in the society. Middle class youth culture tends to be far more political and academic, reflecting their extended opportunities in education. A further criticism of the view that there is a distinct youth culture in Britain comes from surveys by the National Children's Bureau and the magazine *New Society*. Both these surveys found that the overwhelming majority of young people were basically conformist and certainly did not reject society.

To conclude then, the idea that there is a distinct youth culture is too simple. Young people do have some values that are different from the older generation, but they do not disagree on many fundamental issues. There are many divisions within young people which reflect the divisions within society. These divisions are illustrated in the styles of clothes and hair that different youth groups have.

Please note that this is my answer written in the time allowed by the examination board. It is not the only answer possible.

The guided essay

This question is taken from the Northern Examination Association.

'There is an increasing number of professional sportswomen and sportsmen in this country. This reflects a society with more money and leisure.'

Write an essay about leisure. Your essay could include reference to the following:

the difference between work and leisure;
the changing patterns of spending;
the influence of the mass media on leisure activities;
changes in employment patterns;
consequences for employment of a growth in leisure activities.
Credit will be given for any other relevant information.

ANSWER

The division of life into separate spheres of work and leisure first came about in the industrial revolution. Before that time work and leisure were integrated into a pattern of everyday life. As it was an agricultural society mainly, people worked according to the length of the day, the number of tasks to be done and according to the seasons. With the coming of machinery and large factories, workers were forced by employers into a discipline of time. They started work in the early morning, had a break for lunch and continued till the evening. Leisure time was then separated from work time, as work was something that had to be done to earn a living but gave no pleasure.

As the length of time spent in paid employment has declined so there has been an expansion in the amount of time available for leisure. However, it is important to note that work is not an unpleasant activity for a considerable number of people – particularly those in professional or skilled occupations, who gain considerable satisfaction from their work. When it comes to defining leisure therefore, it would be wrong to say that time spent at work is 'work' and time not at work is 'leisure', particularly as much of time spent out of work is engaged in domestic tasks (especially for employed women). There is also the problem of what is defined as leisure for housewives who have no outside employment.

In essence therefore we can say that leisure has a number of elements that distinguish it from work.

Leisure is enjoyable, is usually not paid and involves a large degree of choice. Work is usually less enjoyable, is paid and your freedom is limited. As people have become more affluent, there is generally a lower proportion of income spent on what are usually defined as necessities and more is available for leisure pursuits. This has had a tremendous influence on the growth of the 'leisure industries'. In the past twenty years, there has been the emergence of a wide variety of things to provide leisure interests; these are as diverse as foreign travel, theme parks, discotheques and DIY stores.

The growth of the mass media, particularly the development of television and more recently video, reflects very much the amount of free time people now have. Through their influence there has been the development of pop music and fashion, both of which are industries in themselves.

The consequence of the growth of leisure industries has been a considerable expansion in employment in these areas. They have also allowed people who have an ability in a certain field, such as sport, to make this their 'work'. Thus for some, work and leisure become intertwined into one.

However, for the bulk of people leisure provides an escape from the monotony of work, compensating them for their lack of interest in their jobs. The development of leisure industries in part reflects the dullness of work for the majority of people.

It is also argued that the new forms of leisure are also ways of manipulating people into accepting the society as it is. Most of the modern leisure industries cannot be said to extend people and their personalities – they aim instead simply to amuse.

Also, the unemployed have little opportunity for leisure, as leisure in contemporary Britain usually requires money to pay for the various pastimes. The bulk of the unemployed may be said to have free time which they fill in, but they are excluded from most forms of leisure because of their low incomes. It is true that our society in general is more affluent than ever before, and this is expressed in an expansion of leisure. However, the type of leisure we have may well be viewed as compensation for work. For the unemployed, leisure, like work, may be something they are excluded from.   [30 minutes]

Please note that this is my answer written in the time allowed by the examination board. It is not the only answer possible.

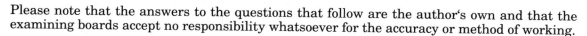

EXAMINATION QUESTIONS

Please note that the answers to the questions that follow are the author's own and that the examining boards accept no responsibility whatsoever for the accuracy or method of working.

Question 1

'Unemployment is killing at least 3 000 people a year, according to a recent analysis. Forty thousand are going to die prematurely before the turn of the century unless something dramatic is done. Unemployed men are more than twice as likely to commit suicide than the rest of the population, 40 per cent more likely to die of cancer, and 75 per cent more likely to die of lung cancer.'

From Dr. R Smith, *Unemployment and Health* (OUP)

QUESTIONS

1 Using the extract, describe one way in which health and unemployment are related.
[1 mark]

2 Apart from poor health, name two other possible effects of unemployment on an individual.
[2 marks]

3 Explain two effects of unemployment on society.
[4 marks]

4 Explain why unemployment exists in a modern industrial society.
[8 marks]

LEAG 1990

ANSWERS

1 One from: unemployment kills 3 000 people each year; 40 per cent more likely to die of cancer; 75 per cent more likely to die of lung cancer.

2 Two from: twice as likely to commit suicide (this is in the extract); more likely to be depressed; more likely to be poor; more likely to become isolated from friends; feel a loss of status; feel bored and frustrated.

3 Two from the following: government loses money from taxes, so it cannot afford the welfare services; it has to pay out social security for the unemployed; employers are able to threaten those still in employment, if they make wage demands, as they know they can replace them; unemployment weakens trades unions; a gap develops between the employed and unemployed, which leads to social tension; there is an increase in the numbers of the poor; crime increases; political extremism increases.

4 Unemployment is caused by the following factors: the changing nature of the British methods of production which increasingly uses automation rather than employees; the extent of competition from imports from abroad; the new jobs in service industries (such as insurance) do not employ the same type of people as those made unemployed; governments through their policies may deliberately choose to make people unemployed for economic reasons.

Question 2

Study item A and item B. Then answer the questions which follow.

Item A

The General Election by votes and seats gained by main parties, 1983 and 1987

	United Kingdom votes 1983	1987	Seats gained	
Conservative	42.4	42.3	375	(−17)
Labour	27.5	30.8	229	(+21)
Alliance	25.4	22.6	22	(−5)
Nationalist	1.5	1.7	6	(+2)
Others	3.2	2.6	18	(−1)

From M Marcus and A Ducklin, *GCSE Sociology* (R S Ball)

Item B

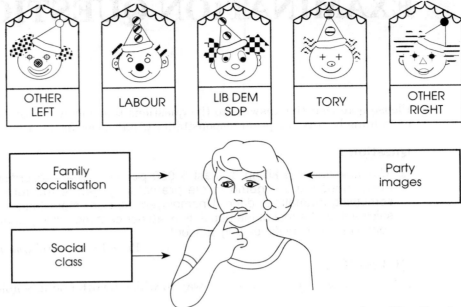

From S Moore, *Sociology Alive* (Stanley Thornes)

QUESTIONS

1 Study item A and state which political party:
(a) had the least change in its percentage of votes between 1983 and 1987;
(b) gained the greatest increase in seats between 1983 and 1987.   [2 marks]

2 Study item B and explain two influences on voting and political attitudes.   [2 marks]

3 Identify and explain two other influences on voting and political attitudes not shown in item B.   [4 marks]

4 Identify and explain two reasons why some people who are registered to vote do not do so at a General Election.   [4 marks]

5 How have links between social class and voting behaviour changed over the last 20 years?   [8 marks]

SEG 1991

ANSWERS

1 (a) Conservative.
(b) Labour.

2 Two of the following:
Family socialisation: attitudes and values are passed on from one generation to another and included in these general values are political ones.
Social class: people are still strongly influenced in their voting preferences by their social class background. This is partially because values vary by social class, and partly because people perceive their political interests differently, according to social class.
Party images: people rarely know exactly the policies of a particular party, instead they have general 'images' of what political parties stand for. The Labour Party stands for the working class and public services, and the Conservative Party stands for business, low taxes and the middle class.

3 The mass media and geographical location.
Mass media: influence people by supporting a particular political party.
Geographical location: people vote differently according to where they live in the country. So those in the north tend to vote Labour and in the south tend to vote Conser-vative. Support for the Liberal Democrats varies across the country but seems to be strongest in the 'extremes' of Britain: the north of Scotland and the south-west of England.
  Also those in cities tend to vote Labour, while those living in the suburbs and the countryside tend to vote Conservative.

4 Two from:
Positive reasons: no candidate standing for the party the person would normally choose; person standing on behalf of the party the voter would normally choose is objected to by that voter; may not bother to vote, as voter considers that the seat is safe; individual objects to all the parties standing.
Negative reasons: apathy; illness; no faith in politicians or politics; does not understand the machinery of politics.

5 The main point you need to make here is that the traditional bonds between the working class and the Labour Party have been broken. Increasingly, the skilled manual workers have chosen the Conservative Party. Also, there has been significant growth in the numbers of floating voters: people who will change their vote to the party they feel will directly benefit them and their families.

Question 3
Extract A

The diary of Nasreen Saddique

Nasreen Saddique is a young Asian woman who lives in the East End of London. She is 20 years old, but was 14 when she started her diary, which gives evidence of six years of continuous harassment.

These extracts are taken from January 1982 and begin when a gang of 40 youths attacked the home where she and her family live.

> *25 January 1982* There was a violent knock at the front door and an enormous crash against the downstairs window. I was upstairs, peering through the bedroom curtains, lights out, hoping they would disappear into the darkness and leave me and my parents alone. Voices echoed through the letter box: 'Pakis out'. they daubed swastikas, gave Nazi salutes and chanted. They did this for six straight hours. When the trouble started, we phoned the police but they never came.
>
> *26 January 1982* Trouble. Got no sleep.
>
> *27 January 1982* Trouble. Got no sleep.
>
> *28 January 1982* Every night we have to call the police but the police didn't do anything. Two youths kick our front door.
>
> *29 January 1982* Three or four youths stood outside and they threw stones at our house and broke windows (three times). The police came and told the youths to go away. When the windows were being broken, the glass just missed my father's head.

From K Thompson, *Under Siege: Racial Violence in Britain Today* (Penguin)

Extract B
Racial incidents reported to London police

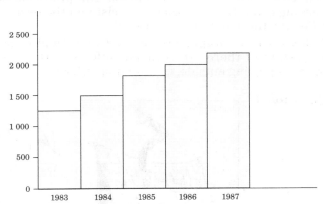

From *Runnymede Trust Bulletin,* March 1986

Extract C

> Of the total 1,937 racial incidents reported to London police in 1985, 286 resulted in arrest.

From *Runnymede Trust Bulletin,* March 1986

Study extracts A, B and C and answer the questions.

1 Sociologists sometimes use diaries (such as that in extract A) as evidence in their research. What do sociologists mean by the term 'evidence'? [4 marks]

2 What value has extract A to a sociologist studying racial violence in Britain today? [6 marks]

3 Name the method of presenting information which is used in extract B. [1 mark]

4 What trend does the information in extract B show? [1 mark]

5 Using information from extracts A and C and your own knowledge, explain why members of ethnic minority groups might be unwilling to report their experience of racial attacks to the police. [6 marks]

6 Explain why members of ethnic minority groups might experience racial attacks. [4 marks]

7 Explain some of the effects which racial attacks might have on the family lives of those who experience them. [8 marks]

ANSWERS

1 They mean evidence as some sort of proof which others can confirm. Diaries are written at the time, and then general conclusions drawn later by the researcher. If another sociologist disagrees with the ideas of the researcher then he/she can study the 'evidence', which is the diary in this case.

2 It provides evidence that racial violence really does take place, and further, gives more details of what form it takes.

It also provides sociologists with a view of racial violence through the experience of the victim. If it was described by an uninvolved individual, for example a white researcher, then they would experience it differently, simply as an observer rather than the subject of the crime, and this would cloud their description.

The description is also more useful because it is written at the time and so is not distorted by memory.

3 This is a statistical representation of the extent of racial violence and it takes the form of a 'bar chart'.

4 It shows that the number of racial incidents reported to the London police has grown from about 1 200 in 1983 to 2 300 in 1987. The trend is therefore one of increasing racial crime.

5 According to extract A, when the police are called, they do not come. Victims of racial violence may therefore lose faith in the police.

Extract C indicates that very few people are arrested for racial incidents, therefore victims may not bother reporting to the police as they think that the chances of the criminals getting caught are too small. Or they may believe that the police are themselves racist.

Members of the ethic minorities may have a perception of the police as protectors of a 'white' law and of the racists. There are often cultural and linguistic barriers which prevent the community and the police understanding the other's point of view.

6 Prejudice, caused by: lack of knowledge of ethnic minorities; fear of them because they are perceived by some as a threat to their jobs and their housing; members of the ethnic minorities provide a scapegoat for the problems faced by certain sections of the white working class; British society is racist and the people who commit racial violence are merely reflecting the 'true' values of Britain.

7 Stress causes arguments; ill health – both physical and mental; fear of going out to shop, to work (and there are economic effects of this), for any social activity; problems about children playing outside, or attending school.

Question 4

Religion as the opium of the people
From M Haralambos, *Sociology – A New Approach* (Causeway Press)

QUESTIONS

1 (a) Who described religion as 'the opium of the people'? [1 mark]
   (b) What links have been suggested between religion and drugs? [2 marks]

2 How may religion be seen as an agency of social control? [6 marks]

3 In what ways may religion be responsible for social change? [6 marks]

LEAG 1990

ANSWERS

1 (a) Karl Marx.

(b) Marx did not mean that religion was really a drug, only that it had the effect of a drug by keeping people mindlessly content and taking their minds off their living conditions. Rastafarians, however, believe that marijuana can bring a person nearer to God, through its effects on the mind.

2 It can be seen as an agent of social control because it stops people from rebelling in certain circumstances. Often religion provides an explanation of why the world is as it is and why apparent unfairness and obvious inequality is really all part of God's plan. Furthermore, people are brought up to believe without questioning the values of a society as they are God given, and therefore there is no reason to question things.

3 Religion can either act as a brake to social change by preventing new ideas entering a society (as the Confucian religion did in ancient China), or it can actually bring about change. This usually occurs when a new religion, or at least a new version of an existing religion challenges existing ideas. The best example of this was the study by Max Weber of the development of industrialisation in Britain, as a result of the values of Calvinism.

Also, a society which is greatly divided by social tensions can often divide along religious lines and radical religious leaders can find justification to overturn the government. This occurred in Iran in the early 1980s.

Question 5

Read items A and B. Then answer the questions which follow.

Item A

A case study is a piece of research which focuses on a single good example. It is somewhat artificial to argue whether one research method is better than another because many case studies which focus on a particular community or group, such as a workplace, in fact use a mixture of methods. Well-known case studies which have analysed documentary evidence, such as media coverage, as well as using interviews and observation, include Tunstall's study of the trawlermen of Hull and Cohen's study of Mods and Rockers in the 1960s.

In *Beachside Comprehensive: A Case-Study of Secondary Schooling*, Stephen Ball describes how he used the following methods during his three year study of one school:

1 He interviewed pupils and teachers.

2 He carried out several small-scale questionnaire studies.

3 He worked through and analysed school records and registers.

4 He also used participant observation to find out about the school.

From Townroe and Yates, *Sociology for GCSE* (Longmans)

Item B

Answer the following:

1 How often do you go to Church?

once a week ☐

once a month ☐

once a year ☐

2 How much do you spend each week on clothes?

3 How much do you spend each week on records or tapes?

£1–£3 ☐

£3–£5 ☐

£5–£6 ☐

More than £6 ☐

4 Do you think that using animals for experiments is wrong?

Yes ☐

No ☐

QUESTIONS

1 Look at item A. What does a case study focus upon? [1 mark]

2 Look at item A. Which groups did Cohen study? [1 mark]

3 Look at item B.
(a) What is missing from question 1? [1 mark]
(b) What is the major difficulty with question 3? [1 mark]

4 Identify and explain one advantage and one disadvantage for a researcher using participant observation. [4 marks]

5 Identify and explain two situations where a sociologist might choose to use a question-naire rather than any other research method. [4 marks]

6 Identify and fully explain one advantage of a structured interview over an unstructured interview. [4 marks]

7 Identify and explain fully one reason why a sociologist conducting a social survey might wish to refer to secondary sources. [4 marks]

SEG 1991

ANSWERS

1 Focuses upon one good example of a particular thing.

2 He studied Mods and Rockers in the 1960s.

3 (a) A box with 'never' beside it.
(b) There are a number of possible criticisms, e.g: people may spend varying amounts each week; if they spend around £3, they could tick two boxes; some people spend nothing.

4 There are a number of each, but the most common advantage is:
the ability to see and understand what is happening rather than just asking questions.

A common disadvantage is: the researcher allowing his/her own values influencing the way in which he/she interprets and explains what is going on.

5 Where the people to be questioned are scattered over a large area, so the questionnaire can simply be mailed out to them.

Where the subject of the enquiry is very embarrassing so that the respondents can complete the questionnaire in privacy and be sure of the anonymity of their answers.

6 A structured interview can be very carefully controlled to ensure that it is almost identical to another interview with a different person. In this way the researchers can be fairly confident that each interview was truly comparable with the others and therefore, as much as possible, biases and own values are eliminated.

7 Secondary sources are extremely useful. In particular the use of secondary sources allows the sociologist to check on the information given in an interview or questionnaire to see if it is true, or to fill in the background to a particular case.

Question 6

A recent survey shows that students from managerial or professional families continued to dominate degree courses, occupying 69 per cent of university places in 1988 despite representing only 32 per cent of the 18 year-old age group.
Similarly, staying-on rates in education after 16 were 'strongly related to social class'.

From *The Daily Telegraph*, 1 November 1989

Duke of Roxburghe and Lady Jane Grosvenor
He is of noble wealth and birth. So is she. Between them they own or have a stake in a sizeable chunk of Scotland and London. Now they have announced their engagement–and one day their fortunes will come together in a multi-million cascade.

From *The Daily Express*, 24 August 1976

QUESTIONS

1 Describe three differences between social classes in Britain. [4 marks]

2 In what ways have opportunities for working class people in Britain increased during the last 50 years? [7 marks]

3 Why do social class differences continue to exist in Britain? [9 marks]

MEG 1991

ANSWERS

1 Three from: different values; different incomes; different levels of wealth; different chances in education; different leisure patterns; different family relationships; different expectations of life; different levels of illness; different dietary patterns; different housing conditions.

2 With the expansion of traditional middle class jobs and decline in the traditional manual labour of the working class, much greater opportunities exist for working class people to enter managerial and professional employment.

Educational opportunities exist, although the gap between the children of managerial and professional employees and those of working class parents, still exists.

Attitudes towards accents and styles of dress are less rigid, therefore it is now possible for children of the working class to penetrate the professions. However, the point needs to be made that differences and opportunities still vary by and are influenced by social class background.

3 They continue to exist because of the economic and political power of the higher social classes to maintain class divisions in British society. The process through which the divisions remain are based upon inheritance of wealth; upon the differences in education provision and attainment; upon different cultural attitudes of the various social classes towards education and in the extent of help that parents can give their children to be successful, and in the ability of the higher social classes through these mechanisms to ensure that their children have a greater chance of entry into higher level jobs.

Question 7
Read item A and item B. Then answer the questions which follow.

Item A

'The growth of cities in Britain really begins with industrialization, around the end of the century. Before 1800 only about 15 per cent of the population lived in towns and cities; 10 years later 75 per cent of the population lived in them.

There has been a move away from the cities, towards the outer suburbs, New Towns and the countryside over the last ten years. Why? People prefer the better standard of housing available and the cleaner, less polluted environment of the suburbs and countryside. Cars and trains make travel into the big cities for work fairly quick and easy. However, firms are also moving out of the big cities, preferring the low costs of the New Towns to the advantage of being in the city centres.'

From S Moore, *Sociology Alive* (Stanley Thornes)

Item B
Regional population changes in percentages (England and Wales) 1981

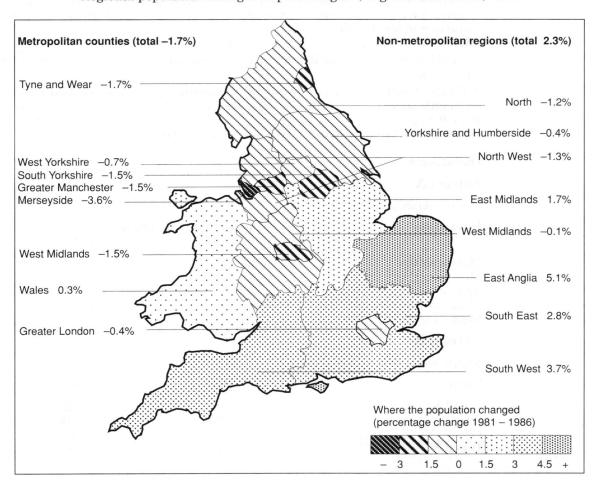

Metropolitan counties (total −1.7%)

Tyne and Wear −1.7%

West Yorkshire −0.7%
South Yorkshire −1.5%
Greater Manchester −1.5%
Merseyside −3.6%

West Midlands −1.5%

Wales 0.3%

Greater London −0.4%

Non-metropolitan regions (total 2.3%)

North −1.2%

Yorkshire and Humberside −0.4%

North West −1.3%

East Midlands 1.7%

West Midlands −0.1%

East Anglia 5.1%

South East 2.8%

South West 3.7%

Where the population changed
(percentage change 1981 – 1986)

− 3   1.5   0   1.5   3   4.5   +

From *New Statesman Society Database, 1987* (Macmillan)

QUESTIONS

1 Look at item A. About what percentage of the population lived in towns and cities before 1800? [1 mark]

2 Look at item A. What was the reason for the growth of cities in Britain in the 18th century? [1 mark]

3 Look at item B.

(a)   Which region had the largest growth rate? [1 mark]

(b)   Which non-metropolitan region had the lowest rate of population loss? [1 mark]

4 Identify and explain **two** factors responsible for the decline in the population of the northern regions of the United Kingdom since 1945, [4 marks]

5 Identify and explain **two** reasons for the increase of the population in some rural areas over the last 20 years. [4 marks]

6 Identify and explain fully **one** factor which might be responsible for the concentration of ethnic minority groups in the inner-city areas. [4 marks]

7 Identify and fully explain **one** social consequence of the heavy concentration of population in the southern regions of the United Kingdom. [4 marks]

SEG 1991

ANSWERS

1 15 per cent.

2 Industrialisation.

3 (a) East Anglia.

(b) West Midlands.

4 Migration towards the south. This is the result of a lack of jobs, which has forced people to move away in search of employment

Low birth rate. This is true for much of Britain, but as younger people move away in search of employment, so there are fewer people of child- bearing age left. As a result the number of births falls.

5 Cheaper housing. The costs of constructing houses in the outer suburbs and the country-side is much cheaper for builders, and these lower house prices attract purchasers. People are also attracted by the possibility of pleasant countryside and unpolluted air. Other reasons include: the relocation of companies; the attraction of lower costs/prices; the attraction of less traffic.

Relocation of companies. Costs are lower. Less traffic

6 Could choose one from: discrimination in housing; poverty; employment; prefer to live in a community.

7 Could choose from: overcrowding and consequent pressure on housing, on traffic levels, on health services, on social services, on transport, on environment due to the building of more houses.

Probably best to take housing issues: high costs, homelessness, poverty etc.

Question 8

Extract A

The ownership of wealth

Population		Percentage of wealth owned	
		1976	1984
Most wealthy	1%	31	21
Most wealthy	5%	52	39
Most wealthy	10%	65	52
Most wealthy	25%	86	75
Most wealthy	50%	97	93

Extract B

Share ownership by social class

Social class	1983	1987
A and B	56	29
C1	26	34
C2	12	26
D and E	6	11

Extract C

How income is divided up:

Income before tax – percentages

	Bottom fifth	Next fifth	Middle fifth	Next fifth	Top fifth
1976	0.8	9.4	18.8	26.6	44.4
1984	0.3	6.1	17.5	27.5	48.6

Income after tax – percentages

	Bottom fifth	Next fifth	Middle fifth	Next fifth	Top fifth
1976	7.0	12.6	18.2	24.1	38.1
1984	6.7	11.7	17.5	24.4	39.7

From M Denscombe, *Sociology Update*

QUESTIONS

Study extracts A, B and C and answer the questions.

1 Look at extract A.

What percentage of wealth was owned by:

(a) the most wealthy one per cent in 1984?   [1 mark]
(b) the least wealthy 50 per cent in 1984?   [1 mark]

2 Look at extract C.

What percentage of income before tax was earned by the top fifth of the population in 1984?
[1 mark]

3 Explain the difference between the terms 'income' and 'wealth'.   [2 marks]

4 Look at extract B.

(a) Give an example of a job which might be done by someone in class A and B.
[1 mark]
(b) Give an example of a job which might be done by someone in class D and E.   [1 mark]

5 Write three statements about share ownership as shown by extract B   [3 marks]

6 Look at extract C.

Write three statements to show the changes between 1976 and 1984 in how income was divided up.   [3 marks]

7 Apart from inequalities in earned income as shown in extract C, in what other ways might people be unequal at work?   [7 marks]

8 These extracts suggest that the ownership of wealth, shares and income has changed in the periods covered by these extracts.

What effects might inequalities in wealth, share ownership and income have on life chances?   [10 marks]

NEA 1990

ANSWERS

1 (a) 21 per cent of wealth.

(b) 7 per cent of wealth.

2 48.6 per cent.

3 Income is the money that a person earns or receives from investments etc. It can best be described as a flow of money. For most people, their income is their salary.

Wealth is the amount of goods, investments and property that a person owns. It is something that can give income but it is something fixed and permanent. For most people their wealth may be the part of their house which they actually own as a result of mortgage payments. Government figures assume that a person's pension is also a form of wealth.

4 (a) A solicitor.

(b) A 'fitter' in a garage (an unskilled mechanic).

5 There are a large number of combinations of statements and the following are some examples:

(a) In 1983, the higher the social class, the greater the proportion of people who owned shares.

(b) In 1987, the largest percentage of share owners were in class C1.

(c) The numbers of shares held by social classes A and B were higher in 1983 than 1987.

(d) For classes C1 and C2, the percentage of people owning shares was higher in 1987 than 1983.

6 There are a number of combinations and the following are some examples:
(a) The top fifth earned more income before tax in 1976 than 1984.
(b) The top fifth earned more income after tax in 1984 than in 1976.
(c) The bottom fifth received less, both before and after tax in 1984 than in 1976.
(d) The three 'lower' groups all lost income both before and after tax in 1984 compared to 1976; the top two groups, however, gained.

7 Differences could include: different quality of workplace environment; provision of free food, canteen, sports facilities, etc; subsidised mortgages; free private health insurance; free or subsidised company car; school fees for children to attend private schools; quality of pension schemes; levels of sick pay; control over one's work; pace of work; different levels of safety; job security.

8 Ownership of wealth, shares and income are very significant influences on a person's life chances, as they allow a person to purchase different standards of housing, and to choose areas of a city/country to live in. It allows people to purchase better standards of food, to have less stress, especially over money matters. These things are directly linked to the different levels of illness experienced by people in different social classes.
Having wealth allows different leisure pursuits. It allows the possibility of purchasing private medicine and private schooling, if the person is unhappy with the State systems.
It should be pointed out that the tables of share-holding are very dubious, as they do not state the value or extent of share holding. Therefore a very large percentage of social classes C1 and C2 may hold shares, but their total value is relatively small per individual. Amongst the classes A and B, the levels **per head** may be much higher and more valuable.

Question 9

Look at item A and item B. Then answer the questions which follow.

Item A

Item B

From *Best* magazine, 16 February 1990

QUESTIONS

1 Study item A and state **two** ways in which it seems to show traditional gender roles.

[2 marks]

2 Study item B. Identify and explain how science may have led to fewer gender role divisions in the kitchen. [2 marks]

3 Identify and explain **two** reasons why women are more likely to have part-time jobs than men. [4 marks]

4 Identify and explain **two** reasons why more women have found paid full-time employment outside the home in the United Kingdom during the last 30 years. [4 marks]

5 How has the increased number of marked women in paid employment outside the home affected family life within the home during the last 30 years? [8 marks]

SEG 1991

ANSWERS

1 Girls playing with dolls, like a stereotype of a mother. Ribbons in their hair. Boy climbing a tree, stereotype of 'adventurous' male – dressed in baseball boots and jeans.

2 Less skill required. Food is prepared and does not require cooking - merely heating in a microwave. There are large numbers of ready-prepared meals now available which allow a person (male or female) to spend the day in employment and then to heat up food in a few minutes. This allows men to share the kitchen work as there is virtually no work!

3 More likely to have family responsibilities and so have to look after children which limits the number of hours they are able to work.

Much of the work offered to women is part-time and they are unable to obtain full-time employment because employers prefer cheaper, more flexible female workers.

4 Two from:

Shift in industry towards lighter industry which requires female labour on flexible shifts; or alternatively towards service work.

Was a labour shortage until 1980s and women were encouraged to enter employment; as a result women working is now regarded as commonplace.

Women are a very attractive source of labour to employers as they are cheaper, more flexible and less unionised than men.

Women have fewer children and in a shorter time span than in the past. This allows them the time to go out to work.

There has been a cultural change in attitudes to women, as they are now seen as having equal or at worst similar status to men and regard it as their right to work if they wish to do so.

You could ask the question whether it is perhaps the changing nature of family life that has influenced the numbers of married women working.

5 Your answer should include discussion of the altered status/relationship between husband and wife. The changing attitudes of wives to their role as wife and mother. The economic independence employment has given women. It should also point out that women still retain the major responsibility for the home and for child care, and therefore things have only changed to a limited extent.

Question 10

Study item A and item B. Then answer the questions which follow.

Item A

Divorce in the United Kingdom

Year	Number of divorces
1961	27 000
1971	80 000
1976	136 000
1981	157 000
1986	168 000
1987	165 000

Item B

Divorce by length of marriage, 1987, Great Britain

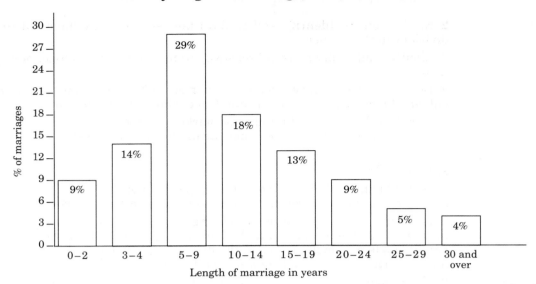

From *Social Trends 19, 1989* (HMSO

QUESTIONS

1 Study item A and state in which of the years given:
(a) there was the highest number of divorces;
(b) the divorce rate fell in relation to previous statistics. [2 marks]

2 Study item B and state:
(a) the percentage of divorces which took place during the first two years of marriage;
(b) between which years of marriage divorce was most likely to occur. [2 marks]

3 Identify and explain **two** reasons why the divorce rate rose sharply from 1971. [4 marks]

4 Identify and explain **two** reasons why the care of children after divorce is more likely to be granted to the mother. [4 marks]

5 Do the increased divorce rates pose a threat to marriage and family life? [8 marks]
SEG 1991

ANSWERS

1 (a) 1986.
(b) 1987.

2 (a) 9 per cent.
(b) 5-9 years.

3 (a) Change in the law: this made divorce easier to obtain.
(b) Changing role of women: majority of divorces are initiated by women. This indicates that they are far less likely to accept what they regard as inappropriate behaviour from husbands.

You could also include that couples have higher expectations from marriage, and that people have different attitudes to marriage than previously.

4 Related to the role of women as being the most important person for children to live with. This depends very much on traditional views on the role of women, as a mother and homemaker.

Fathers are more likely to be the parent who leaves home, either to live on their own or to set up a relationship with someone else.

5 You need to present the cases for and against this idea.

For: reflects changing attitudes to marriage and parenthood. Marriage declining as cohabitation increases. Growth in numbers of lone parents. Women less likely to accept the child-caring and child-bearing role.

Against: marriages stay together because both partners want this. Almost 90 per cent of people still marry at one point in their lives.

The majority of those who divorce under the age of 40 remarry.

There is evidence of a growth in cohabitation to replace marriage until birth of children. This suggests that where people do marry they are more likely to be settled and sure of their partner. Lone parent families can claim to be families just as much as traditional two parent/two child families. There is a move towards a greater variety of family life.

Question 11

'He's a glutton for work – that's as close as he ever gets to a holiday.'

From P Cooper, *Sociology – An Introductory Course* (Longman)

QUESTIONS

1 Explain what is meant by 'work'. [2 marks]

2 Explain why leisure time is important to most people. [2 marks]

3 (a) What is meant by 'intrinsic' job satisfaction? [1 mark]
(b) Why does work fail to provide this for many people [4 marks]

4 Examine the view that what people do in their leisure time is influenced by their work. [6 marks]

LEAG 1990

ANSWERS

1 You need to explain that it is difficult to define work, but at its simplest it is an activity performed for payment.

2 It is important because leisure consists of time or activities in which people are able to choose what they wish to do. Usually leisure reflects people's interests and allows them to express their individuality.

3 (a) When a person gains satisfaction from the actual process of doing the job.
(b) Some people gain little pleasure from actually doing their job. For them, it is simply a way to earn money to buy their preferred style of life. This is described as 'extrinsic' satisfaction. This is because most employment is structured in such as way as to make the most profit for employers, not simply to interest the employees. Another way of describing this experience of work is to call people who only work for the money aspect 'alienated'.

4 To answer this, you should point out that leisure is influenced partially by work and talk about the three relationships of extension, opposition and neutrality. However, you should then go on to argue that other factors are just as important - for example gender, ethnicity, age and social class.

Question 12
People are often reluctant to disclose their true behaviour.

'If an election were held tomorrow, which party…?'   from *Punch,* 11 July 1984

QUESTIONS

1 What is meant by a democracy? Explain, using examples. [4 marks]
2 What aspects of government in Britain might be thought not to be democratic? [7 marks]
3 Social class is known to influence voting behaviour. Why do many working class people not vote in the way they might be expected to? [9 marks]

MEG 1991

ANSWERS

1 Democracy is the political system that allows individuals freedom to choose their leaders, and which also allows them freedom of expression and equality under the law.

2 Some would argue that there are inequalities in power in Britain and that some groups are more likely to influence government decisions. This is related to the differing power of pressure groups, which exist to influence government decisions.

 Secondly, newspapers do not reflect a true range of opinion, but rather they tend to support the views of one political party and therefore are biased.

 It is also argued that the courts and the police forces tend to arrest and punish certain groups of people for certain offences rather more than others. Therefore white-collar and business crime is regarded as less serious than street crime which is performed by young males.

3 You should point out the assumption behind this question is that working class people should logically vote for the Labour Party and the middle class vote for the Conservative Party (Is this necessarily true?). Working class people have been changing their voting patterns over the last 20 years. They are more likely to vote Conservative if they perceive a direct benefit for them in doing so. This has resulted in large numbers of working class voters in the south-east of England preferring the Conservatives.

 There have also been many changes within the working class which have broken the old solidarity. These include such things as moving to new housing developments, greater affluence, changing perceptions of themselves and changing attitudes about leisure, ownership and styles of life. Therefore what might have been seen as 'automatic' support for Labour has in recent years declined.

Question 13

Read items A and B. Then answer the questions which follow.

Item A

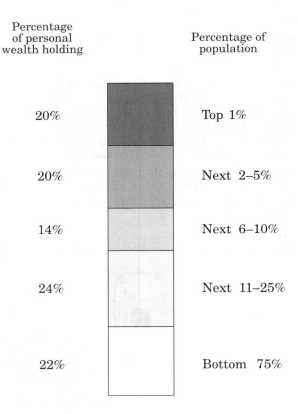

Percentage of personal wealth holding | Percentage of population
20% | Top 1%
20% | Next 2–5%
14% | Next 6–10%
24% | Next 11–25%
22% | Bottom 75%

The information above shows the current distribution of personal wealth in the United Kingdom. However, it is difficult to state exactly what is meant by personal wealth. Generally it is seen in terms of 'marketable assets' which are assets that can be bought or sold, such as land, houses and company shares owned by individuals.

From M Marcus and A Ducklin, *GCSE Sociology* (R S Ball)

Item B

Fathers in managerial and professional jobs

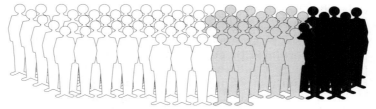

Sons in: Managerial and professional   59%
               Other white-collar   26%
               Manual   15%

Fathers in manual jobs

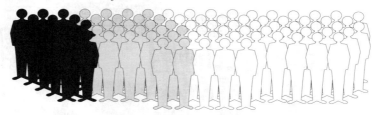

Sons in: Managerial and professional   17%
               Other white-collar   27%
               Manual   56%

From P J North, *Social Science – An Introduction,* (Longman)

QUESTIONS

1 Look at item A. What percentage of personal wealth does the top one per cent of the population own?   [1 mark]

2 Look at item A. Give **one** example of a 'marketable asset'.   [1 mark]

3 Look at item B.
(a) What percentage of the sons of managerial and professional fathers are employed in the same jobs as their fathers?   [1 mark]
(b) Which type of job is the son of a manual worker least likely to be in?   [1 mark]

4 Identify and explain **two** ways in which people can accumulate wealth.   [4 marks]

5 Identify and briefly explain **two** forms of social stratification, other than social class.

[4 marks]

6 Identify and explain fully **one** way in which the social class structure in Britain has changed during this century.   [4 marks]

7 It is often said that education holds the key to a person's opportunities for social mobility. Identify and fully explain **one** reason why this may not, in fact, always be the case.

[4 marks]
SEG 1990

ANSWERS

1 20 per cent.

2 One from: land; houses; company shares.

3 (a) 59 per cent
(b) Managerial and professional.

4 Inherit the wealth from parents or family; earn the wealth through success in business or employment.

5 Two from: caste, estates, race, gender, age.
    Caste: system based on Hindu religion where people are considered to be reincarnated. The type of caste represents the quality and status of the previous life.
    Estates: feudal system in which land was divided according to personal loyalty to a nobleman.
    Race: some people treat others differently according to their perceived racial characteristics.
    Gender: women are often treated in a different (and generally worse) way than men.
    Age: young people and old people have less power in our society, are often the butt of jokes and generally receive their financial support from another person such as the State or their parents.

6 The major change has been the blurring of the divisions between the working and middle classes. The traditional divisions in terms of salary, housing tenure, of leisure patterns and security of employment – all of which used to be better for the middle class – have become less clear and although some differences exist they are certainly not as sharply defined as they were 30 years ago.

7 Your answer should include a discussion of the fact that education itself largely depends upon a person's parents and their social class. Although quality and type of employment is largely determined by educational success, success at school depends upon type of school, parental interest and knowledge, degree of material resources (books, room to study in, etc) that the family is willing to provide to support the learning of the child. Therefore the children of managerial and professional parents are more likely to be successful and to enter similar professions themselves.

Question 14

QUESTIONS

1 (a) Which aspect of democracy is shown above? [1 mark]
(b) Name two other factors that make a society democratic. [2 marks]
2 Why do some people not vote in elections? [4 marks]
3 What factors influence how people vote in British elections? [8 marks]

LEAG 1990

ANSWERS

1 (a) The right to vote (for everyone over the age of 18).
(b) Two from: a free press; a free judiciary (magistrates, judges, police, etc); pressure groups; free speech.

2 People do not vote for either positive or negative reasons:
Positive: no candidate standing in the constituency for the party they prefer; may be one aspect of their favoured political party's manifesto with which they disagree and so they abstain; may be so confident their candidate is going to win that they do not vote; may disagree with all the political parties.
Negative: may simply be uninterested in politics; may be ill at the time of the election; may have no faith in politicians and their promises; may not understand the parties or the political system.

3 This answer needs to include the following factors: social class, ethnic group, gender, age, geographical location, religion (in Northern Ireland). You should stress the importance of political socialisation and the way that people tend to choose parties which would benefit them or their family directly. When a person comes to vote all these factors play their part.

Question 15

Study item A and item B. Then answer the questions which follow.

Item A

> In 1983 'Breadline Britain', a survey carried out for London Weekend Television, looked at 'relative poverty' as 'the minimum standard of living laid down in society'. The survey found that:
> 6 million people could not afford some necessary item of clothing;
> 3.5 million people could not afford carpets and washing machines;
> 3 million people could not afford to heat the living areas of their homes.
> 'Breadline Britain' stated that 7.5 million people (or 13 per cent of the population) were living in poverty.

Item B

Percentage of people who described each of the following items as necessary.

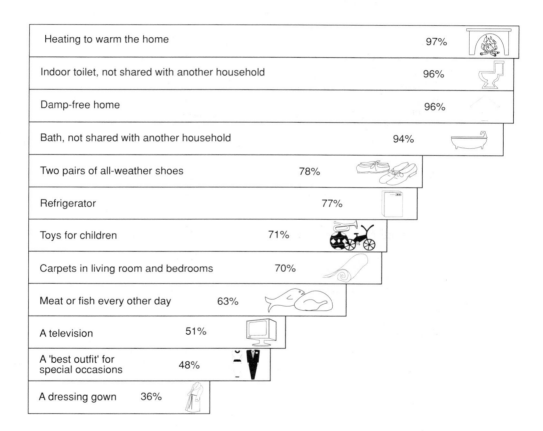

Heating to warm the home	97%
Indoor toilet, not shared with another household	96%
Damp-free home	96%
Bath, not shared with another household	94%
Two pairs of all-weather shoes	78%
Refrigerator	77%
Toys for children	71%
Carpets in living room and bedrooms	70%
Meat or fish every other day	63%
A television	51%
A 'best outfit' for special occasions	48%
A dressing gown	36%

From J Mack and S Lansley, *Poor Britain* (Allen and Unwin)

QUESTIONS

1 Study item A and state:

(a) The number of people who could not afford carpets and washing machines;

(b) The percentage of the population who were living in poverty. [2 marks]

2 Study item B and state:

(a) The percentage of people who considered a television necessary;

(b) Which of the following was considered most necessary: a television, a refrigerator, a dressing gown? [2 marks]

3 Briefly state **three** reasons why women are more likely to be living in poverty than men. [3 marks]

4 (a) Identify and explain any **two** ways in which the Welfare State or voluntary groups may help people in need. [4 marks]

(b) What may be seen as the main causes of poverty in the United Kingdom over the last 10 years? [9 marks]

SEG 1991

ANSWERS

1 (a) 3.5 million

(b) 13 per cent

2 (a) 51 per cent

(b) Refrigerator (77 per cent)

3 Three from: earn less; more likely to be single parent without income (except State benefits); have family commitments; greater proportion of the elderly; greater proportion of the disabled; housewives, who may not be given an adequate proportion of the 'husband's wages'.

4 Welfare State provides state benefits; Welfare State also provides training, housing, counselling, holidays, cheap loans (social fund), employment, etc. Voluntary groups provide goods, financial assistance; services (home helps, meals-on-wheels), child care, clothing.

In Britain the State has tried increasingly to hand these services over to voluntary organisations and to profit-making companies. However, the majority of funds come from the State, with only a small amount provided by charities.

Incidentally, most caring is provided by family and neighbours, not by the State or voluntary organisations.

5 Explanations for poverty are:

The cycle of deprivation: in this parents who are poor raise their children in such a way that they will be poor themselves.

Power: poor people are those who have the least power in society. Therefore they remain poor because their poverty provides others with benefits, and the rest of society does not want things changed.

The culture of poverty: this explanation suggests that people who are poor are brought up in such a way that they lack the values necessary to break out of their poverty.

The structure of society: poverty exists because our society requires badly paid workers, so that those who own the factories and commercial institutions make profits. Unemployment exists through the nature of our society, where profits are more important than jobs.

Question 16

Read items A and B. Then answer the questions which follow.

Item A

Predicted changes in the population of the United Kingdom.

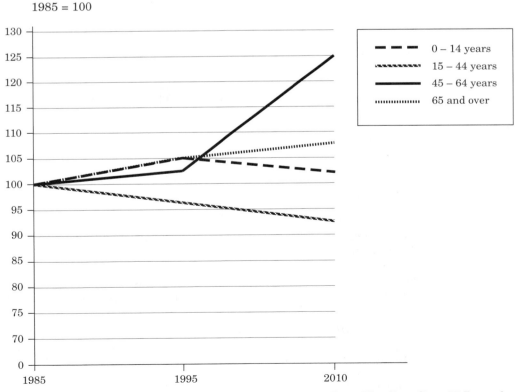

1985 = 100

From *The Guardian,* 22 December 1988

Item B

Reasons for population growth in the United Kingdom

Over the period 1750–1990 the main causes of death changed from the infectious epidemic diseases in the earlier period to the so-called 'degenerative' or chronic diseases of today. In the 1970s and 1980s over 80 per cent of all deaths were caused by heart and circulatory disorders, cancers and diseases of the respiratory system (bronchitis, pneumonia).

Two factors are important in explaining these changes:
1 changes in the environment, making epidemic disease less likely.
2 Changes in food production, distribution and consumption which have improved the diet for some whilst causing difficulties for others.

QUESTIONS

1 What trend is shown, in item A, for changes in the 65 and over age group?   [1 mark]

2 Look at item A. Which age group is expected to increase the most after 1985?   [1 mark]

3 Look at item B.
(a) What were the main causes of death in 1750?   [1 mark]
(b) Give **one** major reason for the decline in epidemic diseases.   [1 mark]

4 Identify and explain **two** problems which might arise from the actual increase in the numbers of elderly people well into the next century.   [4 marks]

5 Identify and explain **two** consequences of a low birth rate in the United Kingdom.   [4 marks]

6 Identify and fully explain **one** way in which governments have acted to reduce the mortality (death) rate in Britain.   [4 marks]

7 There is evidence to suggest that the fall in the number of 15–44 year olds will continue well into the next century.

Identify and explain fully **one** social consequence of this trend.   [4 marks]
SEG 1990

1 A very gradual increase.

2 45–64 years.

3 (a) Infectious epidemic diseases.
(b) One from: changes in the environment; changes in food production, distribution and consumption.

4 Two from:

Increase in the burden of dependency, where fewer people are working and having to support an increase in the numbers of non-working elderly.
Greater pressure on pensions and this will mean higher taxes (or lower pensions).
Greater demands on medical care by the elderly.
Greater increase in the need for social services.
Individuals will experience poverty if the levels of pensions remain as low as they are at present.
Greater demands on care by the families of the elderly.
Greater increase in loneliness of the elderly as friends and family die.

5 There would be immediate changes resulting from the lack of babies, such as a decline in the need for hospital maternity services, but most of the social issues would be slower and longer lasting.

Two from:

The population gradually ages which means that there are fewer younger people to do the jobs, a possible decline in inventive ideas, and gradually an increase in the burden of dependency.
Need to shift health care towards the elderly and away from the young. This shift of services away from the young would occur in all areas of social provision.
Decline in consumer demand.
Smaller families, so change in demand for houses, etc.
Decline in demand for schools.

6 The main ways governments have acted include: improved maternity services to ensure that children survive; improved health services for the population; improved hygiene laws on food sold to the public; improved sanitation and quality of drinking water. Choose one of these.

The other cause in the decline in mortality has been the general rise in the standards of living.

7 You need to choose one of the points covered in the answers to **4** and **5** above.

For example: There is likely to be a problem of over-employment, in that there will be more jobs than the number of young people available to take them. This could mean changing attitudes towards the age of retirement and so people might be forced or might choose to work longer. This would link with the increase in the changing nature of the burden of dependency as the tax levels required to support decent State pensions may just be too high for younger people to accept. This again could be a pressure on older people to continue working to an older age.

Question 17

Extract A

Notifiable offences recorded by the police per 100 000 population in England and Wales, 1982–1988

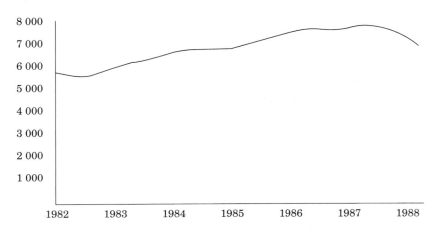

From *Tackling Crime, 1989* (Home Office)

Extract B
Notifiable offences recorded by the police, England and Wales, 1988.

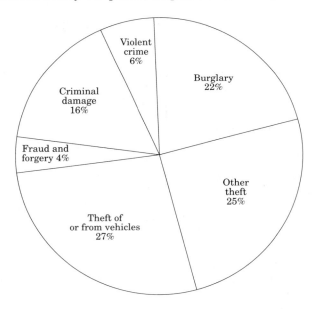

From *Tackling Crime, 1989* (Home Office)

Extract C

Some findings from the second Islington Crime Survey

The Islington Crime Survey is based on detailed interviews with a representative sample of 1 600 people. It covers the London Borough of Islington, a socially and culturally mixed area of north London. This is what they found:

1 More than 90 per cent of women between 16 and 24 years of age often take safety measures against crime. These range from avoiding certain streets to not going out alone at night.

2 74 per cent of women in all age groups stay at home fairly often or very often.

3 40 per cent of men in all age groups stay at home fairly often or very often.

4 Fear of crime is the main reason why people do not go out after dark.

5 In the three years since the first Islington Crime Survey, crime has moved from third place to the top of people's list of problems affecting the neighbourhood.

6 80 per cent of the sample see crime as the main problem affecting the neighbourhood.

7 31 per cent of the sample felt that the police are not doing very well in the fight against crime.

From *The Guardian,* 13 February 1990

QUESTIONS

Study extracts A, B and C and answer the questions.

1 What trends does the information in extract A show?   [2 marks]

2 Look at extract B. What percentage of notifiable offences are violent crimes?   [1 mark]

3 Explain two ways in which official crime statistics might underestimate the amount of illegal activity.   [4 marks]

4 Look at extract C. State **three** ways in which crime may affect the behaviour of people living in Islington.   [3 marks]

5 Why might it be difficult to make generalisations from the findings in extract C?   [4 marks]

6 What do we mean by the term crime?   [2 marks]

7 Give an example of criminal behaviour and explain why it might not always be regarded as deviant.   [6 marks]

8 The mass media are sometimes accused of giving a false view of crime. Using information from extracts A, B and C, and your own knowledge, explain how the media might do this and what effects the media's actions might have.   [8 marks]

NEA 1991

ANSWERS

1 That between 1982–1988, the number of notifiable offences recorded by the police per 100 000 of the population rose slowly until 1987, and then fell.

2 6 per cent.

3 Two from: people may not report crime to the police; police may decide not to record complaints received by them as notifiable offences; the people who have the crime committed against them may be unaware of the crime – for example, in cases of fraud.

4 90 per cent of young women less likely to go out at night; 74 per cent of all women stay at home more often; 40 per cent of all men stay at home more often.

5 It is a sample of only 1 600 people, and only representative of Islington, London. This may well not be representative of other cities, of the rest of London, or of non-urban areas in the rest of Britain.

6 Crime means acts which are defined as illegal by the state. However, crime tends to be linked to theft and robbery by people on the streets, in homes or shops. It is rarely applied to illegal business deals, breaking health and safety regulations, or white-collar crime in general.

7 Tax evasion is an illegal act, yet it is relatively rarely pursued and prosecuted in court. Most people regard evading taxation as acceptable. This could be because it is more of a middle class act than a working class one.

8 The mass media concentrate on lurid, sensational crime - often that which includes elements of sex. They do this to sell newspapers. Although violent crime is only six per cent of all crime, it dominates the crime reporting in newspapers. On the other hand, criminal damage or fraud and forgery are rarely mentioned.

This gives people the impression that there is a lot more violent crime than actually takes place. This has an effect on people's behaviour in that they are frightened of going out of their homes in case they are the subjects of violent crime.

However, this distorts the true picture. For women, for example, the most likely place for violence against them is in their own home, and the most likely source of rape is someone with whom they are acquainted.

Question 18

Boys on a Saturday night in Sunderland, in a group, on a street corner, are aware that they are 'doing nothing' and are bored with it in their own minds, essentially wanting something to happen. They want to have an interesting or an exciting time. (See overleaf)

Question:	What do you do when you just knock around the streets?
Richard:	Sometimes get into fights, or trouble, but mostly nothing much.
Question:	Just try and give me an example.
Richard:	Er…last Saturday we was hanging about and someone kicked a bottle over and it smashed. Then we all started smashing bottles.
Question:	What do you do on an average Saturday evening?
Steven:	Go in the Wimpy, or jump on some boys or something ……kick them.
Question:	Do you ever get into trouble for kicking boys?
Steven:	If we are knocking about in gangs. The police pick on us for just knocking about in gangs. I've been down the police station twice for jut knocking about in gangs.

From P Corrigan, *Schooling the Smash Street Kids* (Macmillan)

QUESTIONS

1 Are the boys described in the source material behaving in a deviant way? [4 marks]

2 Most people conform to what is expected of them in society. How is this conformity and social control achieved? [7 marks]

3 Young working class males are the group which is most likely to get into trouble with the police – why? [9 marks]

MEG 1991

ANSWERS

1 They are according to the rules of normal 'law-abiding' people. However, in the actions they are taking, of simply hanging around a street corner, they are not. It is not just what someone is doing, but how that is defined by someone else.

2 Conformity is achieved through two main ways: by formal and informal social control.

Formal social control consists of the rules that we all have to obey in particular circumstances, and which are enforced by people whose job it is to do that. So, in society in general it is the police, at school the teachers, in the swimming pool the lifeguards, etc.

Informal social control consists of people telling others what to do through their actions and comments. This is closely related to socialisation. The socialisation process is the way in which we are taught what behaviour is acceptable and unacceptable. It begins with our parents and then is taken over by school friends, teachers, employers, colleagues, the newspapers, etc. People who behave 'deviantly' are often punished in some way, such as being 'sent to Coventry' (ignored), or being laughed at and made fun of, etc.

3 This answer has two elements to it. The first is a discussion of the causes of crime and in particular that young males are those most likely to commit crime. Explanations include the subcultural approach, the anomie approach and the Marxist approach.

But another and more general approach is that of 'labelling', whereby police officers expect young men to be troublemakers and therefore 'pick on them'. In doing so they may treat many ordinary and law-abiding working class youths as potential criminals and thus create friction between themselves and the youths.

Question 19

Read items A and B. Then answer the questions which follow.

Item A

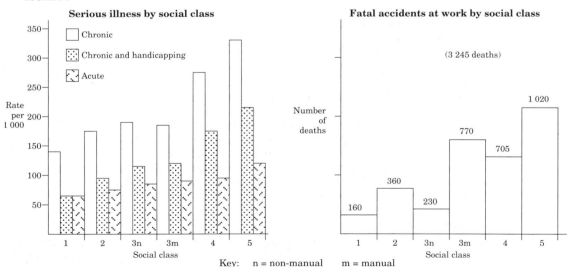

From M Baxter, 'Social Class and Health Inequalities,' C O Carter & J Peel, *Equalities in Health* (Academic Press)

From *Occupational Mortality: 1970–2* (HMSO)

Item B

Education

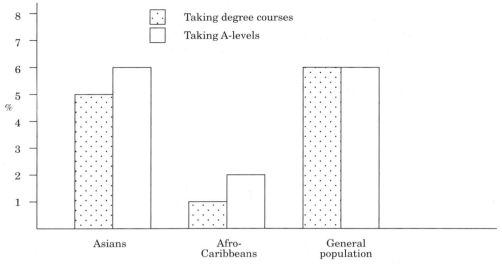

From *Social Trends*, 1985 (HMSO)

QUESTIONS

1 Look at item A. What rate per 1 000 of social class 3n suffer chronic and handicapping illness? [1 mark]

2 Look at item A. Which social class has the fewest fatal accidents at work? [1 mark]

3 Look at item B.
(a) Which group had the highest percentage taking A-levels? [1 mark]
(b) What percentage of Afro-Caribbeans were taking degree courses? [1 mark]

4 Identify and explain **two** ways in which social class might affect a person's life chances.
[4 marks]

5 Identify and explain **two** reasons why some of the elderly continue in employment beyond retirement age. [4 marks]

6 Identify and explain **one** social consequence of the unequal status in the workplace of most women in relation to men. [4 marks]

7 'There are many opportunities for members of ethnic minority groups to achieve a high standard of education and high status jobs in Britain today.'
Identify and fully explain **one** way in which this view can be either supported or rejected.
[4 marks]

SEG 1991

ANSWERS

1 Approximately 120.

2 Social class 1.

3 (a) 'General population' and 'Asians' appear equal.
(b) One per cent

4 Health and education. Health is strongly influenced by the standards of living of a person, by good housing and nutritious diets. These are more likely to occur in higher socio-economic groupings. Education is influenced by parental encouragement and levels of their own education, by schools with a lower student/teacher ratio (often found in private schools), by the possibility of having books at home, and generally enjoying a higher standard of living.

5 Work is both a way of earning money and a means of self-identification.
People beyond retirement age may continue to work for financial reasons, perhaps because they would have only a limited income from a pension otherwise. This occurs particularly amongst the elderly who have only a state pension.
However, others may wish to continue to work after retirement age, because they enjoy the work, or they wish to retain their status.

6 Women are likely to earn less than men, and this has significant consequences for their standards of living. We know that women are far more likely than men to live in poverty, and this has further consequences for their children, in that in nine out of ten single parent families the head of household is a women. Therefore women's low pay condemns children to live in poverty.

7 You can argue either for or against this statement, as the issue really depends upon the particular 'ethnic minority'. As you can see (from item B) there are great variations in the numbers of students from Asian and Afro-Caribbean households taking A levels and degrees.

However, it is more correct to point to the difficulties that members of the ethnic minorities face in having worse jobs, in being more likely to live in poverty, in facing problems of language in schools, in facing the Anglocentric (how 'the British discovered and civilised Africa', etc) nature of the subjects they study at school, and in facing the problem of both overt and institutional racism.

Question 20

Extract

Changes in work and leisure

A recent study by Pahl of the Isle of Sheppey on the north Kent coast looks at the social implications of the decline in manufacturing employment.

> The Isle of Sheppey has a population of 33 000. Most jobs on the island used to be in the Admiralty dockyard until it closed in 1960. Between 1960 and 1981, there was work in private docks (used for importing cars), in some manufacturing industries (mainly steel) and in the holiday trade. Wages were mostly low and opportunities for women were very limited. Jobs were insecure and unemployment rose to 20 per cent by 1983.
>
> Pahl started his study with a concern about how people react to unemployment. There had been a lot of discussion about the unemployed using their 'free' time to work for undeclared income. Pahl found almost no evidence of this. What he did find was that there was an enormous amount of work being done in the home. It was not the unemployed who did this work, despite the extra time they had. Rather, the more people in a family who were in paid employment outside the home, the more work they did inside the home. Households with more than one wage-earner produced more services for themselves. These services included house maintenance and repairs, car repairs and home cooking, as well as routine housework and child care.

From N Abercrombie and A Warde, *Contemporary British Society*

QUESTIONS

Study the extract and answer the questions.

1 What is meant by the term 'manufacturing' as used in the extract? [2 marks]

2 Why has there been a decline in employment in manufacturing industries in Britain? [6 marks]

3 Write **three** statements about changes which have occurred in paid employment on the Isle of Sheppey since 1960. [3 marks]

4 Explain why paid employment opportunities for women were very limited on the Isle of Sheppey. [5 marks]

5 One of Pahl's main findings was that 'there was an enormous amount of work being done in the home'.
(a) Give one example from the extract of work being done in the home. [1 mark]
(b) How far can this example be regarded as 'real work'? Give reasons for your answer. [4 marks]
(c) Which people did Pahl find were more likely to do this work? [1 mark]

6 The extract suggests that there have been important changes in paid and unpaid work on the Isle of Sheppey between 1960 and 1983.

What effects might such changes have on the life styles and life-chances of:
(a) the unemployed;
(b) those with paid employment? [8 marks]

NEA 1991

ANSWERS

1 Production of an object from raw material. As opposed to service or extractive work.

2 Competition from other countries which make the goods at lower prices. Growth in other forms of employment, mainly in service industries such as banking or insurance. Developments in automated technology means that fewer workers are needed.

3 Three from any combination of the following: most jobs used to be in the Admiralty shipyard, but this closed in 1960; between 1960–81 there was work in private docks importing cars, which has now declined; there was also work in manufacturing though this has now declined; there was work in the holiday trade; wages were low and opportunities limited for women; unemployment rose by 20 per cent by 1983.

4 Women are rarely employed in docks and 'heavy' manufacturing industries such as steel. They would more likely have been employed in the holiday trade.

In general, women work in service industries and 'light' manufacturing, such as electronics.

5 (a) One from the following: house maintenance; general repairs; car repairs; home cooking; routine housework; child care.

(b) This is 'real work' as it saves considerable amounts of money by not paying others to do it.

It is difficult to define exactly what work is, but it is not just paid employment outside the home. It could be considered any activity that saves or generates income.

(c) People in households with more than one wage earner.

6 (a) The unemployed are likely to have got relatively poorer and be less likely to undertake jobs in their own home. Therefore their standards of living will have fallen. As there has been a continuing decline in employment, there has been a decreasing opportunity for them to find paid work. Their life-chances have also declined.

(b) The opposite has happened with the employed. They have a higher income, they are more likely to have more than one person earning in the household, and they are likely to do more household jobs themselves. This indicates a rising standard of living and increasing life-chances.

Question 21

Source A

> The 'young' elderly of the future – active, many of them quite wealthy and in their sixties – will become an important and powerful group of consumers, Mr Hobbs said.
>
> The old elderly – frail, and mainly widows – will also provide growing business opportunities in converting houses to meet their needs and health care.

From a speech by G Hobbs, a senior planner with ICI, reported in *The Independent,* 1989

Source B

Minister tells employers to stop competing for young recruits and look to rest of labour market

Simon Beavis
Labour Correspondent

Employers were warned yesterday that they were reacting wrongly to the so-called demographic time bomb by channelling too much energy into recruiting from falling numbers of young people.

The warning came from the Employment Secretary, Mr Norman Fowler, as he explained research results compiled by the National Economic Development Office. The research showed a high degree of ignorance among employers about the changing nature of the market and the population.

Mr Fowler therefore urged employers to look to alternative sources of labour, including women, ethnic minorities, the disabled, and workers aged over 50 to fill the rising number of jobs.

The report will raise worries that employers are not adapting to changes in the population. As a result they will not make the most of new business opportunities as well.

From a newspaper report of a speech by Norman Fowler, the Conservative Government Employment Secretary, in *The Guardian*, October 1989

Source C

To find out how employers are reacting to the changes in the population a large-scale survey was planned. Two thousand structured postal questionnaires were sent to a random sample of larger employers with over 50 employees throughout the UK. However, a low response rate was recorded – only 32% of employers returned the questionnaire.

from an unpublished research study, 1989

QUESTIONS

1 Study sources A and B carefully.

'The falling numbers of young people and the ageing of the population will give industry new business.'

(a) Explain how the evidence in source A supports this statement. [3 marks]

(b) Does the evidence in source B support this statement? Explain your answer carefully. [4 marks]

(c) Sources A and B are examples of secondary evidence taken from newspaper reports. How useful is this evidence to a sociologist studying employers' responses to population changes? You should discuss the strengths and weaknesses of this type of evidence for this purpose. [5 marks]

2 Study source B carefully.

How useful is source B as evidence of the opinions of all politicians about employers' attitudes to recruitment? [5 marks]

3 Study source C carefully.

(a) How is the sample used in this research likely to affect the quality of the evidence collected? You should discuss the strengths and weaknesses of the sample.

(b) In what ways could the use of structured postal questionnaires affect the quality of the evidence collected? You should discuss the strengths and weaknesses of evidence collected in this way. [4 marks]

MEG 1991

ANSWERS

1 (a) It says that there will be two groups: The 'young' elderly who will be quite 'wealthy' and will become important consumers; and the old elderly who will have to have their houses converted to meet their needs and health care.

(b) Source B does support this statement in the final paragraph, but is mainly concerned with the prospects for employment. The article reports a speech by the Secretary for Employment at the time who was stressing the need for employers to go out and recruit older people and those from the ethnic minorities etc.

(c) **Strengths:** gives sociologist an overview of the situation, often provides useful statistics; gives a view of the government's thinking; provides the information in a compact and lucid manner; provides sources where sociologist could go for further information.

Weaknesses: main one is bias. Newspapers often support political parties and therefore may be sympathetic or antagonistic to a particular view.

Journalists are not sociologists, and may have lower standards of proof than sociologists.

2 People often 'plant' information in newspapers for their own purposes, such as companies wishing to gain publicity or a pressure group wishing to gain support for its cause. Therefore the actual content of an article can be unreliable.

Source B does not tell you about all politicians, only about the view of the government of the time. Opposition parties may well have had different views but these were not reported, or even hinted at.

3 (a) The questionnaires were only sent to a sample of employers who had more than 50 employees. Although these employ the majority of employees, they are only a small percentage of all companies. This means that the majority of companies were not questioned. The strengths are that it was a large sample and that the companies were randomly chosen.

(b) **Weaknesses:** postal questionnaires have low response rates; the researcher is never sure if the correct person actually receives the questionnaire; if the questionnaire is too structured it may not allow the respondent the flexibility to explain clearly his/her ideas if they are different from the structured answers in the questionnaire.

(c) **Strengths:** postal questionnaires allow the researchers to distribute the questionnaires to a much greater number of people than would be possible with interviews, and also to a much wider geographical distribution, as it only requires a stamp.

So, structured postal questionnaires could be useful in obtaining a widespread and large sample, as long as people return them. However, they are limited by the inflexibility of the questions and answer format (they are usually 'closed questions', which demand only one simple answer).

Question 22

Read items A and B. Then answer the questions which follow.

Item A

A research method
It has been suggested that a research method should include the following six stages:

1 Identifying an issue.
2 Selecting appropriate methods to study the issue.
3 Collecting relevant data.
4 Analysing the data.
5 Interpreting the data.
6 Reporting findings and conclusions.

One of the most difficult problems, when applying this method in social research, is to ensure that any sample taken is representative of the total population.

From G O'Donnell, *Mastering Sociology* (Macmillan)

Item B

The choice of a research method is dependent upon a number of factors: these include the time available to conduct the study; the size of the population to be studied; whether the researcher chooses a 'scientific' method, or not. Other points for consideration might be the availability of, and access to, research already undertaken, as well as the extent to which the study population is easy or difficult to contact.

QUESTIONS

1 Look at item A. What is the starting point for any piece of social research?   [1 mark]
2 Look at item A. What will a social researcher do when identifying a sample of the population?   [1 mark]
3 Look at item B.
(a) Who decides whether a 'scientific' method is to be used?   [1 mark]
(b) What points need to be considered when using research which has already been conducted?   [1 mark]
4 Identify and explain **two** reasons for using secondary data in social research.   [4 marks]
5 Identify and explain **two** ways in which sociologists might conduct a survey of large numbers of people.   [4 marks]
6 In order to obtain information about small groups in the workplace, sociologists often use participant observation. Identify and fully explain **one** reason why they might choose this method of research.   [4 marks]

SEG 1990

ANSWERS

1 Identifying an issue.

2 Make sure that it is representative.

3 (a) The researcher.
(b) The availability of and access to this research.

4 Two from: historical information needed (for example, family life in the last century): information needed from a society or group that it is impossible to study first-hand (for example, prisoners): information from a geographically remote area (from the perspective of the researcher). It often provides a lot of background information from previous studies to compare one's own work against (for example, from official documents); it may be necessary to include statistical information from very large surveys, which it is impossible for the individual researcher to undertake.

5 Postal questionnaires or large-scale structured interviews, and these could be done in a cross-sectional or a longitudinal way.

6 The most useful answer here is the following: getting to understand the meanings and understandings of people in a particular situation.

By joining in the situation as one of a group, it is possible to understand fully and experience the activities and ideas of people in the workplace. They may alter their behaviour if they feel they are being studied by some official researcher, as the situation of having someone to observe them may alter the way they behave. (You may wish to continue discussing whether the research should be covert or overt, and the extent to which the existence of a researcher influences the situation, and finally the degree of value bias that may creep into the situation if the researcher begins to dislike or like the people being researched.)

Question 23

> If the Ayatollah Khomeini becomes Iran's next ruler, he will set up an Islamic Republic.
>
> The teachings of the prophet Mohammed would mean prohibition of alcohol–wrecking Iran's prosperous wine-making industry.
>
> Gambling would be banned. Cinemas would not be allowed to show 'permissible' Western films. Bikinis could disappear from Caspian Sea resorts.
>
> Khomeini believes that liberalisation and women's rights have undermined the sanctity of the Islamic household.

From *The Daily Mirror,* January 1979

In April 1979, Iran became an 'Islamic Republic'.

QUESTIONS

1 Why do many people obey rules laid down by religions? [4 marks]

2 In what way does religion encourage change and/or stability? [7 marks]

3 Describe three main causes of social change identified by sociologists. [9 marks]

ANSWERS

1 Because the rules are often the very basic rules of the society, and people learn to obey from a young age.

Religion helps provide explanations for the complexities of the world and therefore allows people to make sense of their lives.

2 It encourages stability by providing a clear set of rules and guidelines for living. It also gives a moral justification for these rules. It gives a sense of purpose and belonging, and draws people together in a feeling of sharing common beliefs.

More cynical comments about religion include that it provides a justification for the inequalities of society and keeps people in their places; it is wrong to rebel on Earth if a person is poor or powerless, because after death that person will gain their reward.

Religion promotes change because it can provide alternative sets of values to the dominant ones in a society at any one time. It can also justify these values and provide criticism of existing values.

You could finish this answer by citing as an example the work and beliefs of the Calvinists.

3 Social change can be brought about by:

Changing values and ideas (such as religion): the best example of this is Weber's description of the Calvinist religion and how it brought about industrialisation.

Changing economic circumstances: the best example of this is the Marxist approach, which argues that economic changes eventually bring about social changes.

Political activity: the best example you can use is that of any successful pressure group that brought about the change it wanted.

ESSAY-STYLE QUESTIONS

The degree of depth and length in which these essay-style questions should be answered varies with the Examination Boards: please check the section *'Types of Examination Questions'* on p 181.

1 Socialization

(a) What is meant by the term 'socialization'? Explain how people come to be socialized.

[15 marks]

(b) Human beings are made, not born.

Explain what you think is meant by this statement. Your answer could include reference to the following:

the nature-nurture debate;

the process of socialization;

how the main agencies of socialization operate.

Credit will be given for any other relevant information.   [15 marks]

(Northern Examining Association, Specimen Paper 11)

2 Methods

(a) Describe and explain the uses and limitations of participant observation as a method of sociological research. Use examples where possible to illustrate your answer.   [15 marks]

(b) The local council in an area with a population of over 100 000 people of different ages wishes to spend money on improving local leisure facilities. Before deciding how to spend the money, however, the council needs to find out what kind of leisure activities the people would like.

(i) Describe the methods that could be used to discover the opinions and needs of the local people, remembering the size of the population.

(ii) Suggest how the results of the investigation might be presented.   [15 marks]

(London Regional Examining Board 1983)

3 Family and marriage

(a) In what ways has industrialization affected the family?   [15 marks]

(b) How do sociologists explain the increase in divorce that has taken place this century?

[6 marks]

Does this indicate a breakdown in marriage and the family?   [9 marks]

(c) Describe and explain the changing relationships between members of the family over the last 100 years.   [15 marks]

(d) Describe and explain the changes that have taken place in the family and marriage in the last 40 years.

Your answer might include some of the following:

changing relationships between parents and children;

changing relationships between husband and wives;

female employment and its effects;

the growth of alternative family types.

4 Education

(a) What explanations can you offer for the fact that children from some ethnic minorities do not do as well at school as the majority of children?   [15 marks]

(b) In what ways do influences outside the school influence a child's educational achievement?

Your answer could include reference to the following:

family income and class;

attitudes of parents towards education;

the peer group and the neighbourhood influences;

the language of the home.   [15 marks]

(c) It is often said that the school plays a very important part in forming the career choices of males and females. Suggest why this is so.   [15 marks]

5 Social class

(a) What is meant by social mobility? What are the reasons for a person's mobility in British society? [15 marks]

(b) Describe and explain the importance of social class in influencing people's lives. [15 marks]

6 Gender

(a) 'Women are still treated as second-class citizens in Britain today.' Explain and discuss. [15 marks]

(b) By nature, girls are submissive and domesticated. This is true in all societies.
Explain these statements and discuss them using sociological evidence. [15 marks]

7 Age

(a) What do sociologists mean by 'youth culture'? Is there a distinctive youth culture in Britain today which most young people share? [15 marks]

(b) 'Age is an entirely natural, biological thing and so is the behaviour that we associate with each age group.' Explain and discuss. [15 marks]

8 Race

Explain the sorts of problems that people in ethnic minorities experience in Britain. Can you suggest why this is so? [15 marks]

9 Work

(a) What is the relationship between technology and work satisfaction? [15 marks]

(b) What is automation? Describe and explain the possible consequences of automation.
[15 marks]

10 Unemployment

What are the consequences for people's lives when they are made unemployed? [15 marks]

11 Leisure

Leisure in contemporary Britain is a profitable industry employing large numbers of people. This reflects a society with more money and more leisure time. Discuss.
Your answer could include reference to the following:
the changes in employment;
the changing patterns of consumption;
the relationship between work and leisure;
the increasing professionalism of leisure. [15 marks]

12 Population

(a) Describe and explain the changing pattern of births in this century. [15 marks]

(b) There is a greater proportion of the population over the age of 65 than ever before. Explain this and discuss what the consequences are. [15 marks]

13 Urbanization and community

(a) Discuss the extent to which there are differences between living in urban and rural communities. [15 marks]

(b) What problems are facing people in inner cities today? What explanations can you suggest? [15 marks]

14 Poverty

(a) Some people suggest that poverty is the state when people are so poor that they cannot buy enough to eat; others claim that poverty is not having what others in the same society normally expect to have.
Discuss the problems in measuring the extent of poverty. What are the consequences for social policy of the different definitions? [15 marks]

(b) Why do the poor generally tend to remain poor? [15 marks]

15 The Welfare State

Why has it been suggested that 'the Welfare State is in crisis'? What solutions have been suggested? [15 marks]

16 Power and politics

(a) Describe and explain the role of pressure groups in political decision making.   [15 marks]

(b) What are the main influences on how people vote?   [15 marks]

17 Social control

Conformity to the rules of society occurs partly as a result of social control. Explain the meaning of 'social control' and how it operates.   [15 marks]

18 Crime and deviance

(a) (i) What is meant by the term 'deviance'?   [3 marks]

(ii) Why are some deviant acts criminal and others not?   [12 marks]

(b) (i) Are official statistics on crime a good guide to the true level of criminal activity? Explain the reasons for your answer.   [6 marks]

(ii) What influence on policing and the activities of courts does 'labelling' have?   [8 marks]

19 Religion

(a) What role does religion play in social control?   [15 marks]

(b) Despite declining church attendance, the importance and the influence of religion remains strong. Discuss.   [15 marks]

20 The media

(a) Using examples, discuss how the mass media influence people's attitudes.   [15 marks]

(b) What do journalists mean when they speak of 'news'? Explain why the contents and presentation of newspapers vary.   [15 marks]

ANSWERS

1 Socialization

(a) Socialization equals learning the values and expectations of society, through informal and formal processes. You need to discuss the role of the family, school, peer group, etc. and give examples; a good one would be the way gender roles are learned.

(b) The outline information is listed for you here and you should broaden the points given. Nature–nurture means the debate over the extent to which behaviour is natural or learned. Socialization needs discussing and you should cover the activities of the family, school, and the peer group.

2 Methods

(a) The uses of participant observation are generally in situations (i) where the researcher wishes to study people as they are acting naturally; (ii) in order to achieve greater depth of understanding; (iii) where there is no sample frame or it would be inappropriate to give a questionnaire – as with a deviant group.

Its limitations are that the researcher may lose his/her objectivity, may influence the group, and that no one else can repeat the check on it.

(b) (i) Probably a mail questionnaire, sent to a sample survey of people on the local register of electors.

(ii) They could be presented in the form of a set of clear pie charts and stating what proportion of the population favoured which option. Alternatively, there could simply be a series of tables. However, a wide variety of answers is acceptable.

3 Family and marriage

(a) You would want to base your answer on three areas of discussion: changing structure of the family – the extended/nuclear discussion; the changing relationships in the family, with great emphasis on the role of the wife; the decline in functions.

(b) Changing values concerning marriage; the changing role of women; the changes in the law; the decline in the importance of the church; the weakening of the family; the fact that people from a wide variety of backgrounds marry; the high expectations of marriage.

It does not necessarily indicate a breakdown as people remarry and 90 per cent of people still marry. Divorce rates reflect more the legal availability of divorce.

(c) You need to look at the changing husband/wife relationship; the parent/child relationship and the elderly/younger generation division. Points to stress include the greater degree of equality in the family, the role of the woman especially; the way children are asserting themselves more; the fact that older people are geographically more distant from their children. You need to discuss the concepts of symmetrical family and privatized family life, geographical mobility, smaller families and child-centredness etc. Do not forget to point out that women are still the ones with most of the domestic responsibilities.

(d) This is a general question that requires a full debate on the decline of the extended family among the working class (Bethnal Green) and the increase in the modern symmetrical family. You should point out that there is greater home-centredness and the males have lost their clear role as head of the household, but the woman still is responsible for the home. Discuss the older generation in this context. Point out the increase in divorce, remarriage and the growth of single-parent family life, etc.

4 Education

(a) Mention some facts of different achievement. Point out that not all ethnic minorities do badly – East African Asians, for example, and Jews. Main reasons are direct racism, different family structures and expectations, the deprivations of the neighbourhood, language differences, 'hidden curriculum'.

(b) The outline of the answer is already given. You need to fill these out in some detail. Try if possible to mention some studies. Do not forget to include race and gender differences, not just social class.

(c) This essay is designed to get you to write about the way that schools treat children differently according to their gender. You should talk about the differences in the subjects that males and females take and why this is so (boys – maths, girls – secretarial and domestic subjects). Go on to discuss the 'hidden curriculum' of teachers' expectations. It might be worth arguing that you cannot separate the influence of the school from the wider gender roles of society.

5 Social class

(a) Mobility is the movement up and down the class structure. Reasons include the person's ability, gender, own class background, education, the changing economic structure of society, the reproductive patterns of those in the higher classes.

(b) This covers a whole range of influences including family size, health, length of life, chances at school, type of job, living standards, accents, leisure patterns, etc.

6 Gender

(a) This refers to the fact that women are discriminated against in education and employment; that they are still expected to look after the home and the children; that they are still the object of harassment, both physical and sexual. These points need to be developed. However, do point out the advances made by women legally and culturally, mainly as a result of the feminist movement.

(b) The point of this question is to discuss the way that women are socialized into their roles in our society. Examine the role of the family, the peer group, the media and the school. You should then compare this with examples of female roles in other societies.

7 Age

(a) Youth culture means the distinctive set of values held by younger people. There is not a single youth culture. Instead, there is a variety of youth cultures, based upon the class, gender and ethnic divisions in our society. Your essay should take various examples of this from skinheads to Rastas. Use your own special knowledge of contemporary youth for examples.

(b) This question refers to the way that expectations of age-related behaviour are socially created. You should take the examples of the Ik used in the main text, and the creation of youth in modern society, as the focal points for your essay – to show how behaviour is not directly linked to age but to society's expectation of age. You might also discuss the rites of passage.

8 Race

You should raise the issues of prejudice and discrimination. Examples of these could include the problems over housing, employment, treatment by the police and the mass media. It is useful here actually to know some specific examples. The various explanations for prejudice ought to be covered – authoritarian personality, stereotyping, scapegoating.

9 Work

(a) People tend to get satisfaction from jobs that give them control over their actions, that are interesting, and are varied. It would seem that craft work is most interesting, while machine minding and assembly line work is the least rewarding. In white-collar jobs the routine work on computers and word processors is least interesting. Opinions vary over the use of automation. A good answer would raise issues about alienation and whether it was just the type of technology that caused work satisfaction.

(b) Automation is the control of the complete work process by machines. There are basically two arguments – the optimistic and the pessimistic. The first sees people being liberated from dull, boring work and allowing them greater leisure and freedom. The second sees machines replacing people, so causing high levels of unemployment with all the attendant political, social and economic problems.

10 Unemployment

The point here is first of all to stress that unemployment is bad and that there is a myth of the unemployed scrounger living a high life on social security. Then you should go on to point out how unemployment hits people very differently. Young people and middle-aged people are faced with very different problems, while women may be forced back to the domestic role. In other words the consequences vary according to age, gender and financial resources.

11 Leisure

The outline information is given here in the question. There are the changes in employment and the decline of the heavy industries, which were male orientated; with them has gone a whole style of working class life. There has been a shift in family patterns (not mentioned in the outline answer) towards the home-centred family: this can influence the males' choice of leisure. Also not mentioned is the changing technology of leisure: videos and televisions, etc. Point out the growing threat of unemployment and the differences between those in work and those without it.

12 Population

(a) You need to explain the overall decline in the birthrate – contraception, the desire for a higher standard of living, changes in female attitudes to their role; also the increase after the Second World War, the affluent years of the early 1960s.

(b) People are living longer because they have a higher standard of living and housing and they receive higher standards of medical care.

The consequences of this are the ageing of society; the shifting demands for welfare and health services; the influence on consumer industries; the burden of dependency; a decline in the status of the elderly. The numbers of women living longer might be worth mentioning.

13 Urbanization and community

(a) There are clear differences between life in an urban and in a rural community. Life in urban communities tends to be more superficial; people less often have multiple roles; less sense of community; the people tend to move and do not identify with the neighbourhood. However, you ought to point out that there are strong arguments against this simple division – refer to Pahl's studies. Answers about traffic and pollution are not really comparing 'communities' and would score low marks.

(b) The problems consist of poverty, urban decay, racial tension, drugs, poor housing, the riots. Explanations would centre on the move away from the city of the 'stable' working class and the middle class to the suburbs and the new towns. Industry has declined and the new industries are likely to relocate in out-of-town locations. Lack of housing provision for single people often makes them sleep rough. Inner city areas are therefore deprived.

14 Poverty

(a) This is a debate on the relative definitions of poverty – remember that there are a number of these, and the absolute one by Rowntree. The point here is that depending on where you draw the poverty line, the numbers of people in poverty increases or decreases. This would imply that respectively more or less resources and help should be given. Also the relative definitions of poverty go beyond discussions of money and also talk about resources.

(b) This is a reference to the cycle of poverty and the culture of poverty. Both these concepts ought to be discussed and they could be compared to a Marxist explanation. You should stress that poverty is not just lack of money, but of resources in general.

15 The Welfare State

This question refers to the fact that there are major problems of finance facing the health and social security services. The people who founded the Welfare State never expected this level of social problems to continue so long. There are solutions from both the left and the right of the political spectrum. Those on the left suggest that more money ought to be spent, but that the problems arise out of our economic system, which needs reforming. On the other hand, those on the right talk about cutting back and encouraging people to take out private health insurance policies. They compare the universalistic policies of the NHS with the idea of helping only the poor – in effect a two-tier system.

16 Power and politics

(a) Pressure groups exist to 'fill the gap' that is left by the political parties on specific issues. They are either protective or promotional. They persuade the political parties by various means such as block votes, petitions, demonstrations, etc. You ought to point out the debate on the differences in power and contacts between the various pressure groups.

(b) This is a discussion on class, religion, age, gender and region. It is very important that you point out the changing pattern of class voting in Britain and the way that the automatic loyalty for Labour of two-thirds of the working class has now faded.

17 Social control

Social control is the way that people are persuaded to follow the rules and expectations of society. It operates in two main ways – formally and informally. The main agencies include the family, the peer group, school, religion, the mass media and the police. Take some of these and look at them in some detail.

18 Crime and deviance

(a) (i) Not conforming to expected patterns of behaviour.
(ii) The reasons suggested include reflecting the majority view; the results of moral crusades; and reflecting the interests of the powerful. These should be discussed using examples to illustrate your point. You could also raise the issues of the variation in what is considered deviant/illegal across society and time.

(b) (i) They are only rough guides, little else. The main problems occur with the uneven reporting of crime to the police and the way these reports are subsequently categorized by the police. You should develop the reasons why people report crime or not, and then go on to look at policing practices which also influence the statistics. You might find it useful to refer to the British Crime Survey.
(ii) You should examine the influence of labelling and the role of the media in creating moral panics, which can influence the actions of the police and the judges. You could use the example of Stan Cohen, Jock Young or Stuart Hall. You could go beyond this and comment on the attitudes of the police and courts to female offenders and show why they treat them differently as a result of the label produced by the gender role.

19 Religion

(a) There are different attitudes to this and you ought to reflect the differences in your essay. One group see religion as performing a valuable service for society, holding it together and keeping its central values intact. Others see religion as serving the interests of the powerful – an 'opium of the people'. Finally, others see in religion the power to bring about change. These are the issues and viewpoints raised by Durkheim, Marx and Weber.

(b) This is the debate on 'secularization'. First you ought to go through the decline in the church attendances and then give the reasons for this. After that you ought to run through the arguments that church attendance does not say anything about the religious belief of people; they may still believe in God, but choose not to worship in a church. You ought then to go on and point out the growth in the sects and the newer churches, as well as the growing importance in Britain of non-Christian religions.

20 The media

(a) This is a wide-ranging question. The simplest way to tackle it would be to take a few areas of social life, such as women, politics or crime, and then see how they influence cultural attitudes. You could then go beyond this and look at the way they influence us, either directly through the 'hypodermic syringe' type model, or through the 'cultural approach'. Labelling, stereotyping, moral panics, etc. would all be acceptable here.

(b) The point here is that there is no such thing as news, merely what journalists define as news. They look for the sort of things that would interest the presumed readership of their papers. You must discuss the concept of news values and how they vary according to the paper. You might want to raise the issues of ownership and control.

1 Your coursework will be marked by your teacher and then 'moderated' (checked) by an outsider appointed by your examining board. Your teacher **must** mark coursework according to the guidelines given on pages vii to x. Therefore you know exactly what you must do to achieve high marks. You must bear these marking guidelines in mind when you tackle your coursework.

2 Deciding what topic to do is a difficult task, but do not expect the teacher to tell you what to do. You are expected to study a topic which is broadly relevant to the syllabus, not any topic which interests you. Flick through the topic headings in this book and see if anything interests you.

3 Once you have decided on a topic area that interests you, check whether it is a feasible topic to tackle. For instance, you won't want to do a study on the changing class structure in Britain. This is an enormous topic, which requires resources well beyond the reach of a single student. So keep it small!

4 You should restrict your enquiry to a narrow topic and if you are going to conduct a survey keep the numbers being interviewed (or asked to complete a questionnaire) small. It depends on the subject being covered of course, but 20 good questionnaires are worth a hundred scrappy ones.

5 Always carry out a pilot study – it will help you to see if the study is really possible.

6 Get on with your project at the earliest sensible opportunity. Do not leave it to the last moment. Your teacher will normally tell you when to start. For a two-year course it will probably start at the beginning of the second year, or the summer term of the first year. If you are doing a one-year course, you need to have your plans made by December.

7 Use a diary or notebook to record **everything** you are doing. This helps you and your teacher check the stages of your work and it will probably be sent to the moderator, who can then understand how your project progressed. A small, cheap notebook can be used to record ideas, how things are progressing, difficulties encountered, what is hoped to be achieved through a particular activity and what books have been used. It allows the teacher to see how things are progressing and to make changes he/she thinks are important. It gives the students some feedback.

8 Work out a sensible timetable for tackling all your GCSEs. It is likely that you are doing other subjects besides Sociology. Make sure that you allocate a set amount of time for all your subjects rather than compiling your projects in an unplanned way and finding you have too great a load at the last moment.

9 The enquiry is an opportunity for you to show your ability to research and to come to useful conclusions through analysing data. Do not copy large chunks from books or newspapers. Go out and do some actual research (although you still need to read and take out relevant information from books, newspapers and magazines).

10 Most students seem to think that the only 'primary' research methods they can do are questionnaires and interviews. This is not the case, don't forget that you can do simple observational studies and even experiments. Best of all is to mix the methods, thereby showing the examiner you really understand how to go about sociological research.

11 Normally the enquiry is written but this does not mean you should not use videos and audio tapes you have made yourself, or photographs or even models/displays. Try to be flexible and a little different.

12 You don't have to do the enquiry entirely by yourself, you can do a group enquiry. The only thing to remember is that your personal contribution should be very clear and should fulfill all the marking guidelines outlined earlier.

Checklist for the Enquiry

As I pointed out earlier, the examination boards group the marks to be awarded for the enquiry under specific headings. You must make sure that you have fully covered the specific points mentioned in the 'Marks to be awarded for' listed under your examination board. However, there is a general outline that can be followed which will guarantee a reasonable grade.

GO THROUGH THE FOLLOWING CHECKLIST, TICK EACH ITEM TO ENSURE THAT YOU HAVE DEALT WITH IT IN YOUR ENQUIRY

The introduction

☐ 1 Start with a full discussion of the *aims* of the enquiry.
☐ 2 What area of social life are you examining?
☐ 3 What do you hope to prove (your *hypothesis*) or to demonstrate?

A discussion of the methodology you are going to use

☐ 1 What type of methods are you going to use?
☐ 2 What are the advantages of using these methods?
☐ 3 Why have you chosen them?
☐ 4 What alternative methods could you have used?
☐ 5 Why did you reject them?

The content of your study

☐ 1 What are the findings of your research? (This requires detailed presentation, discussed later.)
☐ 2 Are your findings clear and detailed?
☐ 3 How are they relevant to your original hypothesis?
☐ 4 What sources did you use, other than the piece of research you have conducted yourself?

The presentation of your findings

☐ 1 Have you presented your findings in a clear and detailed manner, using the whole range of means of presentation open to you?
☐ 2 Have you used graphs, tables, bar charts, pie charts, photographs, tape recordings, for example?
☐ 3 Is your work neat and tidy?
☐ 4 Are the pages numbered and in sequence?
☐ 5 Are all diagrams, tables, etc adequately labelled, with title and the source they were taken from?

The evaluation of the content

☐ 1 What conclusions have you come to as a result of your research?
☐ 2 Are your original ideas justified or rejected?
☐ 3 If justified – explain.
☐ 4 If rejected – explain.
☐ 5 Are there any obvious gaps or inconsistencies in the information presented?
☐ 6 Are there any biases which appear?
☐ 7 Have you evaluated the sources?

The evaluation of the methodology

☐ 1 What problems were encountered in the research?
☐ 2 What weaknesses appeared in the methodology?
☐ 3 What were the strengths of the methodology used?
☐ 4 What improvements could be made in further research?

The conclusions

☐ 1 Is there a summary of the main conclusions of the research?
☐ 2 Is there a summary of the methods used?
☐ 3 Is there a note of strengths and weaknesses?
☐ 4 Are all possible links made to other areas of the syllabus?
☐ 5 Is there any other relevant information you have found that can suggest further avenues of research/further insights?

Bibliography

(a bibliography is a list, often in alphabetical order, of all the sources you used in the research)
☐ 1 Have you added a bibliography?
☐ 2 Is it in alphabetical order? *Or*
☐ 3 Have you put a number in the main text to indicate the source of the information and then numbered the bibliography correctly, so the examiner can quickly find the source of your statement?

SOURCES OF INFORMATION

1 The main source of information ought to be your school or college library and if it has not got an adequate supply or range of books for your use you should ask (politely) why not. The main library of your town may also be able to help.

2 You can obtain any book published if you ask for an **inter-library loan form**. By completing this, your library (school/college or public) will ask other libraries if they have the particular book to lend it to them for you. Usually you have to wait for two to four weeks – so think ahead!

3 There are a number of magazines and newspapers which are particularly useful for research. Back copies of the magazine *New Society,* which is unfortunately no longer published, are useful. Other magazines which you may find useful include: *The Social Studies Review* (Philip Allen Publishers); *New Internationalist; New Statesman and Society; The Listener;* and *Nursing Times.* The best daily newspapers for sociology students are *The Guardian* and *The Independent.* You can find them by asking at the library.

4 If you are looking up specific topics ask the librarian to show you how to use *The British Humanities Index.* This lists all the newspaper and magazine articles on particular topics.

5 If you are looking for an organization which may be of use to you, use *The Directory of British Associations.* This contains the names and addresses of virtually every organization in Britain. You should find it in the reference section of your library. When you have decided on your enquiry, it is worth going through this directory to find organizations which may be able to provide you with information.

6 Not all organizations provide information and those that do make a small charge. If you do write, you must always include a stamped, addressed envelope for the reply (make sure the size of the envelope is big enough to take the pamphlet and the stamp is of sufficient value to cover the weight).

7 If you are looking for statistics, the clearest and most comprehensive source available is *Social Trends,* which is a book published every year by HMSO (the Government's publishing house). This covers a wider range of up-to-date statistics and information useful to sociologists. You are strongly recommended to glance through this before starting any research to see if there is any useful background information.

Examination Boards: Addresses

To obtain syllabuses, past examination papers and further details, write to your Examining Group.

MEG   **Midland Examining Group**

1 Hills Road
Cambridge
CB1 2EU

Tel: 01223 553311

NEAB   **Northern Examinations and Assessment board**

Devas Street
Manchester
M15 6EX

Tel: 0161 953 1180

NICCEA   **Northern Ireland Council for the Curriculum Examinations and Assessment**

Beechill House
42 Beechill Road
Belfast
BT8 4RS

Tel: 01232 704666

SEB   **Scottish Examination Board**

Ironmills Road
Dalkeith
Midlothian
EH22 1LE

Tel: 0131 663 6601

SEG   **Southern Examining Group**

Stag Hill House
Guildford
GU2 5XJ

Tel: 01483 506506

ULEAC   **University of London Examinations and Assessment Council**

Stewart House
32 Russell Square
London
WC1B 5DN

Tel: 0171 331 4000

WJEC   **Welsh Joint Education Committee**

245 Western Avenue
Cardiff
CF5 2YX

Tel: 01222 265000